Harvard
Rules

ALSO BY RICHARD BRADLEY

American Son: A Portrait of John F. Kennedy, Jr.

Harvard Rules

The Struggle for
the Soul of the
World's Most
Powerful University

Richard Bradley

HarperCollins*Publishers*

HARVARD RULES. Copyright © 2005 by Richard Bradley. All rights reserved. Printed in the United States of America. No part of this book may be used or reproduced in any manner whatsoever without written permission except in the case of brief quotations embodied in critical articles and reviews. For information, address HarperCollins Publishers Inc., 10 East 53rd Street, New York, NY 10022.

HarperCollins books may be purchased for educational, business, or sales promotional use. For information, please write: Special Markets Department, HarperCollins Publishers Inc., 10 East 53rd Street, New York, NY 10022.

FIRST EDITION

Designed by Nancy Singer Olaguera

Printed on acid-free paper

Library of Congress Cataloging-in-Publication Data is available upon request.

ISBN 0-06-056854-2

05 06 07 08 09 ❖/RRD 10 9 8 7 6 5 4 3 2 1

For Mike, Kate, and Cris

Contents

The Emperor's New Clothes

On the afternoon of Friday, the twelfth of October, 2001, Harvard University prepared to swear in its twenty-seventh president. It was a glorious Indian summer day, almost too warm for the fall, when Harvard's hometown of Cambridge, Massachusetts, is marked by crisp, cool air and the soft, fractured sunlight that hints at the imminence of winter. "With every breeze," a reporter for *Harvard Magazine* would later note pleasurably, "a gentle rain of golden locust leaves showered down on the seated assembly."

Some five thousand spectators were happily milling around Harvard Yard, the historical and emotional heart of Harvard's campus. The women wore sundresses or slacks. The men took off their sport coats and their blue blazers and rolled up the cuffs of their sleeves. The students were clad in the jeans and shorts and T-shirts they normally wore. Students, parents, alumni, professors, journalists, and politicians—all had come to witness this unusual transfer of power. The ritual didn't take place very often at Harvard—only five times in the twentieth century—and, about this new president, there hovered a buzz of excitement and curiosity, and more than a little anxiety.

This would be the first new president of the twenty-first century, and how much the world had changed, how fast, since the happy-go-lucky, all-is-right-with-the-world days of the 1990s. In normal times, anyone could stroll into Harvard Yard through one of its myriad wrought-iron gates. But on this day, police had set up checkpoints and rifled through the visitors' purses, briefcases, and knapsacks. One cop was walking a bomb-sniffing dog on a leash. Police officers stationed at regular intervals kept a close watch on the crowd.

Only a month had passed since the terrorist attacks of September 11, and, at Harvard, what was expected to be a celebratory moment, a coronation of sorts, had assumed a greater gravity. As in the rest of the country, every ceremonial display of American values became both more urgent and more anxious. And the act of installing a new president at this center of learning and diversity, situated just across the bucolic Charles River from Boston, the birthplace of the American Revolution, was really a celebration of Western civilization's most deeply held values. The inauguration of a new Harvard president symbolized America's determined insistence on harmony despite diversity, on peaceful transitions of power, on the need for wisdom in a violent world. That's why there were so many cops. If Islamic terrorists were planning another strike, why not attempt to turn Harvard's day of tradition into a scene of chaos and devastation? You could do a lot worse for symbolism.

Even so, for the new president this day was a moment of triumph. Lawrence Henry Summers—everyone called him Larry, if not always to his face—was taking charge of the university that, by his own account, had rejected him when he was a high school senior. That had been a surprise: Summers came from a truly stellar intellectual family. Both of his parents were economists, and two of his uncles would, after teaching and studying at Harvard, go on to win Nobel Prizes in economics. Instead of Harvard, Summers attended the Massachusetts Institute of Technology, just a couple miles east from Harvard, down Massachusetts Avenue. When Summers was finished at MIT, he did go to Harvard, to earn his doctorate in economics; it was clear by then that Summers was a rising star, and Harvard would not make the same mistake twice. Almost immediately after earning his Ph.D., he accepted a professorship in Harvard's economics department, which made him one of the youngest people ever to receive tenure at Harvard. Twenty-eight years old, and Larry Summers had a job for life at the world's most prestigious university.

Ten years later, Summers would trade the life of the mind for one of politics and worldliness. Like so many of his colleagues in Harvard economics, he left academe for a stint in Washington. But unlike most of them, Summers would not soon return. After taking a position as chief economist at the World Bank, Summers moved over to the Treasury Department, where he would become Treasury Secretary Robert Rubin's right-hand man. Harvard professors are allowed two years' leave of absence before they must resign their positions. In 1993, Summers did just that: he gave up one of the most secure and desirable jobs in all of academia. He reveled in government's mix of power and policy, and as the years passed he became increasingly masterful at understanding both. Together Summers and Rubin, in conjunction with Alan Greenspan, presided over what they so often called the longest period of economic expansion in American history. When Rubin resigned in 1998, Summers stepped smoothly into his place, and served as treasury secretary until the end of the Clinton administration.

And now, at forty-six, Summers was returning to Harvard, poised for another triumph in what was already a remarkable career. It was a move that surprised some who knew him well. "I would never have expected Larry to do this," said his uncle on his mother's side, the Nobel-winning economist Kenneth Arrow. "I thought of him as a scholar." Those who knew him from the Treasury Department would not have been surprised, however. They had seen how desperately Summers wanted to succeed Bob Rubin, how hard he had worked to make himself an acceptable candidate for the job. One thing that everyone said about Larry Summers: he was deeply, hungrily ambitious.

At about three thirty, a procession began winding through the Yard. Clad in a black robe with a scarlet sash, Summers stood at the head of a long line of university officials, deans, and professors. The new president smiled at the applause that greeted him as he walked through the crowd. Occasionally, like a politician working a rope line, he stopped to shake hands with someone he knew, or waved to acknowledge the cheers. But the gestures looked a little stiff, as if they had been rehearsed. Summers was about five feet ten inches tall, but he was not a physically graceful man; his robe could not disguise the fact that he was significantly overweight. The extra weight showed itself in his fleshy cheeks and jaw, softening the line between his neck and head and making his piercing blue eyes look small in his face. As seemed to befit a man of enormous intelligence, Summers had a large, powerful head and a broad forehead. His intermittent smiles looked nervous and awkward, as if he had to consider the gesture before he made it. When he did smile, two deep furrows flanked his mouth, almost exactly perpendicular to his eyes. Larry Summers was too intense for a grin to sit comfortably on his face.

As he walked towards a vast stage erected specially for the occasion in front of the Yard's Memorial Church, a grand, white-steepled Colonial structure, Summers was becoming something both less and more than a scholar. As president, he would forever leave behind the single-minded pursuit of economic truths that was once his life's work. When he was young—younger, for Summers was still youthful, with the energy of men half his age—he was expected to become one of his generation's most important economic thinkers. But that would never happen now. Being president of Harvard left little time for the solitary act of scholarship. Besides, the average tenure of a Harvard president was about twenty years, and after that, most felt more like retiring than returning to academics.

The twenty-sixth president, the one who had preceded Larry Summers, was a scholar of literature and poetry named Neil Rudenstine. He would sit onstage not far from his successor during the ceremony to come. It was too early to say what Rudenstine's legacy was, but everyone knew it would be hard to portray him as a statesmanlike figure. That was neither his appearance nor his nature, and even if it had been, his record wouldn't have supported the description. To his supporters, Rudenstine was a transitional figure who had done all that was asked of him and served Harvard with decency and devotion. But to others, including some of the people sitting onstage with him, Neil Rudenstine was the problem to which Larry Summers was the solution.

As a lone bagpiper played, Summers and his procession approached the stage, ascended a short flight of steps, and took their seats. Here were some of the most powerful people at Harvard—deans, administrators, senior professors, and members of the Board of Overseers and the Corporation, Harvard's two governing boards. In the first rows of the audience sat the university's biggest donors and most influential alumni. Students and other bystanders were relegated to seats farther back. Summers' three children—twin daughters and a son—were on hand, but his wife, Victoria Perry Summers, was not. The new president was in the throes of a painful and less-than-amicable divorce.

Opposite the stage, about a hundred and fifty yards away, loomed the imposing Harry Elkins Widener Memorial Library—Widener, as everyone calls it. If Memorial Church stubbornly insisted on the persistence of spiritual life at Harvard, Widener posed a secular challenge. A massive columned temple with a long, imposing set of steps, Widener was the unintended consequence of human hubris: the library was built in 1914 with money donated by Eleanor Alice Widener, whose son Harry, a bibliophile, had drowned on the *Titanic*. While Memorial Church had really only three books—the Bible, the Book of Common Prayer, and a hymnal—Widener contained almost four million. After the library was built, one of its architects, John McConnell, said, "Harvard was looking around for an empire to imitate. Rome seemed the best idea."

To the right of the stage was University Hall, the gray-stone headquarters of Harvard's powerful academic administration. Designed by 1781 graduate Charles Bulfinch and built in 1814, the blandly named building belied the power it contained, as blandly named buildings often do. University Hall was the seat of Harvard officialdom, deans and associate deans of the Faculty of Arts and Sciences, the people who controlled faculty salaries and the college's academic priorities. On its second floor was the venerable Faculty Room, where about once a month during the school year the president would sit in front of the faculty and hear their concerns and complaints, often delivered with the eloquence of a sonnet and the sharpness of a stiletto. But in recent years attendance at those meetings had declined, a victim of the faculty's waning sense of lifelong allegiance to the university.

Finally, to the left of Memorial Church was Sever Hall, an 1880 building of stone and brick designed by the architect H. H. Richardson. Sever was home to undergraduate classes in the humanities, literature and languages mainly. Of the four buildings, Sever was the least well maintained—the dusty, poorly heated classrooms inside looked like they hadn't changed much since the time of their creation—and perhaps the least noted. Surrounded by the imposing structures that housed church, administration, and scholarship, Sever, a place of teaching, was easy to overlook.

The grassy lawn framed by this symbolic square was called Tercentenary Theatre, because it had been the site of Harvard's three hundredth anniversary, in 1936. Tercentenary is not a word that flows mellifluously off the tongue, but that's partly because it doesn't get much use—few institutions in the United States have been around for three hundred years. Over the course of the 20th century, Tercentenary Theatre had been witness to remarkable oratory delivered by some of the century's most important figures, many of whom spoke of Harvard's role in the world. Franklin Roosevelt, Harvard class of 1904, had spoken there in September 1936, and in that voice so weighty with patrician self-confidence, he had declared, "In this day of modern witch-burning . . . it is the part of Harvard and America to stand for the freedom of the human mind and to carry the torch of truth." It wasn't the first time that Harvard's mission had been equated with that of the United States itself, and it would hardly be the last.

In September 1943, Winston Churchill had ambled up to a crackly public address system in front of Memorial Church and announced, "English and Americans should spread their language all over the globe as a means of promoting understanding and peace. The empires of the future are the empires of the mind." Churchill was, as usual, optimistic. Even as his nation was fighting a war that, whatever the outcome, would inevitably signify the end of Britain's territorial empire, he could speak of a new, Anglo-American empire rising from the ashes. Harvard, a university with English origins that produced the leaders of the United States, was a logical starting point.

In 1947, with the war over, George Marshall spoke at Harvard's commencement and laid out another way for the United States to extend its influence overseas—a policy of aid to Europe that would come to be known as the Marshall Plan. "The United States should do whatever it is able to do to assist in the return of normal economic health in the world, without which there can be no political stability and no assured peace," Marshall said rather stiffly.

And nine years after that, in 1956, Massachusetts senator John F. Kennedy—he graduated in 1940—continued the theme. "The men who create power make an indispensable contribution to the nation's greatness," Kennedy said. "But the men who question power make a contribution just as indispensable, for they determine whether we use power or power uses us." Soon enough, Kennedy would fill his administration with men who may have enjoyed power more than they questioned it—Harvard's best and brightest.

But long before the speakers at Tercentenary Theatre had made history, the graduates of Harvard *were* American history—at least, from the top down. At one time or another, the alumni of Harvard dominated every field in American life that was worth dominating. Their ranks included seven presidents: John Adams, John Quincy Adams, Rutherford B. Hayes, Theodore Roosevelt, Franklin Delano Roosevelt, John F. Kennedy, and most recently, George W. Bush, a graduate of Harvard Business School. Beyond the presidency there were countless Supreme Court justices, members of Congress, bankers, businessmen, lawyers, ministers, scholars, and writers. In the colonial era, Sam Adams, John Hancock, John Adams, and John Quincy Adams had all graduated from Harvard. As the United States moved into the nineteenth century, Henry David Thoreau and Ralph Waldo Emerson went there, along with the great historian Francis Parkman and Henry Adams, grandson of John Quincy and one of the country's most brilliant historians. Robert Gould Shaw, famous commander of the North's first black regiment in the Civil War, was a Harvard man, and so was William James, the philosopher, and W. E. B. DuBois, Harvard's first African American Ph.D., and Samuel Eliot Morison and John Dos Passos and J. Robert Oppenheimer and James Agee and John Updike and Al Gore and Yo-Yo Ma. The names flow like a river of American political and cultural history. Now they are more contemporary, more popular—Tommy Lee Jones, Al Franken, Conan O'Brien, Matt Damon, and Bill Gates (although the last two dropped out). And since 1963, when the women of sister college Radcliffe started getting Harvard diplomas, that list of famous graduates has included prominent alumnae such as Mira Sorvino, Bonnie Raitt, and Natalie Portman.

And now Harvard was getting a new president who would oversee the ongoing creation of American leaders and shape how those leaders would be taught and what they would learn.

As the bell of Memorial Church finished its tolling, a man named Richard Hunt rose to stand behind a podium emblazoned with the Harvard crest—the word *veritas*, Latin for "truth," against a crimson background. Formal and mannered, with tortoiseshell glasses and graying hair under his ceremonial mortarboard, Hunt was the university marshal, the keeper of Harvard's traditions and choreographer of its rituals. Few others knew why Harvard called this ritual an installation rather than an inauguration, but Hunt knew that while *inauguration* referred to U.S. presidents, the Harvard presidency predated the American one, and so Harvard used an earlier term. Hunt had organized this ceremony, as he did Harvard commencements and welcoming rituals for foreign dignitaries. Soon, though, he would unceremoniously retire from the university he had served for forty-two years, effectively ousted after a clash with the man he was at this very moment helping to swear in. But nobody could see that far ahead; this day was far too bright for such ominous foresight.

"I declare this ceremony of installation open!" Hunt said.

Next came an introductory prayer, a bit of cheerleading from an earnest student leader, words of support from a prominent alumna, and congratulations from Rick Levin, the president of Yale, Harvard's chief rival ever since the former's founding in 1701. "Harvard is blessed with the broadest and deepest assembly of intellectual talent and academic resources in the world, and it is to Harvard that the whole world looks for leadership," Levin professed. "These are mere facts, but believe me, these are not easy things for a Yale president to say."

Then Richard Oldenburg, president of Harvard's Board of Overseers, took the microphone. The Overseers is the larger of Harvard's governing boards, and was once the stronger of the two. Now most of its responsibilities are ceremonial, the majority of its powers symbolic. "In an always troubled world, we look to great universities like ours to assert and defend ethical values," Oldenburg said. Turning toward Summers, he added that it was the new president's job to uphold that tradition. "Now, Mr. President . . . in accordance with ancient custom, I declare that you, Lawrence H. Summers, having been duly chosen to be twenty-seventh president of Harvard College, are vested with all powers and privileges appertaining to that office, and I deliver to you these insignia of your authority."

While Oldenburg spoke, a wary policeman stood behind him and watched over the crowd. Terrorism was not the only security concern. Kept at a safe distance by no-nonsense Harvard police officers several hundred yards away, a small group of student protesters stood outside the Yard. They were members of a group called the Harvard Living Wage Campaign, which had organized to pressure the Harvard administration to increase the salaries it paid Harvard workers. "What's outrageous? Harvard wages!" they chanted. "What's disgusting? Union-busting!" They were too far away to be heard, though, which was no accident. In his work at Treasury and the World Bank, Summers had seen plenty of protesters, and he did not appreciate them. To Summers, these young activists didn't understand the forces that were changing the world—forces that he had helped set in motion. He wasn't about to let them ruin this day.

As Summers stood and walked to the podium, Oldenburg turned to him with outstretched hands. "Two silver keys," Oldenburg declared. Representing the unlocking of knowledge and piety, the keys were given to Harvard to celebrate the 1846 installation of President Edward Everett, the man best known for his two-hour speech preceding Abraham Lincoln's Gettysburg Address. Summers displayed the keys to the crowd, but he looked befuddled, as if he didn't know quite what to do with them. The audience was with him, though, and chuckled supportively.

"Two seals of the college," Oldenburg continued. Summers held those up too and clearly gave a little shrug, as if to say, "I know this is silly, and you know this is silly, but I have to do it." The crowd laughed again.

"And finally, the earliest college record book." Summers took the large red volume and opened it to the crowd, at which point a ribbon used as a page marker fell to the ground. Oldenburg hastily picked it up.

Another elderly man approached the podium. Robert G. Stone, class of '45, was head of the Harvard Corporation. A multimillionaire from shipping and international business interests, Stone was one of the people who'd chosen Summers, although Summers hadn't been his first choice. With his gray suit, wire-rimmed glasses, and meticulously slicked back hair, Stone seemed a throwback to the 1950s, the time just before Harvard men like McGeorge Bundy and Robert McNamara headed to Washington to serve John Kennedy. Stone gave off the aura of money and power; he looked like a man who had never doubted his place in the world.

"Mr. President," he said in a gravelly voice, "it is my privilege to hand you one final insignia of authority—a replica of the charter of the university, dated 1650."

Together, Summers and Stone held up the leather-bound charter, which had established Harvard as the oldest institution recognized by Western law in the Western hemisphere. And with that, Summers moved to sit in the President's Chair, an ungainly wooden structure with a square back and a triangular seat, which was a little small for

Summers. President Edward Holyoke bought the chair sometime between 1737 and 1769, although it had probably been made closer to the year 1550, and ever since it had served as the chair in which Harvard presidents sat for their official portraits. Summers was smiling, but he looked impatient. His right leg danced back and forth as if it couldn't wait to get moving.

As Larry Summers gazed out over the enthusiastic crowd on his installation day, he looked upon a university that reigned preeminent in American education. In terms of status, reputation, breadth, money, power, and influence, no other university can equal Harvard—not in the United States, not in the world.

Its dominance is due in part to its age. Founded in 1636, Harvard is the oldest American university by a considerable amount—Virginia's William and Mary, which opened its doors in 1693, is next. Being older than the United States itself gives Harvard as close to an aura of antiquity as you can get in this country. It has also given the university time to experiment, expand, and mature.

But it isn't just age that has contributed to Harvard's preeminence. Geography has helped too. Harvard is just a few miles from Boston, one of the country's most important cities until at least the mid-nineteenth century. Perched snugly in Cambridge and delineated by the picturesque Charles River, Harvard was close enough to benefit from its proximity to Boston, yet far enough away to avoid being overshadowed by urban growth or mired in urban decay. And for more than three centuries Harvard could expand physically without running into the dire space constraints that urban universities such as Columbia, in New York City, have faced.

But age and geography are not the only, nor even the primary, reasons that Harvard has become the world's most important university. Harvard's greatest good fortune has been its success in choosing its presidents. At critical times in its history, Harvard has always managed to locate a leader who would take just the right gamble to keep the university innovative and excellent. It could be argued that Harvard presidents have consistently been more successful than American ones.

For these reasons and more, Harvard has come to occupy a totemic place in the American imagination. The name of no other university carries the cachet that Harvard's does. That is why high school students cram and practice and sacrifice for years to get into Harvard—all those class presidents and star athletes and musical prodigies and budding scientific geniuses—even though they know that in any given year 90 percent of the roughly twenty thousand who apply to the college will be rejected. Because once you're in—well, is there any surer ticket to success in American life than a diploma with the word *Harvard* printed upon it?

Harvard is strong and famous not just because of its undergraduate college but also because of its professional schools. Every year those schools produce the elite of America's white-collar professions, from architecture to education to academia. Most powerful are the schools of law, business, and medicine. If they are not always ranked first in their field, they are always near the top. And they are unrivaled in terms of the connections they provide their students, the status they confer, the aura of success that cloaks their graduates like elegantly tailored clothing.

It is that name, Harvard, that does it—"the best brand in higher education," as many around campus will tell you matter-of-factly, without a hint of irony (or, for that matter, humility). Students describe telling outsiders that they go to Harvard as "dropping the *H* bomb." The name prompts a reaction—sometimes flattering, sometimes awestruck, sometimes resentful, but always a reaction. Going to Harvard, you become part of something bigger than yourself—and in return, you become something bigger, something *more*, than what you were before. Students rarely change Harvard, but Harvard almost always changes its students profoundly.

The farther away you get from Cambridge, the more the name impresses. In New York City, Harvard is respected. But if a boy from Billings, Montana, or a girl from Johnson City, Tennessee, gets into Harvard, it's news for the local paper. Outside of the United States, the name carries even more weight. Harvard students and professors marvel at how they can travel to every corner of the globe—to China or Argentina or Romania—and when they say they come from Harvard, people will nod in recognition and accord them a certain respect, sometimes even awe. That wouldn't happen if you mentioned Yale or Princeton, Berkeley or Stanford, Oxford or the Sorbonne. Harvard is a golden passport that can take its bearer anywhere and everywhere.

And the money: On this campus the scent of money wafts from

between every red brick. The day Larry Summers became president, Harvard's endowment stood at a staggering $19 billion. No other American university—and American universities are the world's richest—could even come close; Yale was second, with a relatively paltry $10 billion. And Harvard's figure didn't even count the hundreds of acres of real estate worth billions more, or the Florentine villa it was bequeathed by a grateful graduate, the thousands of treasures in its twelve museums, or the four hundred thousand–acre lumber forest in New Zealand that the university would purchase soon thereafter. Harvard was reported to be the second-richest non-profit institution in the world. Only the Catholic Church had more money than Harvard—and Harvard was gaining.

And yet, not all was right at the university Larry Summers was about to take charge of. As Harvard faced the beginning of a new century, it looked to the future not with confidence and serenity, but with anxiety and doubts. All that money had brought tensions, conflicts, and questions. It was changing the very nature and identity of the university. How could Harvard be so rich and still teach its students that the life of the mind mattered more than the never-ending quest for cash? When your endowment grew at an annual rate of about a billion dollars a year—and that was a conservative estimate—what differentiated you from the world of big business? And when a university had more money in the bank than any number of countries, did such wealth change the responsibilities of that institution? Its mission? How could a university be so rich without risking the corruption of its soul?

All that money, swirling through the air like what you'd imagine after the crash of an armored car . . .

Maybe that was why, during the 1990s, Harvard endured a growing number of problems with graft and corruption, a string of embarrassing incidents involving both students and faculty. The same kind of thing happened to the rest of America, true, but Harvard wasn't supposed to be like the rest of America. What was it that its twenty-fourth president, Nathan Marsh Pusey, had said? Harvard "was in society but it was set apart and better than that society, and not a corrupt creature of it." You wouldn't know that from looking at Harvard in the 1990s. All that money. *Nineteen billion dollars.*

And Harvard had another problem, one that money alone couldn't fix: its undergraduate education was inconsistent, conceptually flawed, and sometimes just not very good. Harvard College had an aging curriculum that half of its students couldn't explain and still fewer liked. It had professors who didn't want to teach and, what's more, who frequently weren't required to teach, and so they spent their time consulting and lecturing and writing books, activities that garnered them more money and renown than the prosaic duties of instructing undergraduates. Harvard students were paying close to $40,000 a year for tuition, yet the bulk of their scholarly interaction was with teaching fellows—graduate students who, however well-meaning they may have been, weren't what you thought you would be getting when you mailed in that Harvard application. Was that why students were getting such high grades? Something like 90 percent of the undergrads were graduating with honors. No wonder the whispering had become conventional wisdom: it was tough to get into Harvard—brutally tough—but once you were in . . . well, once you were in, you didn't have to work very hard at all if you didn't want to.

And while Harvard was unquestionably on top of the aspirational heap in the public psyche, other schools were catching up. Yale was always a competitor; even people at Harvard were admitting that the undergrad education at Yale was better. Thank God the latter's hometown of New Haven was saddled with a reputation as a depressed and depressing city. That scared people away.

Beyond Yale, though, there was new blood that couldn't be easily dismissed. Some claimed that Princeton had the country's best undergraduate experience. Stanford and Berkeley and New York University were creating buzz. They didn't have the reputation Harvard did—not yet—but they had energy and momentum; they had presidents with *vision*. And if Harvard was losing ground that it had always owned, what was all that money really accomplishing?

That was why the Harvard Corporation had chosen Larry Summers: to take charge; to fix what was embarrassingly wrong and make sure that the gap between the public perception of the university and the reality of Harvard didn't grow so broad that it became a chasm; to revive the image of the Harvard president as a national leader, a figure who spoke out not just to ask for money, nor even to voice his thoughts on higher education, but also to deliver his opinions on issues of import to the nation and the world generally. Not so many years before, Harvard presidents had done that as a matter of routine, but recently, this was less and less the case. For the members of Harvard's governing body, this was unacceptable. If Harvard presidents weren't national leaders, how could Harvard be? Conversely, how could America be great if Harvard was not?

So perhaps it was understandable that Larry Summers looked a little nervous on the day of his installation, a little uncomfortable with all the trappings of history and ritual. Much was being asked of him. The expectations were high, the pressure immense. And Summers was instinctively more comfortable *doing* something than going through the motions of ritual.

Then again, the new president wasn't the only nervous one. Most Harvard professors and students knew very little about Larry Summers, only the bare bones of his biography, really. He hadn't been around campus for a decade. He hadn't even been in the world of academia. All they knew was what they had heard and read, and while some of that was encouraging, some of it was worrisome. Summers was famous not just for being brilliant, but also for being arrogant and hot-tempered. In the past, he'd led more by fiat than by suasion or example, while Harvard presidents traditionally had to rely on all their skills to head such a famously independent and self-assured community. How would Summers fit into a role where he couldn't simply order people to do what he wanted?

It was time for the new president to speak. Summers carefully rose from the ancient President's Chair and strode to the podium. "I accept!" he said. The words sounded slightly forced, but the audience cheered heartily.

Judging from the events of the months and years that were to follow, it is fair to say that neither Larry Summers nor Harvard had any idea what they were getting into.

Harvard
Rules

1

The Remarkable, Controversial Career of Larry Summers

From *Love Story* to *Legally Blonde*, Harvard abounds in American popular culture. Partly this is because the university produces many creative, ambitious, and occasionally dysfunctional graduates whose Cambridge experience provides a natural subject for their work. It's also because the campus is so picturesque, so resplendent with timeless red brick, graceful bell towers, and sleek sculls gliding along a sparkling Charles River. This is cinematic stuff. Setting a story at Harvard conveys history, power, and tradition; Harvard raises the stakes. Little wonder that thriller writer Dan Brown, author of *The Da Vinci Code*, made his hero, symbologist Robert Langdon, a Harvard professor. The label gives Langdon instant credibility.

Nevertheless, much of the literature and film featuring Harvard casts the university in a critical light. Consider perhaps the most famous Harvard drama. In Erich Segal's 1970 novel *Love Story* (the film of which is screened for Harvard freshmen every fall), the university comes across as a cold and uncaring place, aesthetically impressive but officially hostile to the romance of Harvard man Oliver Barrett IV and Radcliffe student Jenny Cavilleri. They fall in love at Harvard, but certainly not because of it. Love distracts from work.

In *The Paper Chase*, the 1973 film about a law student who falls in love with his august professor's daughter, Harvard is a place where excellence takes root not because of its culture of competition, arrogance, and frosty interpersonal relations, but despite it. Then there's 1997's *Good Will Hunting*, the tale of a working-class math genius who falls for a Harvard undergrad. In that film, the typical Harvard student is presented as pompous, effete, and not nearly as smart as he thinks he is. Other, less good movies present Harvard still more cynically. In 1986's *Soul Man*, the only way a young man can afford Harvard is to pretend that he's black in order to win a scholarship. And in the 2002 comedy *Stealing Harvard*, a well-meaning uncle attempts to pilfer $30,000 so that his niece can pay Harvard's costs.

In the realm of nonfiction, there is a sizeable genre of "I spent a year at Harvard" books—memoirs of the law school, medical school, divinity school, and so on. In theme and structure, such chronicles— such as Scott Turow's *One L*—constitute survival narratives. A year at the Harvard Law School is the academic equivalent of surviving a plane crash in the Peruvian Andes or being stranded on a deserted island with only a beach ball for company. As in most Harvard-themed works of culture, individuality is in short supply, spontaneity prompts rebuke, and love is an endangered emotion.

Harvard's administration devotes enormous amounts of time, money, and energy to generating more positive media coverage. The university seems to have more press secretaries than Congress, and they spend as much time shooting stories down as helping them get written. Much of their job involves getting faculty members quoted in newspapers and magazines on issues related to their expertise, and at this they are remarkably successful—helped, no doubt, by the prevalence of Harvard grads in the press. Some years back, a writer working on a book about Harvard asked a group of researchers to count the number of instances in which the *New York Times* cited Harvard over a period of several months. They expected the number to be large, but even to their surprise, they found that the *Times* mentioned Harvard more than all other universities *combined*.

Of course, Harvard doesn't rely on outside press organizations to advertise itself. It publishes dozens of reports, bulletins, journals, and magazines lauding the accomplishments of members of the Harvard community. There's nothing sinister about this—all universities do it—but Harvard does it bigger and better. Among numerous examples, the *Harvard University Gazette*, a weekly newspaper during the school year, profiles Harvard faculty and lists the remarkable number of lectures, exhibits, and performances happening on campus in any given week. *Harvard Magazine* is a slick, professional magazine sent to all Harvard alums six times yearly. The university web page, a more recent innovation, projects a harmonious image of Harvard across the world, twenty-four hours a day.

If, in the summer and fall of 2001, you had read the articles in Harvard publications and on Harvard websites about new president Larry Summers, you would have acquired a meticulously selected and oft-repeated set of facts about him. You would have known that Summers was energetic and "brilliant"—a word repeated so often to describe him that it became almost a third name. You would have known that Summers was an inspiring teacher, often mentioned as a likely winner of the Nobel Prize in economics. And that Summers had spent a successful decade in Washington, capped by his eighteen months as secretary of the treasury. From all the things written about him, you might have gotten the impression that Summers resembled TV's *West Wing*'s President Bartlet, played by Martin Sheen—only smarter.

All the promotion paid off. Summers received glowing treatment in the non-Harvard media, which proclaimed that he was just the man to restore the role of university president to its pre-Rudenstine standing. Larry Summers, wrote one *Boston Globe* columnist, "has the potential to be the greatest president of Harvard since Charles W. Eliot," the nineteenth-century figure generally considered to be Harvard's greatest president, period.

True, it was occasionally mentioned that Summers was a fierce competitor on the tennis court. But if he had other hobbies or interests outside the realm of economics, they went undiscovered. Nor was there mention of Summers' personal life, certainly not of the fact that he was in the throes of a painful divorce. Nor was there discussion of the cancer he had overcome while in his twenties, and the effect that the disease had had on his attitude toward life and work. Also absent was the fact that he would be Harvard's first Jewish president, a cultural milestone whose omission was hard to understand.

In fact, for all the compliments that Harvard's publicity paid him, the career and biography of Lawrence Henry Summers were more conflicted, more complicated, and, above all, more human than the university allowed. Lawrence Summers was not just an intellectual force of nature (though this was clearly an image with which he himself felt comfortable); he was also the product of an immigrant journey, a family crucible, and the classically American story of a man driven by ego and ambition on a ceaseless quest to climb to the pinnacle of American achievement—and beyond.

That Harvard would present such a carefully massaged picture of its new president reflected the competing values within the university. While its scholars pursue the expansion of knowledge, its administrators work to preserve and extend the "brand." And yet, all the flattering publicity about Larry Summers may have backfired. Had Harvard promoted a more balanced picture of him, the new president might have had a more forgiving first year and the university might have spared itself a great deal of shock and unhappiness. Or at least shock.

Lawrence Henry Summers was born in New Haven, Connecticut, on November 30, 1954. He was the first child of Robert and Anita Summers, a husband-and-wife team of economists then at Yale. His paternal grandfather, Frank Samuelson, had been a pharmacist at the Economical Drug Store in Gary, Indiana. His mother's father was named Harry Arrow, and he was an office manager from New York City who struggled for work during the Great Depression.

Robert and Anita Summers were both solid, capable economists, but neither was at the top of the field, and Yale did not offer them tenure. In 1959 they moved to the University of Pennsylvania, where both would teach for the rest of their careers. They raised Larry and his two younger brothers, Richard and John, in Lower Merion, a pretty, prosperous suburb on Philadelphia's Main Line and perhaps best known as the hometown of the blue-blooded lawyer played by Tom Hanks in the film *Philadelphia*.

Of the two parents, Anita was the stronger influence on Larry. Protective, proud, and demanding, she doted on her first son, who had an uncanny knack for absorbing numbers and interpreting information. As a two-year-old, riding in his parents' car, he could identify the names of gas stations. By the time he was seven, he could recite the names of John F. Kennedy's cabinet members. When JFK was assassinated, the nine-year-old spent the entire weekend watching news reports on television. He loved games, especially those that involved statistics and puzzles. "I was a curious kid, not especially outgoing," Summers would remember. Curious—and precocious. At age ten, he appeared on a local sports radio quiz show and answered everything so quickly that the show ran out of questions for him. The next year he devised a logarithm to ascertain whether a baseball team's standing on the Fourth of July could predict its finish at season's end.

Robert and Anita fashioned a domestic environment in which learning and problem-solving were the stuff of daily life, even inventing a system by which the family would vote on what television shows to watch, with votes weighted according to the intensity of one's choices. Larry concocted a system by which he and his brothers could always win the television elections. "His parents deliberately taught the kids economics in family situations," said Harvard historian Phyllis Keller, who knew the Summers family. If the Summers were driving in traffic, Robert and Anita might throw out intellectual puzzles such as, "If there were one more lane, would that eliminate the traffic jam or simply increase the number of drivers who used the road?" A childhood friend would later remember: "Every day [the Summers] would solve a different problem. I liked going over there. But I also liked leaving."

Richard and John were no dummies—they'd grow up to be a psychiatrist and a lawyer, respectively—but Larry was destined to be the standout. In Harriton High School, he focused on math, the subject for which he seemed to have a natural affinity. Outside of the classroom, he played tennis, and was intensely competitive. "He always worked to get the best partner in tennis tournaments, even if that meant dumping the partner he had already played with," remembered Morton Keller, Phyllis' husband and a historian in his own right. Anita Summers liked to tell the story of the time her twelve-year-old son was on his way to a tennis tournament. "Have fun," she called out to him. "This is not about fun," Larry responded. "This is about winning."

Summers' parents were not the only influence on his intellectual life, however, and perhaps not even the strongest. For Summers was born into a truly remarkable intellectual family: two of his uncles ranked among the finest economic minds of the twentieth century.

A graduate of the University of Chicago who earned his Harvard Ph.D. in 1941, Paul Samuelson is Robert Summers' older brother. Samuelson's interests range widely, but perhaps his greatest contribution to economics has been his emphasis on mathematics as the foundation of the discipline. Today's economics students might take this for granted, but before Samuelson, economics was a field that, much like history or philosophy, was characterized by elegant theory and eloquent writing. Samuelson introduced another language. Without advanced mathematics as the basis for economics, he argued, economists were practicing "mental gymnastics of a peculiarly depraved type." In 1948, at the age of thirty-three, Samuelson published *Economics: An Introductory Analysis*, which outlined his vision and became the largest-selling economics textbook ever.

Samuelson helped economists communicate with one another in a way they previously could not. The incorporation of mathematics that he urged helped to establish economics as a powerful analytical discipline, separating it from "softer" academic fields and creating countless new areas to explore, new questions to ask, and new ways to answer those questions. In 1970, he would win the Nobel Prize. "More than any other contemporary economist," the prize committee said, Samuelson "has contributed to raising the general analytical and methodological level in economic science."

Despite his faith in the language of mathematics, Paul Samuelson is very much a public economist who has always wanted his ideas to be accessible. As a younger man, he was deeply ambitious and enjoyed his status as a public figure. He wrote a column for *Newsweek*, consulted for the Treasury Department, and served as an advisor on economic policy to John F. Kennedy and Lyndon Johnson. In his spare time, he was a passionate tennis player.

Ken Arrow, however, is very different, and not simply because he preferred badminton. Anita Summers' older brother is a quiet, gentle, and less outgoing figure whose work is even more theoretical than Samuelson's. Born in 1921, Arrow grew up in New York City and attended City College—then a haven for Jewish intellectuals excluded from other universities due to anti-Semitism—before earning his doctorate at Columbia. In 1951, after spending four years in the Army during World War II, the thirty-year-old Arrow published his most famous work, *Social Choice and Individual Values*. The book's thesis, also known as the "General Impossibility Theorem," is not easily condensed, and it's virtually impossible for a layman to read. Essentially, though, Arrow argued that societies cannot make rational decisions for the general welfare based on the aggregation of individual choices. Abstract though it may sound, the General Impossibility Theorem had enormous implications for public policymaking and helped to start an entire subfield known as "public choice economics." Arrow, who spent his career as a professor at Harvard and Stanford, would win the Nobel Prize in 1972.

Larry Summers was not particularly close to his two uncles, but they and their achievements pervaded the atmosphere around him like the oxygen he breathed. And because of their longevity—both Arrow and Samuelson are well past 80—their achievements were hardly part of a remote past. Samuelson won his Nobel while Summers was in high school; Arrow received his during Summers' freshman year at college. Everybody who knew Larry Summers as a student knew who his uncles were, and because of their stature and his early promise, Larry was expected to do great things. That set the bar high, even for someone as intelligent and competitive as Summers. Within the same field, it would be an enormous challenge just to equal Samuelson's and Arrow's accomplishments, much less better them. Larry Summers' version of teen rebellion may have been the fact that he took only one econ class in high school.

But Larry was not the only member of his family influenced by his famous uncles. Their effect upon his father is an important part of Summers' story. Robert Summers was originally named Robert Samuelson, but as a young adult he changed his surname to Summers. Among economists who know the family—and economics can feel like a very small field in which everyone knows all the rumors about everyone else—it is widely believed that Robert Summers changed his name from Samuelson to avoid constant and diminishing comparisons made between him and his more accomplished brother Paul.

But there is another explanation for Robert Summers' name change: the fear of anti-Semitism and the desire for ethnic assimilation. The Summers family was Jewish on both sides. The rapid rise of Ken Arrow, Paul Samuelson, and Robert and Anita Summers to stature and prominence in American life is a remarkable immigration success story. But, particularly for Paul Samuelson, anti-Semitism was an ugly part of that story.

As a graduate student at Harvard in the 1930s, Samuelson was manifestly brilliant, and that brilliance led to an invitation to join Harvard's Society of Fellows. Founded by President Abbott Lawrence Lowell in 1932, the Society of Fellows is a bit like the academic equivalent

of the military's Navy SEALs or basketball's Dream Team—the elite of
the elite. Fellows are chosen for one reason and one reason only:
because they are astoundingly smart. They receive an annual stipend—
currently around $50,000—but are not required to produce any work
for it. (As the Harvard website puts it, they are "free from formal
requirements.") They are, basically, paid to sit around and think big
thoughts.

But though Samuelson's genius could not be ignored, he was
nonetheless denied prime teaching opportunities. Instead, as historians
Morton and Phyllis Keller write in their book, *Making Harvard Modern*, "he was shunted off with other Jewish graduate students to statistics and/or accounting, generally thought of as 'Jewish courses.'"

Samuelson accepted a professorship at the Massachusetts Institute
of Technology in 1940. Seven years later, with his remarkable textbook on the verge of publication, a tenured position opened up at Harvard, and Samuelson was an obvious candidate. Strangely, he did not
get the job—and anti-Semitism may have been why. Six decades later,
whether prejudice was truly behind the rejection continues to be
argued at Harvard, but the advantage in the debate seems to fall on the
side of those who think it was. For the Kellers, there was no doubt.
"The failure to appoint Samuelson became legendary as the most
destructive consequence of Harvard anti-Semitism," they write. Certainly Larry Summers was struck by the incident. At a lunch at the
Harvard Club of New York in 2004, he would declare that "an uncle of
mine lost the opportunity to be a professor at Harvard because he was
Jewish." Samuelson would stay at MIT, which was, ironically, one reason why the Institute's economics department would rank above Harvard's for decades to come.

Robert Samuelson, Paul's younger brother, was surely aware of his
brother's struggle. Who could blame him for believing that, if anti-Semitism could divert his brother's career, he, a lesser mind, couldn't
afford to take a chance? And so, according to an article in *Slate* magazine
by Paul's grandson, Couper Samuelson, both Robert and Paul's other
brother, Harold Samuelson, "changed their surnames to Summers for
fear that their respective careers might be marred by the anti-Semitism
that their birth name engendered."

Judaism was a part of Larry's youth, but intellectual life was consistently more important to the Summers family than their religious or cultural heritage. Larry Summers wasn't ashamed of or embarrassed about being Jewish, but he grew up in a safe, genteel world far away from his grandfather's drugstore—even if it was only one generation removed. His was a comfortable and prosperous childhood, insulated from the kind of anti-Semitism his uncle Paul had faced. "There were country clubs where I grew up that had few if any Jewish members, but not ones that included people I knew," Summers would say. "My experience in college and graduate school, as a faculty member, as a government official—all involved little notice of my religion."

In 1971, when Summers was in eleventh grade, he applied to colleges a year early. The result was unexpected: Harvard turned him down. Summers has never conceded this awkward fact in print, and the Harvard admissions office will not confirm it, but the question would later provoke so much speculation after Summers became Harvard president that, at a spring 2002 banquet for student fundraisers, one senior woman stood to ask Summers why he hadn't attended Harvard College. "Because I didn't get in," Summers replied in front of a startled crowd. It was, said one person who was present, "an astonishing thing."

So Summers went to MIT, geographically close to Harvard but culturally remote. The Institute is primarily a school for mathematics and the sciences; students who choose MIT tend to have graduate school already in mind. It's a rigorous place filled with hard-working, career-oriented students and a high-pressure atmosphere. One would not attend MIT for the study of the humanities, the social life, or because of its teams' athletic prowess. MIT students are stereotyped as geeks and nerds, and to a certain extent they revel in that identity: An MIT tradition is to play high-tech pranks during the annual Harvard-Yale football game, such as inflating a massive canvas balloon buried underneath the field. (It looked like a whale breaching.) More recently, a group of students built a model plane with a forty-five-foot wingspan and landed it on top of MIT's Great Dome, which is a hundred and fifty feet high. Their intention was to celebrate the one hundredth anniversary of the Wright Brothers' first flight. As the MIT news office succinctly reported, "The model was dismantled by . . . the Institute's hack evaluation and technology team."

Larry Summers thrived at MIT. He grew a heavy beard, more a sign of math-geek nerdiness than hippie rebellion. He joined the debate team and would become a national champion. "I traveled all over the country, attending debate tournaments and debating issues ranging from gun control to national health insurance to control of energy prices," Summers would remember. According to one family friend, Summers wanted not just to travel domestically, but to study abroad; his mother, however, discouraged it, arguing that MIT was too good a place to leave for a semester. That was one of the few arguments Summers lost. Steeped in the intellectual jousting of his home life, he was never afraid to speak his mind or question others, whatever the context. "Larry is in permanent argument mode," said a longtime colleague. "If you say, 'Hello,' Larry will say, 'Why?' For a lot of people, that's very unnerving. But if you say, 'Why not?' he'll come right back at you and engage."

And Summers switched his course of study from mathematics to economics. He realized, he would explain later, that he could not compete with the astonishing students he encountered studying math at MIT. And if he couldn't be the best at something, he didn't want to do it.

As an MIT sophomore, Summers worked as an assistant to economist Martin Feldstein, then a thirty-four-year-old professor at Harvard. Feldstein was politically conservative, but other than that he represented a standard type in the Harvard economics department. He was an impressive, powerhouse figure who was deeply immersed in worldly matters and rather less interested in undergraduates. In later years, he would serve in the Reagan administration, become a director for several corporations, and contribute regular op-ed pieces to the *Wall Street Journal*. Though he was widely considered a soporific lecturer, his introductory economics class—popularly known as "Ec 10"—would become one of Harvard's most widely taken courses, with several hundred students a year enrolled. Students don't take Feldstein's course for his charismatic personality or scintillating presentation, but because they understand that high-paying jobs often require knowledge of economics. One-on-one, however, was a different experience, and Feldstein—so politically unlike Summers' parents and uncles—would become an intellectual mentor to the MIT undergrad.

In 1974 Summers would apply to Harvard again, this time for graduate study in economics, and this time Harvard accepted him. Even if Summers hadn't known Feldstein, it would have been difficult for the university to say no. For one thing, his uncle, Ken Arrow, was teaching in the department. More important, it was clear that Larry Summers was becoming an intellectual force to be reckoned with—capable of absorbing huge quantities of information, constantly questioning, probing a subject from every angle—and fearless.

One of his graduate school classmates, a German economist named George Ziemes, remembered an incident in which Summers challenged his uncle. Arrow was illustrating a problem on the blackboard when Summers interrupted him and said, "Ken, I think you're wrong," then proceeded to explain why. Summers' classmates watched in fascination; Arrow had won his Nobel just a couple years before, and a challenge from any student would have been remarkable. For a nephew to do so added a gripping familial subtext. The class ended before Arrow could address the issue. But at the start of its next meeting, he admitted that "Larry was right."

Summers was "by far the most technically brilliant" of the graduate students in their year, Ziemes said. "I could work for twenty-five hours a day, and not be as smart as him." At the same time, something about Summers made Ziemes uncomfortable. As Ziemes put it, "he was so strong that he could not walk. He was arrogant and ambitious. I believed he wanted to be the first Jewish president"—not of Harvard, but of the United States.

As intense as he was intelligent, Summers often overlooked basic social niceties. When the econ grad students went out for pizza, Summers was an awkward fit, visibly uncomfortable in groups. And his table manners were disconcerting to say the least—he would take a huge bite of pizza and then, before he'd even swallowed, fill his mouth with soda. The other students joked that Summers would wear his meal home.

After finishing his course work, Summers would teach at MIT. Then, in 1981, he traveled to Washington for his first job outside of academia: assistant to his old boss Martin Feldstein, now the new head of President Reagan's Council of Economic Advisers. Summers was hardly an advocate of Reagan's supply-side economics; the experience, said one economist who knew him at the time, was a calculated "résumé-builder."

In 1982, seven years after starting graduate school, Summers completed his doctoral dissertation. (He would have finished considerably faster if not for the teaching and the time in Washington.) His dissertation, called "An Asset Price Approach to the Analysis of Capital

Income Taxation," would win Harvard's David A. Wells Prize for the year's best economics thesis. That same year, Henry Rosovsky, a member of Harvard's economics department and dean of the Faculty of Arts and Sciences, urged President Derek Bok to offer Summers tenure. When Bok did, Summers accepted the offer, becoming, at the age of twenty-eight, one of the youngest tenured professors in the university's history.

Nineteen eighty-two was a good year for Summers, and not just academically. He had fallen for a law school student named Victoria Perry, and she for him. A pretty brunette, Perry was smart and ambitious, although in some ways very different from Summers. She was born in Bangor, Maine, and looked like she was "straight out of an L.L.Bean catalogue," according to one woman who knew her. While the Perrys kept a home in Maine, Vicki mostly grew up in Florida, where her father was an account executive with a securities firm and her mother a math professor. She was smart—she'd graduated summa cum laude from Yale—but interested in becoming a lawyer, not an academic.

Larry impressed her with his mind, and she impressed him by being able to keep up with him; Summers had been raised by a strong woman, and he liked the same in a girlfriend. "Vicki Perry has been a wonderful friend during the late stages of this work," Summers wrote in the acknowledgments of his dissertation. "Her companionship has made the last few months very happy ones." After graduation Perry went to the law firm Hale & Dorr, one of Boston's most upper-crust law firms, and in September 1984 she and Summers were married. Held at the Harvard Club in Boston, the ceremony was conducted by a rabbi and a Congregational minister. Summers was twenty-nine, Perry twenty-seven.

The wedding came at a challenging time: Summers was sick. Eight months before, in January, he'd been diagnosed with Hodgkin's disease, a cancer of the lymphatic system that occurs most frequently in men between the ages of fifteen and thirty-four. A year-long program of chemotherapy followed. It was hard—people who know Summers well say that he could very possibly have died—but he endured by focusing on his work. "I did some of my best research in the year after I was diagnosed," he said. His doctor was a Harvard-affiliated specialist in blood cancers named David Scadden, and in typical fashion Summers turned the experience into a learning opportunity. When it became clear that he would survive, he asked Scadden how recent were the discoveries that led to the treatments that had saved him. The answer—about fifteen years—made a profound impression on him. Fifteen years was not a long time when it was your illness being treated.

In later years Summers rarely spoke of his cancer. He and Scadden lost touch for almost two decades. Many people who know Summers casually, and some who know him moderately well, aren't even aware that he has had cancer. But after being chosen president, Summers told *Harvard Magazine* that the cancer helped him to appreciate family and those less fortunate than himself. According to people who have known him since that time, it did more than that; they say that its greater impact was to leave Summers with a newfound appreciation for the brevity of life. After his cancer, they suggest, Summers possessed an urgency to work as quickly as possible, because he never knew how long—or short—his life might be. And outside of his own field, the work that most interested him was the work that had saved his life—science and medicine. After becoming president of Harvard, he would repay Scadden's aid with a favor of his own.

Over the next years, Summers produced a slew of top-notch papers on issues such as taxes, unemployment, and markets. "Larry was a hive of activity," said Harvard economics professor Larry Katz, a friend of Summers'. "What was amazing was the breadth of his activity—he could work on twenty problems with twenty different people." Politically, Summers was left of center; he was skeptical of the unfettered marketplace and believed that the federal tax code should be structured to promote progressive policy goals. Intellectually, he had a talent for bringing real-world data to problems that economists had previously dealt with theoretically. In a provocative 1986 paper on Henry Ford, for example, Summers and co-author Daniel M. G. Raff examined Ford's 1914 decision to double his workers' wages from $2.50 a day, the industry norm, to $5.00. Why did Ford give his employees such a huge increase? Out of altruism? A desire to burnish his reputation? Both were possible, the authors suggested. But a more powerful motivator may have been that by paying his workers more than he had to, Ford could boost worker morale, lessen labor turnover, and increase profits. The implications were clear. If paying more than the market minimum produced such positive results for Ford, how many present-day firms could—or should—do the same?

Summers was an equally energetic professor. He was demanding and challenging. His Harvard graduate students sometimes felt pressured by him, but they also conceded that he frequently coaxed better work out of them than they had thought themselves capable of. Typical was this 1992 review of Summers from the Harvard Committee for Undergraduate Education (CUE) guide, an annual survey of courses filled out by undergraduates (but published by the college; professors can ask that their evaluation not be printed): "Respondents congratulate Professor Lawrence H. Summers on the overall excellence of his lectures," the entry read. "However, one-fourth of those commenting on his presentations note that he occasionally speaks too quickly." Also, a "significant number of those polled testify to the course's formidable workload." Summers' numeric rating of 4.2 out of 5 was better than average, though not in the highest rank of Harvard professors.

Nevertheless, Summers was restless; he wanted more than the life of an academic. In 1988 he signed up with the presidential campaign of Massachusetts governor Michael Dukakis. Along with economist Robert Reich, who would go on to become Bill Clinton's secretary of labor, Summers advised Dukakis on economic policy. The candidate advocated a proactive role for government in the economy, with tax breaks and government subsidies for companies that invested in high-tech or high-unemployment areas. Rather than raise taxes, Dukakis argued (and Summers agreed) that the government could ease the deficit problem simply by collecting unpaid taxes. Summers was never part of Dukakis' inner circle, however, and today Dukakis doesn't remember much of what Summers did on the campaign. "We met a number of times, but I don't want to exaggerate it," Dukakis says. Nonetheless, Summers made sure to stay on good terms with the former governor. "Every time he gets another important job, Larry writes me a note saying, 'Without you, this wouldn't have happened,'" Dukakis says. "And it's always handwritten."

Dukakis lost that race to George H. W. Bush, of course, depriving Summers of the chance to return to Washington. But the campaign was nonetheless a turning point for Summers. For one thing, he learned that he enjoyed politics; he liked to be not just a student of power and policy, but a player. And during the campaign he met two people who would become very important to his future advancement: a wealthy fundraiser from the investment bank Goldman Sachs named

Robert Rubin, and a rising-star governor from Arkansas, Bill Clinton.

On the surface, Summers was fulfilling everything that might have been expected of him. In 1987 he won the National Science Foundation's Alan T. Waterman Award, which carried with it a $500,000 grant. The award is given to an outstanding young U.S. scientist or engineer; Summers was the first social scientist ever to win it. In 1993 Summers won the John Bates Clark Medal, given by the American Economic Association to the country's outstanding economist under the age of forty. The Clark Medal is often a precursor to a Nobel; Paul Samuelson won it in 1947, Ken Arrow in 1957.

If there was a knock on Summers, it was that he had, perhaps, *too* many ideas. That his mind was so active, it couldn't linger on one subject long enough to produce the big breakthrough that separates an outstanding economist from a truly great mind. There was no lightning bolt, no eureka moment. Both Paul Samuelson and Ken Arrow had experienced such insights before they were forty, the age by which most economists do their most original and important work. As Larry Summers approached that milestone, he'd compiled a formidable record, shown abundant evidence of an agile and powerful mind, produced important insights and valuable papers—but no paradigm shift.

"In the ballpark Larry grew up in, he's not a first-rate intellect," said one prominent economist. "He has not made any major contribution to economics. And you have to understand—his two uncles are not just Nobel Prize winners, they are two of the top figures of the century. Anybody who's in academia knows that there are people who make repeated breakthroughs, there are people who make *a* breakthrough, and there are people who do good economics. His two uncles made repeated breakthroughs. Larry has done good economics. It's two steps down from what his uncles did.

"I think," this economist said, "that Larry knew that." And may himself have come to doubt that he would ever produce the kind of work that wins a Nobel.

If so, it would be an awkward situation. Public expectations of Summers were so high that if he didn't win a Nobel Prize—an absurdly high standard—he'd be considered a disappointment. Maybe, as he approached middle age, he sensed that the likelihood of the prize was slipping away. Especially because he'd already learned that life could be short.

To be fair, economics, especially at its highest levels, is a viciously competitive field, almost entirely dominated by men, many with rapacious egos and cutthroat instincts. Often they are trained in graduate seminars where aggression is encouraged and survival requires attacking your peer's ideas before he slices and dices yours. Surely some of the doubts about Summers arise from the culture of economics and from a personal antipathy toward him. Elsewhere in the field, Summers has his defenders.

"His critics will tell you that there's no one brilliant path-breaking paper," said Richard Levin, the president of Yale and an economist himself. And that's true, Levin admits. "You can't say that Larry ever wrote one paper, or had that one great idea, that everybody just carries around." But, he points out, Nobel Prizes in economics are sometimes awarded for a body of work. "Had Larry stayed an academic, he would have made great contributions to lots of bodies of literature. If Larry had written ten more years of articles of the quality he was writing, I think he would have won the Nobel."

But Summers would not spend the next ten years of his life writing more papers in economics. Instead, at the age of thirty-six, he was headed to Washington again, and this time he would stay for a decade. The economist and professor was on the verge of a profound personal and professional transformation. He was leaving behind the world of the university for, well, the world itself. And in just a few short years, he would become an international figure of enormous importance. Larry Summers—grandson of a druggist and an office manager, child of academia, ivory tower economist—would hold in his hands the fates of nations.

In January of 1991, Summers started a job as vice-president of development economics and chief economist at the World Bank. He took a leave from Harvard and moved with Vicki to Washington, D.C., the home of the Bank.

The World Bank was founded in July 1944 at a meeting of representatives from forty-five countries in Bretton Woods, New Hampshire. Financed by contributions from member nations, the Bank was intended to help fund the postwar reconstruction of Europe. A second, though less explicit agenda was to use financial aid to promote democracy worldwide. The Bank would help pay for public works projects such as highways, hospitals, and dams, facilitating economic growth and fostering political stability.

In its six decades of existence, the World Bank has never been well understood by those most affected by its decisions—usually the world's poorest and least educated people. Some development workers and international policymakers around the world view it as a well-meaning organization doing its best to eradicate poverty. Others, suspicious of its anonymous, bureaucratic culture, think it an avatar for the business and ideological imperialism of the United States. Most Americans, unaffected by its works, don't even know of its existence. But the Bank is an enormously powerful institution, and Summers was joining it just as it was poised to become even more so.

His job at the World Bank was to create economic plans for countries that needed aid. It was a weighty task: Summers would help decide how much money countries would get from the Bank and under what conditions. Though it was a new role for him, he did not doubt his ability, and he had strict ideas about why national economies in developing countries went wrong. "Development failures are the result of national policies," he would argue. "They cannot be blamed on a hostile international environment, or physical limits to growth." Sounding less optimistic about government's ability to effect social change through industrial policy than he had during his stint with Michael Dukakis, Summers articulated a kind of free-market tough love. "National policies have failed when governments thwarted progress, supplanting markets rather than supporting them," he said. Using the kind of provocative imagery he would become known for, he added that countries without a strong central government and vigorous private sector were like "a cripple . . . with no legs, pushing himself around on a crude board with wheels, surviving only with begging and trying to look sympathetic to the potential alms giver."

But it was something that Summers didn't even write that would define his tenure at the World Bank and haunt him for years to come. In December 1991, he signed and distributed a policy memo written by a young aide named Lant Pritchett—though Pritchett's authorship was not indicated on the document. The memo argued that less-developed countries, or LDCs, could benefit from accepting the pollution generated by developed countries. "Just between you and me," the memo read, "shouldn't the World Bank be encouraging more migration of the

dirty industries to the LDC?" Poor countries could earn needed revenue from trade in pollution without losing much in the costs of
increased illness, because people in those countries tended to have a
short life-span anyway. "The concern over an agent that causes a one-
in-a-million change in the odds of prostate cancer is obviously going to
be much higher in a country where people survive to get prostate cancer . . ." The memo concluded that "the economic logic behind dumping a load of toxic waste in the lowest-wage country is impeccable."

Someone at the World Bank leaked the memo to *The Economist*
magazine, which in February 1992 ran an article on it titled, "Let
Them Eat Pollution." Though *The Economist* concluded that "on the
economics, [Mr. Summers'] points are hard to answer," the memo provoked a furor. Then, and for years to come, human rights and anti-
globalization activists, already skeptical of the World Bank, found in
Summers' memo proof of the Bank's hegemonic intentions and callous
attitudes toward the world's poor. And the individual who came to per-
sonify all of their doubts, fears, and hostility to the economic shifts of
the 1990s was Larry Summers.

Summers did his best to explain the memo, claiming that it was
simply part of the free-flowing academic discussion he tried to foster
among his colleagues. He suggested that it was intended to be "ironic."
He insisted that he hadn't read the whole thing before signing it.
Eventually he dispensed with explanations and simply apologized,
quoting New York mayor Fiorello LaGuardia and saying, "When I
make a mistake, it's a whopper." For years, however, Summers never
denied authorship of the memo, which meant that he was being casti-
gated for something he hadn't actually written. But since the memo
sounded like Summers—no-nonsense, aggressively contrarian, cerebral
to the point of sounding amoral—few would have believed such a
denial anyway.

The episode would teach Summers painful lessons about the differences between politics and academia, and about the limits of public
debate. In the field of economics, such a provocative argument was
well within the bounds of acceptable discussion. Unsettling conversations challenged the status quo and promoted new ways of thinking.
But in Washington, the suggestion that the memo was merely an academic exercise didn't fly. It made no sense to float ideas that you didn't
really believe, because special interest groups would inevitably seize

upon your words for political advantage. Some debates were so emotionally charged, you couldn't even conduct them—and certainly not in public. And if one insisted on having such discussions, better not to write them down. Indeed, in the years to follow, Summers became conspicuous for never leaving a paper trail.

Summers also learned how tone and diction can shape public reaction to an economic argument. While the language of the memo, as *The Economist* conceded, was "crass," its content was not as offensive as it appeared at first reading. If you believed that poor countries needed capital to generate economic growth and increase standards of living, then, as paradoxical as it sounded, taking in other countries' pollution might have its positive side. (After all, relatively affluent American states routinely send their garbage to poorer ones, and some environmentalists argue that a marketplace for "pollution credits" would lead to a cleaner environment.) The argument of the memo might have been flawed or even wrong, but it wasn't, as its critics charged, inherently immoral. It was just that, in its clinical language, it sounded that way.

Six years later, in a 1998 *New Yorker* profile of Summers, Lant Pritchett admitted publicly for the first time that he had authored the memo, and he credited Summers with selflessly taking the blame. But the true story might be more complicated. After leaving Washington, Pritchett wound up teaching at Harvard's Kennedy School of Government, and in the winter of 2002 he invited Summers to appear in his class. The week before Summers' visit, Pritchett asked his students not to question Summers on the memo, saying that it was a sensitive topic. The truth, Pritchett said, was that he had always wanted to announce that he'd written the memo, and Summers was receptive to the idea. But others at the Bank advised Summers that if he pointed the finger at Pritchett, he'd look like he was trying to pin the blame on a subordinate, which would make him appear weak. If he took the blame, he'd get hammered by critics outside the Bank. But internally, he'd come across as a stand-up guy, and people would remember that he'd fallen on his sword to protect an aide. (More recently, Pritchett reacted with frustration when asked about the memo, saying that it happened a long time ago and he was tired of the subject. "I feel like Bill Buckner," he said, referring to the Red Sox first baseman whose infamous error may have cost his team the 1986 World Series.)

Summers worked assiduously to transform a painful incident into a humorous, self-deprecating anecdote. As he said at a lecture in January 2000, "I am sometimes asked by friends about the differences between academic life and life as a public official. . . . As an academic, the gravest sin one can commit is to sign one's name to something one did not write. As a public official, it is a mark of effectiveness to do so as often as possible."

In the short term, though, Summers' association with the memo hurt his career. After the election of Bill Clinton in November 1992, Summers hoped to be appointed chairman of the White House Council of Economic Advisers, the three-member board that advises the president on economic policy. (His mentor Martin Feldstein had held the post under Ronald Reagan.) But Summers never got the job; Al Gore, the environmentally minded vice-president, was reportedly so offended by the World Bank memo that he blocked the appointment. "Gore was really pissed off," Summers would later tell students in a Harvard seminar.

Instead, Treasury Secretary Lloyd Bentsen asked Summers to join that department as undersecretary for international affairs, and Summers agreed. In one sense, Treasury was a logical step. The department helps determine the American government's economic policy, and the international affairs section coordinates United States representation in the World Bank and the International Monetary Fund. But in another way, Summers' decision to take the job at Treasury was more radical. Harvard allows tenured professors to take leaves of absence for only two years before they must resign their professorships. So the thirty-eight-year-old Summers, one of the youngest professors ever tenured at Harvard, became one of the youngest professors ever to resign his tenured position.

In the academic world, Summers' decision raised eyebrows. At some point in their careers, most high-level economists engage in public service, often in Washington. In the Harvard economics department, it'd be hard to find an economist who didn't shuttle back and forth between Boston and the nation's capital for a year or so. But such stints are viewed as a temporary respite from academe. The really interesting work—the really *hard* work—is the life of the mind. Moreover, in any academic discipline, it doesn't take long for those who momentarily step aside to start falling behind. The professor who becomes a dean, a university president, or a Washington official will find it difficult if not impossible to return to scholarship. If Summers were to spend more than a few years away from his discipline, then in terms of being a serious intellectual, he would be leaving economics forever.

And so Summers' decision to stay in Washington prompted conversation and gossip. His detractors speculated that he was leaving academia for the same reason he'd switched from mathematics to economics—because he suspected that he couldn't compete at the highest level, the very thin air where great economic minds pondered and clashed. Summers' defenders pointed to his healthy ego and said they doubted very much that he lacked confidence in his abilities. Of course Paul Samuelson's nephew would be interested in a public role, they argued. And anyway, if anyone could play catch-up after years away from academia, it would be Summers.

Whichever the case, the move to Treasury proved to be a very successful decision. Over his eight years there, Summers acquired new stature, new skills, and a new education, becoming, said one observer, "a new kind of geopolitician," a policymaker who "worries about foreigners' economic stability as much as about their arsenals." It is fair to say that even before he was appointed treasury secretary, Summers had become one of the most powerful unelected officials in the world.

Prominently located next door to the White House, the Treasury Department is probably the most elite—and elitist—of federal cabinet agencies. Its vast responsibilities include management of the Internal Revenue Service; the Bureau of Alcohol, Tobacco and Firearms; the Secret Service; the Customs Service; and the Bureau of Printing and Engraving. Treasury also helps to regulate the financial industries and shape international and domestic economic policy. All told, Treasury has about a hundred sixty thousand employees, and the people who work at its highest levels are among the most impressive in government—smart, confident, ambitious, and usually successful in the private sector. Unlike bureaucrats at, say, the Department of Agriculture or the Department of Labor, Treasury aides know that they can quit anytime they want and head straight to a small fortune on Wall Street. As a result, there's a certain swagger to the department culture. As President Reagan's onetime treasury secretary, Don Regan, once said of himself, they have "fuck-you money." And if they don't, they know how to get it.

In some ways, Summers fit in well at Treasury—he was certainly intelligent and confident enough, and his mastery of policy was unquestioned. He was not, however, easy to work with, and sometimes he seemed to forget that conducting endless seminars was not the point of government. In meetings, one former colleague remembers, "there'd be occasions where Larry would take a position and argue it very effectively. And then the next meeting he'd argue the other side, just as effectively. His job was to win the argument at every meeting, not to arrive at a consensus decision."

At the end of 1994, Lloyd Bentsen resigned, and Robert Rubin became the new treasury secretary. Rubin was a judicious, polished veteran of the New York financial world, a graduate of Harvard College and Yale Law School who became a managing partner at the investment firm Goldman Sachs. Rubin exuded an unflappable confidence, almost a sense of existential serenity. If he ever got fed up with public life, he once said, "I could just say good-bye, put on a pair of frayed khakis, and check into a little hotel in St-Germain-des-Prés." Few powerful men could make such a claim without sounding ridiculous. Bob Rubin fostered the impression that he'd be only too happy to quit while he was ahead.

Even as Rubin was taking the helm, a financial crisis was simmering in Mexico. Beset by a falling currency and a massive debt burden, the Mexican government was about to default on some $30 billion worth of bonds. While most Americans couldn't have cared less what Mexico did with its debt, Rubin and Summers knew that a default would have disastrous consequences—other foreign investors would hasten to pull their money out of Mexico, the value of the peso would plummet, and the country could fall into a deep recession. Since Mexico was the United States' third-largest trading partner, the impact on U.S. exports would be grave, and a rise in Mexican unemployment might prompt a surge in illegal immigration. Nor would the effect be limited to Mexico and the United States: a Mexican meltdown could devastate other developing economies around the world, which would, in turn, hurt American exports even more. Strange as it seemed, Mexico might prove to be an economic domino that would tip the world into depression.

Rubin was sworn in by President Clinton on the evening of January 10. When the ceremony was finished, Rubin and Summers lingered in the Oval Office to warn Clinton of the imminent storm. Rubin quickly briefed Clinton, then turned to Summers and said, "Larry, what do you think?" Whereupon Summers spoke for ten minutes on the strategy that he, Rubin, and Federal Reserve Chairman Alan Greenspan had earlier agreed upon.

Clinton immediately understood the urgency of the situation. In the next days, the administration would propose a $40 billion bailout of Mexico. The enormous size of the aid package was a critical psychological component; Treasury wanted to reassure the financial markets that the United States had no intention of letting Mexico go belly-up. In theory, calmed creditors would then stop calling in loans that the Mexican government couldn't pay. But the public and many members of the Republican-controlled Congress couldn't understand why U.S. taxpayers should lend $40 billion to a country to which they usually didn't even pay attention. Said Rubin later, "In 1995, the notion that a poor country's macroeconomic miscalculations could affect the largest economy in the world simply didn't register with a lot of people."

"We felt that by extending a large loan to Mexico—and imposing a set of conditions on that loan—there was a very good chance that we could avert a financial catastrophe with very large consequences for millions of people," Summers said. But if the policy made sense, the politics were crazy. "Eighty percent of the American people were opposed to any kind of loan, and half of the rest were undecided. The Congressional leadership had positioned itself to share the credit if the loan succeeded and blame the administration if it failed."

When it became clear that the opposition of congressional Republicans was likely to doom approval of the loan package, Rubin circumvented Congress by taking the money from a Treasury reserve account. The fine print was hammered out by Summers, who secretly flew to Mexico on an Air Force plane to meet with Mexican president Ernesto Zedillo, a Yale-educated economist. As fraught with tension as the situation was, Summers loved it. This was a high-stakes game, and Rubin trusted him enough to dispatch him on a secret mission involving billions of dollars. Summers had enjoyed teaching and research, but this—this was the stuff of life.

Indeed, the Mexico crisis would become a favorite chapter in Summers' own subsequent accounts of his career. In later years he was always happy to recount the story of the drama—how it exposed him to the backstabbing, duplicity, and intellectual corruption of Washington. The deal "meant eighteen-hour days and quite vicious attacks, and it was less than totally settling to learn that in a real sense, my human capital was peso-denominated," Summers quipped. After a lecture Summers gave at the Kennedy School in April 2002, moderator Graham Allison asked him if he could speak "for a couple of minutes" about the Mexico bailout. Almost twenty minutes later, Summers finished his answer.

There is one part of the story that Summers doesn't tell, however. The success of the Treasury loan package would not be assured for several months, and more than once during that time it appeared that the U.S. initiative wasn't going to stop Mexico's slide. In late February, just a few days after the deal had been signed, things looked so grim that Summers walked into Rubin's office near midnight and volunteered to resign. "He was taking the matter much too personally," Rubin later said, declining the offer. It was a sign of how serious Summers considered the situation—and how expansive he saw his own role in it.

The process of rescuing Mexico taught Summers another lesson: that some matters were too important to be democratically decided. "The Marshall Plan," he would say, "was never focus-grouped." He'd seen how Republican leaders had originally supported the Mexico deal in private, then held their fingers to the wind and demagogued it in public. Congress lacked the guts to pass such an unpopular bill. And why was it unpopular? Because most Americans simply didn't know enough about international economics to have an informed opinion. If you just put smart men like him, Rubin, and Greenspan in a room and left them alone, they could work things out. They could save nations.

It was hard for Summers to mask his impatience with the imperfections of politics and the legislative process. He was still prone to using language that may have been effective in the classroom but was unusually provocative in the offices and corridors of Washington. He also had an unfortunate habit of stating how he really felt. During a 1997 debate over cutting the federal tax on inheritances, Summers remarked that "when it comes to the estate tax, there is no case other than selfishness." That didn't sit well with Republicans, who argued that the estate tax punished families trying to pass on farms and small businesses to their children. "Larry's brain was like a tank powered by a Lotus engine," recalled administration colleague Strobe Talbott. "It purred as it rolled over anything in its way."

It didn't help that Republicans already disliked Summers because of his role in short-circuiting Congress in the Mexico crisis. In the aftermath of that, some GOP members of Congress pushed for Summers' resignation. They didn't get it, and in August, Rubin nominated Summers to be deputy treasury secretary, a position confirmed by the Senate. Twenty-one senators voted against Summers, an unusually large number for what would normally be a routine vote.

"I believe in trying to find the essence of issues, to probe different positions in a very strong way, to discover the right approach," Summers explained. "I'm sorry when that way of thinking gives offense." Or, as his mother would tell a reporter, "He wasn't born to the political arena, where you are always very aware of what you are saying. I think that what many people are seeing is an intellectual form of exploration and underneath is a very kind heart." But even when he tried to say the right things, it was clear that Summers harbored a deep skepticism of, and maybe even a hint of contempt for, the legislative process.

He could also be a difficult boss. "If you're in a meeting, whatever you say, he will make you feel like you're an idiot," said one ex-Treasury aide who worked for both Summers and Rubin. Summers believed that his style would inspire debate on the issues, but more often it only inspired debate about his style. "What was fascinating was to watch how people just shut down after a couple of meetings with him," said another Treasury official. "No matter what people said, he would take them on or demean them in some way. Eventually people would just have nothing to say."

At one point the above-mentioned aide was drafting a relatively minor speech for Rubin. "The Secretary was okay with it," the aide remembered. "But Summers came in and said, 'I just read the draft, and we can't give this speech; this would embarrass the administration!' Just going apeshit. It came down to changing about three words and deleting a paragraph. But he made me feel like I had written a manifesto for the Shining Path."

With people on his level or higher, Summers was more deferential; he recognized that in politics he was the odd man out. "When Larry came to Washington, he started off thinking that he was smarter than everybody else, and soon realized that he was smarter than everybody else at things that weren't always useful in Washington," said one Clinton adviser who worked regularly with Summers. "We had a lot of eggheads in the Clinton White House, and a lot of them just kept banging their heads against the wall until they gave up. Larry looked at it as a learning process, and he kept banging his head against the wall until he began to understand the game. It was kind of Spock-like. He never quite fit in, but he was able to gather enough data that he could get by pretty well. He didn't always make a great first impression, but the more we got to know him and the more comfortable he began to feel, the better he did."

This colleague thought that Summers struggled with the chronic pressure of great expectations. "Al Gore had a similar kind of problem," the colleague said, "when your parents are going to be disappointed if you don't grow up to be president. Larry seemed like if he didn't win a Nobel Prize, he'd be letting down the side."

One person who wasn't troubled by Summers' bellicosity was Robert Rubin. The treasury secretary was secure enough not to mind Summers' oversize ego and smart enough to realize that Summers' intellect was an enormous asset to him. "Having an extremely bright and skillful deputy secretary greatly increased Treasury's effectiveness," Rubin said. "I also thought it made me look good."

"Summers was obviously smarter, more knowledgeable than Rubin about the economy, but Rubin was never intimidated by that," said a colleague of both men. Anyway, they did have their intellectual similarities. Before making up his mind on an issue, Rubin liked to hear every point of view, sitting through hours-long meetings and filling yellow legal pads with notes. Summers explained that he and Rubin were intellectually sympatico because of their shared approach to problem-solving. While some people took data as a conclusion, the two of them saw data as an entry point for new questions; Summers and Rubin shared the approach not just to numbers but to all of life's dilemmas.

In other ways, the two men complemented each other. The slender, elegantly tailored Rubin was the money man with the Harvard pedigree—Harvard College, that is—suave, sophisticated, mannered, charming, and at the time worth about $100 million, according to conservative estimates. Summers was a product of the MIT debate team and Harvard graduate school economics, two forums that encouraged an argumentative nature but not the development of social graces. He'd never made any real money, and he had lousy manners.

He was loud, overweight, impatient, constantly late, and poorly dressed—seeing him with his tie askew and his shirt half-untucked was routine. A caricature of Summers in the *New Yorker* showed a man with a stubby body, a disproportionately large head, and massive, beagle-like jowls, carrying around packets of money like a stork.

But under Rubin's tutelage, Summers began to evolve. He knew that if he wanted to become more than a deputy secretary, he'd have to conform to the Washington way of doing business, and he worked to smooth his rough edges. "Larry just got sick of being called a bull in a china shop," one of his colleagues said. Socially, he started to move in high company. He and Victoria bought a 3,300-square-foot house in Bethesda, Maryland, the affluent suburb bordering Washington, from a Washington lobbyist. The couple started attending the Clintonite "Renaissance Weekends." Summers played tennis with Alan Greenspan and *Washington Post* editor David Ignatius at the tony St. Alban's Tennis Club. Not exactly fleet of foot, Summers wasn't a natural player; his strength was in his strategy, the angles and diversity of his shots, his positioning on the court. "I play a lot better than you'd expect, looking at me," he said.

Sometimes, the same rule applied to Summers' practice of politics. Former Clinton White House adviser Dick Morris recalled an instance in which Summers felt so strongly about a policy, he went behind Rubin's back to promote it. "In early 1996, I met with Rubin and Summers at the Treasury Department to talk about the tax cuts President Clinton was proposing as part of his long-sought budget deal with the Republicans," Morris said. "We had a long talk during which Rubin did most of the speaking. At one point, however, he had to duck out of the office to take a call and left Summers and me alone. As soon as Rubin closed the door behind him, Summers leaned over the table and, in a conspiratorial whisper, said that one of the proposals I had been making—cutting the capital gains tax, which Rubin opposed—might be feasible if the cut were applied only to families selling their homes. . . . Larry told me not to tell Rubin, but he would send me the data. Rubin came back in, and Larry clammed up."

The following day, according to Morris, Summers did indeed send him information that Morris used to make the case for the tax cut to Clinton. "That was the genesis of the current exemption of capital gains taxes on the first $250,000 of profit on home sales per person."

Summers could never become humble, but he could at least act it. So he learned to preface his opinions, as Rubin did, with softening phrases such as, "I'm not an expert on this, but . . ." Or, "It's just one man's opinion, but . . ." Or, "It seems to me that . . ." Perhaps remembering the criticism of the Harvard CUE Guide, Summers began to speak more slowly, biting off words in groups of two or three before pausing, sometimes seeming to catch his thoughts after just a single word. But still, he couldn't hide the effort it took to rein in his opinions. The contrast between the often dumbed-down language of politics and Summers' intellectual impatience was too great to disappear entirely. The effect of Summers' makeover was that "he waits till the end of the meeting to tell you your idea is idiotic, instead of interrupting in the middle of it," said Washington pundit Mara Liasson.

Even as Summers' personal transformation continued, his professional life was increasingly demanding. The Mexico problem, it turned out, was not the end of international financial crises but rather the beginning. Starting in Thailand in 1997, a series of financial panics would sweep Asia, and it would fall to Larry Summers, more than any other individual, to resolve them. At Harvard, few people outside the economics and government departments, the business school, and the Kennedy School were paying much attention to Summers' work. But the deputy secretary was becoming a figure of international renown and controversy, praised as a hero in some parts of the globe, reviled as heartless in others. In fact, Summers may have been better known in Tokyo, São Paolo, and Moscow than he was in Cambridge.

Maybe Harvard wasn't paying full attention, but Summers' experiences with international economics and globalization would shape his attitudes toward the university in ways that the Harvard Corporation might well have understood, but certainly never discussed—not, at least, in public.

After he left the Treasury Department, Larry Summers liked to tell a story about what globalization meant to him. The anecdote reflected his optimism about the phenomenon, as well as his criteria for success in globalization's new, ever-more-competitive world.

"In 1997, I took a trip to Africa to work on debt relief," he said. "We visited a village three hours outside of Abidjan [in Côte d'Ivoire]. We took a kayak there, took a large kayak back. As we were coming back from that village that had just gotten its first water well, somebody stuck a cell phone in my face and said, 'Bob Rubin has a question for you' . . .

"All I could think about was that we were in Africa, in the middle of nowhere, three hours from the capital city, and there was this cell phone. Only nine years before I had been in a car with a cell phone in Chicago, and that was a sufficient novelty at that time that I called my family and I called my friends to say, 'Look, I'm in a car with a telephone.' Nine years later, in the middle of Africa, what does it show? I think it shows a hallmark of a new economy. Globalization—the world is coming together as one. Technology—that's what the cell phone was. And the power of markets, because it wasn't the state-owned telephone company that had put that cell phone service there.

"It seems to me," Summers concluded, "that the nation, the businesses, the individuals that succeed in the next century will be those that grapple effectively with these three forces of globalization, technology, and the power of markets."

Referring to the increasing interdependence of national economies and intermingling of cultures, globalization was perhaps the most far-reaching and passionately debated phenomenon of the 1990s. Summers believed that globalization was generally a good thing, that greater connections between countries would promote economic development and higher living standards all over the world. "It seems to me," he said, "that in the developing world, far more people are poor because of too little globalization rather than too much."

That view was not universally shared. Skeptics suggested that globalization was code for economic and cultural imperialism—primarily by the United States. Globalization, they argued, would lead to environmental pillaging, the extinction of indigenous cultures, a McDonald's in every village, and American-style capitalism—with American bankers and politicians pulling the strings, controlling all the world's nations. Globalization was great if you were one of the haves, they pointed out, someone with the education and training to take advantage of the changes in the world economy. But the have-nots were finding their traditional ways of life uprooted with no apparent payoff.

Both proponents and critics of globalization pointed to the Asian financial crises of the late 1990s as proof of their arguments. The

"Asian flu," as those crises were known, began in Thailand in the summer of 1997 and followed a similar pattern in South Korea, Japan, Indonesia, Malaysia, and non-Asian countries such as Russia and Brazil. In a sense, the crises were a consequence of globalization: improvements in communications and computer technology, combined with changes in domestic law, led to massive influxes of foreign capital into these countries, which in turn led to investment bubbles, particularly in real estate. When the bubbles burst, the holders of the loans—often American hedge funds and investment banks—rushed to call them in, trying to get their money out of the countries before the money ran out. The resulting capital flight inevitably drained the coffers of banks and governments (the distinction between the two wasn't always clear), forcing bank closures and threatening government solvency. As with Mexico, if just one nation defaulted on its loan payments, the aftershocks could throw the rest of the region—and possibly the world—into an economic depression. The result, especially in the developing world, would be higher rates of unemployment, greater poverty, and more disease. In sum, more human misery.

The organization designed to monitor the international economy, the International Monetary Fund, was unprepared for this string of imploding economies. Like the World Bank, the IMF was a product of the Breton Woods Conference, but its mission was slightly different. Whereas the Bank was essentially a fund for international development, the job of the IMF was to monitor the stability of the international economy. Like the Bank, the IMF is dominated by the United States, which has the largest voting percentage at the Fund and dominates IMF policymaking. The government agency that represents American interests at the IMF is the Treasury Department, and the man at the Treasury who told the IMF what to do was Larry Summers. "More than any other single person, Larry [drove] the substance of the U.S. policy response to the Asia crisis," Rubin said.

Summers crafted solutions based on the Mexico model, but using IMF and World Bank funds instead of exclusively American money. He would proffer multibillion-dollar loans, but only with strings attached. Each country had to agree to raise its central interest rate; Summers reasoned that foreign investors could be coaxed back into a country only if they received high rates of return on their investments. Higher interest rates reduced the money supply and lowered inflation.

That was bad for debtors, making it harder for them to pay off their loans, leading to economic slowdowns and higher unemployment. But creditors were repaid in currency that wasn't constantly plummeting in value.

Summers also wanted foreign governments to open their capital markets to foreign investors, lower their trade barriers, restructure the relationships between governments and banks, and even make specific personnel appointments. According to Strobe Talbott, Summers was so deeply immersed in Russian policy, for example, that he controlled the appointments of ministers in the Russian government. "Conditionality in IMF lending was the economic equivalent of the spinach treatment," Talbott wrote in his 2002 memoir, *The Russia Hand*, "and the master chef was Larry Summers."

His opponents said that Summers was taking advantage of the situation to force countries to open their markets to American business on disadvantageous terms. Summers' response was simple: If the IMF was to lend your country billions of dollars—money that might not get repaid—didn't it have the right to dictate the terms? He argued that countries that agreed to the IMF's conditions would be more likely to get their economy back on track, the most powerful means of helping poor people. Yes, IMF conditions would lead to higher unemployment in the short term, but there was no way around that. "Battlefield medicine," Summers would argue repeatedly, "is never perfect."

Summers' approach, known as the "Washington Consensus," was attacked from both the right and the left. Conservatives didn't like the Washington Consensus because it meant using American money to intervene in the internal affairs of other nations. "If it were up to me," said former GOP congressman Jack Kemp in 1998, when Congress was voting on the U.S. share of IMF funding, "I would not give one dime, one nickel, one cent to the IMF, which is asking our taxpayers for [billions]—until it changes its policies and top personnel, without Mr. Summers in the running to lead it."

But perhaps the most vociferous criticism came from liberals who argued that the Washington Consensus was unduly punitive. Ensuring the payback of loans punished the world's poor while rewarding wealthy and irresponsible investors, they said. Why should the IMF bail out Wall Street banks who'd made reckless loans or hedge funds who'd invested in a bubble? "I think it's a mistake to blame the doctor instead of the disease," Summers responded, and, besides, there were no perfect solutions. In the long term, the countries in question would benefit from greater "transparency" in their financial affairs and less "crony capitalism," the dispensing of sweetheart deals to intimates of powerful people.

Perhaps the toughest criticism of Summers came from an unexpected source: the chief economist at the World Bank, an American named Joseph Stiglitz. Unlike most of the anti-globalization activists who still criticized Summers over the World Bank memo, Stiglitz had the academic credentials to take Summers on as an intellectual peer— or perhaps even from an elevated position. A graduate of Amherst who'd gotten his Ph.D. in economics at MIT, Stiglitz began his teaching career at Yale, where he received tenure at age twenty-seven—one year younger than Summers was when he received tenure at Harvard. In 1979, at the age of thirty-five, Stiglitz won the John Bates Clark Medal, the same award that Summers would win at thirty-eight. Stiglitz was a member of the Council of Economic Advisers from 1993 to 1995—the period when Summers had hoped to head the CEA— and then became its chair until 1997, when he moved to the World Bank.

Stiglitz did something that was virtually unheard of for an insider at the World Bank: he criticized it—in public. The Washington Consensus, Stiglitz argued, was a one-size-fits-all program that caused more misery than it alleviated. The Treasury was pushing policies for other countries that the Clinton administration would never tolerate at home. Neither Summers, the World Bank, nor the IMF "wanted to think that their policies were failures," Stiglitz would later explain. "They stuck to their positions, in spite of what I viewed as overwhelming evidence of their failure."

To Stiglitz, Treasury, the World Bank, and the IMF had all become tools of Wall Street, a means of extending American financial interests masquerading as economic benevolence. Summers, once a skeptic of the free market, had become one of its more ardent defenders, and Stiglitz believed that the former was tailoring his positions to please Wall Street, one of Treasury's most important constituencies, so that the Street would support Summers' eventual nomination as Treasury secretary.

Summers bristled at the criticism, but did not respond in public until after he'd left Treasury. "Given the circumstances, I think the advice that we gave . . . was right," Summers said. "Stiglitz would always like there to be a larger audience for his papers, but I think it's not serious to suggest that officials at the IMF or the U.S. Treasury were unaware of the field of microeconomics or unaware of research on credit rationing." In other words, Summers knew that IMF conditionality would hurt the poor. But he still thought it was the best solution for dire circumstances.

There were those, including Stiglitz, who suspected that Summers had actually responded to Stiglitz's criticisms more directly: by forcing Stiglitz out of his position as the World Bank's chief economist. In 2000, when Stiglitz's term was up, he was due to be reappointed by World Bank president James Wolfensohn. But Wolfensohn informed him that the appointment would come only if he promised to silence his criticism, a condition Stiglitz declined to meet.

Stiglitz left the Bank to teach at Columbia University and write an influential bestseller called *Globalization and Its Discontents*. In 2001 he would win the Nobel Prize for his work on "information asymmetries"—the idea that markets are imperfect because their participants have unequal access to information. "Even small degrees of information imperfections can have large economic consequences," Stiglitz explained. As developed by him, it was the kind of big idea that had eluded Summers.

But the memory of his ouster still stung, and Stiglitz blamed Larry Summers. Summers couldn't handle criticism, especially from another economist, Stiglitz thought. He didn't believe in dissent or the public airing of conflicting opinions. Stiglitz believed with all his heart that Summers, with his power over the World Bank, had forced Wolfensohn either to neuter or to exile Stiglitz, but he'd never be able to prove that. Summers, Stiglitz would tell associates, had been careful "not to leave his fingerprints" on the episode.

For the most part, however, Summers received positive press during his Washington years. Reporters appreciated him. He had made himself an excellent source of background information for the beat reporters covering Treasury, and he had a gift for explaining complicated situations lucidly and colorfully. When he did speak on the record, he showed a well-honed flair for the sound bite, as when he compared modern capital markets to the invention of the jet. "On the one hand, it's faster and gets you where you're going more comfortably and more rapidly," he said. "On the other hand, crashes are that much more spectacular." True, Summers tended to repeat his best lines, but they were still more interesting than the usual government monotone.

Anyway, the U.S. economy was roaring along, largely unaffected by the crises abroad. The IMF remedies may have inflicted painful consequences overseas, but the reporters in Washington paid little heed to what was going on in Malaysia or Moscow, and they wrote glowingly about the Clinton economic team. The most egregious example came in February 1999, when *Time* put Rubin, Greenspan, and Summers on its cover, calling them the "Three Marketeers" and "the committee to save the world." In a breathy, you-are-there style, the article's lead portrayed a moment of crisis at which Rubin happened to be bonefishing and Greenspan playing tennis. Of Summers, *Time* said, "You really should calm down about this phone-ringing stuff, but you are the Deputy Secretary of the Treasury, and this past year, for all its chaos and tumult, has been about the most exciting you could imagine. It's the holiday season, and you are eager to get to your family and all that, but boy, this holding the world economy by the hand is even better than advertised."

Summers' presence on the magazine cover raised some eyebrows at the White House, where not everyone thought a deputy cabinet secretary deserved equal billing with Bob Rubin and Alan Greenspan. In the Washington pecking order, deputies were supposed to be anonymous. But the photo did reflect how influential Summers had become and the closeness of his relationships with the other two men. Rubin, Greenspan, and Summers dined together weekly, and their disagreements were as collegial as they were rare.

Summers' presence on the cover of *Time* was also a sign that Bob Rubin was grooming his successor. Though Rubin would not talk about it until seven years later, in 1996 he and Summers had cut a deal. Summers agreed to turn down other job offers and stay at Treasury after Bill Clinton's reelection. In return, Rubin would ask the president to agree to nominate Summers to replace Rubin when he stepped down, which he expected to do in 1998. Clinton agreed to go along with the plan.

As it turned out, Rubin stayed until mid-1999, not wanting to look like he was abandoning the president during the Monica Lewinsky scandal. But the secret arrangement stayed in effect for two and a half years, unknown to anyone except the three men and a handful of their closest staff members. Just as he would five years later with the Harvard Corporation, Rubin had secretly helped Larry Summers acquire a powerful position. When Summers and Rubin dealt with foreign governments, they pushed for transparency. But when it came to their own fortunes, different standards applied.

And Rubin didn't just promote Summers internally; he worked to polish Summers' public image. Both men agreed to cooperate with the *New Yorker* and *Time* in part to promote the perception that Summers was the inevitable heir apparent. So, whereas Rubin used to affectionately tease Summers in public, he now began to refer to his deputy as "Dr. Summers," and conspicuously deferred to Summers at public events. And even before he'd announced his resignation, he suggested to the *New Yorker* that Summers "would make a very good Treasury secretary." The pre-emptive strategy was calculated to defuse resistance to Summers' ascension.

Rubin announced his resignation on May 12, and the Dow Jones instantly dropped 213 points. President Clinton promptly nominated Summers to take Rubin's place, and by the end of the day the market regained all but twenty-five of those points. To the financial community in New York, Summers' appointment meant continuity, competence, and a reliably pro-business treasury secretary. The Street probably wouldn't have felt comfortable with the Larry Summers who had advised Mike Dukakis on industrial policy, but it had no problem with the Larry Summers whom Bob Rubin had groomed.

The Senate Finance Committee held a hearing on Summers' nomination on June 22, and Summers showed how much he'd learned about politics during his years in the nation's capital. He brought Vicki and their three children, twin girls named Ruth and Pamela and a younger son, Harry. "Is it not encouraging that Larry can have such beautiful children?" committee chairman William Roth said from behind his microphone. "Some apples fall far from trees," Summers demurred. When Florida Republican Connie Mack asked Summers if he still felt that "efforts to cut the estate tax are selfish," Summers ate the requisite crow: "No, I do not, Senator Mack," he confessed. "What I said was wrong." Concluded Iowa senator Charles Grassley, "You seem more relaxed now than when I first got acquainted with you, and you smile occasionally." All the smiling, whether it was in a Senate office building or on the cover of *Time*, paid off. The full Senate approved Summers' nomination by a vote of 97–2.

On July 2, President Clinton swore in Summers as treasury secretary at a ceremony in the White House Rose Garden. "I felt ready," Summers said. Nonetheless, it was an emotional moment. As he thanked his parents, his family, and Robert Rubin, Summers was on the verge of tears. "I can't begin to describe how much I have learned from Bob Rubin," he said.

Seventeen months later, the United States Supreme Court would rule on the matter of *George W. Bush v. Albert Gore, Jr.* The decision was heartbreaking for Gore, of course, but it also had a negative impact on Summers. The vice-president, who had once blocked Summers from a White House post, had come to appreciate Summers and was prepared to reappoint him. But now Summers' tenure as treasury secretary would always have the anti-climactic quality of stewardship. There was only so much you could do in the last year and a half of a lame duck administration.

When the Republicans moved in, Larry Summers retreated to a sinecure at Washington's Brookings Institution, a liberal think tank. But his heart wasn't in it; Brookings, a rather dreary building of long, uneventful corridors, is full of public policy wonks grinding away behind closed doors. Worse still, Summers' marriage was falling apart, a victim, some said, of his hectic schedule and obsession with work.

"There are trade-offs in life," Summers said some years later. "You can't be negotiating through the night to prevent Mexico from going bankrupt *and* tucking your kids into bed that night. And you can't get in a position to do that without having worked many long nights at the office. . . . Have I gotten that balance right at every point in my life? There are choices that if I had to do again, I would do differently."

By all accounts the divorce, which wouldn't be finalized until 2003, was deeply painful for both husband and wife. Victoria Summers received the house in Bethesda, custody of the children, and some $8,000 a month in child support. She also took back her maiden name, becoming Vicki Perry again.

Summers had a hard time talking about the divorce. According to several sources familiar with the Harvard presidential search process, Summers did not tell the Corporation of his divorce while it was considering him. An oft-repeated story has that Harvard did not actually learn of the divorce until it received a phone call from Victoria Perry, who pointed out that it had not been necessary to send her an invitation to her ex-husband's inauguration.

At the end of the Clinton administration, Summers could easily have hopped the Delta shuttle to Manhattan and made millions. That's what Bob Rubin had done, becoming chairman of the executive committee at Citigroup and pulling down a reported $25 million a year. But getting rich wasn't what drove Summers. He was a young man, just forty-six in 2001. His energy was remarkable, his drive undiminished. He missed the immediacy, the prestige, the urgency of Treasury—the knowledge that he, Lawrence Henry Summers, was helping to shape the world of the twenty-first century. He missed the limos and the private jets and the one-on-one meetings with foreign leaders. He missed having a rapt audience for every public utterance he made, the heady realization that with one slip of the tongue, he could move markets, make tens of millions of dollars of wealth vanish just like that. He would never do it, of course, but just the knowledge that he *could* . . . He missed that adrenaline-boosting sense of being important. Being powerful. Being *alive*.

But what could he do? He couldn't return to economics, not after a decade away from his chosen field. Even if he could catch up with all the work he'd missed, how could he go back to writing theoretical, abstract papers about economic issues and crises when he'd just spent a decade living through and shaping the real thing? He'd become one of the people those papers were written *about*. He was the most successful academic to go into politics since Daniel Patrick Moynihan or Henry Kissinger—and if you considered that a lot of people regarded Kissinger as a war criminal, maybe Summers was the most successful since Woodrow Wilson.

So Summers weighed his next move, and he waited. And then Neil Rudenstine resigned, and Harvard came calling, and Summers realized that he didn't have to work in Washington to change the world.

2

Neil Rudenstine's Long Decade

On May 22, 2000, Harvard's twenty-sixth president, Neil Rudenstine, announced his retirement. He was tired. A young-looking fifty-six years old when he took the job a decade before, Rudenstine now looked like a man slipping into old age. His dark hair had become heavily streaked with gray, and his face had fallen around the edges, as though life had given it a gentle downward tug. "This has been a good run, and it's time for someone else," he said. Few at Harvard would have disagreed, at least with the second part of that statement.

Neil Rudenstine became president of Harvard in the fall of 1991, succeeding the popular Derek Bok, the wealthy, patrician scholar of labor law who'd been at Harvard's helm for the preceding two decades. Early in his presidency, some saw the handsome Bok as too polished, too Californian. Before law school at Harvard, Bok had gone to college at Stanford, and there was something about him that always made one think he was just about to hit the tennis courts. He was tall, with thick, wavy gray hair and a craggy face that would have worked as well in Hollywood as at Harvard. He had a beautiful Swedish wife, Sissela Bok, an academic in her own right, and three attractive children. Derek Bok made everything look easy.

But Bok's good looks and good fortune belied a canniness about university politics, and over time he showed that his smoothness masked both diplomacy and depth. Perhaps only a man so secure in his own identity could have guided the university from the political and social turbulence of the 1960s into a period of healing, stability, and, ultimately, growth. "Derek took a university stuck for the same reasons America was stuck, and managed the aftermath," said one Harvard professor. "He reminded Harvard of its mission: to train the leaders of a great nation that would navigate the shaping of the world." Derek Bok, said Peter Gomes, the chaplain of Harvard's Memorial Church, "began his presidency like Cary Grant and ended up like Abe Lincoln."

Neil Rudenstine at least looked a little like Abraham Lincoln. He was a slender man with an angular, sensitive face that could appear either thoughtful or anxious but that rarely suggested certitude. He had a floppy handshake and a reedy, singsong voice, and when he spoke he tended to stare at the ground. His body language radiated pliability rather than strength. "Neil Rudenstine looked delicate, like an orchid," said one colleague who knew him well.

He was a surprising choice for president. Asked for their advice, Harvard alumni had suggested 763 candidates for the job, and it was never clear that Rudenstine was one of them. He was not a well-known figure. Unlike Bok, who'd come from an extremely wealthy and socially prominent Philadelphia family, Neil Rudenstine was the product of humble and diverse origins. His father was a Jewish prison guard, his mother a Catholic waitress. The first member of his family to graduate high school, Rudenstine went to Princeton and flourished there, falling in love with its intimate, communal atmosphere. In Princeton's peaceful, village-like world of dining clubs and libraries, Rudenstine found a calling. When he finished, he spent two years in England on a Rhodes Scholarship, then returned to the United States and enrolled in graduate school at Harvard to study poetry. Completing his degree in 1964, he taught in Harvard's English department for two years, then returned to Princeton, where he received tenure. His life was an American dream come true.

Neil Rudenstine was reputed to be an excellent teacher, passionate about his material and skilled at conveying its intricacies to his students. But no one would ever have called him a major scholar; other than his dissertation, Rudenstine never published a work of scholarship. So, like many professors who realize that they are unlikely to revolutionize their field and grow weary of the scholar's solitary life, Rudenstine moved into administration. He became the dean of students at Princeton, then was promoted to a bigger job, dean of the college, and then, in 1977, became Princeton's provost, a sort of right-hand man to the university president. He held that job for eleven years, and by all accounts excelled at it.

Princeton is a small university. It has an undergraduate college and a graduate school for aspiring Ph.D.s, but it does not have the powerhouse professional schools that Harvard does—no law, medicine, or business schools, for example. Located in the affluent, leafy suburb of Princeton, New Jersey, Princeton feels like a school where, if it isn't possible to know everyone else, it may be possible at least to recognize them. Rudenstine liked that. The lover of poetry saw in Princeton an oasis where a scholar's values—tolerance, tranquility, reason—could be cherished and nurtured like a hothouse flower.

After more than a decade on the job, Rudenstine left Princeton in 1988 and became an executive vice-president of the Andrew W. Mellon Foundation in New York City, where his job was to judge the appeals of the money-seeking. He was comfortable in that environment, too. For a man who had grown up poor, and a humanist who studied poetry, Rudenstine was strangely at ease among multimillionaires. "Derek Bok was always very uncomfortable around the very rich, whereas Neil loved it, just loved it," said one member of the Harvard faculty. The very rich, in turn, charmed by Rudenstine's courteous, deferential manner and appreciative of his literary bent, delighted in his company.

In the hunt for a new Harvard president, Rudenstine was an intriguing dark horse; he had sufficient academic credentials and what appeared to be more than adequate administrative experience. The only problem was a rumor that he had once turned down the presidency of Princeton. Would he even be interested in the Harvard job? An offer couldn't be made if it might be rejected; word could get out, and that would be humiliating to Harvard. So an emissary from the Harvard Corporation sat down with Rudenstine and asked. And simple as that, Rudenstine said yes. He would certainly be interested.

Things fell into place quickly. Rudenstine was announced as the new president in March 1991. His installation occurred that October. The mood on campus was upbeat. A weekend celebration devoted to "Values of Education" featured educational symposia, lectures, concerts, and arts performances. Students spelled out "We Love Rudy" in pizza boxes in the Yard—which was a little odd, not just because no one called Neil Rudenstine "Rudy," but also because few at Harvard really even knew Rudenstine, much less loved him.

From an outsider's perspective, Neil Rudenstine probably seemed an odd choice to run Harvard. He was a little-known academic with no national reputation, and he hadn't worked at Harvard in twenty-five years. But in less obvious ways, Rudenstine must have seemed like a promising choice for an immensely difficult job—a job that had changed over the past decades just as Harvard itself had changed.

At the beginning of World War II, Harvard was still what might be called a pre-modern university. All of its students were men. The vast majority of them, about 97 percent, were white, and most of them were Christian. The number of Jews was still small, between 10 and 20 percent—small at least compared with the number of Jews qualified to attend. Slowly, Harvard was opening its door to deserving candidates from both public and private schools, as well as from different regions of the country, but it was a tentative process. Most Harvard students still hailed from New England, largely from the elite private boarding schools of that region.

The wave of social change effected by World War II changed all that. In the war's aftermath, the federal GI Bill helped young men from all over the United States come to Cambridge—the sons of farmers from Kansas, ranchers from Texas, and fishermen from Washington. As the fullness of Hitler's atrocities sunk into the national consciousness, Jewish faculty and students suddenly found Harvard more welcoming also. Though it would never vanish completely, the influence of Andover, St. Paul's, Exeter, and the like began to wane. Harvard, for centuries a bastion of social privilege, was becoming more of a meritocracy—more, theoretically, like the country it predated.

And it wasn't just new blood that poured in, it was money. The postwar years witnessed the growth of the great American foundations—philanthropic, research-minded groups with names like Ford, Carnegie, and, yes, Mellon. Those foundations became an enormous source of revenue for American universities. The federal government would play an even more important role. The government had formed close relationships with university scientists during World War II, enlisting their help with everything from code-breaking to the design of nuclear weapons. Throughout the Cold War, that partnership would continue, as Washington funded hundreds of millions of dollars in scientific and medical research, and the universities built up their labs, departments, and scientific facilities. Both sides benefited. The government employed the nation's finest minds without having to underwrite the entire infrastructure in which they worked. And the universities grew bigger, stronger, and richer, attracting researchers who might otherwise have chosen the private sector and students excited to work with the big names in their field.

But the money did not help only the direct recipients of its grants. At Harvard, the university initiated a tithe on every grant its professors received, ostensibly to pay for overhead. But the tithe was the same regardless of whether you were a biophysicist who needed a multimillion-dollar lab or an English professor writing about John Donne—a little tax that disappeared into the university's gradually swelling coffers.

By the 1960s, in terms of the breadth and caliber of the research they produced, American universities were without question the world's finest, one of the great success stories of twentieth-century America. But that evolution had its downside. To manage such rapid growth, universities began to enlarge their administrations, hiring lawyers and accountants, personnel managers and health care administrators, retirement benefits experts and real estate managers, and public relations gurus and fundraisers galore. They tended to come from corporations and consulting firms, and their style of doing things reflected a corporate culture rather than an academic one. Before Vietnam, and even more so before World War II, Harvard's strongest constituency had been its faculty. But the growth of a central administration shifted power to the office of the president and the anonymous bureaucrats who answered to him. At Harvard, power began to flow away from the people who supposedly represented the purpose of the institution, toward the people who knew how to make it *work*—and, above all, to the people who controlled its money.

Moreover, the ties between the government and universities threatened the schools' independence from the pressures of politics and the marketplace. The richer the universities became, the more they grew entangled with issues of political and social justice that seemed either to coincide with their mission or to distract from it— depending, of course, on one's vision of just how engaged with society the university ought to be. During the tumultuous years of the 1960s the financial and personal connections that universities, and Harvard in particular, maintained with the military-industrial complex would become a major focus of student protest, an issue that has never been completely resolved.

The massive, decades-long cash infusion created another problem: even if the money was suddenly cut off, the infrastructure remained and had to be paid for. If you'd built a new laboratory with a government or foundation grant, you couldn't just shut it down if the grant wasn't renewed. And in the post-Vietnam years, that was exactly what happened at Harvard, as the government cut back its outlays to campuses that now seemed either ungrateful or outright hostile, and alienated alumni slashed their giving.

So when the university was looking for a replacement for Derek Bok, its financial position was less than ideal. On the one hand, it did have an endowment of $4.7 billion in 1991. But the endowment's value had actually dropped $52 million during the previous year, and in 1991 Harvard ran a deficit of about $40 million. Clearly, Harvard's next president would require two skills: management and fundraising ability. If he proved to be an academic leader, well, that would be an added bonus. And to avoid a prolonged learning curve, some institutional knowledge was necessary; if possible, the president should have attended Harvard College. If a College man wasn't available, a Harvard degree from somewhere would have to suffice. (Derek Bok had gone to Stanford, making him the first president since Charles Chauncey in 1654 who hadn't attended Harvard College. That Bok had only attended Harvard Law School caused some alums to wonder if he was really the right man for the job, a slight that rankled Bok even after he retired. "When they cashed my checks to go to the law school, nobody told me that wasn't part of Harvard," he said.) This combination of attributes was not easily found, but Neil Rudenstine had it. And from the very beginning of his presidency, he was charged with the task of fundraising.

Asking for money is the bane of the university president's job. Fundraising means endless schmoozing, sucking up to fat-cat alumni, constantly courting, soliciting, wheedling and, above all, *asking*. No donor capable of writing a seven- or eight-figure check wants to deal with a mid-level flunkie from the fund-raising office. He wants face time with the president—one-on-one meetings, impromptu phone calls, dinner at the president's mansion, and *sotto voce* missives. He wants to hear the president say, "*I need your help* . . ." The gratification of giving money is not only in entering a building with your name carved into it or meeting a student who depends upon the scholarship money you have provided. It's the exhilarating combination of giving to a worthy cause while seeing the most powerful people at Harvard University dedicate themselves to winning your favor.

Not surprisingly, most university presidents want to play the part of a leader, not a petitioner. They like to give speeches, recruit top-notch faculty and students, attend football games, travel abroad, and host international visitors. They seek the collegial approval of the academics from whose ranks they have traditionally ascended. They don't want to be reminded of their dependence upon the business and law school graduates who are now corporate raiders, managing partners, and hedge fund whiz kids whose idea of poetry is the number of zeros in their annual bonuses.

But Neil Rudenstine didn't seem to mind asking for money. On the contrary, Rudenstine threw himself into fundraising with an enthusiasm that couldn't have been faked. In May 1994, Harvard kicked off a massive capital campaign designed to raise $2.1 billion, an amount that would have increased the university's endowment by about one-third of its value at the time. No other university had ever sought to raise anywhere near that amount. Back in 1979, Derek Bok had headed a fundraising drive that aimed to collect $350 million, and back then that had been considered enormous.

The timing, however, was fortuitous. The United States was entering a period of a growing economy and a booming stock market, and the wealthiest Americans were making money faster than they could spend it. Plus, Rudenstine, a genuinely gracious and thoughtful man, proved to be a master fundraiser, brilliant at the art of making personal connections. "He'd ask you about your daughter who was applying to college or your stepmother who was in the hospital," said one Harvard professor who saw Rudenstine at work. And those he was soliciting could tell that he *liked* them. Rudenstine didn't resent donors for being wealthy, or suggest in some oblique way that he found the indignity of their company distasteful. He enjoyed spending time with the rich. And with his passion for poetry and literature, Rudenstine could tell you in the most uplifting ways where your money would go. He would never blather on about a new heating system or a federally mandated ramp for the handicapped. Instead, he'd cite Winston Churchill and talk about how Harvard was "an empire of the mind." It wasn't just building a new dormitory that was at stake; it was building the future itself.

Rudenstine believed in that mission and subordinated himself to it. Because he felt such a commitment to the institution, he set aside his own ego. He never spoke about himself or his own accomplishments; he talked about Harvard. When reporters asked to profile him, he would defer. It was Harvard that mattered.

People often asked Rudenstine why they should give when Harvard was already so rich. That question was a constant irritant for Harvard fundraisers; Harvard always lagged behind schools like Dartmouth and Princeton—smaller schools with tight-knit student bodies—in the percentage of alumni who gave money. Dartmouth and Princeton alumni felt as if those schools truly *needed* their gifts. Moreover, Harvard rarely attracted the big donations, the $50 million or $100 million windfalls that could make a president's job so much easier. (And as the 1990s went on, university fundraisers began to whisper about which institution would first land the new Holy Grail of fundraising, the $1 billion donation.) People with that kind of money wanted to give to a place where their generosity would have a huge impact, but wasn't giving to Harvard like giving gold to Fort Knox?

Rudenstine had a ready answer. First, Harvard was always growing, he said. All those inquisitive minds at Harvard were constantly concocting new projects, new academic centers, new research. And it all required money, a lot of money. Like the people in the development office always said: "Grow or die."

And it wasn't as if the president of Harvard had $5 billion and a checkbook. Instead, that money was divvied up into numerous different endowments. The university ran on an age-old system of decentralization known as "every tub on its own bottom," or ETOB, wherein each school was expected to float or sink on its own. At most American universities, tuition is deposited into a central account. But, at Harvard, each school, and each dean of that school, maintained control of its own tuition revenue. That system created an incentive to expand; the more students a school enrolled, the more money it earned. Thus, those schools in fields that could attract a lot of students—again, law, medicine, and business—became among the largest such professional schools at American private universities. The pedagogy was driven by the money, rather than the other way around. And in turn, the graduates of Harvard became more numerous, and gave more money, so that Harvard's growth could continue.

Another aspect of ETOB was that each school at Harvard raised its own money, and only the deans of those schools could decide how to spend their individual endowments. Thus, those bodies with the richest and most generous alumni made up the lion's share of the endowment. And because they essentially controlled the spending of their endowments, the deans of those schools were powerful figures indeed, veritable dukes in the Harvard kingdom.

Those schools whose graduates went into less lucrative professions, however, had a harder time raising funds and possessed vastly smaller endowments. The John F. Kennedy School of Government, the Harvard Graduate School of Design, and the Harvard School of Public Health have always struggled to stay out of the red. Government service, architecture, and public health are no easy path to riches. At the very bottom of the heap are the Harvard Graduate School of Education and the Harvard Divinity School. Their graduates go into low-paying careers and can give practically nothing—especially since they frequently finish their programs owing tens of thousands of dollars in student loans. It takes a long time to pay back that kind of money when you make $27,000 a year as a public school teacher or prison minister.

ETOB had forced the schools to compete to survive, and that wasn't all bad. Rather than depending on the university for bail-outs, each school had to balance its budget. It was possible that this mandated self-sufficiency had forced them to become better schools—more aggressive, more innovative, forced to take responsibility for the decisions of their deans and faculty.

But ETOB also created an unhealthy imbalance. The rich schools got richer, and the poor struggled just to survive—with little debate about whether business was more important than education, law more important than divinity. Maybe that was the law of the marketplace, but some wondered if it wasn't the duty of the university to redistribute its wealth so that it could produce more teachers and ministers and fewer lawyers and investment bankers. Weren't universities supposed to counter the inequities of capitalism, not merely reflect them?

Part of Rudenstine's mission was to break down the long-standing balkanization of the Harvard campus, which affected the university's life in ways ranging from the minute to the fundamental. Every school had its own calendar, starting and ending semesters on different days. Even if a student got permission to take a course at another school, conflicting schedules made coordination next to impossible. And communication between the schools was minimal at best. Professors at the law school had no idea what was going on at the Kennedy School, even though their missions of training lawyers and developing experts in public policy surely overlapped. People at the business school didn't know what was going on at the medical school, even though both could work together to market the medical discoveries Harvard researchers were constantly making. Another oddity: The presidency of Harvard doesn't actually own Massachusetts Hall, the modest red-brick building that houses the president's office. The Faculty of Arts and Sciences does, and so the Harvard president pays rent to the dean of the FAS.

The problem was the deans, especially the deans of the FAS and the big three graduate schools. As long as they maintained the independence of their schools—and their money—from Harvard's central administration, they remained immensely powerful and largely autonomous figures. Though chosen by the president, once the deans were in power they could—and often did—frustrate his desires. But if the deans let the central administration start dictating policies at the graduate schools—whom they could hire, how to spend their money, or even how to raise it—the power of the president would grow and the deans' status would diminish proportionally. And who gives up power voluntarily? Who was to say that the president even knew the needs of those schools well enough to make such decisions?

Rudenstine's struggle to chip away at ETOB started slowly. He developed some interfaculty academic programs, and he made sure that that $2 billion fundraising drive would be a university-wide campaign, run out of the president's office, rather than a series of individual fund drives by the different schools. Rudenstine would set the goals and priorities, and the deans would have to work together. To an outsider, that might have seemed a small and logical step. But never before at Harvard had it been taken.

Of course, Rudenstine's job wasn't exclusively about fundraising. In his first two years, he was a constant, energetic presence on campus. The peripatetic new president visited the houses to meet with students, walked the sideline at football games, dined at the Faculty Club, and popped in to lectures, banquets, and conferences. Rudenstine was ubiquitous.

So were his thank-you notes. Everybody who contacted Rudenstine would receive a response from the president himself—not just a token sentence or two, but whole paragraphs, sometimes pages, and always handwritten, because Rudenstine wouldn't use a computer. Throughout his ten-year presidency, he didn't send a single e-mail. The thank-you notes were courteous, thoughtful, and appreciated, but sometimes people wondered if they were really the best use of Rudenstine's time. "You thought you were special for getting one, until you wandered around campus and saw that everyone else had received one, too," said Peter Gomes. "They came down like snow in February."

Rudenstine's deferential style—his wet-noodle handshake, the ease of his bended knee—didn't suit many at Harvard, who thought his conduct unbecoming for the president of a great institution. Rudenstine seemed *too* comfortable ingratiating himself with the wealthy, like a scholarship kid who becomes the most passionate pledge in the rich kids' fraternity. "Neil Rudenstine was an aspiring socialite from the working classes," said Martin Peretz, a prominent Harvard alum who is part owner of *The New Republic* magazine, and although the bluntness of that sentiment would have made many at Harvard wince, it was a rough approximation of what many felt.

Rudenstine did have his defenders, who thought that he was guilty only of doing the job he was hired to do "Neil was a man of deep principle," said law school professor Alan Dershowitz. "He didn't really care what people thought, he wanted to do the right thing and be respectful of everybody. You couldn't not like him—you wanted your kids to be like him." Some thought that Rudenstine was smarter, more cunning than his critics gave him credit for. All that hand-wringing, said one supporter, was "a shtick" that masked an underlying toughness. "There's a kind of gentleness about Neil," said another defender. "But it's an illusion. He was perfectly willing to be ruthless. If there was somebody he had to fire, he would fire him. He wouldn't enjoy it, but he would do it."

Perhaps so. But the job took a toll on Rudenstine. He found it lonely and isolating—that was perhaps his biggest surprise, the isolation. Princeton had been smaller, cozier. "He came to Massachusetts Hall and opened for business, and nobody came," said one professor, "and that's when he knew that things were different at Harvard." With about six thousand five hundred undergraduate students, almost nineteen thousand students all told, and, fifteen thousand employees, Harvard was so big that the president couldn't possibly survey all that was happening around him, and so decentralized that many of its deans and professors didn't much care what the president wanted. Then there were the hundreds of thousands of alums, each of whom seemed to want something from him. By the fall of 1994, Rudenstine was working one hundred twenty hours a week.

And then he collapsed. In late November, Rudenstine overslept, missing a meeting with a fundraiser, and realized that something was very wrong. Not only had he missed the meeting; he didn't want to get out of bed at all.

For the next three months or so, Neil Rudenstine simply disappeared, telling only his closest aides how to find him. Where he went, what he did, and what exactly was wrong were all very hush-hush. His aides announced that Rudenstine had suffered a physical breakdown due to overwork and exhaustion. Word was put out that he'd gone to the Caribbean with his wife, Angelica, where he was listening to classical music and reading essays to relax. But inevitably rumors flew that Harvard's president had suffered a nervous breakdown. Rudenstine insisted that he was only physically ill. "I see in retrospect that I still thought I was thirty-five years old and could go three or four years without a vacation," he would explain. "I've realized I'm no longer thirty-five years old." His doubters suggested that the problem may have been more with Rudenstine's head than with his body.

Whichever the case, the breakdown was big news. The media couldn't help but see a larger meaning in Rudenstine's crisis. Referring to him as "the frail Renaissance scholar," *Newsweek* put Rudenstine on its cover for a lifestyle story about Americans collapsing from stress and overwork. Other writers used Rudenstine as a synecdoche for all that had come to plague university presidents, the endless demands that the "multiversity" imposed on them. Education writers suggested that Harvard had grown so big as to be unmanageable. For the university, it was all deeply embarrassing.

When Rudenstine returned in March 1995, he was a changed man—or, at least, a changed president. He delegated responsibilities and cut back on almost all his campus activities. He abandoned his attempts to chip away at ETOB. Instead, he devoted himself almost solely to the primary task for which he had been hired: raising money. By his estimation, he had to raise one million dollars every day to meet the university's target. Who could blame him for deciding that raking in seven figures a day was a task that deserved most of his time?

Some people could, and did. As the years passed and the money in the bank mounted, Rudenstine came to symbolize the decline of an American icon—the university president. And not just at Harvard, but all over the United States. "Who's a university president?" asked the new joke. "A man who lives in a mansion and begs for money." Critics noted that Rudenstine was failing to deliver the kinds of high-minded educational and political pronouncements that a university president—a Harvard president, especially—was expected to make. "University presidents today are eunuchs, shuffling paper by day, grubbing for money by night, and never, never speaking a word about issues of the day for fear of offending donors or alumni or faculty or students," wrote one commentator. Neil Rudenstine, said another, had become "the incredible shrinking college president."

Never mind that much of the country was doing the exact same thing, downplaying politics, spirituality, and ethics to pony up for a national gold rush. American writers and intellectuals expected university presidents to stand above the fray. Many such academics and members of the press had gone to college during the 1960s and '70s, when several notable figures helped shape the image of the activist, idealistic university president. Yale had Kingman Brewster, whose passionate rhetoric about social justice helped prevent the outbreak of violence on a simmering campus. At Notre Dame, Theodore Hesburgh transformed a sleepy, intellectual backwater of a university into a nationally respected institution. As president of the University of California system, Clark Kerr wove a motley collection of colleges and universities into probably the finest state university system in the country, until he was ousted by then-governor Ronald Reagan for being too tolerant of left-wing dissent. Somewhat earlier, Robert Hutchins pioneered a rigorous "great books" curriculum at the University of Chicago, abolished the football team, and criticized American moral hypocrisy. And at Harvard itself, James Conant had crusaded against pre-war isolationism, while Derek Bok fought to prevent the university from retreating into itself after the shock of Vietnam.

By Rudenstine's time, the university president had become a potent symbol in the American imagination, a loftier figure than the politician or businessman. He—and it was almost always a man—was wise enough to know about politics, moral enough to pronounce upon current affairs, but generally humble enough not to throw his hat into the political ring. (Although if he wanted to, he could: Woodrow Wilson and Dwight D. Eisenhower were the presidents of Princeton and Columbia before they were presidents of the United States.) In fact, his self-imposed seclusion gave him the clarity and perspective to remark upon the world around him. University presidents had become secular preachers, using their podiums to spread the gospel of education. "Don't just look at our classrooms," they said in effect. "Look at us." And Americans disillusioned with their political leadership, Americans whose religious leaders often disappointed them as well, did just that. The mission of a university president was not just to educate his students, but to better American society itself, to speak out from his privileged perch, untainted by the seductions and corruptions of American capitalism, and remind Americans of what was noble about their country at a time when the nation seemed to have lost its self-confidence.

In other circumstances, Neil Rudenstine would have loved to play the role of public intellectual. By birth, training, and inclination he was a man who cared deeply about social justice. But there was truth to the charge that his fiduciary obligations had squelched his ability to speak on issues of public import. Wealthy alumni tended to be conservative, and it made no sense to risk offending the very people you were simultaneously asking for money. Rudenstine may have been in love with poetry, but he was no bleeding-heart romantic.

And there was another reason why Rudenstine couldn't speak out with the ease of his predecessors: Harvard's ethnic composition had changed dramatically, making political pronouncements a much dicier matter. After World War II, Harvard had opened itself up to students of different regions, religions, and, to a lesser extent, social classes. Even more dramatically, the social upheaval of the sixties compelled the university to open its gates to underprivileged groups it had long excluded. Women and African Americans came first, followed by Asian Americans and Latinos. Under Derek Bok, the number of foreign students had begun to grow, particularly in the graduate schools, and that trend continued under Rudenstine. And the gay rights movement meant that another group that had long existed on campus gradually made itself both visible and vocal. In the 1920s, Harvard had a secret kangaroo court that drummed suspected homosexuals out of the university; by the late 1990s, gay and bisexual students were holding public "kiss-ins" on the Harvard campus.

All of these groups carried with them diverse life experiences and perspectives that could not possibly fit under a single political umbrella, and the president who dared to venture into political pronouncements now ran a much greater chance of offending his student body than when that student body consisted of khaki-wearing white men from New England. Perhaps the only values that could include all these new citizens of the university were those that Harvard had long insisted upon: a reverence for scholarship, tolerance of dissent, and a belief in the freedom of speech. Derek Bok had argued that a university president should speak out only on issues that had a direct impact on higher education, and when he said anything at all, Rudenstine followed his predecessor's model. Some saw it as a retreat, others as an affirmation of central principles, an attempt to strike a balance between total isolation from the outside world and total immersion in it.

But there was one issue that Rudenstine refused to be quiet about: race in America. Maybe because of his working-class background, Rudenstine felt a genuine empathy for the victims of racial discrimination. That was why he successfully spoke out against a proposed memorial to Harvard's Confederate dead—there already existed a memorial for Harvard's Union dead—and that was why he vigorously advocated for affirmative action.

Since the 1970s Harvard had compiled a record of support for the policy of incorporating race as a factor in university admissions. In the famous 1978 Supreme Court *Bakke* case, Justice Lewis Powell had cited Harvard's admissions policy as a model of a system that incorporated affirmative action in a socially valuable and legally tenable way. Derek Bok vigorously championed affirmative action, co-authoring an influential 1988 book called *The Shape of the River*, which defended the concept. Rudenstine went even further. In 1996, when the U.S. Court of

Appeals for the Fifth Circuit overturned racial preferences at the University of Texas, Rudenstine publicly criticized the ruling. Affirmative action was not simply about helping blacks get into college, he said. Because all students learned from a socially and ethnically diverse campus, affirmative action was in the best interest of all the university's citizens, regardless of their skin color. In 1997, Rudenstine helped author a public statement supporting race, gender, and ethnicity as factors in admissions, which was signed by sixty-one other university presidents. When criticized by some alumni, Rudenstine conceded that the mean SAT score of minority students was indeed lower than that of the average Harvard student. But, he noted, it *was* higher than that of the average alumni child. That comeback tended to silence the critics.

Of all the places where Rudenstine showed his commitment to civil rights, none was more favored than the Department of Afro-American Studies, or Af-Am, as it was known. Af-Am was only about twenty years old when Rudenstine arrived. Its creation had come as a result of student protest in 1969. Black students had demanded it, and, more as political necessity than intellectual imperative, Harvard had agreed to it. But Af-Am had never really prospered at Harvard. Few students "concentrated"—Harvard's term for majored—in Afro-American studies. The field was mostly of interest to black students, and many blacks who had made it to Harvard were more concerned with acquiring the keys to a successful career than they were with academic self-exploration. Afro-American studies, they worried, would marginalize them when it came time to enter the job market. So they majored in economics and government, subjects that they knew prospective employers would regard with approval.

It was equally hard to find professors to staff the department. Scholars in the field were usually African American, but the number of black Ph.D.s in academia was small, and the number of black Ph.D.s Harvard considered good enough to tenure was even smaller. By the late 1980s, Harvard's department of Afro-American Studies contained only one tenured professor—and he was white.

For Harvard, the situation was untenable and potentially embarrassing, particularly at a time when some exciting work was happening in the field of African American studies. So, in 1990, Derek Bok and his FAS dean, economist Henry Rosovsky, hired the man who was doing much of that work: a young, Yale-trained scholar named Henry

Louis Gates, Jr. "Skip" Gates, as he was known, came from Duke University, in North Carolina, along with his longtime intellectual partner, a philosopher named K. Anthony Appiah. Their mandate was to revitalize a moribund department. But they couldn't have done it without the support of incoming president Neil Rudenstine, and that they had in abundance. Rudenstine gave them the resources—money, staff, lavish new offices right across Quincy Street from the Yard—to fulfill their mandate. Rudenstine and Gates recruited other well-known scholars such as the sociologist William Julius Wilson, historian Evelyn Brooks Higginbotham, and, from Princeton, a rising star in philosophy and religion named Cornel West. All told, Rudenstine appointed more than thirty senior and junior black faculty members to Harvard—more than had been hired in the 355 years before he became president.

Not everyone approved. Some faculty members whispered that a department that still had very few concentrators, maybe twenty students a year, didn't merit so much money and attention. They sniped that the players on Gates's "dream team," as the press began to refer to the Af-Am faculty, all seemed to have done their best work *before* they came to Harvard. And the detractors resented Gates' access to the president. If, say, the FAS dean—at the time a chemist named Jeremy Knowles—turned down a financial request from Gates, Gates would just pick up the phone and call Rudenstine. To his critics, this state of affairs reinforced the image of Rudenstine as a weak, easily manipulated president. It didn't matter that he actually wanted to fund Af-Am; he was being played. Rudenstine, however, wasn't swayed by the naysayers and the gossip. For him, and for Skip Gates, it mattered only that a once-moribund department was now alive and kicking, attracting national attention to Harvard.

Af-Am was Rudenstine's major academic achievement, but it wasn't his only one. Rudenstine also brokered a final resolution to a century-old Harvard problem: the integration of its sister school, Radcliffe College. Ever since Radcliffe's founding in 1879—when it was called the Harvard Annex—the women's college maintained an awkward relationship to Harvard, its students increasingly folded into Harvard but its administration largely separate. Women moved into the Harvard houses in the early 1970s, but until 1999 their diplomas still said "Radcliffe." Numerous presidents before Rudenstine had tried and failed to deal with the Radcliffe problem, but Rudenstine negotiated a delicate arrangement by which Harvard would absorb Radcliffe's nine-figure endowment while transforming the college into a think tank for women's studies. Like raising money, it was an unglamorous task, harder to effect than it appeared.

But none of this changed Rudenstine's image; his breakdown and his fundraising ensured that. And in a strange way, the more successful the fundraising was, the more Harvardians grew dissatisfied with their president. Even now there is a certain Yankee primness to much of the Harvard community, and while its members wanted their university to be rich, and wanted to enjoy the benefits of that wealth, they didn't want the outside world to pay quite so much attention to it. Given the financial headlines, that hope was unrealistic. As the stock market soared, Harvard's endowment rose to $10 billion, then $15 billion, and kept going. Harvard's money managers were earning around $20 million annually, about one hundred times what one of the best-paid professors was making. Even those who liked Rudenstine began to worry that the university had grown more concerned with money than with scholarship. "Harvard's goal is to die with the most amount of money," said law professor Alan Dershowitz at the time. "That should not be the goal."

More disturbing but less remarked upon was the way the money lust was trickling down to every level of the university. Beginning in the early 1990s, a number of Harvard students became involved in criminal or allegedly criminal activity. In 1991 and 1992, two students pilfered more than $125,000 from an annual ice-skating charity benefit organized by Eliot House, one of the student residences. In 1995, several undergraduates stole thousands of dollars from the Harvard Yearbook Society and the Krokodiloes, a student singing group. In 1997, another student plundered almost $8,000 from the Currier House treasury. And in 2001, two members of the Hasty Pudding Theatricals, a drama club, embezzled almost $100,000 from the group. One spent his money on drugs and home electronics. The other blew her share on shopping sprees and spa visits.

The Harvard administration dealt firmly with each incident. But with so much money floating around, was it really surprising that a few students would try to pluck some from the air? Was no one at Harvard concerned by the fact that student organizations could be so wealthy that their participants could embezzle a six-figure sum in the belief that no one would notice a missing hundred grand?

And the faculty didn't seem much better. Being a tenured faculty member at Harvard brought enormous prestige and the opportunity to make considerably more money from outside sources than one could earn from teaching. Economics and business professors snapped up lucrative consulting deals with banks and corporations. Law professors marketed their expertise in much the same way, consulting on cases in exchange for substantial fees. Professors of science and medicine maneuvered to steer their research in the direction of drug and biotech companies.

At the business school, Suzanne Wetlaufer, the editor of the *Harvard Business Review*, took this merging of Harvard and commerce to an inevitable extreme. While interviewing Jack Welch for the magazine in late 2001, Wetlaufer commenced an affair with the General Electric chief executive. Welch left his wife and Wetlaufer left her job, but the moral of the story was inescapable: Harvard had, quite literally, crawled into bed with corporate America.

Teaching at Harvard enabled you to do other things: write op-eds for the *New York Times*, get grants from friends in high places, testify before Congress, and land a job in the White House. It was all too easy to view teaching as a nagging obligation. "The nemesis of Harvard is its reputation," lamented Michael Ignatieff, a professor of international affairs at the Kennedy School. "We're much too grand to do what we're supposed to do—teach."

That lack of passion for teaching on the part of many Harvard professors is a chronic problem for the university. The culture of Harvard College in particular reflects this pedagogical ennui. At many of Harvard's competitors, such as Yale and Princeton, professors who teach a lecture course must also teach a discussion section, a smaller weekly meeting with ten or fifteen students instead of the dozens or hundreds enrolled for the twice-weekly lecture. At Harvard, graduate students do most of the hands-on teaching, leading sections and grading papers and exams. Many of those graduate students, known as teaching fellows, are committed, excellent teachers. Many, however, are not, with their skills in English fluctuating as widely as their knowledge of their subjects. But good or bad, the chance to interact with graduate students is not why so many high school students apply to Harvard every year. The lack of contact with their professors is a shock to many entering students and a constant complaint of the rest. In fact, a late-1990s survey of Ivy League newspapers found that Harvard students had the highest level of dissatisfaction with their education of any Ivy League students.

Student dissatisfaction contributed to the gnawing concern that, although Harvard's fame was unequalled, other schools offered an education as good or better. Princeton, Yale, and New York University were all doing an excellent job of teaching undergrads. But perhaps most worrisome was Stanford. The Palo Alto, California, university was younger than Harvard and seemed to be riding the wave of American culture. It had close connections to the entrepreneurs and billionaires of nearby Silicon Valley, creating a steady back-and-forth of energy, ideas, and money. In 2001, the William and Flora Hewlett Foundation gave Stanford $400 million, the largest gift ever given to higher education. Stanford was using its new money to pursue cutting-edge scientific research that would in turn earn still more cash for the university. The affirmation of Stanford's cultural arrival came when Chelsea Clinton rejected the Ivy League for Palo Alto. In the past, a president's child would surely have stayed east, but Clinton's decision to head to the West Coast reflected a new sense of cultural liberation. To join the elite, you didn't *have* to go to Harvard anymore.

Little of this was the fault of Neil Rudenstine, or at least his fault alone; the crisis in Harvard's undergraduate education had been a long time in the making. Nevertheless, Rudenstine was the man in charge, and rather than attend to these increasingly urgent questions, he was off raising money. The students barely saw their president. "Rudenstine knows more about the interests of Harvard's top donors than about the needs of the Harvard undergraduates," editorialized the *Harvard Crimson*, the campus daily. On the announcement of his resignation in May 2000, the *Crimson* declared that "Rudenstine's tenure has stripped Harvard of strong leadership in the presidency and equipped the University with a far quieter voice in American society than his predecessors enjoyed. . . . The University has receded to the shadows of ivy tower and Ivy League obscurity."

Over the course of the twentieth century, Harvard presidents served an average of about twenty years. Neil Rudenstine would serve the shortest stint of any Harvard president since before the Civil War.

Some said that that was because of his apparently gentle constitution; others argued that the president's job had simply become too grueling for anyone to hold it for very long—or even want to. In any event, Rudenstine had told Harvard that he wanted to leave, and Harvard didn't exactly put up a fight.

A year later, Rudenstine would move back to Princeton and a quieter life. Until then, Harvard would search for a replacement. Once again, the qualifications for the job were many and rigorous. The next president had to be bigger, better, bolder than Rudenstine. He had to combine an expertise with money and management with the ability to fix the university's ailing undergraduate education, the toughness to take on the deans, and the drive to be a national leader. Harvard didn't want another underwhelming president.

But who could possibly meet all these requirements, and how would Harvard find him?

3

Searching for Mr. Summers

To understand how Harvard chooses its presidents, you have to go all the way back to 1650, when the General Court of Massachusetts Bay Colony established a legal structure for the university, and if you're going back that far, you might as well push back another fourteen years, to Harvard's very beginning.

In 1636 the General Court, the governing council of the new Puritan outpost, appropriated the sum of £400 for "a schoale or colledge"—a substantial figure for an impecunious body. The promulgation of Puritanism was a priority second only to survival for the colonists, who aimed to found a school for ministers who would ensure the longevity and doctrinal purity of their faith. The new "schoale" would be in "Newtowne," renamed Cambridge in 1638. That was also the year when a young Puritan named John Harvard died and left the princely sum of £780—and, almost as important, a library of 400 books—to the fledgling college. As a measure of its gratitude, and an incentive to subsequent donors, the General Court named its school after Harvard.

Twelve years later, in 1650, the General Court issued a formal charter for Harvard College—the same charter whose replica would be handed to Larry Summers at his inauguration in 2001. That document established the university's two governing bodies, the Board of Overseers and the Harvard Corporation. In a very crude way, the Overseers and the Corporation were like a bicameral legislature. The Overseers would be the larger of the two groups—the House of Representatives, as it were—whose consent was required for college statutes, appointments, and elections to the second group, the Corporation. That body would be like a senate, a small, exclusive panel whose job was to choose and advise the Harvard president. About one hundred and forty years before the United States did, Harvard had a constitution.

Three and a half centuries later, the Harvard constitution has changed less than that of the United States. The university still has its Board of Overseers and its Corporation, and their roles are still more or less what they were in the mid–seventeenth century. The main difference is that the power of the Corporation has grown immense, while the Overseers, once the more powerful of the two, has become a largely ineffectual council. If the Overseers tripped and fell into another dimension, it would take some time for anyone at Harvard to actually notice.

Thirty Harvard alumni sit on the Board of Overseers. Candidates run for office after collecting a certain number of alumni signatures, and winners serve six-year terms, with a 20 percent turnover every year. The Overseers approve presidential choices as well as nominations to the Corporation, which are potentially significant powers. But time and tradition have turned the Board into largely a rubber stamp. The Overseers also conduct fact-finding missions into the status of Harvard College's academic departments, meeting with professors and writing well-meaning reports that are then generally ignored by the deans and president. "We'd write these reports and then never hear about them again," remembered Terry Lenzner, Harvard class of 1961 and a former Overseer. "They just disappeared into a void." However, since an unwritten role for the Overseers is to give and raise money, the task of report-writing creates a sense of involvement among them conducive to giving.

The Corporation, the real power, consists of seven members, including the Harvard president, who are known as "fellows." They meet about once a month, sitting in high-back leather chairs around a long mahogany table in Loeb House, a Georgian mansion on the east side of the Yard. The minutes of those meetings are recorded by a Harvard official known as the university secretary, but they are kept secret. The times of the meetings are also secret. There is no distributed agenda, nothing to inform the Harvard community of what is discussed by its own governing board.

Most universities have an advisory council to assist and oversee the president, but no university has a group that is as powerful, unaccountable, and secretive as Harvard's. (If a public company had a similar governing board, the shareholders would revolt.) Alumni or faculty cannot vote to choose the Corporation members; the fellows serve as long as they want to and choose their own successors. The Corporation's job is to select the president, advise him, and, if necessary, rebuke him—although because they generally choose someone who reflects their values and pursues their agenda, it rarely comes to that. The Corporation also approves the budgets submitted by the deans of the Harvard schools, and that power is substantial. The Corporation doesn't like to fire or scold deans, who often command the loyalty of faculty and alumni, and can cause a stink in the *Boston Globe*. But it can overrule the budget requests of a prodigal dean, making his life so frustrating and joyless that he opts to step down rather than fight, allowing the president to replace him with a more malleable figure.

Partly because of the fellows' life terms, and partly because the Corporation's small size and penchant for secrecy isolate it from the social pressures that inform American society, the Corporation has never reflected the diversity Harvard advocates for its student body. Until 1985, when former FAS dean Henry Rosovsky, who is Jewish, became a fellow, every Corporation member for 350 years had been a white, Christian male. The first woman—a lawyer named Judith Richards Hope—didn't make the cut until 1989. The first person of color was Conrad K. Harper, an African American lawyer who joined the Corporation in the year 2000.

The Corporation isn't just ethnically homogeneous, it is professionally like-minded. Whatever their skin color or ethnicity, Corporation fellows almost always reflect the interests of the American business elite. The twentieth-century Corporation lacked a single fellow from the world of academia until Yale professor John Morton Blum joined in 1970.

The Corporation is culturally homogeneous as well. For most of the past two hundred years, the Corporation represented a microcosm of the Protestant establishment, and even in the twenty-first century the résumés of its members read like entries from the Social Register: *Commodore, New York Yacht Club . . . Member, Trilateral Commission . . . Trustee, Pierpont Morgan Library . . . Member, Council on Foreign Relations . . . Trustee, Metropolitan Museum of Art . . . Director, J. P. Morgan*

& Chase . . . Member, Augusta National Golf Club. Even within the elite
world of Harvard alumni, the fellows of the Harvard Corporation are a
breed apart.

At the time of Neil Rudenstine's resignation, the fellows included
Harper, a 1965 graduate of Harvard Law School and a partner in the
New York firm of Simpson, Thacher and Bartlett. Another recent
addition was Herbert "Pug" Winokur, who graduated from Harvard in
1964 and three years later earned a Harvard doctorate in applied
mathematics. Winokur was a director and chair of the finance committee at the Enron Corporation, and his presence on the Harvard Corporation represented the university's attempt to recognize new energy in
American capitalism, a transition from old money to new.

Old money was represented by D. Ronald Daniel, a 1954 business
school graduate, the university treasurer and a former managing partner at McKinsey & Co., a powerhouse consulting firm that serves as a
repository for Harvard graduates. Another paradigm of establishment
power and wealth was James Richardson Houghton, Harvard '58, Harvard Business School '62, the chief executive of Corning Incorporated,
the manufacturing giant.

But the Corporation was really dominated by two people, a businessman and an academic—the only academic on the board—both
very different but each formidable in their own way. Robert G. Stone,
Jr. was the Corporation's longest-serving member, or senior fellow. An
economics concentrator and captain of the heavyweight crew team,
Stone graduated from Harvard in 1947. He'd gone on to a career in
transportation and finance, heading up shipping companies States
Marine Lines and the Kirby Corporation, and serving on countless corporate boards. Stone made his money quietly, but he made a lot of it. A
longtime Harvard fundraiser and donor—he'd endowed a scholarship
program, the "Stone Scholars," and the position of crew coach—Stone
had been on the Corporation since 1975. A gregarious blue-blood
unrivaled in his devotion to his alma mater, he epitomized the Harvard
man of an earlier time.

On the surface, he could not have been more different from the
other power on the Corporation. Hanna Holborn Gray was born in
Germany in 1930. Before the onset of war, her family fled that country
for the United States. Gray eventually attended Bryn Mawr, a women's
college in Pennsylvania, and earned a Ph.D. in history from Harvard in

1957. She became an assistant professor at Harvard at a time when women professors were an unwelcome novelty in Harvard Yard; the rules of the Faculty Club, for example, stipulated that women could not enter by the front door.

Gray was unfazed by the discrimination—"some of it just seemed comical," she once recalled—and progressed to a remarkable career, teaching at the University of Chicago, Berkeley, Northwestern, and Yale. After a stint as Yale's provost, second-in-charge to president Kingman Brewster, she served as Yale's acting president in the late 1970s. She didn't get the position—Yale English professor A. Bartlett Giamatti did—but instead became president of the University of Chicago, retiring in 1993, after fifteen years.

Over the course of her career, Gray acquired a reputation as a disciplined, demanding teacher with high expectations of students and a hostility toward any suggestion that the university ought to be an engine of social progress, a "change agent." The point of a university was not to reform the world, not to align itself with politics or social movements, Gray argued, but to transmit knowledge and train scholars. Arguing against affirmative action, she once told a friend, "You know, the University of Chicago has only one percent black students. We make no accommodation to anything." Gray was tough; some would have called her cold. At Chicago, she was reputed to have coined the term "tuition-paying units" for students. "Hanna Gray is very impressive, straight off Mount Rushmore," said one member of the Harvard Board of Overseers. "But you wouldn't want to cross her."

In 1988 Gray joined the Board of Overseers, and when Henry Rosovsky stepped down from the Corporation in 1997, Gray stepped up. By 2000, she had garnered more than sixty honorary degrees. She had also been involved in four presidential searches in the previous four years. It was perhaps inevitable that she would dominate this one.

The search for Neil Rudenstine's successor began almost immediately after Rudenstine announced his resignation in March 2000. The *Harvard Crimson* would call it the hunt for "the nation's second most highly contested presidency," which is the kind of line that people at Harvard throw out in a way that at first sounds infuriatingly arrogant, on second thought comes across as at least plausible, and upon further reflection strikes one as the type of remark that, while possibly true, serves no easily identifiable purpose other than showing how seriously Harvard takes both itself and its president.

The search committee consisted of nine people, six Corporation fellows (but not Rudenstine) along with three members of the Board of Overseers, brought on as a gesture of outreach to the lesser board. It would not, however, include any students or faculty, as most such presidential search committees do. Committee members insisted that it was impractical to pick representatives from among the thousands of students and faculty. That explanation didn't convince many students, who noted that much of life at Harvard, starting with getting in, consisted of just such weeding-out processes. Others noted that the same argument could apply to the Corporation itself, yet that body seemed to have no theoretical objections to choosing its own members from the much larger pool of Harvard alumni.

The real reason may have been a fear that students could not be trusted to keep their mouths shut. Because, with the exception of intermittent progress reports—intermittently scheduled but consistently vague—the search would be conducted with the utmost secrecy. And once it was done, its records would be sealed and stashed in the basement of a Harvard library for the next eighty years, until long after everyone involved was dead. University administrators explained that potential candidates for the job would be scared away if the press were involved.

There was some truth to that, but the level of secrecy went far beyond protecting the names of candidates. It seemed equally plausible that this was a group that, having grown accustomed to operating in secrecy, simply preferred it that way. So sure was the Corporation of its ability to pick the right person that no public vetting was believed necessary; so confident was the Corporation in its judgment that it didn't feel the need for outsiders to critique its process.

Rudenstine would stay until the commencement ceremonies of 2001, because choosing a university president takes time. Before the search committee could even begin considering candidates, it had to consider its priorities. Rudenstine's job had been to raise money. What should be the agenda of his successor?

Clearly, the first challenge was reinvigorating Harvard College. Undergrads weren't getting the education that they, and the general public, expected of Harvard. Many students and applicants already knew that, and some didn't much care, because a Harvard diploma was still money in the bank. But sooner or later the gap between perception and reality had to narrow lest a Harvard diploma become like an inflated stock price, dangerously vulnerable to a plunge in investor confidence.

Such a correction would affect more than just Harvard College. Even though undergraduates constitute a minority of the university's students, the college is the bedrock of the university's image. The freshman dorms in the Yard, the stately undergraduate houses along the Charles, the football team taking on Yale in century-old Harvard Stadium—the college is the heart and soul of the university. No graduate gets warm and fuzzy remembering his years at the law school, but Harvard College grads tend to be the university's most loyal alumni and most consistent donors, and they want Harvard to be at least as strong for their children as it was for them. If attending Harvard is part of the American dream, the dream of many Harvard graduates is to have their sons and daughters attend a Harvard that's *better* than the one they knew.

A second priority for the search committee was a heightened emphasis on the sciences, especially the life sciences such as biology, biochemistry, and genetics. Since World War II, the sciences had become the engine of economic growth and prestige at research universities—and the area of the most cutthroat competition. The amount of money flowing to university science departments from the government, foundations, and private donors had soared during the 1990s, the decade of biotechnology and the Internet. In 1996, for example, Microsoft heads Bill Gates and Steve Ballmer had given Harvard $25 million to build a new computer science and engineering building, a drop in the bucket compared with the money available. To get that money—to compete with Stanford and all the other universities busily blurring the lines between academia and the private sector—Harvard needed to invest more in its sciences, build more buildings and laboratories, and recruit more top-notch scientists.

Another priority was expanding the campus into Allston, a gritty Boston neighborhood just across the Charles. For decades Harvard has been pushing the limits of development in Cambridge, and local residents have grown increasingly resistant to further incursions; Harvard's buildings have a way of raising real estate values, forcing out blue-collar locals while corroding the sense of neighborhood and community. By the end of Neil Rudenstine's era, there wasn't much land left to build on in Cambridge, and every time Harvard proposed new construction on what little land there was, community activists roared into action, slashing those plans that they didn't kill outright.

During the Bok presidency, Harvard secretly began to buy land across the river, using a front company to prevent the price gouging that would inevitably follow the disclosure of the buying spree. Allston is a working-class neighborhood, industrial, congested and haphazardly developed, carved up by a train yard and the six-lane Massachusetts Turnpike. Outsiders would call Allston dreary, and so would some of the locals. Unlike Cambridge citizens, Allston residents would happily sell, and did so without ever knowing that the deep-pocketed purchaser was Harvard. By the late 1990s, Harvard owned as much land across the Charles as it did in Cambridge. The question was what to do with it.

Harvard wanted to expand not just across the Charles River, but across the Atlantic and Pacific Oceans. Twenty-five years before, Derek Bok spoke of "internationalizing" the university, launching efforts to recruit more foreign students. As the eighties became the nineties and globalization became all the rage, the idea came to mean more than simply recruiting students from England and France. For Harvard, globalization meant transforming a quintessentially American university into a world institution with overseas campuses, Harvard students coming from and traveling to every continent, and a curriculum that trained students to be citizens of the globe. When Winston Churchill and Neil Rudenstine had spoken of Harvard as an "empire of the mind," they'd spoken metaphorically; now Harvard wanted to make that slogan literal. The university had always trained the leaders of the United States. Who was to say it couldn't train the leaders of the entire world?

Rebuilding undergraduate education, pumping up the sciences, developing Allston, and globalizing the university—those were the official tasks for Harvard's twenty-seventh president. Perhaps equally telling were the subjects that the Corporation did not consider priorities—the effect of the university's great wealth on its self-image, its mission, and its integrity. The fellows of the Corporation were not particularly interested in that wealth's potentially adverse and unintended consequences; most of them were more interested in accruing money than in critiquing it. Instead of considering a president who might present a moral or philosophical counterweight to the economic trends of the 1990s, the search committee wanted someone who could exploit them. That, however, was something they would not say in public.

Nor was another criterion. The committee wanted more than someone who knew Harvard's issues (at least what they considered Harvard's issues). It wanted someone who could restore the luster to the presidency, who could stand up straight and represent Harvard as Harvard saw itself—powerful, strong, sage, and fearless. In short, it wanted someone who was not Neil Rudenstine. "We agreed that we needed somebody more aggressive, more pushy, bolder," Corporation fellow D. Ron Daniel later said.

The committee began by making token gestures of outreach. In September of 2000, it took out a concise ad in the *New York Times'* "Week in Review" section. "President: Harvard University," the want ad read. "Nominations and applications are invited for the presidency of Harvard University." The ad fulfilled a legal requirement about equal opportunity hiring for non-profit institutions, but no one expected anything serious to come of it.

At about the same time, the committee sent a letter to all Harvard alumni, some three hundred thousand strong, requesting their "thoughts on the personal and professional qualities it will be most important to seek in a new president, as well as your observations on any individuals you believe are deserving of serious consideration." The purpose was threefold. First, it gave alumni the impression that their opinions were valued, which helped create the sense of involvement that fostered alumni giving. Second, responses to the letter would give insight into alumni concerns. The third and ostensible purpose of the letter—to generate the names of viable candidates—was in reality its least important. Few believed that alumni would suggest a name that the committee would not otherwise have come up with on its own, or that the vast majority of the suggestions wouldn't constitute a waste of time.

Because in truth, the pool of realistic candidates was minuscule. Harvard's requirements knocked most people out of contention after quick and superficial consideration. Serious candidates had to be able to articulate a vision for the university that encompassed the Corporation's agenda. They had to have a character and personality entirely unlike those of Neil Rudenstine. Finally, they needed a Harvard degree, high-level administrative experience, and, if not a doctorate, then at least a familiarity with academic issues.

Not many candidates fit the bill. "When you actually sit down and want to choose a president at Harvard, you assume that you probably have a long list of very good people," said one person close to the search process. "You'd think people would be just lining up. And then you discover to your enormous surprise that maybe you can find two or three people and you don't like two of them."

In a few months, the search committee had compiled a list of four hundred names, but that number was wildly inflated. It included, for example, Al Gore and Bill and Hillary Clinton, though none of those three met the qualifications or had expressed any interest in the job. "I rather doubt [Gore] will get it," Robert Stone said in a rare public statement intended to slap down the rumor. "He doesn't have the academic and intellectual standing." When Hillary Clinton's name appeared in the press, outraged alums quickly contacted the university to let Harvard know that they'd stop giving if she became president. That was another criterion—the president couldn't be a partisan figure, lest alumni vote with their wallets.

Still, when committee members spoke to Harvard faculty, the searchers made it clear that they wanted a star, a well-known figure who could comfortably master the bully pulpit of the Harvard presidency. Robert Stone stressed exactly that to Peter Gomes in a conversation about the presidency in the fall of 2000.

The teacher of a course in Harvard history, Gomes had strong feelings on the subject and no small expertise; he likes to say that he has known three Harvard presidents and buried two others. Born in 1942, Gomes has worked at Harvard for thirty-five years. A Baptist clergyman, he became minister of Memorial Church in 1970. But if Gomes were only the church pastor, his position at Harvard would be insecure. It is not. In 1974, Derek Bok appointed Gomes the Plummer Professor of Christian Morals. The tenured Divinity School professorship allows Gomes to speak his mind—and not just on issues related to the divine—without worrying about losing his job.

Within the Harvard community, Gomes is something of a celebrity. Balding and portly, nattily dressed when he is out of religious garb, he is an eloquent speaker with a booming bass voice; you could sell tickets to a Gomes recitation of the Lord's Prayer. His volumes of sermons are frequent best sellers, and he was once profiled by *60 Minutes*. He is a one-man band of diversity—a black, gay, piano-playing Anglophile minister who grew up in the blue-collar Massachusetts town of Plymouth (his father farmed the cranberry bogs there) but speaks with a noticeable British accent.

Another source of Gomes' power at Harvard is his popularity with Harvard alumni, whom he frequently addresses at university functions and Harvard clubs around the world. They listen appreciatively to his thoughts on the state of their university and then contribute—or don't—accordingly. At the massive, ornate banquet celebrating the successful end of Neil Rudenstine's $2.6-billion fund drive in 2000, it was not Rudenstine but Gomes who delivered the keynote address. "No one can afford not to listen to me," Gomes once said during an academic debate. "I have the alumni on my side." That alumni constituency, even more than his church pulpit, his professorship, and the politics of his identity, make the Professor of Christian Morals something of a powerbroker, and the presidential search committee had to at least touch base with him.

"One of the questions Stone asked was, 'Do you think the president of Harvard should have a national or international profile?'" Gomes remembered. "And I said, 'Absolutely not. The president of Harvard, if he does his job well, *will* have a national and international profile. But you should not be looking for some colossus, some figure for worldwide education. That is not what makes a great presidency. A great Harvard president is made by doing the ordinary job of the president extraordinarily well. And my reading of history tells me that people are not brought in as great presidents. Harvard *makes* people a great president.'"

But, Gomes added, "I don't think that argument was listened to. It was already settled in the minds of those who make these appointments that they wanted a completely different style. These were pro forma conversations. But they asked my opinion and that's what I told them."

By early December of 2000, the list of four hundred had been chopped down to forty. Eliminating people from consideration was almost too easy. "I look back ten years ago, and I don't see as many really top candidates outside Harvard as I did then," Stone said at the time. The credible candidates would get a phone call from Marc Goodheart, a 1981 graduate and the university secretary, who was helping the committee coordinate its work. Would they be willing to have a conversation about the future of Harvard?

Always, they would—even if they didn't want the job, networking with members of the Harvard Corporation couldn't be a bad thing. But the meetings were never called "interviews." That was in keeping with the search committee's style. Everything was informal, so that everything was deniable.

By January, four names began to crop up with increasing frequency. First was Amy Gutmann, a smart, ambitious political scientist who was the provost at Princeton. Gutmann had the requisite Harvard ties— she had attended Radcliffe and earned her Ph.D. at Harvard, she had taught at Harvard, and her daughter had attended Harvard as well. But her Princeton connections were a problem; Neil Rudenstine had also been provost at Princeton. In the eyes of his critics, he had failed to make the transition from Princeton to Harvard. Could Gutmann? Besides, how would it look if Harvard kept finding its presidents at Princeton? The truth, according to sources close to the search, was that Amy Gutmann was never seriously considered for the job. Instead, her name was floated to give the impression that a woman was a real contender for the Harvard presidency—when, in fact, the opposite was the case. In time, however, Gutmann would have her revenge.

Of the three remaining candidates, only one worked at Harvard. He was Harvey Fineberg, and Harvard was practically in his blood; Fineberg had come to Harvard as an undergraduate in 1964 and never really left. After college, he attended the medical school, then earned a master's degree at the Kennedy School and a Ph.D. at the Graduate School of Arts and Sciences. Except for a brief stint as a practicing doctor, Fineberg had taught at Harvard ever since, serving most recently as Neil Rudenstine's provost.

Fineberg was a generally popular and well-respected man who badly wanted the job. He was smooth, diplomatic, a gifted public speaker and a skilled fundraiser. But his candidacy suffered from the liabilities that dog any insider in an executive search. Over the years, he had made enemies on campus—that was inevitable. Moreover, Harvard's familiarity with Fineberg had bred, if not contempt, then at least a certain limpness of enthusiasm. The Corporation wanted a president whose appointment would instantly signal that Harvard had made a daring pick, a choice that would make headlines and generate discussion. Choosing Harvey Fineberg would not have that effect.

And so the list was down to two: Lee Bollinger and Lawrence Henry Summers. They were successful, accomplished men at the top of their fields, and other than that they were different in every possible way.

A distinguished-looking man with a slim, runner's build and salt-and-pepper hair, Bollinger was president of the University of Michigan. A 1971 graduate of Columbia Law School, he had clerked for Supreme Court Justice Warren Burger in the early 1970s. Joining the University of Michigan Law School, Bollinger specialized in First Ammendment issues. But he first came to public attention when, in 1987, he testified against the nomination of Robert Bork to the Supreme Court. Named dean that same year, he banned the FBI and CIA from recruiting at the law school after courts ruled that the former discriminated against Hispanics and the latter against gays. After serving as dean for seven years, Bollinger left in 1994 to become the provost of Dartmouth. Just two years later, Michigan wooed him back to serve as its president.

Bollinger was a popular and effective president. He successfully launched Michigan's Life Sciences Initiative, a several hundred million dollar plan to expand science facilities. In the arts, he brought England's Royal Shakespeare Company to campus and helped found the six-hundred seat Arthur Miller Theater. Bollinger was passionate about the role of culture in university life. "This is vital to what we are as a community," he said when proposing the theater. "No one can give me a reason not to do it. So let's do it!"

Students loved Bollinger. When hundreds of excited revelers gathered outside the presidential mansion to celebrate the football team's 1997 victory over Penn State, Bollinger simply invited them all inside. Posing as a distant, Olympian figure wasn't his style. Lee Bollinger, said one student journalist, "is like a hyper-articulate version of your best friend's father." He certainly looked the part of a casual authority figure. Sitting for an interview in March 2003, Bollinger wore leather boots, wide-wale corduroys, a button-down shirt with a tie, and a fluffy down vest. About the only thing missing was a golden retriever at his feet.

Politically liberal, Bollinger reacted calmly when a 1960s-style protest broke out on the Michigan campus. In March 1999, thirty students took over his office to protest the use of sweatshops in making university-branded clothing. "They are terrific students," Bollinger said. "They're just the kind of students you want on your campus. They were interested in a serious problem, they were knowledgeable about the problem, and they really wanted to do something about it." He didn't appreciate them taking over his office, but he did respect their passion.

But Bollinger became best known for his handling of two lawsuits brought against the university and its law school, *Gratz v. Bollinger* and *Grutter v. Bollinger*. Targeting the university's affirmative action program, both cases were brought by whites who'd been denied acceptance at Michigan. With the support and advice of his friend Neil Rudenstine, Bollinger vigorously fought the lawsuits, defending affirmative action as essential to diversity, which was, in turn, essential to the fullness of any student's education. The Supreme Court had agreed to hear the cases in the spring of 2003.

At age forty-six, Larry Summers was eight years younger than Bollinger but already had a storied résumé of his own. Summers wasn't a university president, but he brought plenty of relevant experience to the table. He certainly had management experience; the Treasury Department employed more than one hundred sixty thousand people. Summers knew Harvard well, having spent years there as both a student and a professor. And though fundraising would not be the next president's priority, were Summers chosen he would instantly become the best-connected fundraiser in the university's history—after all, who has more experience with big money than the head of the Treasury Department?

Summers had something else that was appealing—an intangible but definite aura of star quality. He was an unconventional man, a brilliant academic who'd quit the cloistered world of his profession to pursue public service in Washington. Along the way, he'd acquired power and fame. In the Internet-age jargon of the 1990s, choosing Larry Summers would constitute thinking outside the box. The genius economist and former Treasury secretary as president of Harvard? No question, that'd generate some press.

On Sunday, February 18, 2001, the search committee interviewed Bollinger at the Hôtel Plaza Athénée, on East Sixty-fourth Street and Madison Avenue in New York City, a tony, discreet place where rooms start at $500 a night—the perfect locale for such a delicate mission. Things were long past the point of pretending that this was not an interview; it was Bollinger's third meeting with Harvard officials. Eight members of the committee dined with him that Saturday night, and on Sunday morning they convened a meeting at a $3,600-a-night penthouse suite, ate lunch, then reconvened for another short session.

The committee, Bollinger recalled, "had a very strong concern with undergraduate education, with attention to undergraduates right down to advising policies. How do you make this undergraduate experience richer than it is, and more fulfilling?" The Harvard emissaries also wanted to talk to Bollinger about where he would invest in the sciences, the development of the Allston campus, and the globalization of Harvard.

The meetings went well. Bollinger was comfortable addressing the questions and impressed his audience with the breadth of his knowledge. Harvard needed to focus on its undergraduate life, he argued, making the student-professor relationship more relaxed and accessible. He spoke of the need for university presidents to be engaged in society, and argued that they could do so without risking alumni contributions. In his years fighting the affirmative action lawsuits, Bollinger said, he couldn't remember a single instance in which an alum had refused to donate as a result. But after the interview was over, something happened. A small incident, but still, it said something about how Bollinger's style and Harvard's were different.

Two enterprising reporters from the *Crimson*, a junior named Garrett McCord Graff and a first-year named Catherine E. Shoichet, had tracked down the committee at the Plaza Athénée. The presidential search was the year's biggest story for the *Crimson*, which was pulling out all the stops to scoop the national press, and several times did. Graff and Shoichet had been tipped off that the Corporation was meeting in New York; they just didn't know where. So they showed up at the Manhattan offices of various Corporation members, doing their best to look youthful and innocent, whereupon they'd announce, "We're from Harvard. We're here for the Harvard meeting." Eventually, they got lucky. An unwitting secretary said, "Oh, it's not here," and directed them to the Plaza Athénée.

When the reporters reached the hotel, they rode the elevator to the penthouse, where the committee was meeting. Almost immediately, Shoichet and Graff bumped into Marc Goodheart. "Who are you?" he asked. They told him. Goodheart, an important but little-recognized administration official, asked them to leave. Was he a hotel employee? the reporters asked. No? Well then, they weren't about to leave. But, just in case, the students rented a room so that they couldn't be thrown out of the hotel for loitering. (The *Crimson*, which has an endowment of its own, could afford it.) Then they staked out the lobby.

At the conclusion of its interview, the committee asked Bollinger to avoid the reporters by taking the freight elevator and exiting by the hotel's back door. "I'll leave by the front door, thank you," he replied, bemused. Shoichet and Graff caught up to him just outside the hotel entrance. Bollinger wouldn't answer their questions, but they took his picture, and two days later the *Crimson* broke the news of his meeting with the search committee.

The veil of secrecy was lifted, if only for a moment.

Six days later, the committee met with Larry Summers.

A chauffeured limousine whisked him from Logan Airport to the Boston Harbor Hotel, taking Summers through the underground garage so that he could ride the freight elevator up to the sixteenth-floor, $2,500-a-night presidential suite. Summers would spend the next five hours talking with the search committee, going over much the same issues that Bollinger had. He agreed that Harvard needed to hire more professors, in part by awarding tenure to junior professors who were coming into their own rather than to stars from other universities who might already have done their best work. And, because the committee didn't want to have to go through this process again anytime soon, he vowed his devotion to Harvard. Even if Federal Reserve Chairman Alan Greenspan were to step down, Summers said, he wouldn't leave Harvard to take the job.

It was, by all accounts, an impressive presentation—lucid, wide-ranging, and backed by a broad sense of the world beyond Cambridge that Summers had developed over a decade of jet-setting around the globe. "What we saw was a powerful intellect and understanding of the university and a university's mission and purpose, and a tremendous taste for excellence," Hanna Gray said later.

Gray was Summers' most ardent supporter, in large part because of her disappointment with Neil Rudenstine. Although she publicly praised Rudenstine, she was privately impatient with him, and his collapse in 1994 had offended her. In Gray's eyes, not only had the episode embarrassed Harvard, but there was something damningly effete about the act. It represented the lack of toughness, the absence of rigor that she felt permeated academic culture in the 1990s. "Hanna didn't like Neil at all," said one professor who knew them both. "Like many successful women in our world, she didn't like unmanliness, because she's had to be pretty manly in her career. So, from her point of view, Neil's breakdown was disaster." Larry Summers, Gray was confident, would never pose such problems. He had been tested in the pressure-cooker worlds of Washington and international finance, and the tests only seemed to have made him stronger.

Robert Stone, though, was reputed to be leaning toward Bollinger. The Michigan president had the temperament and experience to step smoothly into the job. He was affable, likeable, a familiar type. Along with at least three other members of the search committee, Stone was worried about Summers' reputation as hot-headed and haughty.

No one was asking the faculty's opinion, but if they had, Bollinger would have been the likely favorite, a known quantity under whom the University of Michigan was prospering. Summers was obviously a man of enormous capability, but he had question marks. He hadn't been a well-known figure when he was at Harvard; he'd hung around with other economists and hadn't gotten involved in larger university issues. And he'd been away from academia for a decade.

"Bollinger was in many ways a much more intellectually appropriate figure" than Summers, said Everett Mendelsohn, a Harvard professor of the history of science since 1960. "He was someone who had dealt with issues of the university in the modern world in a way that Larry had not. Summers was known as someone with a hot temper, with strong ideas on some things but no reflections, as far as anyone knew, on what a university is or ought to be. Bollinger had dealt with issues of affirmative action, of student activism, of faculty salaries. Almost to a person, I don't think anyone on the faculty would have been a strong supporter of Summers."

That assertion may be too strong, but in any event, it was moot. In the committee's eyes, faculty support might actually have been a negative for a candidate; the Corporation wanted to shake things up. And to some search committee members, Bollinger had his drawbacks. He had no Harvard degree—though his daughter had attended the college, Bollinger matriculated at the University of Oregon before Columbia Law School, and for some members of the Corporation, "UO" was not quite Harvard material. According to sources close to the search process, Treasurer D. Ron Daniel was adamantly opposed to putting the university in the hands of someone who hadn't gone there. Plus, at fifty-four Bollinger was a little older than the committee would have preferred, almost as old as Rudenstine was when he took the job. That made it less likely that he'd serve the fifteen or twenty years the committee wanted.

In fact, there were hints that Bollinger was too much like Rudenstine in a number of ways, especially to Hanna Gray's taste. Rudenstine had been known for his promotion of the arts and African American studies, along with his defense of affirmative action; Bollinger too was a patron of the arts, and was fighting two lawsuits on behalf of affirmative action that were attracting national attention even before the Supreme Court heard them. Some Harvard officials were already uncomfortable with the amount of attention the Af-Am department under Skip Gates was attracting. Would Lee Bollinger change that trend—or continue it?

Larry Summers was pulling ahead. Only the question of his disposition remained. Could the committee entrust Harvard to a man famous for his brilliance but notorious for his temper?

So Summers' old mentor Bob Rubin stepped in. The widely respected former treasury secretary, Harvard class of '60, had enormous credibility. He was judicious, discreet, thoughtful, and enormously wealthy—a thoroughly impressive combination of old-school values and new-world money. Rubin didn't want to be president of Harvard, but if he had wanted the job, he probably could have had it. Instead, he wanted the job for Larry Summers.

So Rubin called three members of the search committee who had particular doubts: Stone, D. Ron Daniel, and James Richardson Houghton. It was true, Rubin admitted, that Summers had once had what Rubin would call a "rough-edges" issue. But he'd mellowed, Rubin insisted. This was a man who'd successfully negotiated with congressional leaders and foreign treasurers, who'd survived and prospered for a decade in a viciously partisan Washington environment. His temper existed more in legend than in reality.

Rubin's seal of approval worked. "Rubin made us confident that we weren't getting a bull," one member of the committee later said.

On February 26, 2001, the search committee met in its Loeb House conference room and unanimously chose Larry Summers as Harvard's next president. Robert Stone called Summers to ask if he would take the job, then flew to Washington, where Summers lived, to press the issue. Summers took a week to officially say yes. Then, on Sunday, March 11, he and the search committee met with the Board of Overseers on the sixty-fourth floor of 30 Rockefeller Center. The search committee members explained their reasons for choosing Summers, and then Summers gave a brief talk, laying out his vision for Harvard. As expected, the Overseers voted unanimously in favor of Summers.

After nine months of searching, Harvard had found a new president.

About five weeks later, fifty students took over Massachusetts Hall.

On Wednesday, April 18, they gathered secretly in the basement of a nearby freshman dormitory. They carried backpacks containing toiletries, cell phones, and paperbacks of Henry David Thoreau and Martin Luther King, Jr. Their leaders gave them last-minute pep talks on what to do if the police arrested them. A few minutes after five o'clock in the afternoon, they sprinted the one hundred feet or so from the dorm to the red-brick building that houses the Harvard president's office, flung open the green door at the front of the building, and rushed past an astonished secretary. Amid the chaos that ensued, Neil Rudenstine escaped out the back of the building. Provost Harvey Fineberg, whose office was next to Rudenstine's, did not. Fineberg refused to talk to the protesters, and the students refused to leave. It would be almost three weeks before they did so.

The occupation of Mass Hall, as the building is commonly known, was the most sustained piece of student activism at Harvard since the 1960s, and had been years in the making. It began with a small and seemingly innocuous act. In the early 1990s, Harvard, like numerous other universities, had copyrighted the name "Harvard," so as to prevent other companies and organizations from profiting off it, even as the university itself explored money-making opportunities. Through its Trademark Licensing Office, Harvard vigorously enforced that copyright, threatening lawsuits against, for example, the brewer of Harvard Beer. At the same time, Harvard was licensing its name to sportswear companies such as Nike and Champion to produce collegiate-themed clothing—T-shirts, sweatshirts, hats, and the like. Harvard was far from the only university to enter into such arrangements: By the late 1990s, college-affiliated clothing was producing about $3 billion a year in revenues for its manufacturers. But as American labor unions and campus activists discovered, one reason the business was lucrative was that some of the clothing was manufactured in Asian sweatshops. Outrage over universities' ties to the sweatshop trade inspired nationwide protests, such as the one that had resulted in the occupation of Lee Bollinger's Michigan office.

At Harvard, the anti-sweatshop drive led to the creation of a activist group called the Progressive Student Labor Movement. The members of PSLM soon came to feel that it wasn't just foreign workers who were being vastly underpaid, but Harvard employees as well. They had some justification for their belief. In May 1999, the Cambridge City Council had passed an ordinance requiring city contractors to pay what it considered a "living wage"—not just the minimum wage of $5.25 an hour, upon which it was impossible to support a family, but the more plausible amount of $10.00 an hour. Even that amounted only to an annual salary of about $21,000.

But according to the PSLM, thousands of Harvard workers—janitors, security guards, dining room workers—made considerably less than ten dollars an hour. (Harvard claimed that the number was in the hundreds.) In fact, throughout the 1990s, the wages of such workers had actually decreased, and many Harvard jobs had been outsourced to non-unionized workers, who didn't receive health or retirement benefits. As janitor Frank Morley put it, "You don't need a degree to know when you're getting screwed." Over the course of 1999 and 2000, PSLM's attempts to meet with Rudenstine and the Harvard Corporation had been repeatedly denied.

It was hardly the first time that Harvard had been accused of exploiting its blue-collar workers. Back in 1930, President Abbott Lawrence Lowell had refused to pay a group of "scrubwomen" more than thirty-five cents an hour, even though a state labor commission had instructed the university to pay the women thirty-seven and a half cents hourly. Instead, Lowell offered the women a daily twenty-minute rest break. Not until a group of embarrassed alumni raised $3,000 in "back pay" did the university retreat from its hard line. Similar fights occurred periodically for the next seventy years, according to Morton and Phyllis Keller, authors of *Making Harvard Modern*. Harvard, write the Kellers, cultivated an "almost feudal relationship" with its staff.

But the living wage movement brought a new element to an ongoing fight—globalization. With Harvard's endowment approaching $20 billion, idealistic students saw similarities between a sportswear corporation that exploited workers and a Harvard Corporation apparently doing the same. That link between the anti-sweatshop struggle overseas and the living-wage fight at home galvanized students, and the Harvard administration's recalcitrance only energized them further. Instead of offering to negotiate wage increases, the administration boasted of the free classes it offered workers. Joe Wrinn, a Harvard spokesman, claimed that such courses were the best way "to raise people into better-paying jobs." The workers pointed out that since they often had to work two jobs to support themselves, they really didn't have much time left over to take classes in English lit.

For lame-duck president Rudenstine, the sit-in was agonizing. With only weeks to go before his retirement, he had little power to affect the situation. And he was genuinely torn. Though he considered the sit-in a threat to the sovereignty of the university, he was not entirely unsympathetic. His own mother had been a cafeteria worker who, he once blurted out in frustration, had never made ten dollars an hour in her life. So while Rudenstine refused to negotiate with the students, neither would he allow them to be evicted or arrested. "He made it very clear that he would not call the police," said Everett Mendelsohn, who served as an informal liaison between Rudenstine and the protesters. "No matter how long it took, he would not call the police." The students, who had expected the worst, were shocked. "We couldn't believe our luck," said one.

Day after day, Rudenstine came to work, stepping over and around the increasingly smelly protesters. His own office had been locked when the students originally rushed in, apparently by an electric lock controlled by his secretary. So Rudenstine shifted to an office on the second floor. At one point he was joined for a meeting by president-elect Summers, who, according to sit-in participants, looked alternately annoyed at having to walk past the protesters and incredulous that they were still there. They didn't know yet just how strongly Larry Summers felt about student protest.

For the administration, the ties between the living wage movement and anti-globalization protests were clear and constituted an additional reason to take a hard line. When Bradley S. Epps, a professor of Romance languages and literature who supported the sit-in, asked if he could visit the protesters, Harvey Fineberg firmly said no. "They're involved with the anti-globalization protests in Seattle and elsewhere," Epps remembered Fineberg warning him. "They're going to tear down the gates."

Outside Massachusetts Hall, the campus was slowly being engaged by the sit-in. Cafeteria workers passed boxes of pizza through the windows of the building. Ted Kennedy and Jesse Jackson came to campus to protest, and the national media wrote stories and aired segments about the sit-in. Worried that their classmates couldn't actually see them except for brief glimpses through the windows, the protesters encouraged sympathizers to pitch tents in the yard around Mass Hall, and the early spring grass was soon decorated with a makeshift village of about seventy tents.

Harvard Yard is routinely described as a beautiful place, but that description is not quite accurate. A pigsty (literally) for much of the seventeenth century, the Yard is impressive, historic, and grand, but it falls short of beautiful. Perhaps it is the buildings—crammed together like hotels on a Monopoly board and radiating so much history that they celebrate the dead more than the living. Then there is the fact that the space is bisected by University Hall into the Old Yard (mostly dorms and Mass Hall) and the New Yard (mostly Tercentenary Theatre and its surrounding buildings).

Another dehumanizing element is the paved walking paths that crisscross the Yard like airport runways. The macadam stripes carve up the Yard's grass into small, asymetrical sections, and much of the year, the grass is either covered with snow or so muddy that it resembles the pigsty of yesteryear. When spring finally comes, usually not until May, the unpaved sections are cordoned off with ropes and coated with a green spray that improves the aesthetics until the real grass shoots up. The grassy chunks aren't big enough for the kind of athletic activity—

touch football, Frisbee, hackysack—that you'd normally find on a freshman quad. And even if they were, Harvard rules ban such recreation in the Yard. They also ban parties in the Yard's freshman dorms (even without alcohol, which is, of course, illegal for freshmen to drink).

Such rules exist partly for the peace of mind of the tens of thousands of tourists who stroll through the Yard every year, invariably posing for pictures in front of an 1884 statue of John Harvard. But they also reflect a larger truth about the culture of the university: Harvard is not a place where students are encouraged to relax. The Yard is not tranquil; it is fragmentation and constant motion. Seen from above, it would look like a series of conveyor belts constituting a sophisticated assembly line, a metaphor reinforced by the fact that in all of the Yard's twenty-five acres, there is not a single bench, nowhere for students or passersby to sit, chat, and simply slow down for a while. That absence puzzled one student—Josiah Pertz, class of 2005—so much that he wrote a Mass Hall administrator about it. The aide wrote back, "The University has historically shied away from placing structures in the Yard. This may be due to the fact that the Yard is meant to be a thoroughfare, rather than a gathering place." By "structures," the administrator meant places to sit.

During the occupation of Massachusetts Hall, however, the Yard did become a gathering place—the tent city made it one. It created a sense of community that many students said was as welcome at Harvard as it was rare. During the day, the colorful tents looked like the set for a piece of performance art. At night, students sat outside their tents and talked or played guitar, hanging out in a way that students don't do very much at Harvard. The tents were small, fragile, temporary shelters, yet, if only for a few days, they held their own against the silent disapproval of the historic buildings surrounding them.

After about two weeks of steadily building pressure, Neil Rudenstine still adamantly refused to talk to the protesters or soften the university's position. "I'll resign before I give in," he said, a threat that, given that he already had resigned, was more rhetorical than suasive. Students who had never seen Rudenstine play the heavy—who had never seen Rudenstine, period—were surprised. It seemed so out of character; he must be parroting the Corporation's party line, they decided. If so, the Corporation wasn't saying.

One week after Rudenstine issued his threat, the Harvard administration announced that it would raise the minimum salary of its hourly
employees to $10.83 an hour, with equal wages for outsourced workers,
and create a commission to study its employment practices. After
twenty-one days inside Massachusetts Hall, shortly after five P.M. on
May 8, twenty-three jubilant protesters poured out of the building.
Neil Rudenstine was nowhere to be seen.

It was Larry Summers' time now.

4

The President versus the Professor

It was the summer of 2001, and Skip Gates was getting worried.

The fifty-year-old chairman of Harvard's department of Afro-American Studies had heard that the new president was making the rounds on campus, chatting with professors about their interests, their needs, their concerns. But Larry Summers hadn't called Gates or anyone else associated with Af-Am, and the department members were growing concerned. Afro-American Studies may have been a small department, but it was still the best-known, most respected African American studies department in the country. How could Summers not want to meet with them, and quickly?

Gates wasn't used to getting the cold shoulder. Back in 1991, when Neil Rudenstine was taking over, the incoming president sent Gates a handwritten note asking if they could meet, and in short order the two were having lunch in New York. Rudenstine asked Gates to jot down the scholars he wanted to hire. Then, over the next few years, the two men went out and hired them.

A decade later, as Rudenstine was preparing his exit, Gates helped put on a farewell dinner for the outgoing president. Toasting Rudenstine, Gates called him "our president," meaning the president of black people at Harvard. "Neil," he said, his voice catching, "although you are far too modest to know this, you are, and shall always be, a hero to our people. And for us, your most loyal and dedicated constituency and your unshakably devoted friends, you should always be 'the President.' You shall always be the Man."

Rudenstine felt equally fond of Gates. He'd given the professor a copy of his book of essays with a heartfelt inscription: "To Skip, I write very slowly, so this cannot possibly rival your own fertile, eloquent, and always grand stream of prose. But it's all I have to offer, and it comes with a sense of deep gratitude, steady friendship and a rare feeling that does not come often in life—of having worked together to achieve something truly transcendent."

For Henry Louis Gates, Jr., feeling the odd man out is an unusual situation; he lives to be in the mix. Gates is a networking master, particularly by the standards of academe, where, after too many hours in the library or laboratory, social graces are often neglected or just plain underdeveloped. But Gates, a light-skinned black man with an easy smile and a quick laugh, is comfortable, funny, self-deprecating, and charming. Even people who find him a bit of a rogue can't help liking Skip Gates. Back when he was writing regularly for the *New Yorker*, editor Tina Brown threw a party with him at Harvard's Eliot House packed with luminaries from Cambridge, Boston, and New York. When a friend asked Gates if he was enjoying himself, he threw back his head and laughed. "Man," he said, "it's like shittin' in high cotton."

When conservative columnist George Will visited Harvard, Gates threw a dinner party for him with guests that included former dean Henry Rosovsky, conservative political scientist Harvey Mansfield, and the liberal philosopher Cornel West. Normally, George Will and Cornel West wouldn't have been found within one hundred yards of each other. But Gates is all about building bridges—between liberal and conservative, white and black, academics from different fields—so that everyone benefits.

Same thing with the bash he threw every fall at his house on Francis Avenue in Cambridge, an elegant home just down the street from that of legendary Harvard economist John Kenneth Galbraith. Gates had bought the home in 1995 for $890,000, then had it extensively renovated by the internationally famous architect Moshe Safdie, and he liked to show it off. There was great food, lots of booze, a band in the yard out back. This kind of thing wasn't done at Harvard—throwing a big party for no particular reason. For one thing, the cost was prohibitive for most professors. A top salary for a tenured professor at Harvard is around $200,000, far from extravagant given the many years of training and the high cost of Cambridge-area living. And that comes only to a select few.

But money wasn't the only obstacle; Harvard just isn't the kind of community where people relax easily. "People at Harvard aren't used to being treated like human beings," said Peter Gomes. "A colleague is someone lashed to the same mast. We're surrounded by subordinates whom we tell what to do, or superiors to whom we suck up." Socializing usually has a purpose—something official and work-related, like a going-away banquet or an award ceremony. But Gates' parties united people from all over the university. And, not coincidentally, there would just happen to be more African Americans present than at any other Harvard gathering one could think of. It was just like back in 1957, when seven-year-old Skip would watch Nat King Cole, the first black with his own TV show. Cole would have black guests on his program as well as white ones. That way, the black people could advance without threatening whites and prompting a backlash.

Skip Gates had come a long way since then. He was born on September 16, 1950, in Keyser, West Virginia, a small, rural town about two hours west of Washington, D.C. His father worked at the local paper mill in the first half of the day, then went to a second job as a janitor at the phone company. His mother raised Skip to speak English the way whites did and to dream of going to an Ivy League school. She wanted him out of Keyser, where racism was a fact of everyday life. "I was called 'nigger' so many times, I often thought I had a sign on my back," Gates recalled. In high school, he broke his hip playing football. When he made the mistake of telling the white doctor that he too wanted to go into medicine, the doctor decided that young Skip was faking his injury and declined to treat it. As an adult, Gates would have seven operations on that hip, culminating in a replacement joint. He now walks with the help of a cane.

Limping or no, he did get out of Keyser. Gates went to Yale and graduated summa cum laude in 1973, just two years before Larry Summers graduated from MIT. There weren't a lot of black students in New Haven then. But rather than feeling alienated, Gates wanted to make Yale his own. He read and appreciated Sam Greenlee's 1969 novel, *The Spook Who Sat by the Door*, a satire about a black CIA agent. "We all wanted to be spooks who sat by the door," Gates later remembered. "We all wanted to be inside the system, integrated into historically elite white institutions of America, transforming them from the inside."

Gates earned his Ph.D. in English at Cambridge University, then returned to Yale to teach. But his route to professional stardom really began in 1981, when he won a MacArthur Award, the so-called "genius" grant given by the MacArthur Foundation. Even though Gates didn't get tenure at Yale, the MacArthur, a $156,000, no-strings-attached prize, made him nationally known, and in 1985 Cornell University granted Gates tenure at age thirty-three—and for a humanist, whose research tends to take longer than that of scientists and economists, winning tenure at thirty-three is virtually unheard of. Gates spent five years at Cornell, until he was lured away by Duke University in 1990. But he wouldn't stay long in North Carolina. Gates was then married to a white woman named Sharon Lynn Adams, a fact that seemed to make some North Carolinians uncomfortable, which, in turn, made Skip Gates very uncomfortable. So when Harvard's Derek Bok and Henry Rosovsky let their interest be known in 1991, Gates was amenable to a move back north.

Gates began his career as a literary theorist aiming to show that black Americans had written books just as deserving of serious critical analysis as were books by white Americans. His best-known work of scholarship, *The Signifying Monkey*, argued convincingly for the existence of an independent black American literary tradition. But with the MacArthur and now Harvard, Gates became more than a mere scholar; he was an academic entepreneur. Gates was co-editor of the encyclopedia *Africana*; co-founder of a website called Africana.com; historical consultant to Steven Spielberg's film *Amistad*; and star of print and television ads for IBM. He became a judge for various career-making awards, including the Pulitzer Prize. His list of publications—a growing number of which he edited or just introduced—was longer than some people's dissertations. Skip Gates was a celebrity, a brand. And he was powerful. Gates could get people jobs—and keep people out of them. A phone call from him to a publisher could land a book contract for a young scholar; a blurb by Gates signified establishment approval; a Gates recommendation could mean the difference between winning a grant or changing careers.

Inevitably, his scholarship suffered. The wheeling and dealing kept him busy: he was always on the phone, constantly traveling, near impossible to schedule. Everyone who knows Gates can tell a story about his chronic tardiness or canceled appointments.

Also inevitably, he aroused skepticism and envy among both whites and blacks. Other academics resented the bidding wars that Duke and Harvard engaged in to lure him, reportedly paying him some $200,000 a year—a pittance by the standards of, say, Wall Street, but a lot for a professor of literature. And salary was just for starters; Gates got staff, prime office space, generous department budgets. Harvard, Duke, and Cornell had even hired his intellectual colleague and close friend, a Ghana-born philosopher named K. Anthony Appiah.

Some whites—some of the same people who didn't much care for Neil Rudenstine—thought that Gates exploited white guilt, that he was a 1990s mau-mauer who solicited money not by threats of street protest but by playing the race card in subtler ways. Certainly for a small department, Afro-American studies seemed to get an inordinate amount of Neil Rudenstine's attention, and Gates wasn't shy about letting it be known that he had Rudenstine's ear. Some blacks, on the other hand, argued that Gates was too accommodating, a modern-day Booker T. Washington, the black educator who thought that the only way for blacks to get ahead in late-nineteenth-century American society was to shun politics and learn a trade. For Washington, money had been foundational power, the basis of all other social gains, and Gates did seem to enjoy the fruits of his labors. Some African Americans wanted him to be more confrontational, more in-your-face—especially since he was now at the top of the world's most powerful university. They thought that Skip Gates was enjoying his success just a little too much. His defenders responded that Gates' rising tide was lifting a lot of boats.

Gates may have picked his battles carefully, but he did pick them. In 1991 he testified in defense of 2 Live Crew when the rap band went on trial for violating Florida's obscenity laws. Yet Gates was no apologist for all of black culture. In 1992 he wrote a famous *New York Times* editorial, "Black Demagogues and Pseudo-Scholars," in which he attacked black anti-Semitism and decried the deteriorating relationship between blacks and Jews.

Anyway, no matter how much Gates had become accepted by whites, he never forgot where he came from or that, to some whites, it didn't matter how light his skin color was. When Gates first came to Harvard, he and Sharon lived in the suburb of Lexington, a few miles northwest of Cambridge. Shortly after moving in, Gates paid a visit to the local police department. I travel a lot, he told an officer, and my wife will be alone. Are there any special security measures I should take?

Truth was, Gates wasn't particularly worried about his wife's safety in the tranquil suburb. He just wanted to introduce himself to the local police—because, otherwise, he suspected, a black man driving a Mercedes in Lexington, Massachusetts, was going to see a lot of flashing blue-and-white in his rearview mirror.

Gates took enormous pride in the department that he, Anthony Appiah, and Neil Rudenstine had built. They'd recruited scholars such as the eminent sociologist William Julius Wilson; jurisprudent Leon Higginbotham and his wife, historian Evelyn Brooks Higginbotham; legal scholar Lani Guinier; and Cornel West. Gates himself had raised an astonishing $40 million for the department's endowment, tapping his network of friends and business partners. Who else but Skip Gates could have convinced Time-Warner CEO Gerald Levin to donate $3 million of his company's money to endow the "Quincy Jones Professorship of African-American Music"? Outside his office, Gates had hung a framed note that Jones had written during a "celebration of African-Americans in Paris." It read: "A Skip Gates, le meilleur professeur du monde, et mon cher bon ami et frère. Avec toute ma gratitude et mon coeur. Je t'aime, inconditionnellement. Quincy Jones, July 4, 2000."

Gates knew that by building this department at Harvard, he'd achieved something historic. He had taken something that was historically white—profoundly white, in its composition, its outlook, and culture—and had made it, in a small but significant way, black. And because this was Harvard, you could see the ripple effects at the nation's finest universities—at Princeton, Columbia, Yale—the awareness that if Harvard was making African American studies a priority, they had to compete. It gave Gates a deep appreciation of Harvard's power; the university was like an enormous megaphone.

So when Larry Summers didn't call, Skip Gates, not a man to sit and wait, decided he'd better do something. In late June, he was in his sunny office on the second floor of the Barker Center, home of several humanities departments, meeting with Corporation member Herbert "Pug" Winokur. The two men were discussing the creation of fellowships for minority graduate students in honor of Neil Rudenstine. Attracting black students to graduate school in the humanities was a chronic struggle. If you were a black kid from a poor background, with the brains and education to attend grad school at Harvard, wouldn't you want to go to the business school or the law school and make some real money? Spending six or seven years working on a doctoral dissertation was an uncertain road to success, especially for someone whose modest origins made financial security that much more appealing.

In the midst of that conversation, Gates let slip that he hadn't heard anything from Larry Summers, but he was uncomfortable saying anything to the new president—after all, the president called you to say he wanted to meet, not the other way around. Could Winokur mention to Summers that Gates would be interested in a meet-and-greet? Winokur could mention it, and did. Before long, Summers was on the phone.

Why didn't you call me before? Gates asked. I could have helped introduce you around. Gates was taken aback by what Summers said in response.

"Because," Summers answered, "everyone told me to."

Soon enough, Gates would get his face time with the president. But it wouldn't turn out exactly as he'd hoped.

The meeting between Larry Summers and African American faculty members took place in early July, in the Alain Locke seminar room in the Af-Am department at the elegant new Robert and Elizabeth Barker Center, just across Quincy Street from the Yard. Af-Am used to be tucked away in a slightly decrepit house on a small side street a few blocks away, but Neil Rudenstine had helped raise $25 million to transform what had been the freshman dining hall into a stunning humanities complex. Afro-American Studies was a proud resident, along with the English department, the Committee on the History of American Civilization, the Committee on the Study of Religion, and others. The symbolism was important: Just as the proximity of federal agencies to the White House reflects their importance (or lack thereof), Harvard departments want to be as close as possible to the Yard. After being stuck on the outskirts of town, Af-Am had been integrated into prime real estate on campus.

It was about a month after graduation, and Harvard had settled into the rhythm of summer, when the campus feels considerably more easygoing than it does the rest of the year. Perhaps a dozen African

American faculty and staff members had come to this meeting, including Gates, Anthony Appiah, law school professor Charles Ogletree, Evelyn Brooks Higginbotham, William Julius Wilson, and Charles Willie, a professor at the Graduate School of Education. They had gathered in the seminar room, a small but cozy space with room for about twenty and a blackboard at one end.

When Summers arrived, Gates gave him a tour of the department and presented him with a gift, a CD-ROM of *Encarta Africana,* the Microsoft-published encyclopedia that he and Appiah had edited. Higginbotham, a soft-spoken, dignified scholar of black religion and history, gave Summers a copy of *The Harvard Guide to African-American History,* for which she had served as editor-in-chief. Summers himself arrived bearing a gift of sorts. As he had wandered around campus, he said, he'd noticed the prevalence of academic centers devoted to the study of specific subjects—the Ukrainian Research Institute, for example. It seemed odd that there was no African studies center.

For the professors sitting around the seminar table, this was a welcome sign. Gates in particular had long wanted to expand the focus of his department to include Africa. How could you study African American history without studying Africa? But that would require more faculty, more staff, a travel budget—it was a major commitment.

The good start did not last long. Charles Ogletree, a law school professor known for his civil rights activism, asked Summers where he stood on the issue of affirmative action. Harvard had a tradition of supporting affirmative action, Ogletree said. The university had written an *amicus curae* brief in the fabled 1978 Supreme Court case *Regents of the University of California v. Bakke,* in which a white man named Allan Bakke sued after being rejected by the medical school at the University of California at Davis. Justice Lewis F. Powell, Jr., the critical swing vote in the decision to uphold affirmative action, had singled out Harvard as a practitioner of constructive and legal affirmative action. Now two more cases attacking affirmative action were headed to the Supreme Court, the ones involving Lee Bollinger and the University of Michigan. Would Summers align Harvard with the defense of affirmative action once more? And would he appoint blacks to top positions in the lily-white Harvard administration?

Until this point Summers had been civil, if not exactly warm. But he looked prickly at the questions, as if surprised that the subject had come up. "That's one of the things that I need to think about," he said. "I need to look at all the relevant data and decide what position Harvard will take, and that is something I plan to do in time."

This was not the answer those assembled were expecting to hear. "I thought that, whatever your views, you should have not have allowed yourself to become president of a major university and not have made up your mind on affirmative action," said one participant later. "It was very odd."

Ogletree, a handsome, elegantly dressed man who can be as intense as he is smooth, did not look happy. Affirmative action was essentially a settled matter at Harvard, he continued. Former president Derek Bok had co-written an entire book articulating the need for affirmative action. How could Summers not have a position on it?

"I've read parts of that book, and I didn't find it convincing," Summers said. He wanted to look at more data before making up his mind.

"Come on, Larry," Gates said, "that sounds like something you'd hear at a Washington press conference. I don't think I heard you make a commitment to diversity."

It was meant to be a joke to cut the tension, but Summers didn't laugh. "He was coming to tell us that we weren't going to get special treatment anymore, and he was upset by Ogletree's style," said one person present.

Visibly upset. "I believe in diversity, but I also believe in excellence," Summers snapped.

If the mood in the room had been precarious before, this remark pushed it off a cliff. Neil Rudenstine had believed that diversity was a prerequisite for excellence; Summers seemed to be suggesting an incompatibility between the two.

"In retrospect, he might not have meant that," remembered Higginbotham. Possibly Summers had simply misspoken. Still, when he inserted the *but* between *diversity* and *excellence*, then "all of a sudden, we looked at each other and thought, 'Oh dear, I wonder if he thinks these two things don't go together. Because we certainly think that excellence and diversity go together, and we don't want anybody here who isn't excellent.'"

Gates changed the subject by telling Summers about *Transition*, a journal devoted to black studies, which Rudenstine had funded with monies from the president's office. Gates hoped that Summers would continue to support *Transition*. Still annoyed, Summers wrapped up, saying, "I'm judging everything on a case-by-case basis. Make the case."

After less than half an hour, Summers was gone, and the professors' moods ranged from puzzled to anxious to grim. "My God," said one, "it's not just that he's not going to help us; it's that he wants to destroy us."

For the next several months, Gates didn't hear from Summers. Then, one day, in early October, he got a phone call from the president. There was something on his mind. He had been hearing some worrisome things about Cornel West, things that made him wonder if West was upholding his responsibilities as a faculty member. There were rumors that West had skipped classes to campaign for New Jersey senator Bill Bradley in the 2000 Democratic presidential primary. That he was contributing to the problem of grade inflation at Harvard. And that he was neglecting his scholarship, publishing popular books rather than serious academic works.

Summers was very concerned. He wanted to meet with West as soon as possible.

In the months to come, Cornel West would be labeled an egomaniac, a con man, a charlatan, a tenured radical, and a media whore. None of these caricatures explained him. West's story did not easily translate onto the pages of the daily newspapers whose columnists and editorial writers were so quick to judge him.

West was born on June 2, 1953, in Tulsa, Oklahoma, the son of an Air Force administrator and an elementary school principal who had met at Fisk University, an all-black college in Nashville, Tennessee. His paternal grandfather was a Baptist minister. When West was just a few years old, the family moved to Sacramento, California, where he was raised.

Growing up in the 1960s, West was a dissident and nonconformist from an early age. When he was just nine, he refused to stand and salute the American flag along with the rest of his fourth-grade class. His teacher slapped him. He slapped her back, and was promptly suspended from school.

But whether in school or not, West had a passion for learning. As a kid, he spent countless hours reading in a traveling bookmobile, a public library bus that traveled to neighborhoods whose residents didn't have easy library access. One of the books he read was a biography of Harvard graduate Theodore Roosevelt, whose story so inspired West that he decided he wanted to go to Harvard after finishing at Sacramento's John F. Kennedy High School. Harvard accepted him, and in 1970 West began his freshman year in Cambridge. He lived just across the hall from William Samuelson, the son of economist Paul Samuelson and Larry Summers' cousin. One year later, Larry Summers would begin his first year down Massachusetts Avenue at MIT.

Thirty-five years ago, there weren't many students at Harvard like Cornel West, a lower-middle-class black man whose enthusiasm for scholarship was as urgent as his commitment to social justice. He loved Harvard and all its riches—brilliant professors such as the philosophers John Rawls and Robert Nozick, gifted classmates, libraries with their millions of volumes, like nothing he'd ever seen before. "You could get lost in Widener Library for two years," he remembered. "Man, you'd come out *knowing* something." At the same time, West wanted to make Harvard more responsive to the social exigencies of the era. He became president of Harvard's Black Student Association, a radical student group at the time, and in 1972 the group took over President Bok's office in a protest over Harvard investments in Angola.

West worked to help pay his way through school, washing dishes and working "dorm crew," a job that still exists at Harvard. Rather than having students clean the bathrooms inside their suites, the university pays other undergraduates to do the dirty work. It's one of the better-paying campus jobs, so dorm crew slots tend to go to the neediest students. As have hundreds of Harvard students before him and after, Cornel West literally cleaned the shit of his more affluent classmates.

Even so, he ran out of money. Unable to pay for four years of college, West took sixteen classes in his junior year, twice the usual eight Harvard students take per year. He graduated magna cum laude in June of 1973 and headed to Princeton to start graduate work in philosophy. After finishing his doctorate in 1980, he taught at New York's Union Theological Seminary, Yale, and Princeton over the next decade.

As a young professor, West cut a charismatic figure. He is tall and slender, with a large afro and heavy, black-rimmed glasses. Following the model of 1950s jazz musicians, he wears three-piece black suits with black wingtips, a black tie, and a white shirt. And he has a physical intensity and a contagious passion for his material. A West lecture can glide smoothly from Dante to Nietzsche to Chekhov to Duke Ellington. Onstage, West sounds more like a preacher than a professor. It is a performance, but not an act; for someone so dramatic, West is strangely lacking in self-consciousness. "He is always the same—completely guileless," said one scholar who knows West well. "There's a kind of public Cornel," the man you see at a lecture or conference. "And then you go have a drink with him afterward, and he's exactly the same person."

West's 1993 book, *Race Matters,* accelerated his growing renown and popularity. Written in response to the Rodney King riots in Los Angeles and the nomination of Clarence Thomas to the Supreme Court, the book is a manifesto for black progress and racial healing— criticizing, for example, black anti-Semitism and calling for improved relations between blacks and Jews. It also attacks American capitalism and the market economy, which West sees as a kind of drug dealer to black America. He warns of "unbridled capitalist market forces . . . that have devastated black working and poor communities. . . . The common denominator is a rugged and ragged individualism." *Race Matters* sold half a million copies, and West acquired a reputation as a public intellectual—a scholar who used his learning to address a popular audience on topics of current interest. He began popping up on the television talk-show circuit, making the rounds on CNN, PBS, and C-SPAN.

Gates and Appiah wanted West at Harvard, and in 1994, with Rudenstine's support, they got him. While West had liked Princeton and appreciated the intimacy of a small community that valued undergraduate teaching, what was going on in Af-Am at Harvard felt too important to miss. "I wanted to be part of the team," he said. "Skip's team."

Four years later, Rudenstine elevated West to the position of University Professor, the highest status a scholar can attain at Harvard. President James Bryant Conant created the position in 1935 because, in the words of Harvard historian Richard Norton Smith, Conant wanted the University Professor to "roam as he wished across disciplinary bounds, teaching as he saw fit, conducting research or simply pondering." West and sociologist William Julius Wilson would be the first two blacks appointed University Professors, and West certainly roamed: he taught in the college, the divinity school, and the law school.

West's promotion prompted subterranean grumbling among the faculty, some of whom took it as another sign of Rudenstine's favoritism towards African American Studies and sniped that West's record of publications didn't merit the position. Though he had published more than a dozen books, the most recent ones were popular works, more journalism than scholarship. Sometimes he had a co-writer; other times he was only the editor. He'd co-written or co-edited three books with Skip Gates alone.

Even as West's scholarship grew shallower, he broadened his political activities. In 1995 he supported and attended the "Million Man March" organized by Nation of Islam minister Louis Farrakhan. In 2000 he campaigned for Bill Bradley, who was running for the Democratic nomination for president. After Bradley dropped out, West stumped for Green Party candidate Ralph Nader. And in August 2001, the controversial New York activist Al Sharpton announced that West would be heading his presidential exploratory committee.

At the same time that West was involved with black political figures whom many critics considered anti-Semitic, he was vigorously speaking out against black ant-Semitism. If it wasn't a contradiction, it was certainly a gray area. But West argued that such moral absolutes were a luxury he could not afford. Like Skip Gates, he walked a tightrope between blacks and whites, albeit in a slightly different way. Gates liked high society, and it liked him; West felt out of place amid rich white people. He was oriented toward the streets, the neighborhoods. That was where he could make a difference. And sometimes that meant that you had to mix with flawed characters.

In 2001 West recorded a spoken-word CD called *Sketches of My Culture*. It sounded like a Beat poet riffing to a hip-hop soundtrack. Though the album would, in subsequent months, repeatedly be described as a "rap" record, with all that that label implied to many whites, its inspirational themes were intended as an unambiguous rebuke of the misogynistic, violent side of rap. "Since black musicians play such an important role in African-American life," West argued, "they have a special mission and responsibility: to present beautiful music which both sustains and motivates black people and provides visions of what black people should aspire to."

It was all about communication, West said, about teaching young people. If you were a black academic from the inner city, you couldn't just lecture to upper-crust kids at Harvard. You knew *they* were going to make it. You had to remember where *you* came from—and who was still back there. It was your responsibility to be an intellectual, a well-dressed black man who carried himself with dignity, because black youths needed to see the choices they had, that they were capable of becoming other than basketball players and hip-hop artists. But you also had to speak to them in a way that they could relate to. Maybe white professors didn't—couldn't—appreciate the position West was in.

And, yes, ego was a factor too. Cornel West was human. He liked being recognized on the street, liked the sight of a rapt audience. And, yes, West was making money. When he charged it, his fee for speaking at universities and conferences had risen to $10,000 an appearance. But would it make more sense to live in an ivory tower, to cede young black America to Suge Knight or other apparent apostles of the thug life? For West, that would have been an abdication of responsibility, a betrayal of self. After all, he was a man who had learned to read great books in a bookmobile, a traveling public library. That's what Cornel West wanted to be—a traveling public library that could change kids' lives the way that, decades before, a bus filled with books had changed his.

Depending on your point of view, that self-image was either imperative or egocentric—and, no question, West's persona and politics were making him enemies. Two of them were Martin Peretz, then a Harvard professor and owner of *The New Republic,* and Leon Wieseltier, the magazine's literary editor. Peretz had been a civil rights activist while earning his doctorate at Harvard in the 1960s, a true believer in the political solidarity of blacks and Jews. In the aftermath of that decade, he had grown markedly more conservative, somewhat disillusioned, generally distrustful of left-wing politics, and ever more deeply steeped in his Jewish faith and culture. In 1993 Peretz endowed a Harvard professorship, the Martin Peretz Chair in Yiddish Literature, with a gift of several million dollars. He is a force to be reckoned with around Harvard—wealthy, part-owner of one of the last mainstream journals in the country to review academic books, absolutely fearless and unafraid to make enemies, while at the same time socially active, throwing catered dinner parties at his tasteful home in an expensive neighborhood near campus. For many years he taught undergraduate seminars at Harvard, often taken by ambitious young men who wanted to work at *The New Republic.*

Like Peretz, Leon Wieseltier takes faith seriously; a former member of the Harvard Society of Fellows, he is a scholar of Jewish culture. Like West, Wieseltier has an attraction to the dramatic; West had bit parts in the second and third *Matrix* movies, while Wieseltier had a cameo on *The Sopranos*. He is a striking man, the Lou Reed of literary editors. Tall and so thin as to be almost gaunt, Wieseltier has long, flowing white hair and dresses in untucked shirts, black jeans, and cowboy boots. And, like Peretz, he uses his position at *The New Republic* to reward those writers and politicians of whom he approves and rebuke those who do not meet his standards.

Cornel West was a member of the latter group. In 1995, Wieseltier wrote a scathing essay, "All and Nothing at All," portraying West as an incoherent thinker obsessed with his public persona—an essay that, by several accounts, greatly influenced Larry Summers. "Since there is no crisis in America more urgent than the crisis of race, and since there is no intellectual in America more celebrated for his consideration of the crisis of race, I turned to West, and read his books," Wieseltier began. "They are almost completely worthless . . . monuments to the devastation of a mind by the squalls of [literary] theory."

Wieseltier noted that many American writers had been lamenting a paucity of public intellectuals. They fretted that scholarship had grown too obtuse, too removed from public discourse. But, Wieseltier asked, was being a public intellectual mostly an excuse for avoiding the hard work of serious thinking? "Perhaps we have been asking the wrong question," Wieseltier suggested. "Where are the *private* intellectuals? Philosophers have for too long been trying to change the world. Perhaps it is time to think about it."

Wieseltier's essay was eagerly consumed in the halls of academe, where, as in all fields of human endeavor, a juicy takedown of a successful colleague appeals to people's baser instincts. And, to be sure, Wieseltier put into words what some academics already felt but did not care to state in public.

Yet even when they had their political differences, many of West's Harvard colleagues liked him. Alan Dershowitz, ever vigilant about anti-Semitism, didn't think much of his colleague's empathy for Al Sharpton, but he never believed that West was anti-Semitic and he considered West an inspiring teacher. Government professor Harvey

Mansfield, a conservative, had known West since the latter was an undergraduate, when he'd taken courses taught by Mansfield. "I like Cornel," Mansfield said. "The way that he presents himself to the world—his hairstyle, the black suit—doesn't offend me, as it does some."

Nor did Wieseltier's attack hurt West among Harvard students; West remained one of the university's most popular professors. Behind a lectern, he was motion, energy, and intensity—the polar opposite of, say, Martin Feldstein. "He resonated with people," said a student named Johanna Paretzky, who graduated in 2003. The daughter of a black father and white, Jewish mother, Paretzky emphasized that West's appeal wasn't just to African American students. "White, black, it didn't matter. He was just completely invested in what he had to say."

West's primary course, African American Studies 10, was a survey of blacks in American history and literature. But "he would stand up there and say, 'None of this is history, it's all *now*,'" Paretzky remembered. West's emphasis on the current-day relevance of his material made Paretzky feel greater enthusiasm for studying it; this wasn't just stuff you talked about in class and then discarded when you went out into the real world. The annual CUE Guide reviews showed that many students shared Paretsky's feelings: West consistently earned a 4.6 or 4.7 out of a possible score of 5, significantly higher than Larry Summers had scored among his undergraduate students.

West's importance extended beyond the classroom. At an institution where students chronically complain that the faculty are too busy and self-important to care about them, West was one professor who would actually engage with undergraduates. "He was a pop star, but in the small ways of creating community, he was important," said Krishnan Subrahmanian, the 2003 class marshall. "You'd see him walking down the street and he'd say, 'What's up, brother?' He was inspirational, passionate. He made people care." West seemed to know everyone—he'd call you "brother" or "sister"—and when he saw someone he knew, he'd give that person a warm hug, get immersed in an impromptu conversation about anything from a new translation of Virgil to the latest Prince CD. It could take Cornel West half an hour just to make the five-minute traverse across Harvard Yard, so many people wanted to talk to him—and he to them.

Harvard professors have a reputation for not being particularly grateful when students come to their office hours, the allotted time students can visit them to discuss material in person. Some professors make students call for appointments weeks in advance; students quickly get the message that they have to be crammed in amid higher priorities. But West's office hours frequently lasted as long as the students wanted to stay. He hosted reading groups with graduate students that went on until late in the night. "He'd talk about things you don't often hear on campus," said John McMillian, a graduate student in American history, "like how to be a decent person."

Despite all the diversity of its student body—and in terms of geography, ethnicity, religion, and culture, Harvard probably has the most diverse student body of any university in the world—the majority of Harvard professors are white men. And almost all of the people who run Harvard are white men. In 2001, every single dean of a Harvard school, with the almost mandatory exception of the Radcliffe Institute, was a white male. (The university does have several female vice-presidents of substantial power, but they are largely behind-the-scenes figures, unknown to students.) The men who run Harvard preach diversity among the students, but do not practice it within their own ranks. So Cornel West mattered.

"He's the kind of inspiring teacher that people have as a fantasy of the Ivy League," said one Harvard professor. And in the fall of 2001, he was more popular than he had ever been. Af-Am 10 had some seven hundred students, making it the third most popular course at Harvard; in fact, West had clashed with university administrators who wanted him to cut the class size in half—they couldn't seem to find a classroom big enough to hold all those students. West had refused, and wound up teaching in the basement of St. Paul's, a local Catholic church.

Maybe, West thought later, that fight was a sign of things to come. Perhaps he was being paranoid, but it seemed that suddenly the powers-that-be wanted him to be a little less popular. He couldn't help but think that this would never have happened when Neil Rudenstine was president, and he wondered if Larry Summers was trying to show that he would use his power very differently than Rudenstine had.

Among the ranks of people who might be considered for the job of a university president, the presidency of Harvard has long been seen as a

structurally weak position. Harvard's every-tub-on-its-own-bottom tradition makes its deans unusually powerful figures. But the powers of
the presidency do create opportunities for a president with sufficient
energy, determination, and diplomacy to change the institution in radical ways—especially if he focuses on Harvard College. After the Civil
War, Charles William Eliot abolished the prescribed curriculum and
introduced elective courses, probably the most crucial step in making
Harvard a world-class university. In the 1910s and 1920s, Abbott
Lawrence Lowell imposed a system of undergraduate concentrations
and built the Harvard houses, which physically and psychologically
transformed the campus by eliminating the "Gold Coast," the luxurious private housing where rich students isolated themselves. And in
the years before and during World War II, James Bryant Conant began
the transformation of Harvard from a school for New England's social
elite to an undergraduate meritocracy, with students from private and
public schools all over the country.

Some of the powers of the Harvard president are tangible. He has
the power to appoint university vice-presidents, the administrators who
perform the corporate functions of the university—finance, community
relations, real estate planning, and the like. Those are relatively anonymous positions within the university, but they are powerful ones, and
the larger a university becomes, the more power accrues to the people
who know how to administer its bureaucracy.

The president also appoints new deans when the old ones step
down, another method of solidifying his power. For many academics,
deanships are desired positions. They bring larger salaries than professorships, higher profiles, and power of their own; the deans set salaries,
allocate office space, approve sabbaticals, raise money, and shape the
academic agenda for their schools. Sometimes deans are visionary figures with concrete agendas and administrative skills; other times they
are academics who've wearied of the hard, lonely life of a scholar.

Not surprisingly, the president can compel promises of allegiance
in exchange for appointments. His challenge is to find people who will
submit to such quid pro quos, but are nonetheless able enough to run
their schools. If he desired, the president could appoint an obeisant
hack to head, say, the Kennedy School, but the coherence and morale
of the school would inevitably suffer, especially if the dean lost the

confidence of his faculty. So the power to appoint deans is a substantial one, yet must be carefully wielded.

The president also raises money from and fosters healthy relations with alumni. Although Harvard's individual schools conduct their own fundraising campaigns, the president is expected to help. Of course, some schools need the president's help more than others. "A responsible president will spend a certain amount of time helping the divinity school and the design school and the education school raise funds," said Derek Bok. "But he wouldn't walk across the street to help the business school raise funds. If the dean can't raise funds with that constituency, you'd better get a new dean."

The president also has a self-interest in fundraising. He has his own slice of the endowment at his disposal—it falls under the rubric of "central administration"—and although most Harvard alumni don't realize this, about five percent of every dollar they give is tithed and redirected to the president's monies. That way the president can support projects of particular importance to him, whether it be funding for a faculty endeavor or fellowships for scholars he wants to support. The money to initiate projects and reward the favored is another form of the president's power.

The president also meets with the other Corporation members to discuss university priorities and—another tangible power—sign off on the budgets of the various schools. It's rare for a president to intervene significantly in a school's budget, because any self-respecting dean would probably quit after such an incursion upon his autonomy. But it does happen, especially if the school is in shaky financial shape.

Perhaps the most important of the Harvard president's powers is that he makes the final decision on candidates for tenure. Every professor up for tenure at Harvard College or at some of Harvard's graduate schools—the school of education and the divinity school, for example—must be approved by the president. This gives him direct control over the makeup of a department and the intellectual direction of the university. Again, withholding approval is rarely done; a president who vetoed too many tenure nominations or who rejected them for dubious reasons would likely prompt faculty rebellion.

And then, of course, there are the intangible powers of the Harvard president, the ones that flow from his bully pulpit. An activist president can set the academic agenda of the university as a whole and Harvard College in particular. Since the college is Harvard's crown jewel, by tradition the president gives it the lion's share of his attention. He sets his agenda by garnering the support of the Corporation and the Board of Overseers, giving speeches, appointing committees, reaching out to the alumni, using the tangible powers of his office, and exploiting his unparalleled access to the press, granting interviews with favored publications and meeting with the editorial boards of newspapers and newsmagazines. The president of Harvard can make national and international headlines anytime he wants to—again, a power most effective when used judiciously. Even people with a bullhorn will eventually be ignored if they overuse it.

The success of a Harvard president depends not only on the powers he has but also his leadership style. He can try to impose his will upon the Harvard community, but if its members don't accept the validity of his mandates, or the manner in which they are applied, the university will grind to a halt, sputtering with dissatisfaction and unrest. Faculty, students, alumni, and staff all place enormous weight on leadership style. They want their president to be eloquent and erudite, poised and polished, sophisticated and witty—for, more than anyone else, he personifies Harvard and communicates the character and values of the institution to the outside world.

At the same time, they want their leader to be personable, accessible, likable, and strong in a velvet-glove sort of way, a sage father figure who is also a man of the people—or, at least, of the people who study and work at Harvard. Many universities are now so concerned with the proper administration of their financial affairs that they hire business executives with no academic background to serve as presidents. At Harvard, such a move would be inconceivable (one reason why Robert Rubin, who had never been a professor, would have been a controversial choice). Harvard presidents are supposed to be scholars first and administrators second.

Since World War II, no man has filled that multiplicity of roles more successfully than Derek Bok. As law school dean from 1968 to 1971, Bok made a reputation for himself as a conciliator with a diplomatic touch. In the spring of 1968, a group of several dozen law students staged a sit-in at the law school library. Bok responded by bringing the students coffee and donuts. Standing on a table, he addressed their concerns and took their questions. But as Bok was clambering down from his podium, blood rushed to his head and he fainted.

"When I woke up I was surrounded not by angry student radicals, but by anxious student radicals who thought they might have given me a heart attack or something," Bok remembered. "They were very solicitous—eat this, eat that. They drove me home, and for the rest of the term, I got treated pretty well. Then, after the summer, they felt free to be cranky again."

As president from 1971 to 1991, Bok maintained an image that was somehow both aristocratic and democratic. He was fit and handsome, with a rumpled, tweedy look. He drove a Volkswagen Beetle. He waited in line at the local Harvard Trust bank, listening to suggestions and complaints about Harvard from other customers even as he deposited his checks. He bought his lunch at the Au Bon Pain on Massachusetts Avenue, across Harvard Yard. With an equally attractive, accomplished wife—Swedish philosopher Sissela Bok—Bok appeared to have a charmed life. And yet he seemed such a fundamentally decent man that few could resent his good fortune.

Now seventy-five years old, Bok bears the title of president emeritus and retains an office in the Kennedy School, which he helped to create; he once dreamed of serving in the Kennedy administration and is a longtime advocate of public service who championed the cause of a school to train people for work in government. He spoke about the leadership role of the Harvard president on the condition that his remarks not be interpreted as bearing on any particular president.

"You can't get good books written and classes taught well by issuing orders," Bok explained. "Even if, theoretically, you have the power to do that. But you can influence the agenda, get people to focus on your issues. You can try to exhort, teach, persuade. It's all those gentle arts.

"There are presidents who try to lead with fear," Bok continued. "They are very tough and they push their powers to the limit. And there are presidents who try to lead in other ways, by winning the respect or even the affection of the faculty.

"A lot depends on this intangible relationship you have with the faculty. If you can't at least persuade yourself that you have some reasonable amount of respectful attention from them, the job for anybody—any satisfaction they get from the job—is seriously impaired. Of course, you're the president for all the constituencies of the university, but especially for the faculty. You're one of them. You're killing your-self to make this a better place for them. And then they turn around and say, 'You're a trivial person. I don't believe what you say. That windbag.' It just takes the guts out of you. If they don't have respect for you, if they don't trust you, that's fatal.

"It's not every bit of faculty opposition that should discourage you. If they don't like the fact that you've taken a position that makes them uncomfortable or challenges their authority in some way, it may be very important to stand your ground.

"You have to be very discriminating about when you get disheart-ened and when you don't," Bok concluded. "It can feel the same. But some of these occasions are the mark of a really distinguished presi-dency, and others are the mark of a hopeless presidency."

In September and October 2001, Larry Summers was wasting no time in showing Harvard that he had a very different agenda and style than his predecessor—than any of his predecessors, in fact. Perhaps the first public sign of this came when he addressed the incoming freshmen on September 2 and warned them not to be intimidated by their new sur-roundings. "Harry Truman said of the United States Senate that 'the first six months, I wondered why I was there. And ever after, I won-dered why all my colleagues were there.'"

Summers' remark struck an odd note, and was interpreted by some campus observers as a shot across the bow, a sign that he would not be daunted by his return to a place where continuity and tradition were venerated. Some listeners heard a hint of skepticism, if not disrespect, for the Harvard faculty in Summers' words. Possibly they were reading too much into it—but then, for scholars, this is an occupational hazard.

Just nine days later, the terrorist attacks on New York and Wash-ington occurred, and on September 21 Summers delivered a somber address in Memorial Church. Peter Gomes' church has a long-standing tradition of a brief morning service known as Morning Prayers, which is characterized by a hymn, a prayer, and a short talk by any member of the community on a matter of moral and spiritual concern. The Morning Prayers service is normally held in Appleton Chapel, a small sanctuary at the very front of the church separated from the main nave by a wooden partition. It contains merely a pulpit and about six rows of pews on each side. But in the days after September 11, people at Harvard, like people all over America, were seeking solace, and so Summers delivered his Morning Prayers talk to a church filled to overflowing.

"I expected, in the first month of the term, to visit many parts of this university," Summers began. "This pulpit was not one of them."

For Peter Gomes, who was sitting near Summers in the church that day, this seemed an odd remark. Gomes believed that, even in a secular university—perhaps *especially* in a secular university—a spiritual haven was essential. Faith, whatever form it took, infused the work of Harvard with morality and conscience. Not to mention humility. Having a church in the middle of Harvard Yard reminded Harvardians not to get too cocky. So at a time when thousands of community members were seeking the solace of Memorial Church, Summers' remark struck Gomes as gratuitous.

Summers spoke then of the difficulty of grieving and the importance of moving on. He reminded his audience that "the time we spend with our loved ones is most precious," and he emphasized that Harvard had its own distinctive role to play in the fight against terrorism. "With what's going on in the world, does it matter if I do my calculus homework or go to field hockey practice? With all that is going on in the world, is it right to carry on with my work of managing accounts or teaching my small class?"

His answer was, it mattered more than ever. In a time of war, the work of a university—the daily rituals of teaching and learning—might seem less urgent. But over the long run it constituted the road to peace. "We will not succumb to the temptation of nihilism," Summers said. "We will carry on our work." From his own experience with cancer, Summers knew how immersing oneself in work helped one carry on even when staring death in the face.

Summers' official inauguration was held three weeks later. The timing was slightly awkward, and not just because of the heightened security that the terrorist attacks had prompted. On October 7 and 8, two long articles on grade inflation at Harvard appeared in the *Boston Globe*. Reporter Patrick Healy found that an astonishing 91 percent of Harvard students graduated with honors. At Yale, by comparison, the number was about 51 percent; at Princeton, 44 percent. Healy wrote that the easing of the standards required to earn an A was Harvard's "dirty little secret," and it was corroding the value of a Harvard diploma.

The *Globe* articles caused consternation on campus. Many professors thought that the origins of grade inflation could be traced to Vietnam, when professors were reluctant to grade harshly because of the
risk that failing students would become eligible for the draft. Others,
such as Shakespeare scholar Stephen Greenblatt, argued that because
Harvard students were outstanding, one would expect them to get
good grades. (Not surprisingly, this belief was widely shared by students.) Another possibility was that grade inflation stemmed from the
fact that most grading at Harvard was done by graduate student teaching fellows, who might have had a different idea than professors did of
what constituted honors-level work.

The most controversial explanation was advocated by government
professor Harvey C. Mansfield. Mansfield was old school—literally.
He'd been at Harvard since 1949, earning his bachelor's degree and
then, in 1961, his Ph.D. A scholar of Machiavelli, he'd joined the faculty in 1962 and earned a reputation as a proud conservative. One of
Mansfield's longtime frustrations was grade inflation. He'd been talking about it for so long that students started calling him "Harvey
C-minus Mansfield." Mansfield joked that the C stood for compassion,
explaining that "that's what I lack when it comes to grading."

For Mansfield, grade inflation was directly attributable to the influx
of black students at Harvard that occurred in the late 1960s and 1970s.
These students weren't prepared for Harvard's rigor, Mansfield argued,
and liberal professors didn't want to stigmatize them with bad grades.
"White professors, imbibing the spirit of affirmative action, stopped giving low or average grades to black students and, to justify or conceal it,
stopped giving those grades to white students as well," Mansfield said.

Mansfield's explanation disturbed many on the faculty, and one
man in particular strove to rebut it: Harry Lewis, the dean of Harvard
College. Though Lewis oversaw the non-academic side of college life,
he felt strongly enough about the issue to speak against Mansfield. He
too was a Harvard man through and through, a computer scientist
who'd earned his Harvard B.A. in 1968 and his doctorate in 1974.

The numbers didn't support Mansfield, Lewis argued. Data Lewis
had compiled showed that grades had been rising at Harvard since the
1920s; in fact, the only fifteen-year period during which grades did *not*
go up was from 1970 to 1985. The idea that grade inflation had stemmed

from the lenient grading of black students was the result of gossip, Lewis said, and "gossip is a dangerous basis for a social theory."

Nonetheless, the statistics in the *Globe* articles resonated. Ninety-one percent! Regardless of the nuances of the situation, the perception that Harvard had become far less academically rigorous than its competitors was devastating. An incoming president would be compelled to address the issue.

On the afternoon of October 11, after the pomp and circumstance was done—the transfer of the symbolic keys, the display of the 1650 charter—Summers stood on the stage in Tercentenary Theatre and talked about Harvard's importance to the world. Universities are sometimes "derided as remote or not relevant," Summers admitted. But that was wrong. Universities, and Harvard in particular, internalize creative tensions that promote their vitality and relevance.

"The university is open to all ideas, but it is committed to the skepticism that is the hallmark of education," Summers said. "All ideas are worthy of consideration here—but not all perspectives are equally valid." Though universities ought to be places of passionate moral commitment, they were also places devoted to seeking knowledge regardless of its moral implications. Above all else, "We carry ancient traditions, but what is new is most important for us." Every year a new crop of students brought new energy and ideas to the institution. Now, Summers implied, he was going to do the same—and in the rest of his speech, he talked about what that meant: A renewed emphasis on undergraduate education. A revamped curriculum. A new campus across the river in Allston. Greater emphasis upon the sciences at Harvard. Globalizing the university.

The new president's language was lofty and rhetorical, but the implications of his words were clear. Summers was proposing changes that would shape Harvard for decades to come—for the next century, really. If he could effect his agenda, Summers would go down in history as one of Harvard's greatest presidents.

Which meant that things really were going to change at Harvard. The old traditions didn't matter to Larry Summers. Why, when he'd been handed the symbols of Harvard's tradition—the keys, the charter—he'd held them up to the crowd with an expression that was half smile, half grimace.

Summers would run things his way. And those in the audience—
the faculty, administrators, and students who stayed after the parents
and friends had left—could either get onboard or get out of the way.
Starting now.

Larry Summers and Cornel West met at 3:15 P.M. on October 24 in the
president's office in Massachusetts Hall.

Mass Hall is a deceptive building. Just inside Johnston Gate, the
main entrance to the Yard, it's a four-story brick structure in the Early
Georgian style, about one hundred feet long and forty feet wide. Dating to 1721, Mass Hall is the oldest extant building at Harvard, and
was used to house soldiers of the Continental Army during the Revo-
lutionary War. The first two floors consist of administrative offices,
meeting rooms, and the president's office. The third and fourth floors
house freshmen said to be randomly chosen for these prime living
quarters, although precisely no one on campus believes this. (Mass
Hall freshmen have a reputation for being unusually studious and
equally quiet.) The students enter by a dedicated side entrance; everyone else comes in through an unadorned green door in front. The president's corner office is at the end of a long, blue-carpeted corridor on
the left-hand side.

Mass Hall gives the appearance of democratic access while in fact
making the president's office considerably more isolated than those of
his counterparts at other universities. That the entrance has only one
purpose discourages the curious from peering in; you wouldn't simply
wander into Mass Hall. Inside the front door is another, alarmed door
that appears to be made of shatterproof glass. Next to the door is an
electronic keypad and an intercom. An eye-level sign instructs, PLEASE
ANNOUNCE YOURSELF TO THE SECRETARY. Below it a smaller, more discreet sign warns against trespassing.

Though the president's office is located on the ground floor, white
interior shutters seal off the bottom half of every window. Members of
the Harvard men's basketball team might be able to peer over them,
but for passersby of conventional height, the office of the Harvard
president is, like Poe's purloined letter, invisible in plain sight.

Behind the shutters, Larry Summers' office is perhaps thirty-five
feet long by fifteen feet wide, with a fireplace in the middle of the interior long wall. It is tastefully decorated, with a crimson-colored carpet,

half-moon wall lights, and a grandfather clock. A seating area in the rear half includes a lowback couch, three brown-leather chairs, and a coffee table. Summers' desk and computer nook are in the front. Opposite them is a bureau containing some of the numerous framed photographs that decorate the office: a portrait of Summers' three children, a picture of him with Bill Clinton and Al Gore, a framed dollar bill bearing his signature from his time as treasury secretary. There are two doorways, one near Summers' desk and one in the far corner of the office, so that visitors can be whisked out the back even as others are ushered in the front.

On that October day, Cornel West and Larry Summers sat facing each other in two of the leather chairs. It was just the two of them, which was a little unusual. Numerous people who'd already met with Summers had been struck by the fact that he seemed to do nothing without an aide present, meticulously taking notes in the background.

After a few moments of small talk, Summers got down to business. "I want you to help me fuck Harvey Mansfield," he said.

West was shocked. He knew right away that Summers was playing a head game, trying to enlist him in the fight against grade inflation by presenting the matter as a way of undercutting the man who blamed the problem on affirmative action. Summers apparently didn't know that Mansfield and West were friends.

You don't know me from Adam, West thought. There's no need to swear. Don't assume that because I'm a black brother with an Afro that that's going to make me more comfortable.

"I don't need that kind of talk about a colleague," West said.

Well, Summers replied, I am a little upset that the grades you're giving out might be contributing to the problem of grade inflation. But I'll get back to that.

I'll get back to that? West was already feeling blindsided. There was more?

Summers then moved to the subject of West's alleged absences from campus, accusing him of missing three weeks of classes while campaigning for Bill Bradley in the 2000 primary. "I'll have none of that," he said.

West adamantly denied the charge. "Man, you must be kidding," he said. "My calling as a teacher is primary and paramount. I haven't missed two classes for over twenty-seven years. Bill Bradley is my dear brother, I would do anything for him—other than that. I wouldn't do that for anybody."

West wanted to know who had told Summers that he skipped classes. Summers said he had three reliable sources, but declined to name them. Anyway, Summers said, now you're supporting a candidate whom nobody respects.

He didn't name names, but West took that as a reference to Al Sharpton, and argued that he had the right to support whatever political candidate he wanted to.

I'm concerned about you being a "good citizen" of the university, Summers continued—a phrase West would later jot down in his journal—because of your travels away from campus giving lectures or campaigning.

West pointed out that over the past year he'd given more than thirty talks to campus student groups. Could Summers name another professor who'd given so much of his time?

The two men were flat-out arguing now, their voices raised. Instead of backing off, Summers was actually growing more animated. More intense. Rocking back and forth, but never looking West in the eye. West had never seen anything like it. Larry Summers seemed to be energized by this. *Enjoying* it.

Summers abruptly switched subjects. He said that he was concerned about the level of West's scholarship. It was too popular and insufficiently serious. He wanted West to write books that would be reviewed in scholarly journals, not the *New York Times* and the *New York Review of Books*.

In fact, only a few of West's books had been reviewed by those organs. Frankly, West said, he wouldn't mind it if the *Times* reviewed more of his work.

No, Summers reiterated, he was very concerned about this issue. As a University Professor, West had an obligation to set an example of high scholarship. If he wasn't setting that example, he shouldn't spend his time messing around with politics and social activism. Summers wanted West's work to be "purely scholarly"—another phrase that West wrote in his journal.

His concern, Summers added, was really a compliment. Just look at economist Robert Reich, Summers' former Dukakis campaign colleague and Bill Clinton's secretary of labor, now a professor at Brandeis

University who had unsuccessfully run for Massachusetts governor in 2000. Reich, Summers said, wasn't even capable of the level of work Summers wanted West to perform. Reich was just a popularizer. West wanted to be more than that, didn't he?

West didn't see why you couldn't be both a scholar and a popularizer.

But that rap CD that you recorded, Summers said—it's an embarrassment and it has nothing to do with the Harvard tradition.

"I am as much a part of the Harvard tradition as you are," West shot back, "and we all have our distinctive interpretations of it." After all, both of them carried Harvard degrees.

Summers wouldn't let it go. He told West that he wanted him to write an academic text that wrestled with and interpreted a particular philosophic tradition.

West couldn't believe it. What right did Summers have to tell him what he should write about? Summers was an economist. To suggest that he knew enough about another field to tell a Harvard professor what to work on—that was just hubris. If West had told Summers what to research, Summers would have laughed in his face, and appropriately so.

Summers said that he wanted West to do two things in their subsequent meetings.

Subsequent meetings? West thought. "What's that?" he asked.

Summers wanted West to bring him every grade that he'd ever given in Af-Am 10.

"You can get that yourself," West said. "Just ask the registrar."

No, Summers said, I want you to get every grade you've given and bring them to me.

West was reeling. He couldn't think of any reason Summers would make such a request—other than to humiliate him.

And, Summers said, he wanted to see West again in two to three months, to see how he was progressing on that book. His assistant would set it up.

At 4:05, fifty minutes after the meeting had begun, Cornel West walked out of Larry Summers' office and past his secretary. He didn't bother to make a return appointment.

In time, Larry Summers' meeting with Cornel West would receive a massive amount of press attention, most of which focused on the disparate personalities of the two men and the possibility that the tension between them was racially based. On campus, however, professors and students debated another issue, one that was hard to understand for people unfamiliar with the culture of a research university: the nature of academic freedom.

Perhaps no one at Harvard knows more about the subject than former FAS dean Henry Rosovsky. Rosovsky is in his late seventies now, with a quiet, serene demeanor that belies a sharp and inquisitive mind. Though he was once a professor, a dean, and a member of the Harvard Corporation, he now has no official role at the university. But such is the respect in which Rosovsky is held that he retains an office on the second floor of Loeb House, where the Corporation holds its monthly meetings. The Moshe Safdie–designed headquarters of Harvard Hillel, built in 1992, is named Rosovsky Hall.

Rosovsky is a modest, self-deprecatory man, proud of his accomplishments but uncomfortable talking about them. He does, however, care deeply about universities—their operation, their excellence, the strength of the social contract between them and the American public whose tax dollars support them. So, in 1990, he wrote a book on the subject called *The University—An Owner's Manual*. He meant the term "owner" to refer to anyone who feels some stake in the university: students, professors, parents, alumni, staff. Or just Americans who believe that the American system of higher education is one of the things that makes the United States a unique and special place.

In the book, Rosovsky explains how Harvard's tenure system works and how it protects academic freedom at Harvard. When a tenured position comes open, the members of the relevant department are charged with finding the best person "in the world" for the job. The senior faculty in the department—that is to say, tenured professors—spend months searching for a candidate. After a leading candidate emerges, the department chair sends out a letter to scholars at other universities asking for their evaluations. The letter includes the names of the person being considered and of other scholars tossed in as camouflage. (It's generally believed that this cloaking device fools no one; everybody knows who the real candidate is.) If the responses to this letter are encouraging, the department nomination goes to the FAS dean.

If the dean approves, he then sends the nomination to something called an ad hoc committee, a group made up of the president, the dean, three scholars in the field from other universities, and two Harvard professors *not* in the relevant department. Ad hoc committees meet to weigh the merits of every person nominated for tenure at Harvard College. These can be tense gatherings. "I have seen distinguished older scholars treating one another with icy courtesy only barely masking contempt," Rosovsky writes.

The Harvard president must approve or reject every tenure recommendation for the Faculty of Arts and Sciences. That enormous power gives the president the tangible authority to shape the intellectual composition of his university—and to slap down department heads making choices of which he disapproves. (Imagine if, say, Congress nominated Supreme Court justices, and the president had the power to veto them.)

Deciding upon tenure nominations is also an enormous burden. Every year, there are about twenty ad hoc meetings at Harvard College, each requiring hours of preparation on the part of the president, who must intimately familiarize himself with the candidate's work. The meetings themselves last about four hours. The president must weigh a decision which has required months of work by members of his faculty—or, in the case of the candidate, a life's work. Rejection is devastating. "From that point on, the scholar is marked with a scarlet letter, always having to explain the basis of a presumably mistaken negative judgment," Rosovsky writes. "In every case with which I am familiar, the result is a scar that may not even be wiped out by the award of the highest professional honors."

But the end result of this arduous gauntlet, Rosovsky argues, is that Harvard accumulates a remarkable group of scholars who have survived the most rigorous weeding-out process the university can devise.

And then, once someone is granted tenure, they are left alone to write and research as they see fit. This is the very point of tenure—to guarantee academic freedom; to protect professors from the Joe McCarthys of the world, whether inside or outside the university. True, once in a while, you get a dud. Maybe 3 percent of the people chosen turn out to disappoint, to be unproductive, never to write another book. But Harvard can live with 3 percent. The benefits of tenure more than justify a minuscule failure rate.

Besides, "failure" is hard to define. Scholars are human beings—sometimes quirky, often high-maintenance—who work on their own schedules. Rosovsky remembered one professor who didn't publish a thing for years and years. His colleagues began to whisper: What was with this guy? Yet Rosovsky never pressured the man, giving him his customary annual raise without question. In 1971, after almost two decades of virtually nothing, the professor, whose name was John Rawls, published a book. It was called *A Theory of Justice*, and it would be considered perhaps the most important work of political philosophy published in the last half-century. When Rawls died in 2002, he was remembered as one of Harvard's greatest professors. The fact that he'd gone some twenty years without publishing any major work was largely forgotten.

Tenure isn't just about giving people the freedom to publish what and when they want; it creates a secure environment in which professors can freely speak their minds, on any subject, so that they can push the envelope of thought without fear of penalty. Such freedom is the very heart of the university, and Harvard has a long tradition of defending it. "There is no middle ground," Abbott Lawrence Lowell, who was president from 1909 to 1933, once said. "Either the university assumes full responsibility for permitting its professors to express certain opinions in public, or it assumes no responsibility whatever, and leaves them to be dealt with like other citizens by the public authorities according to the laws of the land."

Derek Bok also wrote eloquently on the subject. "Brilliant and creative people are sometimes eccentric or even irresponsible . . ." he argued when he was president. "As a result, in institutions whose overriding purpose is to discover and transmit knowledge, it has often seemed best to tolerate unpopular opinions and questionable behavior for the sake of giving the most talented individuals the opportunity to publish and teach."

In an interview with *Newsweek* about seven months before his meeting with West, Larry Summers himself endorsed the notion that professors' politics were their own business. Asked whether it was appropriate for a university president to take political stands, Summers responded, "Universities—*as distinct from the scholars who work in them*—have to be very careful about political involvement" (emphasis added).

Of course, the Harvard president has the authority to meet with University Professors. James Bryant Conant, who created the position, wanted University Professors to be answerable *only* to the president, as opposed to the FAS dean. That chain of command was not the issue in the case of Cornel West. The problem was that the concerns Summers raised with West seemed to undermine long-established ideas about the nature of tenure at Harvard. Criticizing a professor over the pace of his scholarship? His political opinions? It just wasn't done. For one thing, if you chastised every professor who went a few years without publishing a major book—or a minor one, for that matter—you'd run out of voice long before you ran out of professors.

And there was another problem. On the facts in question, Summers was simply wrong—and he had been warned that he was wrong. In the days before West's meeting, Skip Gates had written Summers a long memo in which he rebutted the allegations Summers had mentioned. West missed classes? Not true, Gates wrote. If Cornel West had missed three weeks of classes, you'd have read about that on page one of the *Harvard Crimson*. Grade inflation? That wasn't true either, and outside sources agreed. "Cornel was not the biggest offender," one high-ranking Harvard administrator said. "If you went down the list of who was giving all As, Cornel would not be high on the list, and certainly no worse than a lot of people." Even if the charge were accurate, grade inflation was clearly a systemic problem; you didn't address it by attacking one professor.

What, then, explained Summers' decision to lambaste one of Harvard's most esteemed professors?

After Cornel West left Mass Hall that afternoon, he called Skip Gates to tell him what had transpired. Gates couldn't believe it. "That man is going out of his way to demean you," Gates said. Then West called his old friend, the writer Toni Morrison, who teaches creative writing at Princeton. "Summers has lost his mind," Morrison said.

For the next two months, West would ponder his meeting with Summers, discussing it with only a few close friends. He couldn't make sense of it. Why would a new president make calling West on the carpet one of his first official acts? Why would he attack an African American professor to whom his predecessor awarded Harvard's highest honor, the title of University Professor, and a member of the department that Neil Rudenstine considered his most important legacy? Why would he embarrass West with allegations he had good reason to believe were untrue? And why would he instruct West to appear for mandatory intellectual check-ups when he must have known that no Harvard professor would accept such babysitting?

The more he thought about it, the harder it was for West to avoid the conclusion that Larry Summers wanted him gone. West had tenure; it was virtually impossible for Summers to fire him. But he could make Cornel West's life at Harvard so miserable that West would leave of his own volition.

Over the next days and weeks, rumors began to fly, first within the Af-Am department and then beyond. West's colleagues knew that something bad had happened between the professor and the president, but they didn't know exactly what—except that whatever had gone on, it was upsetting enough that West was thinking of quitting. Soon a reporter from the *Boston Globe* showed up outside West's office door. West wouldn't talk to him. The rumors were also circulating down south, at Princeton. And when Princeton provost Amy Gutmann— whose name had been leaked as a candidate for the Harvard presidency to make it seem that the Corporation was seriously considering a woman—called West to see if he would consider returning, West took that call.

There are academic departments at Harvard whose members are competitive with one another, don't like one another, and don't trust one another. In recent times, for example, the Department of History has been so bitterly divided that it couldn't agree on tenure candidates, and the senior professors grew older and older until the department fell into decline. The Departments of Government and Economics, two of the more powerful groupings of faculty, are also known for their internecine tensions.

But Afro American Studies is a small department whose members care about one another, take an interest in one another's work, and socialize with one another outside of their official duties. "I have been in lots of departments" at other schools, said Evelyn Brooks Higginbotham. "I have been in history departments, I have been in other African American departments. I have never been in a department where people like each other so much. It is truly a community."

For months, this community tried to persuade Cornel West that he should not head to Princeton. What had happened with Summers could be patched up, Gates and others insisted. And if it couldn't,

West should stay to act as a thorn in Summers' side. "Don't break up the team," Gates urged West.

But West was pessimistic. Not once after their meeting had he heard from Summers. The president must have known that West hadn't scheduled another appointment, but he didn't seem to care—which only reinforced West's conviction that Summers wanted him out.

West was also distracted by tensions in his personal life. Recently diagnosed with prostate cancer, he would soon undergo an operation to remove the tumor. He was also going through a difficult divorce. As his marriage had begun to fall apart, he'd become romantically involved with a thirty-eight-year-old woman who was studying at the Kennedy School on a journalism fellowship. The woman had become pregnant and would decide to keep the baby. Although she and West would not stay together, West was determined to be a good father to his new daughter. Still, it was a messy, painful situation, and the tongues of campus gossips were wagging. "There was a rumor that the mother of my precious daughter was a twenty-one-year-old junior," West said. "I heard it from friends—even Skip and others were saying, 'Corn, I don't know what the heck is going on, but there's this thing . . .' I said, wait a minute, I haven't touched an undergraduate in twenty-seven years of teaching."

On December 22, a *Boston Globe* reporter named David Abel—the one who'd shown up at West's office—broke the story: Skip Gates' Dream Team was in turmoil because of tensions with new president Larry Summers. West was thinking of heading to Princeton. So was Anthony Appiah, whose significant other lived in New York City. If West and Appiah left, could Gates be far behind? Charles Ogletree spoke on West's behalf, saying that it would be "a miscarriage of justice if for any reason Cornel were no longer at Harvard." Summers, meanwhile, explained that he had not meant to offend West. "It's a very unfortunate misunderstanding," he said. Just to reaffirm the point, an anonymous Harvard official called the situation "a huge misunderstanding." Summers and his aides would use that term again and again over the next weeks, months, and years. West thought that was kind of funny. There was no misunderstanding; Summers had made himself perfectly clear.

One week later, the story of the president and the professor appeared on the front page of the *New York Times*, and after that in newspapers across the country and the world. The *Times* account enlarged the issues at stake. West and Gates, wrote reporter Jacques Steinberg, were considering leaving because "Mr. Summers . . . has yet to speak out forcefully enough in favor of affirmative action and diversity."

That wasn't quite true. Summers' disastrous meeting with West was by far the most pressing issue at hand, and people on both sides of the matter suspected that Charles Ogletree had just piggybacked on the West controversy to pressure Summers on affirmative action. If that was his intention, it worked. On January 1, Jesse Jackson arrived in Cambridge to proclaim that "Harvard must be a beacon of light for the nation, not a shadow of doubt." Al Sharpton announced that he, too, would be paying a visit.

This was not the kind of attention that the Harvard Corporation hoped for when it hired Summers. Though Bob Rubin had assured them that Summers was a changed man, this was just the kind of ugly episode others had warned of. And so Corporation member Conrad Harper, the only black on the Corporation, called Summers and strongly urged him to defuse the crisis.

On January 2, Larry Summers released a public statement reaffirming his commitment to a diverse campus. "I take pride in Harvard's long-standing commitment to diversity," his statement said. "I believe it essential for us to maintain that commitment . . ." But privately, Summers was furious. He had never expressed doubts about the value of diversity; he'd only questioned the merits of affirmative action as a means to that end. Summers had never anticipated that chastising West could lead to such an uproar and leave him exposed to charges of racism.

On January 3, Summers and West finally met again in Mass Hall, this time an evening meeting, at Summers' request. At first they spoke of personal matters; Summers asked about West's illness, and shared his own experience with cancer. West appreciated the concern, and he was impressed with the strength that Summers had shown during his treatment. Summers then thanked West for not having made their disagreement a racial issue, which startled West a little, because he believed that, at least in part, it *was* a racial issue.

Over the course of the meeting, Summers repeatedly apologized to West. He cited Richard Posner's recent book, *Public Intellectuals: A Study of Decline*, which called West one of the most often-cited scholars in the country. As the rest of Harvard would learn soon enough, with Summers, it was all about the data. Arguments from the heart didn't move him; he wanted to see numbers. And he hadn't seen these numbers before his and West's first conversation. He confessed that he wished that he had; he would have reconsidered some of his earlier remarks.

Neither of them may have realized it, but the two men were similar in ways besides their experiences with cancer. Each was a charismatic figure who had attracted numerous admirers and a subset of equally fervent critics. Each was living through the pain of a failed marriage. And both were academics who may have compromised their intellectual potential for a career in the public eye. For all his gifts, Cornel West had never had "a single compelling idea of his own," author Sam Tanenhaus would later write in *Vanity Fair*—the exact same criticism that many economists applied to Summers.

West was heartened by Summers' outreach for all of about twelve hours. The next morning, he picked up the *New York Times* and read an account of their meeting—an account that had not come from him. "Summers resolved the last issue with the Afro-American Studies department when he met with Dr. West and cleared the air, though he made no explicit apology," the article said. *No explicit apology?* West couldn't believe it. He called Summers and demanded an explanation; Summers said that the *Times* must have misquoted him. West didn't buy it. He decided that Summers had lied to the *Times* and was now lying to him.

"That's when I decided to leave," West said. "I can't deal with a place where people stab me in the back." That apology had mattered to West. Everyone in the world, it seemed, knew what Summers had accused him of. It was only fair that they read that it wasn't true.

Three weeks later, on January 25, philosopher Anthony Appiah announced that he was leaving Harvard to teach at Princeton. The decision was made for personal reasons, he said—he wanted to be closer to his partner. But the West affair surely contributed to his decision. "I don't think Anthony would have left if all this hadn't happened," said Evelyn Brooks Higginbotham. Appiah didn't want to break up the dream team, but "this opened a door that Anthony could go through." Meanwhile, Ogletree announced that he was weighing a possible offer to be dean of the law school at Washington's Howard

University. And one newspaper article after another suggested that Skip Gates had one foot out the door as well.

In some venues, though, Summers was winning the PR war. "In all politics, one needs an enemy, and preferably an incompetent, misguided, or socially adverse one," Harvard economist John Kenneth Galbraith once wrote. Summers had chosen an enemy who could be easily caricatured. With his afro and black suits and street slang—indeed, by the very color of his skin—West hardly looked or sounded like the stereotype of a Harvard professor. Quoted out of context, his writings were easily lampooned. And then there was that "rap" CD.

And so cultural conservatives—both white and black—cheered Larry Summers. He wished only to restore "excellence," they said, and Cornel West was, well, less than excellent. To them, West epitomized the kind of tenured radical who had torn apart universities in 1960s protests, then found sinecures drinking cappuccino and preaching revolution from within the security of ivy walls. The *Wall Street Journal*, the *National Review*, and the *New Republic* all praised Summers for calling West on the carpet. (As a general rule, the fewer the number of black staffers at a news organization, the greater was its hostility to West.) *Forbes* magazine suggested that if West left Harvard, he could be replaced by the rapper Eminem. In the *New York Times*, black academic John McWhorter criticized Harvard's Af-Am scholars for "shooting a gun at Larry Summers' feet and making him do the 'I'm not a racist' dance." Another black conservative, Shelby Steele, wrote in the *Wall Street Journal* that Summers' "rebuke [of West] for failing to deliver excellence was an act of social responsibility." Since none of these critics appeared to know what had actually transpired between the two men, their conclusions seemed drawn from their own politics rather than from any fact-based interpretation of the situation.

On campus, students were dismayed and the professoriat divided. In early April, 1,200 students petitioned West not to leave. But few professors outside of Af-Am spoke on his behalf. Some agreed with Summers that West deserved to be criticized; others simply did not want to get involved. They didn't know exactly what had happened, and saw no gain in picking a fight with the new president. Every tub was indeed on its own bottom.

Meanwhile, Harvard alums—particularly those who had graduated before, say, the mid-1960s—rallied round their school's new president.

"There's an enormous reservoir of goodwill out there" for any Harvard president, explained Derek Bok. "You can feel it when the alumni come back for reunions or when you go speak in different cities. These people want him to succeed, and they want to love and respect the institution, and to respect the president, simply because they assume that if he was chosen, he's the guy."

When many Harvard alumni looked at the situation, they saw a white man who was the former secretary of the treasury, a man of Nobel-level intelligence—after all, Harvard had told them that—taking on a black professor who supported Al Sharpton and recorded rap CDs. Letters to the university ran three-to-one in Summers' favor. Still, staffers who worked in alumni affairs weren't entirely happy about the mail they were getting. A number of the letters—a substantial enough number that the staffers were genuinely disturbed—could only be described as racist.

West could not imagine a scenario in which he could remain at Harvard without seeming to endorse Summers' aspersions. And he didn't want to stay just to make things difficult for Summers. Life was too short for that. West wanted to be somewhere that wanted him.

On April 12, Skip Gates sent around a short e-mail to his colleagues in Af-Am and elsewhere. Cornel West would be joining Anthony Appiah at Princeton in the fall of 2002. If you had happened to walk into several departments around Harvard that day—Af-Am, history and literature, English—you would have seen people crying after they'd read that e-mail.

And that wasn't even the end of the matter. With West leaving, would Gates be next? If Skip Gates left, the whole thing—the department that Neil Rudenstine had cherished and built up for a decade—would implode. No one would stick around in a department that had lost Anthony Appiah, Cornel West, and Skip Gates. That'd be like buying a ticket for the Titanic *after* it hit the iceberg.

In the months and years following Cornel West's departure, Larry Summers would largely avoid the subject, refusing to get into the specifics of what had happened. When asked about it by the *Crimson* in October 2002, he said, "I have not talked about the content of that meeting and certainly do not intend to start now."

But that wasn't quite true. At an off-the-record meeting with the editorial board of the *New York Times* that same fall, one *Times* editor asked Summers what had *really* happened with Cornel West. According to several people familiar with the exchange, Summers coolly replied, "What would you do if you had a professor with a sexual harassment problem?"

The remark, apparently an inaccurate reference to West's relationship with the visiting journalist, made its way back to several professors who were friendly with West. They did not mention it to him, and indeed, West did not learn about the comment until asked about it for this book. Those who heard of the accusation were stunned. It was one thing to confront a scholar face-to-face, but this rumor felt deliberately planted in the press, meant to be spread behind the scenes, without accountability. The new president was obviously versed in the ways of Washington. What did that bode for Harvard?

5

Washington on the Charles

According to several people professionally close to him, Larry Summers little regretted the departure of Cornel West. True, the way that the drama played out wasn't entirely to his liking. The controversy had been embarrassingly public, and on campus, most student opinion ran against Summers. The president knew that he had overplayed his hand, and now he had to worry about the possible departure of Skip Gates, a man harder to caricature than West and impossible to replace.

On the whole, though, Summers considered West's exit a victory. The high-profile professor was gone, and that was good. Plus, much of the media coverage surrounding the fracas had lauded the new president. In general, the press had portrayed Summers as a take-charge, reform-minded newcomer who wasn't afraid to break a few eggs to make an omelet, and Summers knew that many Americans had a deep, almost primal affinity for such men of action—particularly when juxtaposed against hand-wringing, nervous-nellie egghead academics. "[Summers' critics] kept calling him 'a bull in a china shop,'" James Traub, a *New York Times* reporter who wrote about Summers, said in a 2003 lecture to the Harvard Club of Westchester County, New York. "But who wants to work in a china shop?" Traub did not appear to realize that the Harvard faculty was not the origin of that simile; it was a Treasury Department aide who had first described Summers thusly, and the Treasury Department is not usually thought of as a haven for gentle souls.

No matter. Many outsiders and some campus conservatives saw West and his allies as defenders of the status quo, digging in their heels to fight a new president's desire to raise standards and impose account-ability. Summers had immediately framed the debate in a way that put *them* on the defensive. Like the soundbite slogans of a political cam-paign: Change versus more of the same! Excellence versus mediocrity! Mainstream values versus tenured radicals! Such reductive dichotomies were standard operating procedure in Washington, and Summers knew how to exploit them far better than did the residents of Harvard.

Many members of the Harvard community—on both sides of the schism—were left wondering why Summers had picked such a risky fight so early in his tenure. The idea of singling out a popular black professor for criticism seemed so fraught with hazard, they found it hard to believe that Summers' stated reasons were his only motive—especially those who believed that the criticisms were of dubious merit. Instead, most people believed there was some other, deeper factor at work in Summers. An impulse to define himself in opposition to Neil Rudenstine? The alleged ear-whispering of Martin Peretz, Leon Wieseltier, and FAS dean Jeremy Knowles? Ethnic retribution for West's support of Al Sharpton?

Such theories are perhaps best left for psychiatrists to ponder—and Harvard's did—but there was one interpretation for which tangible proof did exist. Rebuking Cornel West was really only a microcosm of Summers' larger purpose: to prepare Harvard for an expansive future by eradicating what Summers perceived as the noxious remnants of an unhealthy past—the tumultuous, divisive, corrosive 1960s. Only by moving beyond the legacy of that decade, Summers felt, could the uni-versity embrace the magnificent future he envisioned for it.

Larry Summers may have left the Treasury Department, but he had no intention of disappearing from the circles of the world's power elite. He no longer had hundreds of billions of dollars at his disposal to pro-mote American influence and his own power, but Harvard had its own distinctive assets. Summers was presiding over probably the greatest collection of brainpower anywhere, backed by one of the world's most powerful brands. Like a corporation with foreign subsidiaries, the uni-versity had outposts all over the globe—offices and partnerships with other universities in Asia, Europe, South America, and the Middle East. Summers knew that by further extending Harvard's influence around the world—and by shaping the content of that influence—he could extend his status as one of the globe's most influential citizens.

He would never say so explicitly. Unlike Neil Rudenstine, Summers would not talk about Harvard's destiny as an empire of the mind. But that was partly because the two men approached public speaking very differently. Rudenstine slaved over his writings and struggled to make each new speech clear and meaningful. "Neil doesn't delegate," said one man who knew him well. "If Neil was giving a speech to his three nieces, he'd stay up the night before to write it." Rudenstine thought that serious, painstaking writing was part of the job of university president. He believed in leaving a paper trail.

Plus, Rudenstine could get away with calling Harvard an empire. He was so mild-mannered, so self-effacing, no one would suspect him of grand personal ambitions. Summers did not have that luxury. He'd already been accused of exactly that. Nor could Summers forget "The Memo" from his days at the World Bank. To him, leaving a written record of his actions and ideas, whether they dealt with toxic waste or anything else, entailed more risk than benefit. As a result, the speeches that he did give were circumspect, containing rhetorically powerful lines but a notable lack of specifics—more the speeches of a cabinet secretary than a university president. It was no coincidence that Summers enlisted David Gergen, a Kennedy School professor who had served both political parties as a communications adviser in four White Houses, to help write them.

But in more intimate settings—in question-and-answer sessions, dinner parties, meetings with alumni, and talks with colleagues and aides—Summers made clear that a Harvard stretching out across the globe was exactly his intention. He did not want to rule the world, of course. But he did want to guide it, to shape it, to influence its development, just as he had during the 1990s. Harvard would be his power base, a knowledge factory exporting hundreds of soon-to-be leaders every year. And he would run the factory.

"You know," he said in more than one speech, "I was overwhelmed during the time that I was at the treasury by the fact that I would travel all over the world and I would meet the deputy finance minister of this country or the foreign minister of that country, and half the time his reaction would be, 'Well, it's nice you're here from the U.S. Treasury Department, Mr. Summers, but you were a professor at Harvard, weren't you?' And I'd say, 'Yes, I was.' And then the person would say, 'In 1977 I spent a year as a fellow at Harvard University and it was the most important year of my life, because of what I learned, the connections I made, the experience that I had.'

". . . The network of people who have been through our campus and have become leaders around the world is something that I could not have conceived of when I was a professor here, and would not have believed if I had not met these people through my travels.

"What will shape this world is the people who come forth to lead it," Summers said on another occasion. "And the group of 1,650 people [in every freshman class] from every state, from dozens of countries, from every possible background . . . is every year the most remarkably talented group of young people that has ever been assembled in the history of the world.

"The years in which students are here at Harvard College are the years of tremendous malleability in their lives," he said. "We have such a wonderful opportunity to shape and prepare what these students do."

Again and again Summers returned to the idea that, more than any other place, Harvard created the earth's leadership class "The world is really shaped by what its leaders think," he said on another occasion. "What they think . . . depends on what happens in the years in which they are being formed. Harvard College will do its part."

And Summers explicitly linked the future of the United States in its fight against terrorism with the success of Harvard. As he said to students at a Florida high school, "There is . . . nothing that would give greater support in the long run to countries that are adversaries of the United States, than for us to have the situation where members of every group don't feel like they have a chance to be at places like Harvard."

Of course, all teachers hope that they will have a lasting influence on their students; on a much larger scale, the same was true for Summers. During his time in Washington, he had become convinced that the single most important factor in how politicians made decisions was their education. Now Summers ran an institution containing the world's best and brightest students, and he was determined to teach them how to lead. "Harvard exists for only one reason—the future of the world depends more than anything else on what young people learn and go forth and do," he said.

For someone who had thought as long and hard about globalization as Summers had, the opportunity was inescapable and inevitable—not just for Harvard, but for himself. Once he had been able to prod, cajole, and sometimes even bully world leaders using billions of dollars in IMF loans and "conditionality," the implementation of specific, pro-American policies attached to all those loans. Now he could shape the world in a different way—by training its elite. Through his paradigmatic textbook, Paul Samuelson had influenced generations of economists; Larry Summers wanted to influence generations, period. He had called the students of Harvard "the most remarkably talented group of young people in the history of the world." *In the history of the world.* And every year another group, equally or more impressive. And he was now the president of this, the elite of all elites.

First, though, he had to wipe the slate clean. To purge Harvard of the bonds that kept it from realizing its enormous potential and seeing itself in a new way—*his* new way. And that meant eradicating the influence of the 1960s.

What was that influence? Larry Summers had one decidedly negative view. In the years to follow, those who held a different perspective would become Summers' most ardent critics. They did not disagree that Harvard should shape the world's future leaders. But on the question of how those leaders should be shaped, what they should be taught, what their *values* were, they could not have disagreed with Larry Summers more. As Summers moved to remake Harvard in his own image, these people would become his most passionate opposition.

The man who had been president of Harvard during the decade of Vietnam, civil rights, student protest, and political assassination had been tragically out of sync with his era. Nathan Marsh Pusey was a classics scholar who'd graduated from the college in 1928 before earning his Harvard Ph.D. in 1935. (He enjoyed, according to one report, a "passion for Athenian law.") Pusey was a deeply pious man, a regular attendee at Memorial Church who was committed to improving the lot of the chronically impoverished divinity school. Minister Peter Gomes called Pusey "the last Christian," by which Gomes meant the last Harvard president profoundly infused with and motivated by faith. ("It's a problematic title, but one that I can get away with," Gomes joked.) Pusey's conviction showed in his broad, resolute face, which never looked creased by doubt—or, for that matter, flexibility.

When James Bryant Conant announced in the spring of 1953 that he would leave his office to become the U.S. high commissioner to Germany, no one at Harvard expected Pusey to succeed him. How could they? Few even knew who Pusey was. The leading candidates were McGeorge Bundy, then a thirty-three-year-old associate professor of government, strikingly young but manifestly brilliant, and John Houston Finley, a professor of Greek literature who had helped author the famous "Harvard Red Book," a blueprint for education in postwar America. In different ways, both were men of gravitas and stature.

Pusey, who had in the interim become president of Lawrence College, a small liberal arts school in Appleton, Wisconsin, was not—at least, not to many Harvardians. A native of Iowa, he would be the first Harvard president born west of the Hudson. Unlike Abbot Lawrence Lowell, he didn't have family money. Unlike James Bryant Conant, he wasn't married to a Harvard professor's daughter. Pusey had never even been a member of the Harvard faculty. He was so anonymous around campus that, after the choice was announced, a joking refrain sprang up: "Pusey? Who's he?" Once the students and alums answered that question, they concocted another rhyme: "We couldn't be choosy, so we took Pusey."

But for most of his presidency, Pusey confounded his skeptics. He smartly appointed Bundy dean of the FAS, bringing into the fold a man of enormous intelligence and energy who also possessed the disposition of a potential rival. Pusey also proved to be a master fundraiser, leading what was then the largest capital campaign in the history of higher education—$82 million. And he wasn't afraid to use his bully pulpit to rebuke an American bully. During his time at Lawrence College, Pusey had been a fearless critic of the increasingly dangerous Joe McCarthy—on Pusey's appointment, McCarthy remarked that "Harvard's loss is Wisconsin's gain"—and he would play the same role at Harvard. "Someday I am sure we shall all look back on the hateful irrationality of the present with incredulity," he told one journalist. A 1954 faculty citation said that Pusey confronted McCarthy "with a serene and quiet courage," and called Pusey "the president of Harvard both in name and deed."

But the moral certitude that served Pusey so well in the 1950s proved less suited to the 1960s, when the greatest threat to Harvard came from within. As student protest began to embroil campuses nationwide, Pusey refused to believe that Harvard might become infected by the unrest. Why attack the university for problems that were so clearly the result of external forces? "The number of undergraduates who get excited about political problems is not large," he declared. "Most of them are above that sort of thing."

As it turned out, they weren't—though at first the students' protests seemed more hormonal than political. In 1960 the faculty voted to publish Harvard diplomas in English rather than the traditional Latin, and a horde of some two thousand cranky undergraduates marched on Loeb House, then the president's residence. "Latin Si, Pusey No," the students chanted. The president came out of his house and addressed the crowd—in Latin. Since virtually none of the students had any idea what he was saying, the protest quickly fizzled.

Pusey had a sense that the students either weren't dealing with important issues or didn't understand the complexity of the matters they were going on about, and the events of the next years did nothing to dissuade him. In 1963 students protested a plan to cut down sycamore trees along Memorial Drive, the four-lane road that runs parallel to the Charles River. The protest succeeded; the trees were spared. A 1966 attempt to block the introduction of WALK/DON'T WALK signs in Harvard Square did not. Trivial though these little flare-ups seemed, they had an underlying consistency—a reaction against the incursions of unwelcome "progress" into Harvard's tradition-minded community.

Nor was all the student activism at Harvard so slight, and Pusey failed to distinguish between jejune rebellion and genuine political anger, or to recognize how potent the two combined could be. In 1966 Secretary of Defense Robert McNamara, a 1939 graduate of the business school to whom the university had awarded an honorary doctorate in 1962, was invited to speak on campus. He never got the chance to deliver his speech. A shouting mob of students corralled him outside Quincy House, on Plympton Street. McNamara responded with bravado—"I was tougher then, and I'm tougher now!" he shouted, referring to his own student days—but the situation verged on chaos. A young student (and future congressman) named Barney Frank hastily led McNamara to safety through a labyrinth of underground steam tunnels. The ugly incident only hardened Pusey's conviction that student protest subverted the sine qua non of the university, a respect for free speech and civil debate. The students argued that extraordinary times required exceptional behavior. Without concession, Pusey disagreed.

As the war in Vietnam escalated after 1965, the tension at Harvard also rose. Some students, perhaps the majority, were not particularly demonstrative. But others grew angrier and angrier—over the war, the draft, racial injustice, on-campus recruiting by military contractors such as Dow Chemical, and the campus presence of the Reserve Officers' Training Corps. The fact that Harvard had numerous connections to the Johnson administration—including the since-departed Bundy, now special assistant to the president for national security affairs—fueled many students' conviction that their university was complicit in the war.

Students weren't the only ones torn between their reasons for being at Harvard and the pull of social unrest outside the campus gates. A politicized faculty split into liberal and conservative caucuses (both tilted considerably more to the left than either term now connotes). So broad was the divide that members of the two groups stopped speaking to one another. At the Faculty Club, who ate lunch with whom was meticulously scrutinized. Professors aligned themselves with or against the students. When the radical group Students for a Democratic Society threatened to burn the Widener Library card catalogue, several members of the conservative caucus camped out in the library for months keeping watch.

The collegiality that bound Harvard together was crumbling under the combined assaults of war and protest, mistrust and incivility. Still, most professors thought that widespread civil disobedience was unlikely. Hundreds of demonstrators might have seized buildings at Columbia and Berkeley, yet the faculty firmly believed that Harvard was different; Harvard was too old, too venerable, too *good*. Harvard had always thought of itself as exceptional among universities, in both senses of the word—better than and apart from the mass. Student uprising could not, would not happen here.

It did. On the afternoon of April 9, 1969, some three hundred students and outside activists, angered by Pusey's refusal to evict ROTC from the campus, raced into University Hall, the administration building that sits between Memorial Church and Widener Library. Shouting, swearing, and ransacking file cabinets, the protesters infiltrated the offices of the college deans. The stunned administrators were pushed, threatened, and forced to leave, subject to a torrent of verbal abuse and the threat of worse. One, Archibald Epps, Harvard's first African American dean, refused to depart. The protesters carried him feet first out of the building, unceremoniously dumping him on the ground. Epps, who considered himself someone who could sympathize with the students because of his own groundbreaking position, would never quite recover from the sense of violation and betrayal he felt.

Over the course of the afternoon, shocked university officials debated how to respond. While they talked, two to three hundred more students, most more curious than committed, joined the original protesters in University Hall.

Pusey had no intention of waiting out the sit-in or negotiating with student leaders. Instead, he called the cops—and not just Harvard police, but Cambridge and Boston troopers as well. In the gray pre-dawn light of April 10, they took University Hall back. About four hundred masked policemen filled the building with tear gas and waded inside, liberally wielding their nightsticks against anyone who didn't get out of the way fast enough. Coughing, crying, and gasping for breath, the demonstrators rushed out doors and jumped out windows. Less than twenty-four hours after it began, the occupation was over.

The immediate consequences were a ten-day campus strike, vociferous denunciations of the president, and media portrayals of a bitterly divided university. Those would pass. But in the longer term, the assault on University Hall—both assaults on University Hall—scarred the campus for decades. The trust between students and faculty was shattered. Relationships between some professors would never fully heal. And no longer would the students see the Harvard president as an Olympian figure to whom they deferred, but as a flawed and fallible individual against whom they protested. After all, the students may have taken over a building, but Pusey unleashed armed outsiders upon them. Not all trespasses were equal.

Most seriously, perhaps, Harvard's self-confidence, that invisible armor that had cloaked the university since the seventeenth century, had been profoundly shaken. If its own students could hate Harvard so much—and could such a treason stem from anything other than hatred?—then what was the very point of the university?

Not everyone thought that this was an improper question to ask. The events of the 1960s prompted a still-ongoing debate about the role of universities in American society. How engaged should they be with the world beyond their walls? Given their status as redoubts against the increasing materialism and ever-growing competitiveness of American society, should they infuse their students with an idealistic enthusiasm for reforming American life? Or would doing so corrupt the integrity of universities' fundamental mission—to seek and impart knowledge?

Given Harvard's prestige, power, and wealth, these questions were all the more urgent in Cambridge. With the nation's eyes on Harvard, as was always the case, didn't Harvard have a responsibility to serve as a university on a hill? Harvard thought it was better than every other university, so shouldn't it set a standard of idealism to which other universities should aspire? After all, Harvard had so much money, how could anyone pretend that its decisions did not have profound social and political ramifications?

If it took a little revolution to bring these issues to the fore, so be it. That, at least, is what many defenders of student protest believed. Many Harvard students and professors thought that the tangible consequences of the sixties were, on the whole, good ones. The concept of in loco parentis—that universities played the role of parents to the students they enrolled—was severely weakened, leading to greater student freedom and, theoretically, greater individual responsibility. Restrictive social mores were loosened. Men at Harvard were no longer compelled to wear coats and ties to dinner; women and men would live in the same dormitories. The faculty voted to banish ROTC from campus and created a committee on Afro-American studies, which would eventually become the department run by Skip Gates. Meanwhile, the college pushed to increase the diversity of its student body, using affirmative action to recruit African American students in particular. Cornel West, who came to Harvard in 1970, might have been a beneficiary of just this effort.

This emphasis on ethnic diversity and social justice also opened up enormous new fields of inquiry, particularly in the humanities. No longer were DWMs—dead white males—the sole legitimate area of interest. Scholars of history, literature, anthropology, sociology, and the like turned their attention to women, the poor and working class, blacks, native Americans, and other groups traditionally neglected by scholars. This was new and fertile material whose exploration helped detail a richer, more nuanced portrait of American history. It also brought new faces into the academy. Part of Skip Gates' reputation rested on the fact that he had unearthed the first novel ever written by an American black, *Our Nig*, by Harriet Wilson, *and* the first novel ever written by a female slave, *The Bondwoman's Narrative*, by Hannah Crafts.

Still, 1969 was a traumatic year for Harvard, and professors present at the time wince and sigh when they reflect upon it now. Nathan Pusey retired in 1971, widely seen as a casualty of the protest but insisting that his actions were proper. His successor was Derek Bok, the conciliator.

For the first years of his presidency, Bok aimed simply to keep the peace. One of the conditions for his taking the job was that he not have to live in Loeb House. Its location in the Yard made it vulnerable to further student turmoil, and Bok had young children. So the president's office bought the FAS dean's mansion on Elmwood Avenue from the Faculty of Arts and Sciences.

Bok took the question of the university's role in society seriously, and over the course of his two-decade presidency, he struggled to define the appropriate political role for Harvard and its president. A university president, he argued, should address political issues only when they had direct relevance to the mission of the university—teaching and learning. In the 1980s, Bok employed that argument in rejecting student demands for the university to divest its investments in South Africa as a protest against apartheid.

Bok also moved to redress an institutional shortfall that some Harvardians felt contributed to the unrest of 1969: a paucity of administrators. Improbable though it may seem today, Nate Pusey primarily depended upon two secretaries to run his administration, and some members of the faculty and administration felt that the lack of a broader management structure contributed to his loss of control over the students. Bok agreed that the university needed more professional management, if only because it had grown so much in the boom years after World War II. Harvard needed more experts in law, finance, political affairs, public relations, real estate, and so on. Bok hired them.

"One of the things that I faced, which my predecessor deliberately left for me to do, was coming to terms with how we administered a much more complicated institution," Bok said. "[Pusey] was old-fashioned in that respect . . . but we couldn't wait any longer. We had one vice-president for the whole institution, and we had massive complaints about the way in which buildings and grounds operated, the way the budget system worked, faculty pensions. . . . And so we entered a period that could be described as bureaucratization."

"Bureaucratization" changed Harvard in profound and unexpected ways. The growth of a corporate infrastructure that reported to the president diminished the power of the faculty while boosting that of the central administration. The culture of the university changed as well. Harvard's dominant values had once been those of scholars, but increasingly the university was defined by the bottom-line standards of corporate lawyers and MBAs. At points in Harvard's history, the faculty had essentially run the institution. Now they became more and more like mere employees, with less and less of a sense of investment in the university as a whole. For many, their greatest allegiance to Harvard was due to the fact that it was lucrative to be affiliated with the best brand in higher education. Some might criticize people like Skip Gates for hopscotching from university to university, but the diminished stature of faculty at universities everywhere was partly to blame.

Along with their other demands, the student protesters had sought greater democracy in Harvard's governance. The growth of a management culture took the university in just the opposite direction. Bureaucratization created a corps of behind-the-scenes powerbrokers whose decisions had great impact on both the students and faculty—yet the students and faculty frequently didn't even know who those decision-makers were. Looking back at 1969, these administrators and the members of the Corporation saw ample cause to shut students out of decision-making. As was also the case at the World Bank during the 1990s, transparency was a concept praised in theory, but largely ignored in practice.

If the Bok years were considered an era of healing at a university burned by its engagement with the political world, the Rudenstine decade that followed saw what might be called the normalization of the sixties. With his commitment to the Af-Am department and affirmative action, Rudenstine endorsed some of that decade's inheritance. Another, perhaps less constructive consequence was the growth of identity politics, with students fighting turf battles over ethnicity, gender, and sexual orientation. The importance of the world outside campus had diminished; the canvas of activism had shrunk to the individual body.

None of this recent history appealed to Larry Summers. Both by training and by temperament, the economist felt a profound skepticism toward the youth movement of the sixties. He thought of himself not as a product of that decade, but a response to it. Born in 1954, he was a little too young to be swept up in the turmoil of the time. As something of a loner, he wasn't a movement type. He wasn't a cool kid, a rebel who'd feel comfortable smoking a joint and listening to Jimi Hendrix. He was too driven, too disciplined, and too ambitious for that. A physically ungainly young man, Summers relied on his strength—his enormously powerful intellect.

Nor did he have to worry about being drafted; he was a student throughout the entire 1960s and '70s. Even after graduation, Summers was not inclined to save the whales or freeze the nukes or end aid to the Contras (or continue it, for that matter). He was a scholar in a field not known for its radicalism. "The reason I decided . . . to become an economist is that I wanted to work on solving what felt to me the most important problems in the world: poverty, unemployment, helping poor people," Summers said in a 2001 speech. "But I knew that I didn't want to just shout and rant about them. . . . I wanted to carefully study what worked and what didn't work."

If anything, Summers had a visceral distaste for the actions of people just a few years older than he. His academic training instilled in him what he called an "economic rationalism," and he looked upon activism as if it were something to scrape off his shoe. Sixties-style protest, whether it occurred at Harvard in 1969 or at the Seattle meeting of the World Trade Organization in 1999, struck him as anti-intellectual and, therefore, of dubious value. At a meeting with students in October 2004, Summers said regarding the war in Iraq that "If this was the 1970s, [Harvard] students would be protesting the war every day, but as it is, youth apathy means they focus on the important things—their studies—and that can only be a good thing." He disliked the way protesters simplified complex issues, turning them into chants or slogans to be scrawled on pieces of cardboard. And he thought that the emotion-fueled acts of protesters often worked *against* the causes they supported. The best example was their anger and dismay over globalization. Summers had no doubt that globalization would lead to higher living standards and greater longevity for people all around the world, as well as a cleaner global environment. If the anti-globalization protesters—the people who would never let him forget The Memo—couldn't see that, then it was an intellectual failure on their part, an argument for the primacy of logic over passion, data over faith. He referred to those people as "espresso-drinking Westerners."

Same thing with sweatshops, the original source of 2001's living-wage protest. Liberals thought that sweatshops were bad. Summers thought that it was better to work in a sweatshop than, for example, to walk the streets as a prostitute. If sweatshop jobs were really so terrible, people wouldn't take them. Activists who tried to shut down sweatshops were hurting the very people they claimed they wanted to help. That might sound contrarian, but it was really just thinking with your head and not your heart.

Summers was not devoid of passion. During his years in Washington, he became increasingly patriotic and started referring to the 1990s as an "American decade." But his patriotism took the form more of admiration for American capitalism more than, say, a lump in the throat upon hearing "America the Beautiful." The more Summers traveled around the world during the 1990s, the more he appreciated the American economy and the political framework that allowed it to thrive. In the trouble spots he visited, he saw how corruption stymied economic development and lowered the quality of life for ordinary people. Conversely, the economic policies that he, Rubin, and Greenspan had crafted and implemented had helped "save the world," as *Time* had declared. The anti-globalization protesters who listened to Rage Against the Machine and rioted in the streets may not have understood, but the wise men of Washington knew what they were doing.

When he returned to Harvard, however, Summers saw the flotsam and jetsam of the 1960s wherever he looked. He had to step over it on his way through the student-occupied Mass Hall in the spring of 2001. The incoming president was shocked that Rudenstine had allowed the occupation of the president's building. And when the sit-in was over and the students got off with punishments so light you could barely call them slaps on the wrist, Summers couldn't believe that either. He considered such timidity a direct and unfortunate result of the 1969 riot, and he didn't hesitate to make his feelings known.

In September 2001, a Harvard undergrad named David Jonathan

Plunkett came to talk with Summers at the president's office hour, which Summers scheduled every month or so. Plunkett had been one of the living-wage activists involved in the 2001 occupation, and as he sat down in Summers' office, he said, "You know, I used to sleep outside this door." Summers responded, "If I were president then, I'd have suspended you for at least a year." Plunkett pressed on, raising the issue of Harvard's outsourcing of union jobs to non-union workers. "I don't feel any obligation to buy a union-made trash can," Summers told him. "Why should I feel an obligation to hire union workers?" Plunkett couldn't tell if Summers was serious or just trying to start an argument, but either way, he found the comparison offensive.

Summers was not only surprised that the occupiers hadn't been punished, he also believed that they felt they *shouldn't* have been punished. What gave him that idea was unclear. The protesters had fully expected to be disciplined and probably arrested, and were happily surprised when their assumptions proved wrong. But because they had anticipated being hauled out of Mass Hall, most of them hadn't even brought changes of clothes, sleeping bags, and the textbooks they needed to keep up with their course work.

Still, Summers was convinced that the living-wage activists wanted the moral high of protest without the morning-after hangover of punishment. "The living-wage campaign and the way it was carried on did not engage me as a step toward social justice," he told one student who asked him about the Mass Hall sit-in. "If you read Gandhi or Martin Luther King or any other thoughtful proponents of civil disobedience . . . they will all tell you that the punishment of the civil disobedient is integral to the concept of civil disobedience. So the position that's been taken by some in this community that civil disobedience is so noble that it shouldn't be punished seems to me a misleading proposition."

In February 2002, Summers announced a new "Interpretation" of an existing rule, the "University-Wide Statement on Rights and Reponsibilities." Passed after the takeover of University Hall, the 1970 statement said that a member of the Harvard community enjoyed "free expression, free inquiry, intellectual honesty, respect for the dignity of others, and openness to constructive change." Interfering with these freedoms was a "serious violation of the personal rights upon which the community is based." The Orwellian-sounding "Interpretation" that

Summers instigated added that "any unauthorized occupation of a University building, or any part of it . . . constitutes unacceptable conduct . . . and is subject to appropriate discipline."

The Interpretation didn't actually change anything; it only emphasized extant policy. But it was widely seen as a sign of Summers' determination to break the spirit of campus activism. Students got the point. First Larry Summers had called Cornel West on the carpet—a warning to the faculty that Summers would not hesitate to castigate them. Now he was sending the students a similar warning: Neil Rudenstine might have tolerated protest. Larry Summers will not.

Summers not only disagreed with Rudenstine's decision not to have the Mass Hall occupiers arrested, he also found it hard to respect. In his opinion, Rudenstine's restraint reflected a post-sixties crisis of confidence that had weakened the presidency and degraded Harvard's intellectual life. Summers believed that the sixties had promoted what he called an "identity-based politics" in which the ideas people advocated were inextricably linked to their own cultural identities—the color of their skin, their religious belief, what social class they belonged to. He felt that scholars and students were afraid to say that one idea was better than another, lest they be accused of cultural insensitivity. Someone who criticized the value of African American studies, for example, risked being dubbed a racist. This way of thinking was so different from Summers' experiences in graduate-level economics seminars, where every idea was fair game and the thin-skinned did not fare well.

Summers blamed the professors more than the students. In the 1960s, he believed, the average Harvard student was to the political left of the faculty. Today it was the professors who were the knee-jerk liberals. He estimated that in 2000, 85 percent of the Harvard faculty voted for Al Gore, while the rest split their votes between Ralph Nader and George W. Bush. Perhaps 70 percent of the students voted for Gore, 25 percent for Bush, and 5 percent for Nader. Granted, both groups were more liberal than Americans generally, but the faculty was more monolithic and less open-minded than the students. If, as Summers believed, the decisions of adults were fundamentally the result of their education as young people, then Harvard students were too often being shaped by tenured professors infused with the anti-intellectual, counterculture spirit of the 1960s.

Summers was more hopeful about the undergraduates. They were, as he put it, malleable. Most of the freshmen during his first year as president had been born in or around 1983. Because they were some years removed from the sixties, they were less instinctively hostile to authority. Summers was particularly interested in those who wanted to enroll in ROTC, but were unable to do so at Harvard. The university's original ban on the officer training program had been extended in 1994, to emphasize the faculty's opposition to the military's discrimination against homosexuals. Now Harvard students wishing to participate in ROTC had to take the subway to MIT, which did conduct an on-campus program. The cost of training Harvard cadets, about $135,000, was picked up by anonymous alumni donors. Summers disapproved of that state of affairs, and he called for the return of ROTC to Harvard Yard and a reconsideration of Harvard's relationship to uniformed authority in general.

"There are still many people who, when they think of police, think too quickly of Chicago in 1968, and too slowly of the people who risk their lives every day to keep streets safe in America's major cities," Summers said at a Kennedy School dinner in October 2001. "It is all too common for us to underestimate the importance of clearly expressing our respect and support for the military and individuals who choose to serve in the armed forces of the United States." Perhaps, he suggested, the terrorist attacks of the previous month could have a silver lining. "If these terrible events and the struggle that we are now engaged in once again re-ignite our sense of patriotism—re-ignite our respect for those who wear uniforms and bring us together as a country in that way—it will be no small thing," Summers concluded.

In February 2002, Summers made a cameo appearance in an Army recruitment video. Standing in front of the Yard's famous statue of John Harvard, which tour guides describe as "the third most widely visited statue in the country after the Statue of Liberty and the Washington Monument," he announced, "I am proud of the Harvard ROTC students who participate in the ROTC program. . . . Their work is America's work."

Eradicating the corrosive legacy of the 1960s also meant re-building the trust between the president and students. One undergraduate who asked Summers' opinion of the 1960s got this response: "As you and I meet today," Summers said, "I think there is a kind of mutual respect between us. I talk with the assumption that you're not going to turn around and write an editorial in the *Crimson* tomorrow saying that Larry Summers is an asshole for [espousing] the following ideas, and you hold the assumption that I'm listening carefully to you and responding thoughtfully. Those assumptions would have been the exact opposite in the 1960s." Just in case, Summers always had an aide sitting in on his meetings with students, partly so that he could keep track of their concerns, but partly so that if they did talk to the *Crimson*, he could ensure the veracity of their memories.

Summers wanted students and faculty to know that he could listen to them. But during his first year as president of Harvard, many students and faculty members began to wonder if he really *was* listening. Judging from his actions, it certainly didn't look that way.

Part of the problem—a large part—was stylistic. Summers had come to Cambridge after a decade in Washington, and he carried the culture of his former city with him. At Treasury, Summers had enjoyed the trappings of power, and at Harvard he replicated as many of those perks as possible. When star-struck students approached him bearing dollar bills for him to autograph—bills that already bore his signature from his time as treasury secretary—the new president was delighted to oblige. Image was important. He hired a decorator to redo the president's mansion, Elmwood, and printed up elegant stationery with "Elmwood" written on it. The stationery looked like "a wedding invitation," said one of its recipients. He replaced the aging Lincoln Neil Rudenstine had used with a brand-new Town Car. That shiny black sedan was all over campus—outside the Faculty Club, the Kennedy School, Loeb House, with Summers' driver waiting patiently inside, often for hours at a time. Though cars are generally banned from Harvard Yard, Summers' Lincoln was constantly idling on the macadam in front of Mass Hall, a charging cell phone and a can of Diet Coke—a Summers addiction—perched in the rear-seat cup holders. Its license plate read simply "1636," the year of Harvard's founding.

Summers quickly surrounded himself with Washington veterans, including several who had lost their jobs when George W. Bush took office. Familiar though they were with Washington's corridors of power, they had little or no Harvard experience. For his chief of staff, Summers hired a thirty-year-old former Treasury staffer named Marne

Levine, a graduate of Miami University, in Ohio. A former Hillary Clinton aide, Sharon Kennedy, was hired as an event planner and alumni liaison. Alan Stone, once a speechwriter for President Clinton, became the vice-president for government, community, and public affairs. An aide to senator Ted Kennedy, Colleen Richards Powell, became another Summers staffer. For his "special assistant to the president"—no such position existed under Rudenstine—Summers brought in Michael O'Mary, a 2000 Harvard graduate who'd been an advance man for Al Gore. Lucie McNeil, a young press aide to British prime minister Tony Blair, would later sign on as Summers' personal press secretary. Her title was Senior Communications Director, Office of News and Public Affairs, but McNeil really had only one job: to promote Larry Summers in the media. This too was a position that had not existed in the Rudenstine administration.

The newcomers did not go over well. By and large, they knew little about Harvard, and their sometimes clumsy attempts to get up to speed rankled. To avoid just that learning curve, Harvard presidents customarily hired Harvard graduates. Alumni not only possessed helpful institutional memory, but they were also devoted to their alma mater; their loyalty to Harvard was the foundation of their work for its president. By hiring Washington politicos, Summers sent the message that he wanted an inner circle that was loyal, first and foremost, to him.

For people who had worked at Harvard for years, often decades, this was not a good omen. Yes, it was true that the Corporation wanted Summers to shake things up. And, yes, it was also true that Summers was the first Harvard president who might plausibly consider the job a demotion. But the citizens of Harvard did not see things that way. For them, there could be no better job in the world than to be president of Harvard. Harvard's traditions, its way of doing business, set a standard for others and kept the university from being swept up in the great onrush of American materialism. They did not appreciate staffers who considered their boss more important than the institution that employed him. "He travels with an *entourage*," said one longtime member of the community. "No Harvard president before Larry ever said, 'I'll talk to my people about that,'" noted another. No Harvard president had ever had "my people" before—there were only Harvard people. And as Skip Gates had said to Summers, such language sounded like political flimflam—dilatory and disingenuous. It irritated

Harvardians that Summers could bring Washington-style politicking to their campus and still enjoy a reputation as a straight shooter. Most of the time when he talked to the *Crimson,* it was off the record or not for attribution—a university president who didn't want to be quoted by his own campus newspaper! But when the *New York Times* called, Summers was certain to pick up the phone.

Summers not only hired cultural strangers, he used them in ways more reminiscent of Washington than Cambridge. Cell phones glued to their ears, his staffers followed Summers around campus, scribbling notes, snapping photos of him, and fetching him Diet Coke, pizza, and chicken wings. If Summers was giving a lecture or attending a meeting, an aide preceded him to the site, scoping out the room like a White House advance team. When Summers spoke at Memorial Church, a staffer arrived early to ensure that the president would find a glass of water waiting for him. Summers, however, was always late. Certainly he was busy, but his tardiness wasn't always accidental. He never wanted to be seen waiting for a room to fill up; it made a person look like he had spare time. Instead, he'd stride into a crowded room, giving a thumbs-up to a face he recognized in the crowd, reaching into a row of seats to shake someone's hand. Waiting drove him crazy. When Summers traveled internationally, according to one source familiar with his travel arrangements, he'd have a staff member call up the customs officials at Logan Airport so that Larry Summers would not have to wait in line with the hoi polloi.

Sometimes Summers relied on his staff in ways that struck the community as just bizarre. At one event later in his presidency, Summers met the freshmen who lived in Mass Hall. Before the gathering began, aide Colleen Richards Powell informed the students that she didn't want the conversation to be awkward, and so she asked them to suggest questions for Summers to ask them. They decided that Summers should ask, "What surprised you about Harvard?"

When the president arrived, he seemed bored and distracted until Powell handed him a slip of paper. Summers read it, cleared his throat and said, "So, tell me, what surprised you about Harvard?" Sitting in a circle, the students, one by one, answered the question, all the while having to pretend that they weren't expecting it.

In Washington, such gestures signal a person's importance and are so commonplace among high-level politicians that the lack of them is more notable than their presence. In Cambridge, they felt like the hallmarks of a hostile takeover. Summers' use of political tactics and political people suggested that he distrusted the community. That, in turn, bred suspicion and dislike among Harvardians used to a less "imperial" leadership style, as it was often described. One high-level administrator quickly dubbed Michael O'Mary "Summers' yes-boy," because, although he played the role, he wasn't old enough to be a yes-man.

The insult was a small complaint suggestive of a larger issue: a widespread feeling that Summers was not hiring aides strong and independent enough to tell him when they thought he was making a mistake. Some observers saw a gender-based pattern. As had been the case at Treasury, Summers' closest staff members were female. He seemed to feel most relaxed in the presence of women. "Larry surrounds himself with these women who see the vulnerable side of him and think they can change him," explained one White House aide who worked closely with Summers. Conversely, whether at MIT, Harvard, or in Washington, virtually all of the colleagues whom Summers felt intellectually challenged by were men.

Yet Summers didn't get many positive reviews for spending time with one woman who probably did challenge him. As early as September 2001, the campus was buzzing with the rumor that Summers was dating conservative writer and radio host Laura Ingraham, a furiously anti-Clinton partisan about a decade younger than Summers. The relationship had apparently begun before Summers left Washington. In July, the pair had lunch at the Palm steakhouse, a hangout for D.C. celebrities. "What shorthand phrase will future historians use to describe the Clinton administration?" Ingraham joked. Summers didn't know. "Sex between the Bushes." Then, in early September, the two were spotted jogging along the banks of the Charles together, and the *Washington Post* reported that Ingraham had helped Summers lose twenty pounds.

It was, admittedly, a difficult situation for Summers; Harvard hadn't had an unmarried president since John Thorton Kirkland, who served from 1810 to 1828. There was no modern precedent for a bachelor president, no existing social code to help Summers adjust to the situation. But it is safe to say that even if there had been, Laura Ingraham wouldn't have been Harvard's choice for an appropriate presidential girlfriend. She is a graduate of Dartmouth, where she had been an editor of the arch-conservative *Dartmouth Review*. After serving as a speechwriter in the Reagan administration, she attended the University of Virginia Law School, after which she clerked for Supreme Court Justice Clarence Thomas. For an article on young conservatives, she had posed on the cover of the *New York Times Magazine* wearing a leopard-print miniskirt. And she'd authored a book trashing Hillary Clinton.

Part of the campus' skeptical reaction was political. Harvard liberals didn't like the idea of their president dating a right-wing bomb-thrower, even if she was a bombshell. Many found it odd that one of the highest-ranking members of the Clinton administration would date one of its most vociferous critics. But perhaps the larger objection was cultural. Laura Ingraham is a very modern figure, a Washington player who straddles the worlds of politics and media. She was a dramatic change from Sissela Bok, a scholar, or Neil Rudenstine's wife, Angelica, a patron of the arts. And, for that matter, she was a drastic departure from Summers' ex-wife, Victoria Perry. To many Harvardians, she was another sign of how Summers was bringing Washington style to a campus that had always believed Washington needed it more than it needed Washington. After all, Harvard predated Washington by one hundred and sixty years.

Summers' relationship with Laura Ingraham didn't last long, so it was only a blip on the campus radar screen. A much more enduring issue was something the campus found hard to discuss. Harvard had a new president with—there was no other way to put it—bad manners. When students came to see him, Summers propped his feet up on his coffee table or desk, sometimes with his shoes off, regardless of the condition of his socks. He often appeared in public with a toothpick dangling from a corner of his mouth. If someone said something he found uninteresting or foolish, he'd conspicuously roll his eyes. He seemed incapable of looking an interlocutor in the eye. "I went to shake his hand, and he never made eye contact," said undergraduate Johanna Paretzky, who met Summers after she sang at a concert for his inaugural. Paretzky demonstrated by turning her head so that she was looking over her right shoulder. "It was really dramatic, like he was looking for someone else." Dozens of students and faculty tell essentially the same story.

Other times Summers would simply stare into space when you were talking to him. "Larry's always looking away," said one junior professor who has met him on several occasions. "At first you think he's scanning the room for someone more important; but no, he's just looking away." Summers frequently mangled the names of people he was greeting or introducing, with ethnic-sounding names giving him particular trouble. For an entire year at faculty meetings, Summers mispronounced the name of Michael Shinagel (Shi-*nay*-gull), the dean of the extension school, calling him Shin-*ah*-gull. His behavior at faculty meetings troubled the faculty in other ways. One of the most venerable traditions at these highly formal gatherings is something called the "memorial minutes," in which professors read brief remembrances of colleagues who have passed away. The readings are short, but they matter; they're a sign of respect for the Harvard past, and faculty members take them very seriously. But during the readings, Summers closed his eyes and drummed his fingers. He looked bored, impatient, and disrespectful, as if honoring the dead were keeping him from more important tasks.

Summers had another tic that those conversing with him found unsettling. While he was thinking or listening, he'd trace circles around his mouth with his right forefinger—on and on, apparently compulsively. He gave no sign of being aware of the habit. "He's like a free-throw shooter in the NBA," said 2003 graduate Krishnan Subrahmanian. "When he talks, he has to do these little rituals." It made those conversing with him feel as if Summers wanted to be somewhere else—or wanted them to be.

The president's social deficiencies even extended to alumni he was soliciting for money. On several occasions when Summers was talking with prospects for donations, he simply wandered away in mid-conversation—in mid-*sentence*—as if he couldn't muster the energy to feign interest. To an observer, it looked like Summers had a sort of mental radio. When he'd heard enough from one station, he simply twisted the dial to another. The fundraisers tried to work around the problem by, for example, scheduling him to play tennis against prominent alumni. Summers grew conspicuously more interested in his environment whenever an element of competition was introduced.

But it wasn't just individual interactions that were a problem; Summers wasn't always good with crowds, either. On a trip to London early in his tenure, he arrived late and tired to an alumni banquet, and was not pleased when he wasn't able to eat before his speech. According to several people who were present or subsequently heard about the incident, Summers cracked a joke to the effect that a nation that couldn't serve a salad on time was doomed to second-tier status. That started the trans-Atlantic phone lines humming.

Food was a recurring problem. Summers was a prodigious and sloppy eater. The first time he visited the editorial board of the *Harvard Crimson,* in the fall of 2001, he dispatched an aide to Pinocchio's, a beloved campus pizza place. When the aide returned, Summers talked to the editors as he wolfed down bites of pizza, much of which found its way onto his shirt. The students watched, transfixed. On another occasion Summers went out to dinner with several graduate students. After one excused himself to use the restroom, Summers started choking on a piece of meat. The student returned from the restroom to find another diner standing with his arms around the president, preparing to give him the Heimlich maneuver. Summers coughed up the meat before the emergency measure was necessary. And then there was the general problem of eating and talking at the same time, which sometimes resulted in Summers spraying saliva on his audience.

Tellingly, the beat reporters covering the Treasury Department had never reported on such social peccadilloes, though many were aware of them. "He had the worst table manners of any cabinet head ever," claimed one *Washington Post* reporter who socialized with Summers on several occasions. But readers of the paper never heard about that. Any beat reporter who made note of it would quickly find his access at Treasury much diminished.

At Harvard, however, the student press had no such compunctions. This was not because the *Crimson* is a tabloid rag. On the contrary—it is so concerned with its professionalism, so aware of its hundred-fifty-year history, that it often comes across as deferential to the Harvard administration. (It's a far cry from the *Crimson* of 1969, which editorialized in support of a North Vietnamese victory.) Yet Summers' manners were so widely remarked upon that student reporters were really just transcribing an omnipresent campus conversation. Putting his feet on the table, staring into space, rolling his eyes—all these small gestures seemed to symbolize a larger lack of respect that Harvard's new president had for the university.

The *Crimson's* columnists repeatedly noted how Summers' lack of social graces impeded his interaction with students and faculty. Columnist Vasugi V. Ganeshananthan wrote that Summers' "best efforts to demonstrate his interest in us fall miserably short . . . because they literally look terrible. (The man even fidgeted at his own installation, and I'd guess he was pretty interested in that.) . . . It's at the root of every major problem he's had this year."

Farther down the road, after relations between the *Crimson* and Summers had deteriorated, the paper ran a photo essay chronicling Summers' fluctuating weight. And the *Crimson* was gentle compared with some student publications. "This just in from Mass Hall," announced one anonymous column in a student humor magazine called *Demon*. "Larry Summers is really, really fat. He's not the same size as the average human—he's fatter! He's *above average in fatness!*"

Quickly, the outside press picked up on the problem. On November 10 that first fall, the Harvard football team played the University of Pennsylvania at Harvard Stadium, and, along with a number of professors, Summers participated in a halftime contest of the children's game "Red Rover." But as Summers ran across the field, his sweatpants plunged down to what the *Boston Herald* called "the upper-thigh area." The *Herald* quoted one observer saying, "He was wearing crimson-colored briefs that were in a wedgie!"

Trivial though such incidents might sound to an outsider, Summers' odd behavior mattered in Cambridge. Students and faculty puzzled over how a man could rise to such a powerful position without developing the social niceties that most people in high-profile jobs possess—gracious manners, a gift for small talk, a knack for putting people at ease. Harvard students and faculty are well aware how much their campus interests the outside world, and they consider their president their most visible ambassador. That was why Neil Rudenstine's breakdown had been a source of such acute embarrassment. But no matter what other criticisms they had of Rudenstine, no one at Harvard would have said that he wasn't polite, even charming when the situation called for it. Rudenstine certainly had no trouble making other people feel that they were more important than he was.

Summers, by contrast, had just the opposite effect; he always reminded people that he seemed to think himself more important than they were. For one thing, he had a bizarre habit of falling asleep in public. Eyewitnesses reported Summers dozing at a temple service, a festival celebrating cultural diversity, a talk by Pakistani president Pervez Musharraf, a lecture by United Nations head Kofi Annan, and again at a speech by Mikhail Gorbachev in Sanders Theatre, Harvard's largest classroom. "He was sitting in the front row, and he just dozed off," said one Kennedy School student who sat directly behind Summers at the Musharraf speech. Asked if it was possible that Summers was simply closing his eyes, the woman said strongly that she didn't think so. Besides, she added, whether or not Summers was actually sleeping was a moot point. If she was sitting right behind Summers and *she* was convinced he had nodded off, how could Musharraf, about fifteen feet away, not think the same?

On repeated occasions Summers showed a similar lack of tact when he interacted with questioners. At one fall 2001 meeting with the law school faculty, a female professor asked a question Summers didn't think much of. "That's a stupid question," he responded. ("It *was* a stupid question," another law school professor subsequently admitted. "But still . . .") His aides explained that Summers' style was typical of the intellectual free-for-all that characterized economics seminars, and people shouldn't take it personally. That argument convinced few.

Then there was the time Summers had to give an award to a student director who'd made a documentary, called *Occupation*, about the Mass Hall sit-in. In front of a large crowd under a tent outside the Science Center, Summers announced sarcastically, "I admire the cinematography [of *Occupation*] more than the content. I look forward to [the director's] upcoming documentary on grade inflation, though I expect it'll be some time in coming." The audience did not seem to understand why the president of Harvard was insulting a student to whom he was handing an award. (The answer was because *Occupation* presented the sit-in in a positive light.)

So great was the bewilderment over Summers' lack of basic social skills that some in the Harvard community speculated that there might be a clinical reason for his deficiencies: a neurobiological disease called Asperger Syndrome. A form of autism, the disease was first described by a Viennese physician named Hans Asperger in 1944, but only really started being diagnosed in this country after it was officially recognized by the American Psychiatric Association in 1994. People with Asperger

Syndrome, which affects mostly boys, don't have any cognitive or physical disabilities; on the contrary, they sometimes show "an astonishing grasp of the most arcane subjects," according to a report in *Time*. Little wonder that the illness is sometimes known as the "geek" or "little professor" syndrome. Some scientists believe that Asperger has a genetic basis, often present when a child is the product of two intellectually similar parents. As *Time* put it, the theory goes that in university towns and research-and-development corridors such as Silicon Alley, many highly intelligent but ill-socialized men are marrying women with similar characteristics, "leading to an overload of genes that predispose their children to autism, Asperger's and related disorders."

People with Asperger's may be unnervingly smart in specific modes of thinking but have trouble functioning in rudimentary social situations. They have difficulty handling change or transition. They don't work well in teams. One on one, they won't make eye contact, instead staring at a wall or into space. They may have repetitive physical mannerisms. While they may have an excellent vocabulary, they can also be linguistically tone-deaf and use words that convey a different meaning than they intend, which can result in their sounding brusque, dismissive, or simply as if they're not really listening to an interlocutor. Similarly, they have trouble feeling empathy.

"It's important to remember that the person with AS perceives the world very differently," wrote one Asperger's specialist. "Therefore, many behaviors that seem odd or unusual are due to those neurological differences and not the result of intentional rudeness or bad behavior."

To some viewers, Larry Summers at one time or another manifested all of these characteristics. No one raised the issue publicly, but to a number of faculty observers—who did not appear to have spoken to one another—Asperger's would explain virtually everything about Summers that seemed inexplicable. On the other hand, what were the implications of having a president whose ability to empathize may have been clinically limited? Whether at Treasury making decisions that affected millions of people, or at Harvard shaping the leaders of the world, shouldn't someone with such power be able to connect with the emotion of human experience?

Half gossip, half scientific speculation, and fueled by an intense consternation over the president's behavior, the Asperger's theory bubbled beneath the surface of Harvard life. Meanwhile, Summers' aides responded to the oft-stated complaint that their boss was a terrible listener by repeatedly insisting that he was willing to consider any argument from any source. The truth of that claim, however, was not always obvious. Timothy McCarthy, a lecturer in the Department of History and Literature, remembered a meeting with Summers in August 2001 during which the president showed a nasty temper. McCarthy had organized an e-mail petition supporting the living-wage movement, and the meeting agenda was to discuss worker salaries in the aftermath of the University Hall sit-in. Also present were other faculty members, some physical plant workers, and a couple of students. As usual, Summers was late, and he didn't look happy to be there. When one student, a sophomore, questioned him about a university "policy" that was in fact just a proposal, Summers blew up. "Summers interrupted him and went for the jugular," McCarthy said. "He kept battering the student with questions based on the slip-up. He was going after him, pointing his finger at the guy." According to another person present at the meeting, "Summers just dismantled this kid. It was like he was taking apart the deputy finance minister of some Third-World country." Finally, McCarthy intervened. "I said, 'Larry, you know what he means.'" The president stopped abruptly and looked at McCarthy with a surprised expression, then changed the subject.

Summers liked to say that because he asked tough questions, he was also happy to answer them. But people who took him up on the offer sometimes found that that wasn't the case. While giving a guest lecture at the business school in early 2002, Summers criticized Malaysian prime minister Mahathir bin Mohamad, who in September 1998 had imposed capital controls to stop the flight of foreign investment from his country. Some economists thought that such measures helped prevent Malaysia from succumbing to the Asian economic flu, but the move ran contrary to the free-market policies advocated by Summers and the IMF. So, in his lecture, Summers accused Mahathir of practicing crony capitalism, promoting policies that enriched his political and personal friends.

During the subsequent question-and-answer session, one contrarian student raised his hand and asked Summers if he didn't have essentially the same relationship with Bob Rubin. Wasn't Summers' opposition to capital controls just a sop to Wall Street banks, which wanted to recoup their risky investments regardless of how doing so affected the country in which they had invested? "Summers just lost it," said one audience member, a business school student whose version of events was supported by others who were present. "He looked at the person and said, 'You don't know what you're talking about and how dare you ask this question of the president of Harvard?' The whole class was disturbed by what happened."

Perhaps Summers' most widely talked about social gaffe was the one involving Bill Clinton and the football. On November 19, 2001, the former president came to Harvard to give a speech. Standing before six thousand listeners in the Albert H. Gordon Track and Tennis Center, Clinton joked, "I've got so many former staff members here [at Harvard], I can't keep up with them all." The ex-president then spoke about the world after September 11. There is "a war raging within Islam today," Clinton said. "It is rooted in the frustrations so many Muslims have with the modern world, which they see as a threat to their values, destructive of their way of life. . . . We cannot engage in this debate without admitting that there are excesses in our contemporary culture, and that no people have ever been able to live forever only with their rational facilities, without any spiritual nourishment and non-logical belief systems."

It was a good speech, delivered with poise, humor, and confidence to a warm and welcoming audience. But if you asked students what they remembered most about the event, they'd tell you about the football. After Clinton had finished speaking, the captain of the Harvard football team, Ryan M. Fitzgerald, presented him with a football from Harvard's victory against rival Yale three days before. Clinton tossed the ball to himself a couple of times, then casually lobbed it about five feet over the podium to Summers. The Harvard president looked stricken. He threw his hands up palm first, bobbled the football, bobbled it some more, and then dropped it. The audience groaned. "For a second you thought, oh my God, it's that nerdy kid in middle school," said one observer.

It was, of course, a small incident, with no tangible impact. Trivial, really. But the dropped football resonated with students because it exposed something true about Summers—an inability to be spontaneous, to act with a natural grace, especially compared with Clinton, whose instinctive leadership gifts only highlighted the contrast between the two men. No one would say that Summers wasn't working hard to master the issues and learn the requirements of his new job. But he made it look like work—and if you took him by surprise, all the practice fell away and the new president was revealed to be, as the students would put it, a geek. Uncool. Like the sarcastic term at Harvard that undergrads use to describe the inevitable sycophant who won't shut up in class discussions—"that kid in section."

And that wasn't entirely fair. For one thing, the students would never have gotten to see so much of Summers if he hadn't been making a concerted and sustained effort to visit the houses, drop in on courses, and generally make himself a ubiquitous presence on campus. And when Summers was interested in what you were saying, a conversation with the president could be an intellectual delight. He questioned every assumption: In a conversation with Harvard graduate and famed cellist Yo-Yo Ma, he asked Ma if it was really necessary for Harvard libraries to spend tens of thousands of dollars buying original musical scores. Why wouldn't photocopies serve? You couldn't always tell if Summers really believed what he was saying or if he was just trying to play devil's advocate, but he asked questions that made you rethink things you'd always taken for granted.

He solicited opinions: At one dinner party at Martin Peretz's home, he engaged the table in a discussion about the virtues and demerits of a Harvard-branded credit card. It could make money for the university—but would it ultimately cheapen the Harvard brand? Or, given the nature of American society, might a Harvard credit card actually extend the Harvard brand in a positive way?

He conducted informal research: As Summers thought about the nature of the possible Allston campus, he repeatedly asked audiences which campus buildings they liked and disliked, wryly noting that their favorites were generally the opposite of architectural critics' favorites, and vice versa.

He posed provocative questions: To try to determine the value of a Harvard degree, Summers asked hospital workers how they tested the value of their hospital. How did they measure whether their hospital saved more lives than other hospitals did? And was there something about their measurement techniques that could be applied to how Harvard compared the value of its education to that of other universities?

He took material from one area and considered its application to others: After reading Michael Lewis' book *Moneyball*, about how Oakland A's general manager Billy Beane used statistics to choose over-looked baseball players and sign them for less money than big name stars, Summers weighed what Harvard could learn from Beane. "Being a good baseball scout is now about doing econometrics," he told one academic audience. When they laughed politely, he insisted. "It's true—the A's win as many games [as other league champions] with one-third the payroll. That's a two hundred percent productivity improvement, and it must have applications elsewhere." It did. One reason Summers was interested in offering tenure to younger professors was because Harvard would have to pay them less than it would estab-lished scholars.

Summers' intelligence was sometimes mixed with a clinical can-dor. At a forum with graduate students, one aspiring scholar rose to tell Summers that his Harvard stipend had expired, and the teaching load he was offered in its stead didn't pay him nearly the amount of the stipend. Why would Harvard actually reduce the amount of money it had once offered him as incentive to come to the university?

For the same reason, Summers responded, that Polaroid sells it cameras cheaply, but not its film. Once a consumer bought the camera, he was locked into purchasing the film. Similarly, when Harvard was competing with other universities for the best graduate students, it had to offer them the most attractive financial aid package. But as soon as that student had committed to Harvard, the university was free to low-ball its subsequent offers; at that point, the student wasn't likely to transfer.

The graduate student sat down, enlightened but not assuaged.

When Summers delivered a lecture, he spoke confidently, without a hint of nervousness. Still, his body language sent an entirely different message. His head rotated deliberately back and forth, making contact with each section of the audience. The gesture looked stiff and unnat-ural, as though a public speaking coach had made him practice it. Often he gripped the podium with one hand, while his right leg mean-dered back and forth as if it had a life of its own. As he bit off his words in clumps of three, two, and even one before taking deliberate pauses, he sounded eerily like Al Gore—a little pinched, a little lockjawed. Sometimes, at the end of sentences, he'd slur a word, so that it sounded like an old cassette tape sticking in its player.

But when Summers took questions, his demeanor changed entirely.

His body relaxed, his expression grew animated. As he listened to a questioner, he'd wander so far away from the podium, one could be forgiven for thinking he was simply about to leave the room. He'd absorb the question, ponder it for a few seconds, wander back to the mike, and deliver an answer that sounded like a well-written newspaper editorial. He seemed to know something about everything. Ask Summers questions ranging from presidential politics to the economy of Bolivia, from the nuances of educational policy to the merits of the graduate student dental plan, and he always had an answer, often one that sounded steeped in an expertise most people would have developed only if they had specialized in the subject.

Summers' mind was like a computer, with the memory not only to store vast amounts of information but also to access that information whenever it was needed, lift it, turn it, examine it from myriad angles and manipulate it in unexpected ways. In April 2003, he gave three hour-long lectures on globalization at the Kennedy School over three consecutive nights. Not surprisingly, the pro-globalization arguments he advocated would have prompted disagreement in some quarters. Still, the sheer volume of information he wielded was staggering. Though he brought notes to each lecture, he placed them on the podium and subsequently ignored them. As he usually did, he began with a couple of jokes. "When I left Washington, I did not leave politics," he said.

Over the course of those three hours, Summers spoke concisely, provocatively, and logically, his arguments following crisply from one to another, without digression or hesitation. He did not appear to have memorized the lectures. Rather, it looked as if, while part of Summers' brain was delivering his words, another part was forging ahead, like a scout, considering the path of his argument and making a decision in plenty of time to report back. In three hours of lectures without notes, Summers did not once utter an incomplete sentence.

Being what Washingtonians might call "wonky" wasn't inherently a bad thing at Harvard. Certainly the community could appreciate, even embrace, a geek—Harvard is, after all, an institution that respects intelligence, accomplishment, and power, three things that Summers had in abundance. But the community also hoped that he would have humility, a sense of humor, and some self-awareness about his own nerdiness.

Not likely. Accurately or not, Larry Summers came across as arrogant, patronizing, disrespectful, and power-hungry. And nothing the Corporation or the university flacks had told the community about the new president before his arrival had prepared them for this unfortunate combination of personal qualities. Inevitably, its members wondered how the Corporation could have chosen a man of such a temperament. Did its members not know? Or not care? The former seemed impossible, but the latter was more alarming—because if the Corporation had known what Larry Summers was like and had still chosen him, what did that say about its opinion of the institution it governed?

Doubt began to pervade the campus. Some students and faculty decided that Bob Rubin had simply deceived the Corporation when he assured its members that the rough-and-tumble Larry Summers was a thing of the past. Others who had followed the presidential choice process began to speak wistfully of Lee Bollinger, who had since become the president of Columbia University, and wonder if he would not have been the superior choice. Some students looked enviously at Princeton and Brown, where presidents Shirley Tilghman and Ruth Simmons, the latter the first African American president of an Ivy League school, were leading their campuses with a less combative, more inclusive style.

In the spring of 2002, with the chaos in the Af-Am department ongoing, and a community ill at ease with its new president, Larry Summers' first year was coming to a rocky end. An oncoming controversy over the limits of speech in the post-September 11 world, set against the magisterial backdrop of Harvard's commencement, would make the conclusion of the 2001–2002 school year even more turbulent.

Zayed Yasin, class of 2002, was a model of the modern Harvard student: a bright, thoughtful, motivated young man from an international, multicultural background. His mother was an Irish Catholic nurse from southern California. His father was an engineer, a Muslim from Bangladesh who had immigrated to the United States in 1971 and worked as a designer of power plants. Before college, Yasin had lived in Chicago, southern California—his parents met at UCLA— and Indonesia. But he spent most of his youth in the small town of Scituate, a fishing village turned white-collar suburb about twenty miles southeast of Boston. An international student and a local kid at the same time, Yasin would be the first member of his family to attend Harvard.

Dark-haired, clean-cut, and slender, with a manner that was mature yet earnest, Yasin was always interested in public service. As a boy, he became an Eagle scout. While a high school senior, he won a scholarship from the Navy Reserve Officers Training Corps that would pay for his Harvard tuition in exchange for military service after college. But he turned down the scholarship because, he said, "I didn't want to go to MIT all the time" for training, and he was worried about committing himself to the military until he was in his thirties. Yasin intended to make up the financial difference with help from his parents and aid from Harvard, but the lost ROTC scholarship was a big hit. "We're not poor, but we're not filthy rich," Yasin said.

Like most Harvard students, Yasin was active in extracurricular pursuits. He wanted to be a doctor, and as a freshman he worked as an emergency medical technician. For a while he was president of Harvard-Radcliffe Friends of the American Red Cross, a group that taught first aid and helped in disaster relief. Before his senior year, he worked on a public health program to try to eradicate malaria in Zambia.

But perhaps his most challenging work came during his junior year, when he became president of the Harvard Islamic Society. HIS was a small but growing group on campus, in proportion to the small but growing numbers of Muslim students from South Asia and the Near and Middle East. Yasin hadn't been particularly devout before college, but at Harvard, he started to become more serious about his faith. "The people that I liked the best at Harvard, the people that I respected for the way they lived their lives, were Muslims," Yasin explained. "I really admired the people who did have that moral and religious compass. And I saw the difference between people who did live that way and people who didn't."

The Harvard Islamic Society didn't have the numbers, the money, the alumni, or the tradition that Harvard Hillel did. For evening prayer, HIS members met in the lounge of a classroom building in the Yard. The Jewish cultural and religious organization, by contrast, was housed in the multimillion-dollar Rosovsky Hall. But Yasin did what he could with the resources he had, and one of his priorities was to build bridges between the different religious organizations on campus. During his year as president, he held several inter-faith meetings with

Hillel and initiated a discussion series with Hillel and the Catholic Student Association.

One activity, however, would come back to haunt him: During Yasin's tenure, HIS threw a fundraiser to benefit the Holy Land Foundation for Relief and Development, a U.S.-based Muslim group that raised money for Muslims around the world who needed health care—particularly Muslims in the West Bank and Gaza Strip. From what Yasin knew, HLF was a legitimate, valuable group. Before his junior year, he had spent a summer working for Balkan Sunflowers, a nongovernmental health organization in Albania, which has a largely Muslim population. "I saw the HLF doing good work there," he remembered, delivering health care to the stream of refugees flowing back into Kosovo.

But after the fundraiser, there were news reports that HLF was funneling money to Hamas, the Islamic terrorist organization. (In December 2001, the Bush administration froze HLF's assets for just this reason, although the group vigorously denies the accusation.) So, instead, the Harvard Islamic Society gave the money it had raised, about $900, to Red Crescent, an international relief organization affiliated with the Red Cross. "We wanted to avoid any murkiness," Yasin said.

As president of HIS, Yasin had gotten to know Harry Lewis, the dean of the college, and Rick Hunt, the university marshall who was also head of the faculty committee on religion, a group that set university policy regarding religious issues. Both Lewis and Hunt were impressed with Yasin. They liked his positive attitude and admired how he struggled with the problems of the world at such a young age. And so both administrators encouraged him to try out for one of Harvard's biggest honors: the position of undergraduate commencement orator.

The Harvard commencement ceremonies, which take place in Tercentenary Theatre, are so filled with history and ritual, they're like a performance art piece for scholars. Commencement is divided into two parts. On Wednesday's Class Day, a humorous speaker addresses the undergrads. Recent Class Day speakers have included Conan O'Brien, Al Franken, and actor Will Ferrell. Day two on Thursday sees diplomas conferred upon the cap-and-gowned graduates, not just the college seniors but students from the graduate schools as well. Though it's ostensibly for the graduates, the afternoon of commencement's second day is actually called the "Annual Meeting of the Harvard Alumni

Association." That's because Harvard hosts its reunions at the same time. The idea is to fill returning alums with school spirit, and then—boom!—hit them up for money. Simultaneously, the new graduates transition instantly from tuition-paying students into the ranks of gift-giving alumni.

The second day of commencement is by far the more formal of the two. Before the degrees are officially awarded, the morning ceremony kicks off with the Harvard band playing; a procession of the president and members of the faculty and governing boards filing onto the stage, and an opening address delivered entirely in Latin.

After the morning ceremony, the undergraduates go to their various houses, and the graduate students to their schools, to receive diplomas. And in the afternoon, everyone is supposed to reconvene in Tercentenary Theatre to hear the university's commencement speaker. (It was on this occasion in 1947 that George Marshall outlined his plan to aid postwar Europe.) In June of 2002, that speaker was scheduled to be Robert Rubin; Summers had shown his gratitude to his former boss by asking him to speak at Harvard's commencement. But he had done more than that for Rubin. He had offered Rubin the seat on the Harvard Corporation being vacated by Herbert "Pug" Winokur. (The Enron-affiliated executive had resigned from the Corporation to spare Harvard bad publicity.) With Winokur gone, Larry Summers and Bob Rubin would be a team again.

As part of the Thursday morning rites, every year one undergraduate delivers an address to the assembled crowd. Called the "Senior English Address," it's usually about five minutes long. Being chosen to deliver the undergraduate oration is considered a high honor. On the most public, elaborately choreographed occasion of the university year, one undergraduate is entrusted with the opportunity to stand before the university community and speak his mind. It was this responsibility that Harry Lewis and Rick Hunt wanted Zayed Yasin to compete for. "I had rough ideas," Yasin said. "I wanted to talk about graduation from Harvard in a post-9/11 world. But I didn't think I had a shot. I just figured, why not go for it?"

So Yasin wrote a short essay about the tensions between being Muslim and being American, and how in fact they weren't really tensions at all. How both the Koran and the Constitution promoted peace, justice, and compassion. "As a Muslim, and as an American, I am commanded to stand up for the protection of life and liberty, to serve the poor and the weak, to celebrate the diversity of humankind," he wrote. "There is no contradiction."

Yasin focused on "the constant struggle to do what is right." That, he claimed, was the true meaning of the word *jihad*—a word that had been "corrupted and misinterpreted" by Muslims and non-Muslims alike. In fact, jihad was a universal concept, even an American one. "The American Dream," Yasin wrote, "is a universal dream, and it is more than a set of materialistic aspirations. It is the power and opportunity to shape one's own life; to house and feed a family with security and dignity; and to practice your faith in peace. This is our American Jihad."

The judges were a committee of five: Peter Gomes; Rick Hunt; Nancy Houfek, an acting teacher at Harvard's American Repertory Theatre, a classics professor named Richard Thomas; and the dean of the extension school, Michael Shinagel. Together they had more than a century of Harvard experience, and they took the university's traditions seriously. Competing against about twenty other students, Yasin had to submit a draft of the speech in advance and then make it through three rounds of auditions. But in early May, he got the news that he had been chosen to speak at commencement on June 6. There was really only one concern—his speech didn't have a title. "I was slow on the title bit," Yasin remembered. So Michael Shinagel suggested one that he thought summed up the speech in a concise way: "My American Jihad."

About three weeks later, the *Crimson* ran a short piece on the student commencement speakers. The article listed the title of Yasin's speech. After that, all hell broke loose.

The protest began with some discussion on the house bulletin boards, websites that each undergraduate house uses to disseminate news and events. Each site has a discussion forum, and in the days after the *Crimson* story, several students began posting messages to the bulletin boards in which they questioned the appropriateness of a Muslim student giving a commencement speech called "My American Jihad." They didn't know what the speech said, as it was customary not to disclose the contents of such speeches before they were delivered. But they didn't like the sound of it, and some began to circulate a petition requesting that the Harvard administration let them read the speech before commencement.

On May 29, Patrick Healy, the *Boston Globe* reporter who'd authored the grade inflation articles, wrote a piece on Yasin. Almost instantaneously the media swarm descended. The *New York Times*, the *Washington Post*, all the print heavyweights. "Harvard's Holy War," proclaimed an editorial in the *New York Daily News*. Next followed the TV acronyms: ABC, NBC, CBS, CNN, MSNBC. Many of the stories and articles questioned Yasin's definition of *jihad*. On the *Today* show, Katie Couric said to Yasin, "In fact, Jayed . . . Zayed, the dictionary definition describes jihad as 'a Muslim holy war or spiritual struggles against infidels.'" Couldn't Yasin understand "why some people might be unnerved by the title of your speech?"

"You're using an American dictionary to try to find a definition of an Arabic word," Yasin shot back.

Larry Summers was livid. "The controversy took him by surprise, and he was furious," said one person familiar with his thinking. This was his first commencement as president. He'd invited his closest professional friend, Robert Rubin, to speak. He'd spent much of the year talking about the importance of patriotism and the university's respect for military service. And now all anyone was discussing was a five-minute undergraduate speech that he hadn't even known about. But he was taking heat for it. Summers was receiving hundreds, perhaps thousands of e-mails through his public address, lawrence_summers @harvard.edu. Many of them contained similar language, as if they were part of an organized campaign. Jewish alumni in particular were furious, and some were threatening to withhold donations.

"The speech was obviously an assault," said Ruth Wisse, the Martin Peretz Professor of Yiddish Literature, who is known for her uncompromising pro-Israel views. "Primarily an assault on the Jews, secondarily an assault on America," she said. "You could so obviously see the professoriat thinking, 'Oh, isn't this wonderful? Here we're really going to show our bonafides as multiculturalists by taking the most unpopular minority view of the moment.' But jihad is serious. This was an act of contempt for the sensitivities of Jews and Americans."

Summers was irritated with Yasin, but he was furious with the people who had chosen him. He thought that the members of the commencement committee were just the kind of aging radicals for whom he had no use—classics professor Richard Thomas, for example, was one of Harvard's most liberal faculty members—and Summers blamed the committee for provoking an unnecessary controversy. Rick Hunt, who organized the commencement ceremonies, bore the brunt of Summers' outrage. The president couldn't understand why Hunt could have permitted such apparent insensitivity. Summers felt blindsided. "My guess is, Larry didn't even know there was a committee on commencement," Marty Peretz said. "Why would anyone care?"

Summers cared now. He wanted the university on message, just like the White House would be. Harvard staged a commencement to salute its graduates and advance its fundraising and public relations goals, not to ignite international controversy or celebrate freedom of speech. If he could have, Summers would have replaced Yasin as speaker, but he knew it was too late for that—if he ousted Yasin, he'd only provoke more publicity. To regain control, Summers forbade members of the administration from speaking out about Yasin. "Larry told all his top administrative people not to say anything in support of me," Yasin said.

Privately, Harry Lewis and the members of the committee were appalled. To them, Summers was leaving a Harvard student in the lurch. The president had read the speech; he must have known that its intended message was one of healing and reconciliation. Yet Yasin, a twenty-two-year-old student, one of the best Harvard had to offer, was being ripped to shreds in the press. On MSNBC, Chris Matthews announced that Yasin was a supporter of terrorism who had once thrown a fundraiser for Hamas. People were calling him an anti-Semite. And Summers' official response was to say that no one could speak on his behalf?

"His attitude about Zayed Yasin was just about the most un-American thing any Harvard president had done in years," said one faculty member involved in the controversy. Harry Lewis told colleagues that Summers had personally forbidden him to say anything in support of Yasin. Lewis obeyed that command, but he didn't feel right about it. Later, he would decide that in all his forty years at Harvard, that was the decision he most regretted. "I should have resigned right then," he told one friend.

As commencement approached, Yasin was under mounting pressure. The debate on campus was only getting hotter. Jewish students were particularly upset, and the angriest among them announced that, to protest Yasin, they would hand out twenty thousand red-white-and-blue ribbons at commencement. That way, twenty thousand people could show Yasin that they were patriots and he was not. An e-mail chain letter was urging attendees to stand up and turn their backs on Yasin when he spoke. Another e-mail petition called on Yasin to publicly condemn "all organizations that directly or indirectly support terrorism anywhere in the world," and urged his ouster as commencement speaker. Some five thousand students, faculty, parents, and alumni were reported to have signed the petition.

Someone sent Yasin a death threat in the form of a Blue Mountain Arts e-card. The card showed a cute bunny rabbit pulling itself out of a hat. "It seems that you want to die early by making such a sucked-up speech on jihad," it said. "You can jolly well take you and your pig religion elsewhere. After september 11th—take this as a warning: Your life will be in danger if you choose to go ahead. You should really go back to whichever country you came from. America does not welcome Moslems. Eat pork and die sucker."

It was signed, "One Shot One Kill." The police traced it to a small town in Colorado, but couldn't identify the sender.

Another e-mail mentioned that "your University allowed Muslim groups to hold fund-raisers on your campus . . . linked to the support of terrorists. At the same time you do not allow ARMY ROTC classes on campus because you do not like their 'don't ask don't tell' policy toward homosexuals. Sounds like your University is out of touch with the zeitgeist of America. Get with it. You are either fer' us or agin' us."

Yasin, who was thin to start with, was losing weight. He wasn't sleeping. He kept misplacing his commencement cap and gown. His brother Tariq, a Harvard sophomore, had to keep finding them for him. The members of the committee told him that Summers was convinced that he planned to hijack commencement—that on that special and important day, Yasin was going to walk up to the podium in front of tens of thousands of listeners, throw away his speech, and deliver some fire-breathing pro-Palestinian, anti-American screed. That pissed Yasin off—he'd worked hard on his speech; he wasn't about to just discard what he'd written—but it also demoralized him a little. He'd never intended to provoke such bitter words.

So he compromised. He changed his title from "My American Jihad" to "Of Faith and Citizenship: My American Jihad." "I was naïve," Yasin said. "There was more than I realized when we came up with the title—it was a little incendiary. At the same time, I couldn't just get rid of the word *jihad*, because that would have been backing down too much." In a sense, though, the word was removed for him; the Harvard commencement program and every official Harvard publication would simply delete the subtitle.

On May 29, about a week before commencement, Summers released a statement about the controversy. It read as follows:

> Concerns have been raised about the planned commencement speech of Zayed Yasin, who was chosen as one of this June's student Commencement speakers by a duly appointed faculty committee. We live in times when, understandably, many people at Harvard and beyond are deeply apprehensive about events in the Middle East and possible reverberations in American life. Yet, especially in a university setting, it is important for people to keep open minds, listen carefully to one another and react to the totality of what each speaker has to say. I am pleased that there have been a number of constructive conversations that have addressed potential divisions in our community associated with his speech.
>
> Finally, I am told that Mr. Yasin recently received a threatening e-mail from an unidentified source. Direct personal threats are reprehensible and all of us who believe in the values of this university should condemn them in the strongest terms.

To Yasin's supporters, Summers' statement was far from a vigorous defense of the values of tolerance and civil discourse in a university setting—not to mention of a student who'd done nothing wrong. "It was basically like saying, 'It would be good if you don't kill Zayed Yasin,'" said one faculty member. The first paragraph felt like an expression of sympathy toward those who were angry. And that line about Yasin being "chosen . . . by a duly appointed faculty committee" was clearly Summers' way of distancing himself from the brouhaha.

"The statement was weak," Yasin said. "Especially when you consider that he's not the kind of guy to mince words. There was no reference in it to me, or to the content of the speech. There was only reference to 'constructive conversation,' when there was no constructive conversation going on." In fact, Summers hadn't even called Yasin. Throughout the entire controversy, the university president never said a word to the beleaguered undergraduate commencement speaker.

On June 5, the day before commencement, Summers gave a short address at the ROTC commissioning ceremony for Harvard students. "You know," he said, "we venerate at this university—as we should— openness, debate, the free expression of ideas, as central to what we are all about and what we should be. But we must also respect and admire moral clarity when it is required. . . ." Those words, too, seemed to indicate where Summers' sympathies lay.

The morning of June 6 dawned cold and gray, but there were still some thirty thousand people on hand for commencement. The ceremonies had traditionally begun with Harvard-themed music from the university's history. On this day, at Summers' instigation, "The Star Spangled Banner" would be played. "That is as it should be," Summers had told the ROTC cadets, adding that it was always "a thrill" for him to hear the national anthem.

Security was tight. For the first time ever, visitors had to pass through metal detectors to get into the Yard. For Zayed Yasin, security was even tighter. He spent the morning shadowed by an officer from the Harvard University Police Department, just in case any of those threats were real. And when the time came for him to deliver his speech, he was so nervous his legs were shaking underneath his gown. But he was a little angry, too. Looking out over the crowd, he could see the protesters wearing their red-white-and-blue ribbons. In anticipation of that, he'd donned a red-white-and-blue ribbon of his own. No one was going to take his patriotism away from him. He remembered that Summers thought he was going to throw away his speech—the suggestion still insulted him. The whole experience, he said later, "pulled some of the veneer of civilization off of Harvard. I saw how thin that veneer was—and underneath it was raw power politics."

By commencement tradition, just before the undergraduate orator gives his speech, he turns to the university president and bows. With Summers' suspicion in mind, Yasin improvised a little. Just as he turned toward the president and began his bow, he gave Summers a quick but clearly visible wink. As if to say, I know what you think I'm going to do . . . and probably I won't. But maybe I will. Seated in the president's chair, Summers did not appear to react.

Yasin didn't ad lib, of course. Giving his speech as he'd written it had become a point of pride to him. "Harvard graduates have a responsibility to leave their mark on the world," he said, trying to make himself heard over the pelting rain that had begun to fall. "So let us struggle, and let us make our mark. And I hope and pray that our children, our grandchildren, and those who take our seats in the years to come, will have cause to be proud."

It was hard to tell because of all the umbrellas that popped up, but when the speech was done, a large part of the crowd appeared to be giving Zayed Yasin a standing ovation.

Summers, however, was neither impressed nor amused. Several times at dinners and cocktail parties in the days and weeks following commencement, he would relate the story of Yasin and the wink. When he did, according to people who heard his account, Summers referred to Yasin as "the little shit."

In his second year as president, Summers would make sure that such unfortunate incidents would not be repeated.

Harvard Law School dean Derek Bok became president in 1971 and inherited an angry and divided campus.

Twenty-year-old Lawrence Summers in his 1975 yearbook photo from MIT, where he was captain of the debate team.

(Nicola Kountoupes/Cornell University Photography)

As Harvard president from 1991 to 2001, Neil Rudenstine raised
$2.6 billion but was criticized for devoting too much time to fundraising.

(Republished with permission of Globe Newspaper Company, Inc.)

Henry Louis Gates Jr.
and Cornel West
were part
of Rudenstine's
"dream team" of
African American
scholars but were
resented by some
members of the
Harvard faculty.

Treasury Secretary Lawrence Summers in front of dollar bills bearing his signature. At Harvard, Summers would autograph bills for eager students.

"A new kind of geopolitician": Summers in the White House briefing room with Clinton economic advisers Gene Sperling (*center*) and Jack Lew in July 1999.

Now president of Columbia University, Lee Bollinger was said to be the faculty's favorite to be Harvard's twenty-seventh president.

(Courtesy of Columbia University)

"I accept!" Lawrence Summers at a March 11, 2001, press conference at Harvard's Loeb House to announce his selection as president.

(AP Photo/Lawrence Jackson)

Lawrence Summers with U2 singer Bono at a Harvard dinner in June 2001. The two men had met to discuss the issue of international debt relief while Summers was at the Treasury Department.

Cornel West with freshmen at Princeton University in the fall of 2002. After leaving Harvard due to an altercation with Summers, West taught a Princeton seminar called "The Tragic, the Comic, and the Political."

Harry Lewis, the dean of Harvard College until March 2003, clashed with Summers over the college's direction—and lost.

(Justin Haan/Harvard Crimson)

Memorial Church pastor Peter Gomes, here speaking at the Boston State House in February 2004, worried that Harvard's new president didn't appreciate the importance of spiritual life on campus.

(Jim Bourg/Reuters/Corbis)

(Brian M. Haas/*Harvard Crimson*)

Faculty of Arts and Sciences dean Bill Kirby, here in his University Hall office, was charged with leading Harvard's curricular review, but some wondered if Summers wasn't really calling the shots.

Mathematician Benedict Gross replaced Harry Lewis as dean of Harvard College in a spring 2003 shake-up and soon reported feeling "overwhelmed."

(David E. Stein/*Harvard Crimson*)

Timothy Patrick McCarthy, co-teacher of "American Protest Literature, from Tom Paine to Tupac," speaking at a rally against the war in Iraq on March 20, 2003.

(Courtesy of Timothy Patrick McCarthy)

(David E. Stein/Harvard Crimson)

William Kirby, Lawrence Summers, and Benedict Gross sing "Fair Harvard" at the freshman opening exercises in September 2003.

(Courtesy of Brian Palmer)

Lecturer Brian Palmer, shown here teaching in the spring of 2004, thought that Summers was making Harvard more competitive and materialistic.

Lawrence Summers celebrating his third commencement as president of Harvard on June 10, 2004.

(AP Photos)

6

Larry Summers and the Bully Pulpit

At the beginning of Larry Summers' second year, Harvard was in a state of upheaval. Summers was shaking up the status quo, but few could tell whether the change was for the better, might make things worse, or was simply change for its own sake, so that the president could claim its existence as an accomplishment in and of itself. Intentionally or not—and people argued it both ways—everything Summers did divided the university. Mostly, the divide was Larry Summers and the Harvard Corporation against everyone else. And the Corporation was aloof, invisible, which left Summers as the source of division.

Dressing down Cornel West was a good example, but hardly the only one. Calling for the return of ROTC and a renewed patriotism had also split the faculty and students. First, Summers seemed not to care that the military discriminated against gays. He generally did not mention the issue when talking about ROTC, though this, more than any Vietnam-era hangover, was now the main reason why Harvard did not want military recruiters on campus. His emphasis on patriotism also struck many faculty as anti-intellectual. Harvard's mission was to search for truth, regardless of whether that truth was considered patriotic by newspaper columnists and Washington politicians. Importing the leadership style and perks of a D.C. powerbroker further irritated a culture that prioritized the university over its president. Even Summers' lamentable manners and aggressive conversational style had people splitting into camps. His supporters argued that such behavior reflected refreshing candor; what you saw was what you got. Critics responded that Summers' manifest lack of respect for underlings was simply an arrogant man's way to bully and manipulate.

These debates were not easily resolved because, in part, Summers' tangible accomplishments were still few. He spoke frequently about the importance of the new campus in Allston, but there were as yet no major public developments on that front, just behind-the-scenes planning. Nor had the much-hyped curricular review taken form. The faculty, not Summers, had attempted to curb the problem of grade inflation by adopting a curb on honors effective with the class of 2005. (Under the policy, only 50 percent of any given class could be awarded honors.) And while Summers' rhetoric about ROTC had made national headlines, the president hadn't actually done anything to bring ROTC back on campus. Doing so would have required a vote of the faculty, which appeared to take the anti-gay discrimination issue more seriously than Summers did, and Summers didn't want to stake political capital on a vote he would probably have lost. Instead he spoke at the ROTC graduation ceremonies and persuaded the editors of the *Harvard Yearbook* to allow seniors to list ROTC in their blurbs of activities. (In the past, students could list only university-sanctioned activities.)

Of course, it was to be expected that a new president would spend his first year learning about the university, and Summers had certainly done that. Even his fiercest critics gave him credit for immersing himself in the details of Harvard life, getting up to speed on the operations of the graduate schools, reaching out to undergraduates, and keeping a daunting schedule. Summers even found time to travel to China, Japan, and London, trips that promoted Harvard's global presence while boosting Summers' own international profile.

The president was also making progress on another crucial front: filling the university's high-level academic positions with his own people. In October 2001, Summers had named as provost Steven Hyman, a former Harvard professor of psychiatry and the well-respected director of the National Institute of Mental Health. Generally described as a university's chief academic officer, the provost is roughly comparable to the role of the United States vice-president, which is to say, poorly defined but potentially powerful depending on how much responsibility the president delegates: Hyman quipped that his job was "to do whatever Larry doesn't want to." By appointing Hyman, Summers signaled his determination to emphasize the sciences, and particularly the life sciences such as biology, neurobiology, and biochemistry. He was convinced that Harvard had missed out on the high-tech gold rush of the nineties that had helped enrich Stanford. Biomedicine, Summers often said, would be the next scientific frontier to combine research, life-saving discoveries, and profit, and this time Harvard would not miss the opportunity.

The Hyman appointment also compensated for the loss of another influential scientist, Faculty of Arts and Sciences Dean and chemist Jeremy Knowles, from Summers' administration. In May of 2002, Knowles had stepped down from the deanship, telling colleagues that one year into the new presidency was an appropriate time for him to go. Summers replaced Knowles with William Kirby, a historian of China who had also served as chairman of the history department. With Kirby, Summers showed his zeal for focusing the university on the world beyond the United States. "History teaches us that the relationship between great powers shapes eras, and the relationship between the United States and China will shape this next era," Summers said before appointing Kirby. Plus, Kirby had long advocated study abroad, another of Summers' globalization-related priorities.

Still, there were those who thought that Summers might have had another reason for choosing Kirby—because Summers considered him malleable.

Traditionally, the FAS dean is a locus of enormous power, a figure who can set his own agenda and parry a president's attempts to encroach upon his authority. The dean's primary responsibility is to serve as the faculty's intellectual leader. Regardless of his own academic specialty, he is expected to promote the academic values and interests of the seven hundred or so scholars over whom he presides. In order to do that, the dean must have the intellectual respect of his colleagues on the faculty. After all, he leads perhaps the greatest body of scholars in the world.

The FAS dean wields powerful tools. For one thing, he has money—more money than the president has. FAS owns by far the largest share of the Harvard endowment, about 40 percent of the current $23 billion total—the numbers fluctuate—and its dean draws up the FAS budget, which is approaching $1 billion a year. From his office in University Hall, the dean doles out space to faculty and departments, approves salary increases, helps find jobs for faculty spouses—or does not. He has veto power over all tenure recommendations, and virtually nothing can be more damaging to an academic's career than to have his nomination rejected before it even gets to the Harvard president—that's a clear sign that he might want to consider another career.

The dean's donor pool, the alumni of Harvard College, is both loyal and, on the whole, rich. And fundraising has benefits other than cash: an adept dean can build a constituency with alumni who are more devoted to the university than are those of any other Harvard school. Harvard College alumni can have an enormous impact on internal university disputes, whether by giving money for targeted purposes or by threatening to withhold it.

The FAS dean under Larry Summers would, in theory, possess one more critical power: the mandate to shape a new curriculum for the college. Revising its undergraduate curriculum is an act of self-examination Harvard performs about every twenty-five years, and it means that, academically speaking, everything is up for grabs. What courses would be required, and which diminished in importance? Would professors have to teach more or less frequently, and how would that affect their research? What kind of teaching would be most valued—the ability to deliver a spellbinding lecture to hundreds of students, or the knack for leading a small, intellectually intense seminar?

The structure, priorities, and requirements of a new curriculum affect the status of every Harvard College professor, leading to greater or lesser intellectual influence, prestige, and earning power. And as the leader of the faculty, the FAS dean is the traditional head of a curricular review. He guides a process that affects the futures of every single member of his faculty. They can make his job extremely difficult, either by opposing his agenda at faculty meetings and other forums, or simply by refusing to buy into it. Faculty lethargy can be as devastating to a dean as faculty opposition.

During a curricular review, a dean has two other advantages. First, he—for Harvard has never had a female FAS dean—can use the review to promote himself in the media, which inevitably pays attention to a revamping of the Harvard curriculum. Those advertisements for himself are helpful if the dean has higher academic ambitions. In addition, the dean can exploit the curricular review as a fundraising vehicle, meeting with alums to discuss his new priorities—more faculty, innovative new programs, that sort of thing—and solicit their support. The one pitch guaranteed to make Harvard alumni pull out their checkbooks is the argument that the university needs money to improve undergraduate education. Everyone wants the Harvard that their children will attend to be even better than the one they went to.

Two of Kirby's recent predecessors proved how important the dean's role was. Erudite, worldly Henry Rosovsky, dean from 1973 to 1984, and again for a year in 1990 and 1991, was immensely popular with the faculty, whose prerogatives he protected and whose shortcomings he addressed with tact and discretion. Rosovsky's close bond with Derek Bok also helped. He rarely challenged Bok because the two men rarely disagreed. The patrician Bok was secure, even ambivalent, about power; he was not averse to sharing it. Emerging from the 1960s, Bok knew that any perception that he monopolized authority could invite resentment and opposition.

British, highly intelligent, and charming, Jeremy Knowles, dean during the Rudenstine years, was considered a shrewd practitioner of academic politics. After Neil Rudenstine's breakdown, he did little to challenge the authority of his deans, and everyone knew it. So Knowles benefited from the perception of power, which helped make the autonomy he did have even more tangible. Knowles had a reputation for telling people what they wanted to hear, and he was not entirely trusted. But he could and did stand up to Rudenstine when he felt the president was encroaching on his and the faculty's authority. "He was a fierce defender of the faculty's independence," said one of Knowles' colleagues. Further strengthening his position, Knowles also had a healthy relationship with the Harvard Corporation. Fellow James Richardson Houghton, former chief executive of Corning Incorporated, was so impressed with Knowles that when Knowles resigned as dean, Houghton appointed him to Corning's board of directors.

About Bill Kirby, though, there was concern.

A boyish-looking man with square glasses and salt-and-pepper hair cropped almost crewcut short, Kirby looks like a G-man from the 1950s. His humor sometimes feels similarly dated. When speaking to alumni, he likes to joke that when he was an undergrad at Dartmouth, his "idea of study abroad was a weekend at Wellesley College." Visiting that all-female school not far from Cambridge, Kirby sometimes adds, "I could date girls who dated Harvard men."

Soon enough, Kirby would become a Harvard man himself, enrolling in graduate study of history in Cambridge. After earning his Ph.D. in 1981, he spent eleven years teaching at Washington University in St. Louis before Harvard brought him back in 1992. Students considered him a committed and enthusiastic teacher, and as chair of the history department from 1995 to 2000 Kirby was widely credited with rebuilding a department that had fallen into deep decline due to bitter internal feuding.

Some of his peers, however, thought that Kirby was perhaps too anxious for advancement within Harvard's ranks. He happily performed all the thankless tasks that signal a professor's desire to become a dean, such as chairing the search for a Harvard librarian and serving on the board of the Harvard University Press. Such activities inevitably take time away from scholarship, and to Kirby's colleagues, they gave off an unmistakable whiff of ambition—not intellectual ambition, which was certainly commonplace among Harvard professors, but rather a lust for administrative power. Larry Summers would have recognized that scent. He would also have known how useful it might be to choose a dean who longed for the job—who might accept impositions, burdens, even degradations that other, less aspiring candidates would not tolerate.

Many of Knowles' colleagues believed that he resigned because he saw which way the wind was blowing. Larry Summers, some said, had more respect for those who chose not to work for him than for those who did. Certainly by the end of Summers' first year, the signs of his intention to micromanage undergraduate education and diminish the dean's authority—the Cornel West matter being the most blatant among them—were hard to miss. Bill Kirby either disagreed, or did not detect those warnings, or simply chose to disregard them.

The appointment of a new provost and dean were not the only personnel matters that required Summers' attention. As his second year in office began, he wanted to make sure that one faculty member did not leave and that one administrator did.

In late June, Summers met with Skip Gates to discuss Gates' future. The chair of the Af-Am department had publicly vacillated on the question of whether he would remain at Harvard. Already he missed West and Anthony Appiah. He wasn't sure whether Summers even wanted him to stay. So at their meeting, according to people who were told about it, Gates asked Summers for financial support for some small department projects. Under Rudenstine, such requests would have been quickly granted. Much to Gates' surprise, however, Summers turned him down. For Gates, that refusal meant only one thing: Summers did not care whether he stayed, and perhaps even wanted him to leave, to clean the slate.

Skip Gates enjoys the fruits of his labors: the posh offices, celebrity friends, substantial salary and frequent travel to exotic places. He enjoys French wines, Italian suits, and German luxury cars. But his needs are not all material. Perhaps more important, Gates needs to feel wanted, valued, and needed. As high as he has risen in his field, he still loves to be courted; it's one reason why he's changed jobs numerous times. Larry Summers, however, is a man who does not like to admit— not to himself, not to the person in question—that he needs anyone. Skip Gates wanted to be wooed by a man who found the process of courtship self-abasing.

So, when he realized that Summers was not prepared to give him what he wanted, Gates readied himself to say good-bye to Harvard. Envisioning a move to Princeton or perhaps the up-and-coming New York University, he began house-hunting in Harlem. If Gates had to go, he wanted to relocate to a crucible of intellectual, corporate, and media life—which was, after all, exactly what he was in microcosm. He'd also been thinking more and more about the responsibility of educated, successful blacks to serve as role models to less fortunate African Americans, to re-immerse themselves in the black community. Buying real estate in Harlem would transform an idea that was increasingly important to him into physical reality.

In July, Gates was relaxing at his summer house in Oak Bluffs, a small, affluent African American community on the island of Martha's Vineyard, when he received a phone call from his summer neighbor, Vernon Jordan. Gates and Jordan, the Washington lawyer who had served as chairman of Bill Clinton's presidential transition team in 1992, had known each other for years. As two of the most prominent black men in the United States—men who between them knew just about everyone in the stratospheres of American intelligentsia, business, and politics—that was inevitable.

Jordan wasn't calling to talk about the summer weather. He'd been asked to make the call by Bob Rubin, who was acting with the knowledge of, and possibly at the request of, Larry Summers. Jordan wanted to know how Gates was feeling about Harvard. Would he stay or would he go?

Gates told him he was leaving. Summers didn't want him, he said. The president wasn't supporting the department, and he certainly wasn't making an effort to woo Gates.

Thinking about leaving sounded understandable, Jordan said, but maybe he shouldn't go. He needed to be careful about looking greedy. Any perception that Gates wanted to start a bidding war between Harvard and Princeton might damage his reputation. He did not want to be seen as mercenary.

Gates didn't think he would change his mind, but he agreed to think it over. Sure, he wanted more money. Given what Summers was putting him through, he thought he deserved it. But he certainly didn't want it to look like his motivation was pecuniary. Gates was genuinely angry about losing two colleagues who also happened to be his best friends. It had taken him ten years to put together that collection of scholars, and it seemed as though Summers was hell-bent on dismantling it.

About forty-eight hours later, Jordan called back with news: Summers wanted to talk to Gates. Badly enough that he was willing to come to the Vineyard to do it. Gates could hardly say no.

So, one morning in early August, Summers boarded a Cessna operated by Cape Air, a small airline that flies from Boston to Martha's Vineyard. Gates picked him up at the airport, and for the next three to four hours, the two men had an intense and emotional meeting at Gates' house. Summers said that Gates had the wrong impression, that Summers very much wanted him to stay. Referring to Summers' meeting with West, Gates told Summers that in forty-five minutes he had tried to destroy what Gates had spent over a decade building.

Both men had grievances. Summers had heard through the grapevine that Gates had repeatedly called him "an asshole," and he asked him to stop—Gates' words carried weight around Harvard, and his unflattering comments were making Summers' job more difficult. Gates responded that *asshole* wasn't a word he would use. He would have called Summers a "motherfucker," and, yes, he probably had. So what? Summers had played a part in Gates' two best friends leaving

Harvard. He should have expected to be called some names. Gates was surprised that Summers was so thin-skinned.

Besides, Gates had his own reason to be annoyed at Summers. He believed that someone in Mass Hall had leaked to the *New York Times* a document about a job offer he'd received from Princeton. Because the document had contained a specific salary number, the leak appeared intended to make it look that Gates' talk about the damage done to Cornel West was merely a smoke screen for asking for more money. Although Gates suspected that Summers had been spinning reporters with background information, he didn't think Summers was the leaker—the president was too smart to be directly involved in such an act. But Gates also believed that whoever had leaked the document wouldn't have done so without Summers' consent.

Each man, however, knew that he needed the other. While Harvard could recover from the departure of Cornel West, losing Skip Gates would have caused Summers long-term damage; the establishment media embraced Gates in a way that it did not West. For his part, Gates knew that Harvard was still the academic world's greatest bully pulpit, and if he left now, the department he had worked so hard to build would slide downward. The conversation ended around noon in a mutual understanding: depending on the successful outcome of future negotiations, Gates would stay.

Neither man would speak of their agreement for months, and neither ever spoke of the specifics publicly. But signs of their rapprochement were evident in early November, when Gates held his annual party at his elegant home on Francis Street. After most of the guests had arrived, he announced that Summers would be attending. Several people booed. "Gates held up his hands and said, 'No, no, we need to work with this guy; he's making an effort,'" said one guest. Soon after, Summers arrived—"without a tie and with his shirt untucked," another partygoer noted. Gates escorted Summers around the party, introducing him to people, and Summers did, indeed, seem to be making an effort. More than one guest gave him credit for venturing into what he must have known would be an extremely hostile environment.

They gave Summers that credit in part because, as far as anyone knew, Gates had still not made up his mind. In hosting Summers at his party, Gates could simply have been paving the way for a graceful exit from Harvard. The students had started a petition drive urging him to stay, and the *Crimson* published an editorial in the form of a letter to him. "The *Crimson* staff hope that you stay at Harvard," it said. "Our community would be much poorer without you."

Before the school year began, there was one other notable personnel development. Richard Hunt, the university marshal, announced his retirement in the middle of August. "I did it a little bit quickly, but I've been thinking about retirement for some time," Hunt told the *Crimson*. His departure meant the loss of a repository of institutional memory and Harvard tradition. Hunt had been at Harvard since 1956, earning his Ph.D. there in 1960, and working and teaching at the university for the next four decades. He had known or met every Harvard president since James Conant, and he was co-writing a encyclopedia-like book called *Harvard A to Z*.

Most campus observers saw Hunt's departure as a direct consequence of Summers' anger over the Zayed Yasin affair. The president didn't fire Hunt, but he made his job so unpleasant that the university marshal had no desire to stay. "He just wanted to stand up for the values of freedom of speech and open expression that he believed the university stands for," Zayed Yasin said. But Hunt was not a young man. He had been thinking about retirement anyway, and he lacked the will to fight the new president.

His departure would never make national news; Hunt was not important enough for such recognition. He was the type who knows he will never be a celebrity academic or a pathbreaking scholar, and perhaps because of his self-awareness, he appreciates the genius of the university all the more, and devotes himself to the institution. Every great university has and needs such figures. Though they are easily overlooked and often underappreciated, they provide continuity, humanity, and a stability in which greater minds can do their work and win their glory.

To many Harvardians, Hunt's retirement meant a loss not just of a colleague, but increasingly, of a sense of decorum and dignity on campus. "Rick represented a strain of graciousness and humanity that was important to the university," said a Harvard professor who is friendly with Hunt. "He was deeply, deeply wounded by what happened during the Yasin affair."

Supporters of Larry Summers were not sorry to see Hunt go; his exit marked a new era, one in which people fell into line behind the president or got out of the way. For Ruth Wisse, the professor of Yiddish literature, Hunt's defense of Zayed Yasin represented political correctness and moral relativism, and Summers was right not to have tolerated it. "The marshal was summarily gotten rid of," she said, "and everyone understands that that was cause and effect."

In an official statement, Summers said, "Rick has served Harvard with a combination of grace and sophistication that will be hard to replace." He announced that Harvard would immediately start a search to find that replacement. But Summers would not fill the position for sixteen months, by which point it was clear that subsequent commencement orators would have to meet with the president's approval. With the possible exception of the Harvard-Yale football game, commencement was the university's largest public event, and now Summers picked the commencement speaker, monitored the student speeches, and mandated changes in the ritual. Summers was turning commencement into a bully pulpit for himself.

Meanwhile, in the heated political climate of post-9/11 America, a new college cause had flickered into life: the idea that universities should divest from Israel. On campuses such as Yale, Princeton, and Columbia, the organizers of these fledgling divestment movements argued that Israel's treatment of Palestinians constituted gross violations of human rights. While numerous governments violate the human rights of people under their domain, Israel, they said, is a special case. Because the United States has such a close relationship with Israel, and because it sends Israel billions of dollars a year in aid, that country "is practically the fifty-first state," explained J. Lorand Matory, a Harvard professor of anthropology who supported the divestment movement. "We have to criticize them more because they're us."

The professors and students who felt this way argued that, as was said of South Africa in the 1980s, universities could play a constructive role by pulling their money out of Israel, making a moral statement by the act of disassociation. If the trend caught on and actually inflicted economic damage to the country, fine—that might pressure Israel to change its policies regarding the Palestinians. But even if it didn't, at least the universities that divested could claim that they had done their part in fighting a political evil.

In Cambridge, the divestment movement—more a flutter than a

movement, really—began in the spring of 2002 with a website, www.HarvardMITdivest.org, and an online petition launched by a handful of professors from Harvard and MIT. The petition called for divestment and said, "As members of the MIT and Harvard University communities, we believe that our universities ought to use their influence—political and financial—to encourage the United States government and government of Israel to respect the human rights of the Palestinians."

The divestment drive did not exactly take Cambridge by storm. By June, some five hundred people had signed the petition, including about a hundred faculty members from the two universities. Many of the signatories were of Middle Eastern and South Asian descent and/or Muslim, but a significant number of Jews signed as well. Still, the push to divest had little chance of reaching a critical mass. A counter-petition opposing divestment was signed by about ten times as many people, including more than four hundred Harvard faculty members. The onset of summer vacation diminished any momentum the divestment petition might have had.

Weak though it was, the push to divest concerned Larry Summers. He worried that it was part of a surge in anti-Israeli sentiment that was circling the globe, and wanted to make sure that neither he nor Harvard had anything to do with it. In late August, he called Kennedy School professor Michael Ignatieff, the director of the Carr Center for Human Rights, to do a background check on Mary Robinson, the former president of Ireland and former United Nations High Commissioner for Human Rights. Summers was slated to introduce Robinson at a Kennedy School event in September. But in September 2001, Robinson had headed the United Nations World Conference against Racism in Durban, South Africa, an event widely seen to have been overwhelmed by campaigns to denounce Zionism as racism. Summers wanted to know whether Robinson was complicit in the conference's anti-Semitic elements.

"Summers asked me if Robinson was associated with the 'Zionism is racism' resolutions at the Durban conference that she organized, because if so he didn't really want to have much to do with her," Ignatieff said. "I said she wasn't, but I thought that was appropriate for the president to ask." Summers did introduce Robinson.

Summers had never felt particularly anxious about anti-Semitism before, nor had he ever had a podium from which it was appropriate to speak on the subject. But he felt intellectually and morally engaged by September 11 and its aftermath. It frustrated him not to be in Washington at such an important moment in history. Anti-Semitism, he thought, was not just something taking place overseas. You could find it even at Harvard.

He may also have been thinking about the issue because he had a new girlfriend who was deeply engaged with her Jewish heritage. Pretty and warm, with curly black hair and a quick, slightly nervous smile, Elisa New (known as Lisa) had been dating Summers for a little under a year. A professor of English and American literature, New was very much a product of post–World War II, Jewish-American culture. As a child in Washington, D.C., she had attended Hebrew school, and later described herself as "one of those tormented Jewish girls . . . that loves the tradition but hates the rules." She attended college at Brandeis University, which bills itself as "the only non-sectarian Jewish-sponsored college or university in the country." Graduating in 1980, New earned her doctorate at Columbia in 1988 and taught at the University of Pennsylvania for ten years before coming to Harvard in 1999. She was a potent mix of sensuality and rigor. Describing her approach to poetry, the *Harvard Gazette* called her "a rule-breaker . . . who reveres the idea of discipline," but "also a seeker of pleasure." New could come across as absent-minded, sometimes breathy. When she spoke of poems, she often struck a rapturous tone, as if she were reciting them by herself on a mountain top. But she was tougher than she looked, highly opinionated on academic matters, and very much interested in the operation of the university. Though some on campus saw only differences between her and Summers, the two had more in common than was immediately visible.

Dating a member of the faculty would later create problems for Summers, but Harvard certainly considered New a more appropriate presidential partner than Laura Ingraham. She was an intellectual, not a partisan flamethrower. Like Summers, New was divorced, with children—he had twin girls and a boy; she had three daughters. In her mid-forties, she was closer to Summers' age of forty-eight. It was unlikely that Elisa New would pose in a leopard-print miniskirt on the cover of a national magazine. She preferred long, flowing dresses.

But if they were at a similar point in their personal lives, Summers and New were very different when it came to ethnicity. Judaism had never constituted a large part of Summers' self-consciousness, and not just because he fell asleep in temple. When, for example, one Jewish student asked him if he had ever turned to the Torah for help in making important decisions, Summers looked startled by the question, as if the idea had never occurred to him, and he answered with an emphatic no. Though steeped in two professional environments that were heavily influenced by Jews—economics and academia—Summers was little interested in exploring that side of his identity. The language of faith was foreign to him; he preached the secular religion of economics.

Judaism, however, was a central theme of Elisa New's life. When she and Summers met, she was working on a book about Jewish immigration from Eastern Europe to American port cities that was partly inspired by the history of her own family. One of New's great-grandfathers had run for Congress as a Socialist in 1914. She had always thought he was from Austria, until one day she discovered a cane that had belonged to him. On it were carved the names of several different towns in Lithuania, none of which were the places he was supposed to have come from. The revelation startled New into reconsidering her family's origins.

Whether New influenced Summers' thinking on the question of anti-Semitism is unclear, because neither of them will discuss their relationship. But as the 2002 school year began, Summers decided to address what he saw as a growing problem. He would speak out against anti-Semitism, both at home and abroad, from the pulpit of Memorial Church. Barely two weeks into his second year as president, his words would spark another controversy, one that illustrated what a massive audience a Harvard president could command when he chose to address issues of public importance. Especially when his own evolving ethnic awareness was at the heart of the matter.

Over the course of the twentieth century, as the number of Jews attending Harvard grew, the university compiled a distinctly uneven history of tolerance and acceptance. To put it another way, Harvard first tolerated Jews, then discriminated against them, and finally welcomed them—until Jews were clearly such a vital and powerful influence upon the university that discriminating against them was not only morally intolerable, but, as a practical matter, impossible.

The first Jews to attend Harvard in large numbers arrived during the presidency of Charles W. Eliot, in the latter half of the nineteenth century and the first decade of the twentieth. As evidenced by his abolition of required courses, Eliot had a broad and open mind and little patience for restrictions, whether intellectual or social. Jewish students, primarily the sons of Germans overseas or immigrants living in the Boston area, found Eliot's Harvard a surprisingly welcoming place. By the end of his presidency, Jews constituted about 20 percent of Harvard College students, a remarkable number for the time.

Eliot's successor, Abbott Lawrence Lowell, was not so open-minded. A wealthy Bostonian from a socially prominent family, Lowell did not much approve of Jews—nor of blacks, Catholics, and other non-Brahmins. He considered Jews shiftless, plebeian, and amoral, and was convinced that Jewish students lacked the honor he ascribed to his own caste. But he was perhaps most concerned about Jews because they seemed so adept at earning their way into Harvard. "An educational institution that admits an unlimited number of Jews will soon have room for no one else," Lowell warned.

In 1922, Lowell proposed a quota that would limit Jews to 12 percent of the student body. Wary of a formal policy, the faculty nixed the quota but established a special committee to consider how to restrict Jews without actually coming out and saying so. By 1930 the number of freshmen who identified themselves as Jewish had dropped to 10 percent, from 25 percent in 1924—although part of that drop was probably due to students' being increasingly leery, given the mood on campus and geopolitical events of the time, about identifying themselves as Jewish.

James Bryant Conant, who took office in 1933, was better, but barely. An early supporter of quotas, Conant was the type who wouldn't make anti-Semitic remarks but didn't object when others did. Throughout the 1930s and into World War II, he offered little help to refugee Jewish scholars and students. During his presidency, house masters instituted a policy of placing an asterisk next to the names of Jewish students. That way, Jews could be tracked, to ensure that no one house master would have to endure too many of them under his roof.

At the same time, Conant passionately believed that Harvard needed to move away from its history as a school for posh young men from New England prep schools and become a meritocracy. So, while he didn't exactly proffer a helping hand, Conant decided that those Jews who qualified to be at Harvard ought to be welcomed. And in the aftermath of the war, as the horrors of the Holocaust became known, the idea of restricting Jews became unpalatable. Moreover, any university that wished to retain or improve its competitive position, as Harvard certainly did, had to recognize the wealth of brilliant minds among the exodus of Jews from Europe. Harvard hired Jewish professors not so much because it was the right thing to do, but to prevent rival universities from snapping them up.

By the 1950s, concern over what one university official once termed "the snowballing New York contingent" had virtually disappeared. Anti-Semitism at Harvard remained only in lingering pockets and occasional outbursts. One was the 1948 tenure battle involving Larry Summers' uncle, Paul Samuelson. Another involved Memorial Church. The Congregational church had been used for Christian weddings since 1932, but in 1953, Willard Sperry, the chairman of the board of ministers that ran the church, prevented a Jewish couple from getting married there. The prohibition against Jewish weddings continued for five years, until 1958, when the *Crimson* editorialized against it. Then-president Nathan Marsh Pusey supported the ban, but backed down in the face of opposition from the Corporation.

In the decades following, fights over the status of women, blacks, and gays became far more common than battles over anti-Semitism. After the 1960s, as the WASP establishment fell out of fashion and into decline, Jews became probably the most powerful ethnic bloc at Harvard. So far had the question of anti-Semitism receded from sight that when Larry Summers became Harvard's first Jewish president, the event was barely remarked upon.

Until Summers himself raised the subject.

He spoke from the modest pulpit of Appleton Chapel, the warm, peaceful space at the front of Memorial Church, at about 8:50 on the morning of Tuesday, September 17, 2002—the first day of classes at the college. Only a few dozen people were seated in the stained wooden pews flanking the pulpit, mostly regular churchgoers but also a few visitors curious to hear what the president had to say. Often speakers at Morning Prayers used a biblical passage to discuss some aspect of life at

Harvard, or simply tried to bring a spiritual perspective to questions of daily life. One year before, Summers had spoken at Morning Prayers about the healing power of learning after the attacks of September 11. This talk would prove to be less therapeutic.

"I speak with you today, not as president of the university but as a concerned member of our community, about something that I never thought I would become seriously worried about—the issue of anti-Semitism," Summers began.

"I am Jewish, but hardly devout. In my lifetime, anti-Semitism has been remote from my experience . . ." Indeed, the Clinton administration economic team—including Summers, Rubin, Greenspan, and trade representative Charlene Barshefsky—was "very heavily" Jewish, and no one had even mentioned the fact.

"But today I am less complacent," Summers said. "Less complacent and comfortable because there is disturbing evidence of an upturn in anti-Semitism globally, and also because of some developments closer to home."

Summers cited synagogue burnings in Europe, anti-Semitic political candidates in France and Denmark, and the UN conference on racism—the one he had asked Michael Ignatieff about. "I could go on," he said. "But I want to bring this closer to home. Of course academic communities should be and always will be places that allow any viewpoint to be expressed. And certainly there is much to be debated about the Middle East and much in Israel's foreign and defense policy that can be and should be vigorously challenged. But . . . profoundly anti-Israel views are increasingly finding support in progressive intellectual communities."

Summers' next line would prove particularly controversial.

"Serious and thoughtful people," he said, "are advocating and taking actions that are anti-Semitic in their effect if not their intent."

At the same rallies where protesters criticized the International Monetary Fund and denounced globalization, "it is becoming increasingly common to lash out at Israel," he said. And the problem was hardly limited to mass demonstrations. "Events to raise funds for organizations of questionable political provenance that in some cases were later found to support terrorism have been held by student organizations on this and other campuses . . ."

This was a reference—carefully worded, but factually inaccurate—

to the fundraiser held by the Harvard Islamic Society while Zayed Yasin was its president, whose proceeds had gone to the International Red Crescent.

Finally, Summers continued, "some here at Harvard . . . have called for the university to single out Israel among all nations as the lone country where it is inappropriate for any part of the university's endowment to be invested. I hasten to say that the university has categorically rejected this suggestion . . .

"I would like nothing more than to be wrong," Summers concluded. "It is my greatest hope and prayer that the idea of a rise of anti-Semitism proves to be a self-denying prophecy—a prediction that carries the seeds of its own falsification. But this depends on all of us."

With that terse declaration, Summers ended his comments.

If the audience for Summers' talk had been limited to those few people who heard it, his jeremiad would probably have attracted little notice. But Summers wanted the speech to get attention, so later that morning a member of his staff called the *Harvard Crimson* to make sure that its reporters knew of the speech and to signal that Summers thought it should be covered. Ordinarily, Summers discouraged the paper's efforts to report upon his activities.

The *Crimson* did cover the speech, then the *Globe's* Pat Healy wrote about it, and then the *New York Times* followed up on the *Globe* piece. It didn't take long before Summers' warning about a resurgence of anti-Semitism made news all over the world—and again, as with the Cornel West incident, the majority of commentary was positive. This was what university presidents were expected to do: take a stand on issues of public import. Certainly, many Jewish alumni were pleased, but supporters were hardly limited to Jews. Their ranks also included many people who liked the idea of a public intellectual as president or who thought that divestment was a wrongheaded idea, and conservatives who disliked the political left—the *National Review's* William F. Buckley, for example—which had become so critical of Israel's government.

But what played as a clear-cut morality tale beyond Harvard Yard was more subtly argued within. Scholars who made a living out of deconstructing texts or analyzing DNA applied their critical faculties to Summers' speech, and some of them came to feel that the president possessed, in addition to a sincere concern about anti-Semitism, several less high-minded agendas. According to sources familiar with his thinking, Summers was still angry about the Zayed Yasin speech three months earlier and wanted to make amends to Jewish alumni, who'd let him know that they had felt insulted both by Yasin's choice as speaker and the title of his speech. Now Summers would personally redress the wrong.

Others thought that his choice of venue was telling. In certain circles, it was believed that Summers did not much like the idea of a Christian church smack in the middle of Harvard Yard and that the centrality of the university's Protestant heritage, both literally and figuratively, made him deeply uncomfortable. Churchgoers thought that Summers seemed ill at ease with Christian ritual and WASP tradition, as evidenced by his visible discomfort with the ceremonies of his own inauguration. This was a club that he could not join, no matter how impressive his achievements.

Moreover, Memorial Church was a tub on its own bottom. It had its own endowment, its own community, and its own alumni relationships, all of which was a challenge to Summers, who wanted to centralize power in the presidency. Those active in the Memorial Church community believed that if he had had his druthers, Summers would have converted the church into some sort of non-denominational community center. As evidence, they pointed to the fact that Summers had skipped a service Peter Gomes had arranged for him on the day of his inauguration—"my mother would never forgive me" for going, Summers was said to have explained.

Relations between Summers and Reverend Peter Gomes could be charitably described as tense. (Gomes, who agreed to be interviewed regarding Harvard history and culture, declined to address this subject.) Although Gomes happily opened the church for Jews to use during Jewish holidays, he fiercely believed in maintaining its fundamentally Christian identity, partly because he thought that that was the very point of the church, and partly because any diminution of its Christian primacy would mean a concurrent decrease in his own power. So Gomes, who is twelve years older than Summers, had taken to telling friends that he would "outlast" Summers at Harvard. Gomes, normally a courtly man, had a hard time hiding his antipathy to Summers. At least once while teaching his class on Harvard history, when the suit-and-bowtie-clad Gomes referred to Summers, he untucked his shirt and yanked on his tie in imitation of the president's sartorial lapses.

Gomes was worried not only about Summers' apparent lack of interest in spiritual matters, but also about Summers' politics and the way the president seemed to be aligning Harvard with the military goals of the Bush administration. Before Zayed Yasin's speech the previous June, Summers had publicly declared that while the university must venerate freedom of speech, "we must also respect and admire moral clarity when it is required as in the preservation of our national security and the defense of our country."

In a sermon on October 6, Gomes spoke words that appeared to be a direct rebuke to Summers. "How can we have an intelligent conversation on the most dangerous policy topic of the day without being branded traitors, self-loathing Americans, anti-patriotic, or soft on democracy?" he asked. ". . . We hear much talk of 'moral clarity,' but it sounds more to me like moral arrogance, and it must not be met with moral silence." Gomes himself would never acknowledge that the "moral arrogance" line was a shot at Summers, but many in his audience—both within and outside Harvard—interpreted it as such.

The reverend was right about one thing: Summers would have loved to trim his authority. But taking on a black, gay minister was a sure way to offend multiple constituencies, especially after the Cornel West imbroglio. Even so, according to one source close to Summers, the president wanted to needle Gomes a bit. He knew of the fight over Jewish weddings at Memorial Church, and of course he was aware of Gomes' insistence on the church as a Christian space. And so he provocatively chose Memorial Church to deliver fighting words on anti-Semitism.

These were deep currents, signs of underlying power struggles over the direction of Harvard and the relevance of the university's heritage and tradition. Many on campus were disturbed by Summers' speech for a more readily apparent reason. Despite the praise Summers had won from outsiders who applauded a university president acting as a public intellectual, these critics believed that his speech was, in fact, inappropriate for a university president. In their minds, Summers had crafted his talk not to promote debate, but to silence it. And that was exactly the *wrong* way for a university president to speak out on current events.

Of first concern was Summers' assertion that he spoke not as president of Harvard but as "a member of our community." To many, this was an untenable distinction, so clearly unsupportable that they doubted that Summers himself believed it. No one could hear Summers speak and not understand that they were hearing the president of Harvard—especially when he used Harvard employees to publicize his speech and had it posted on his Harvard website. You couldn't simply slip off the robes of power and pretend to be an ordinary citizen whenever the mood struck. Hamlet and Henry V could disguise themselves and mingle with ordinary people, but they could hardly speak from a public pulpit and not expect their words to carry the weight of their station. As Carl Pearson, a lecturer in the history of science department, pointed out in a letter he wrote to Summers, "You seem to recognize this yourself, when you respond to calls for divestment by saying, 'I hasten to say the University has categorically rejected this suggestion.'" Certainly a former treasury secretary, whose most casual remark could wreak financial chaos around the world, would have known the power inherent in a highly visible office. Even professor Ruth Wisse, who called upon Summers to fire Harvard professors who had signed the petition, admitted that "he should have been speaking as president, and in fact he was perceived as speaking as president."

This mattered, of course, because the Harvard president's words had weight and consequences, and Larry Summers had just called everyone who had signed the divestment petition anti-Semitic, including nearly seventy Harvard professors.

That, at least, is what the petition signers believed. Summers would not have agreed; he'd have said that he'd called only their actions anti-Semitic. But by his own logic, even if this was not his intent, this was his effect. Several professors named in news accounts were promptly bombarded with hostile e-mails and anonymous phone calls calling them anti-Semites and Nazis. Even the act of defending oneself, of insisting that one was not anti-Semitic, could now be considered anti-Semitic. An unsigned item about the speech in the *New Republic*, Martin Peretz's magazine, posed the question, "Why would anybody who is not anti-Semitic recoil from a speech against anti-Semitism?"

"I signed the petition believing that the policies of [Israeli Prime Minister Ariel] Sharon were terrible and misguided," said professor of Spanish literature Bradley Epps. "I signed it in part worrying about just this reaction, that the act might be reduced to anti-Semitism. I am not anti-American or anti-Semitic or anti-Israeli. It was utterly irresponsible on Summers' part to resort to labels."

The subject became so polarizing on campus that many simply refused to talk about it. "I found it extremely uncomfortable after Summers' talk, because it was very divisive," said another professor who signed the petition but subsequently wished to remain anonymous. "Anybody who says that it didn't cause critics of Israel on this campus to think twice about what they could say—not just to the president, but to colleagues—is kidding himself."

Law school professor Alan Dershowitz vigorously supported Summers, arguing that the president was exactly right: it *was* anti-Semitic to target Israel among all the world's alleged human rights violators. "To single out the Jewish state of Israel . . . is bigotry pure and simple," Dershowitz said in a letter to the *Crimson*. "Those who sign the divestment petition should be ashamed of themselves. If they are not, it is up to others to shame them." Dershowitz took it upon himself to do just that. He challenged one signatory, a professor of Middle Eastern studies named Paul Hanson, to a public debate. After Hanson, who was also the master of Winthrop House, declined, fearing that the debate would devolve into a public referendum on whether he was or wasn't a bigot, Dershowitz publicly repeated the challenge, "either with Hanson present or with an empty chair on which the petition which he signed would be featured." In part because of Dershowitz's words, the climate in Winthrop House became so bitter and angry—at commencement time, one Jewish student would refuse to accept a diploma from Hanson—that Hanson came to feel he could no longer function as master. After resigning his position, he promptly left Harvard for a sabbatical.

Muslim and Middle Eastern students were devastated and demoralized by Summers' speech. Some had supported the divestment movement, and virtually all of them advocated vigorous debate about the Middle East. They now wondered which comments about Israel would earn them the anti-Semite label, or if the very act of questioning Israeli policy was now ipso facto anti-Semitic. "Criticizing the actions and laws of a country is very different from attacking people for their religion, nationality or ethnicity," wrote three self-described "students of Middle Eastern descent" in the *Crimson*.

Such students did not see Summers' speech as a statement of morality, but as a flexing of ethnic power. To them, the speech was an exercise in identity politics, that same brand of ethnic politicking Summers scorned when others practiced it. From their perspective, Jews at Harvard were powerful; there were Jewish members of the Corporation, Jewish deans, and, of course, a Jewish president. Jewish names were carved into buildings all over campus. Muslims, however, were clearly not powerful at Harvard. As a more recent ethnic presence, they occupied none of these positions—no deans, no Corporation members, few faculty members, obviously no president—and their numbers were considerably smaller than those of Jewish students. And so, from their tenuous position, Summers' speech meant simply that a Jewish leader had used his position of power to stamp out opposing viewpoints. In addition, many of them knew Zayed Yasin, and were still angry about Summers' treatment of him.

Some Muslim students had left authoritarian countries to come to a university where they could speak their minds. But now they were afraid to do that. After all, in the wake of 9/11, Muslim students were already worried about attracting attention to themselves—even at Harvard. Now, perhaps, especially at Harvard.

Certainly Summers' talk at Appleton Chapel raised legitimate questions. A significant number of liberal members of the Harvard community had not signed the divestment petition, concerned that it could be exploited by anti-Semites and uncomfortable advocating a tactic that seemed to equate Israel with South African apartheid. And who could doubt that, after the devastation of 9/11 and with war in Iraq imminent, anti-Semitic acts and advocates were growing in number, especially overseas?

But in implying that those who advocated divestment were anti-Semitic, Summers used a stigmatizing label to characterize and isolate a small minority of the Harvard community, the petition signers, and an even smaller minority group, Muslim and Middle Eastern students. In the process, he had raised his visibility outside of Harvard, winning praise from pundits and politicians. But he had also heightened the growing conviction on campus that the president of Harvard used his power to reward those who agreed with him and punish those who did not.

His talk had its desired effect. While debate about the speech itself raged, debate about divestment fizzled out, and very soon the issue became a dead letter. As the drive to divest from Israel ground to a halt, so, largely, did any ongoing campus debate about Israeli policy toward Palestinians. "Unpopular opinions have become even more unpopular in recent times at Harvard, and that troubles me," said Peter Gomes shortly after Summers' speech. "We seem to have lost the mechanism by which strong and differing views can be stated and dealt with in a pluralistic community."

In his discussions about economics, Summers had always preached a vigorous competition of ideas, an intellectual meritocracy. But now, from the bully pulpit of the Harvard presidency, he had won an argument not on its merits, but on the force of words backed up by sheer power. The results were predictable. Summers had already alienated African American students; now Muslim and Middle Eastern students also felt that the president of Harvard was not their president.

For his part, Summers moved on. He rarely raised the issue of anti-Semitism again, except fleetingly or in response to questions—years later, he still made the "in effect if not intent" argument. When he was inaugurated, though, he had not wanted to be thought of as Harvard's "first Jewish president." He was not comfortable being labeled. Now he did not want to be known as "the Jewish president of Harvard." He knew too that, by responding, he could get drawn into an endless debate, and though Summers loved debate, he saw no point in getting mired down in this one.

And so he did not publicly extend or clarify his remarks. The Morning Prayers speech would speak for itself, by itself.

"I wrote three e-mails to Larry Summers [about his speech]," said Bradley Epps, who has successfully corresponded with Summers on other matters. "He responded to none. He never has, and he never will."

But before the year was out, the question of anti-Semitism would resurface in ways that Summers had never expected, ways that showed how difficult it is for a university president to speak out on public issues without finding himself in conflict with the activities of his own university.

In February 2001, an Irish poet named Tom Paulin wrote a poem called "Killed in Crossfire." Published in *The Observer*, an English newspaper, it read:

We're fed this inert
this lying phrase
like comfort food
as another little Palestinian boy
in trainers jeans and a white teeshirt
is gunned down by the Zionist SS
whose initials we should
—but we don't—dumb goys—
clock in that weasel word
crossfire

A professor of English at Hertford College, Oxford, Thomas Neilson Paulin is well known for his inflammatory political opinions. Born in England in 1949 but raised in Belfast, Paulin is a rare combination in Ireland, Protestant but pro-republican. Literary critics consider him a serious poet, and many admire his work. With the help of a substantial grant from the English government, he is writing an ambitious, multi-volume epic poem about World War II called *The Invasion Handbook*. But despite his impressive output, Paulin is best known in England for his appearances on *Late Review*, a feisty talk show about the arts aired on England's BBC2 channel. On one episode, Paulin called the British soldiers involved in the Bloody Sunday killings of 1972 "rotten racist bastards." Such intemperate declarations had turned the poet into an intellectual bad boy welcomed in certain left-wing circles. One sympathetic newspaper writer dubbed him a "sexy curmudgeon." A mildly successful English pop band named itself "tompaulin."

But many readers thought that "Killed in Crossfire" crossed a line into anti-Semitism, particularly in Paulin's equation of Israelis with Nazis. Then, in April 2002, the Egyptian English-language weekly newspaper *Al-Ahram* published an interview with Paulin in which the poet expressed his sympathies for Palestinians and his opposition to the state of Israel. Brooklyn Jews who had become Israeli settlers "should be shot dead," Paulin said. "I think they are Nazis, racists. I feel nothing but hatred for them."

The interview provoked an instant uproar in England, where critics called for Oxford University to dismiss Paulin. The poet testily defended himself in a letter to London's *Daily Mail*. "My views have been distorted," he wrote. "I have been, and am, a lifelong opponent of anti-Semitism and a consistent supporter of a Palestinian state. I do not support attacks on Israeli civilians under any circumstances." It was true that Paulin had publicly lambasted literary critics who white-washed the anti-Semitism of T. S. Eliot. But Paulin did not claim to have been misquoted in *Al-Ahram*, nor did he explain how his opposition to the killing of civilians could be reconciled with his suggestion that Jewish settlers "should be shot dead."

The controversy over Paulin's remarks attracted little mention Stateside. Only a handful of American writers noticed it, much less remarked upon it. One of the few who did, Martin Peretz, wrote in the *New Republic* that Paulin was "a lousy but famous poet" who spewed "venom towards Israel." The first assessment was debatable; the second seemed undeniable.

Soon enough, Tom Paulin's anti-Semitism problem became a problem for Harvard. Sometime between the publication of "Killed in Crossfire" and the *Al-Ahram* interview, the Harvard English department invited Paulin to campus to deliver the Morris Gray Lecture, an annual reading. In November 2002, about seven weeks after Summers' anti-Semitism talk, the fracas over Tom Paulin came to Harvard.

Three professors had chosen Paulin for the honor. One was Helen Vendler, probably the doyenne of American poetry critics and a University Professor, just as Cornel West had been. The other inviters were poets named Jorie Graham and Peter Sacks. Graham and Sacks are partners both in life and in politics; they are one of Harvard's more left-wing couples. But none of the three professors, they would all insist later, had been aware of "Killed in Crossfire" when they invited Paulin to speak, nor had they read or heard about the *Al-Ahram* remarks.

Someone else, however, was aware of Paulin's feelings toward Israel—a Harvard lecturer named Rita Goldberg. When she received an e-mail invitation to the Paulin lecture, Goldberg was shocked that it said nothing of his controversial background. And though Goldberg was not particularly influential on campus—lecturers are non-tenure track teachers hired for three years to fill in curricular gaps—she was married to someone who was: Professor Oliver Hart, then the chairman of the economics department. On Thursday, November 7, just a week before Paulin was scheduled to lecture, Goldberg and Hart attended the annual department dinner. Economics is Harvard's most popular under-graduate concentration, and as a sign of the department's wealth and status, the dinner was held at Harvard's imposing Fogg Art Museum. Larry Summers was on hand, and Goldberg buttonholed the president to tell him about the poet whom the English department had invited to campus. "That sounds pretty bad," Goldberg recalled Summers saying. She suggested to Summers that the English department either disinvite Paulin or publicize his remarks on Israel. Summers cautioned her that opposition to the event would raise issues of free speech.

The next day Goldberg took a step that would ordinarily have been done *before* protesting to the university president. She e-mailed Lawrence Buell, a scholar of American transcendentalism and the English department chairman, to complain about the Paulin reading. "I assume that the people who selected him . . . know about the reputation he has recently made for himself," Goldberg wrote. "In the minds of many thoughtful people both in England and here in the U.S., Paulin's vitriolic attacks have crossed a certain boundary between civilized discourse and something much more sinister. You ought at least to attach a warning label to your announcement of the reading." Buell, a respected and well-liked figure, responded that he had not known about Paulin's background and would look into the matter.

But things were already progressing beyond Buell's dominion. Goldberg sent a similar e-mail to a contact at Harvard Hillel, who forwarded it to other interested parties. By November 11, on the Internet and over e-mail, the Paulin problem had erupted. Within the English department, there was instant concern about the emerging public controversy—and about Summers' reaction. Tom Paulin was exactly the kind of figure the president had warned them about, apparently the paradigm of the left-wing European intellectual who glibly tosses off anti-Semitic comments at radical chic dinner parties.

Perhaps inevitably, several professors asked Elisa New what her boyfriend thought. New's colleagues had become wary of her presence during their conversations on the Paulin matter, fearing that she would share their comments during pillow talk with Summers. Rather than avoid the subject, they decided simply to ask her directly. Their requests put New, who did not want to serve as a conduit to or from her boyfriend, in an awkward position. She answered, "If you want to know what Larry Summers thinks, you should ask Larry Summers."

On Monday evening, the eleventh of November, Larry Buell picked up the phone and did just that.

Telephoning the president of Harvard to ask for his feelings about a controversial lecturer was not a normal thing for a department head to do. The university, after all, has hosted plenty of divisive figures, from Robert McNamara in 1966 to Colin Powell in 1993. (The award of an honorary degree to Powell was protested because of his recently announced opposition to allowing gays to serve in the military.) Tom Paulin's lecture was a minor event compared with, say, the November 1997 talk by Chinese president Jiang Zemin. That visit, the most hotly debated in recent years, prompted thousands of demonstrators to rally outside Sanders Theatre in Memorial Hall, just beyond the rear gates of the Yard, where Zemin spoke. To ameliorate the protest and promote a different kind of discussion, the university organized "China Debate Week." Neil Rudenstine issued a statement articulating why such a visit affirmed "the traditions and purposes" of Harvard. "The invitation does not represent an institutional endorsement of the speaker's particular point of view," Rudenstine said. "Rather, it reflects a broader belief that we are ultimately stronger—as a university committed to education, reasoned discourse, and mutual understanding—if groups within our community have broad discretion to invite speakers of their own choosing."

It was one thing to involve the president when the authoritarian head of state of the world's most populous nation was coming to Harvard; but for Larry Buell to contact Summers four days before the arrival on campus of a relatively unknown poet-provocateur—anti-Semite or no—showed just how edgy the campus had become. Rather than risk the president's anger, Buell preferred to ask Summers' opinion, even if it meant sacrificing a part of the faculty's autonomy.

During that phone call, Summers reportedly told Buell that while *he* certainly wouldn't have invited Paulin, he would defer to the English department as to how to handle the visit. Summers apparently believed that withdrawing the invitation would create an appearance problem, and that his Morning Prayers talk would be seen to have discouraged free speech on campus. But he also thought that the Department of English should explicitly disassociate itself from Paulin.

The next morning, Helen Vendler called Paulin, who was teaching at Columbia University while on sabbatical from Oxford. She told him of the situation that had developed and the pressure the department was under. She suggested that perhaps there should be some sort of panel discussion or question-and-answer session in which the charges of anti-Semitism could be discussed. Whether because he found the invitation half-hearted or because he did not want to engage in such a discussion, Paulin declined.

Later that day Larry Buell posted a message on the English department website saying that the Tom Paulin reading "will not take place." Moreover, he wrote, the department regretted the "widespread consternation that has arisen as a result of this invitation, which had been originally decided last winter solely on the basis of Mr. Paulin's lifetime accomplishment as a poet."

If Summers had indeed asked for a disavowal, there it was: Harvard's English department wanted nothing to do with Tom Paulin. For his part, the president released a statement saying, "My position was that it was for the department to decide, and I believe the department has come to the appropriate decision."

Then something unexpected happened. The "appropriate decision" prompted almost as much controversy as did the original invitation. Some suspected that the decision had been made under pressure from Summers—that as soon as the president stated his opinion, he'd given Buell an implicit command. Others thought that the canceled appearance was a lost educational opportunity regarding the exercise of free speech. Law school professor Charles Fried sent the *Crimson* a letter, co-signed by his colleagues Alan Dershowitz and constitutional scholar Laurence Tribe, lamenting the cancellation. "What is truly dangerous is the precedent of withdrawing an invitation . . ." Fried wrote. "Now [Paulin] will be able to lurk smugly in his Oxford lair and sneer at American's vaunted traditions of free speech."

The law professors were hardly the only ones who thought that the English department had buckled. Many of its own faculty felt that however misguided the original invitation had been, it should have been honored. Professors of literature, they suggested, ought to be especially sensitive to free speech issues, since many of the works they taught had been banned or continued to be the objects of censorship. In Paulin's appearance, the English department had had a chance, however inadvertent, to practice what it preached, and it had instead skulked away from the opportunity.

On Tuesday November 19—a few days after Paulin was to have lectured—the entire department convened to discuss what had happened. Larry Buell conducted the meeting, and Helen Vendler walked the faculty through exactly what had transpired. Peter Sacks, who had been Paulin's strongest advocate, apologized for conducting insufficient due diligence. But the gist of the meeting was what to do about the fact that a department devoted to freedom of expression appeared to have caved in to political pressure. Skip Gates, who also taught in the English department, noted that Harvard had hosted white supremacist David Duke and black nationalist Malcolm X and survived. Why not Paulin?

A vote was taken: though two professors abstained, the rest of the department—including Lisa New—voted to re-invite the poet. Two days after announcing that Tom Paulin would not be coming to Harvard, Larry Buell posted another announcement saying that Paulin was being asked back. But the invitation was less than enthusiastic. "The department in no sense intends to endorse the remarks by Mr. Paulin that have given offence," Buell wrote. "We are glad that Mr. Paulin has in fact gone on record as regretting those remarks, stressing that they do not represent his real views"—which was not exactly what Paulin had said.

Summers quickly produced a statement of his own. "Invitations to Harvard departments are commonly extended by those departments," it began. His language was awkward, the tense passive, because the intent of the sentence was to remind the reader that he had nothing to do with inviting Paulin—just as he'd wanted people to know that he'd had nothing to do with Zayed Yasin.

Summers continued, "We are ultimately stronger as a university if we together maintain our robust commitment to free expression, including the freedom of groups on campus to invite speakers with controversial views, sometimes views that many members of our community find abhorrent . . .

"On another occasion, I have made clear my concerns about speech that may be viewed as lending comfort to anti-Semitism."

That was a subtle piece of historical revisionism. In his Morning Prayers remarks, Summers had not warned about speech that might be "lending comfort to anti-Semitism"—he had decried speech that he considered anti-Semitic. The new formulation soft-pedaled his original argument.

"I hope," Summers said, "that people who choose to attend the planned reading will respect the rights of those who wish to hear the speaker. And I hope that people with differing points of view will feel free to air them in responsible ways."

The differences between Neil Rudenstine's statement regarding Jiang Zemin and Larry Summers' on Tom Paulin were subtle but significant. For Rudenstine, a controversial speaker represented the kind of educational experience that brought people to Harvard in the first place. Summers was more pragmatic. For him, such incidents were something to be tolerated, because universities needed to be tolerant places, but ultimately they were a distraction from the work of the university, rather than *being* an important part of a university education. Readers of Summers' statements would have no difficulty discerning how the president really felt about controversial speakers coming to Harvard.

In the end, Tom Paulin never did come. After finishing his sabbatical at Columbia, he returned to Oxford to write and teach. Declining an interview request, he said, "I wouldn't speak about *Ulysses* now." But in January 2003, Paulin did publish a poem that appeared to be in response to the Harvard incident. Called "On Being Dealt the Anti-Semitic Card," it included the lines:

> *the programme though*
> *of saying Israel's critics*
> *are tout court anti-semitic*
> *is designed daily by some schmuck*
> *to make you shut the fuck up*

The episode was an unexpected blessing for Larry Summers. In September he had warned against an anti-Semitism that most people thought did not exist at Harvard—until the English department invited Tom Paulin to speak and made Summers look prophetic. Even better for Summers, Paulin had not actually come to Harvard. Summers got the result that he wanted—the result everyone knew he wanted—without having actually done anything.

Across the campus, however, the perception was that fear of Larry Summers had caused the English department to renege upon and then waffle about an invitation to a controversial speaker. Fear of Summers had become so great that the president had only to suggest his displeasure and professors flinched.

The perception of power is power, and after the Tom Paulin affair, Larry Summers was a more powerful president than he had been before it.

His popularity, however, was another matter.

Barely a year and a half into Larry Summers' presidency, there was already hopeful talk among faculty members and administrators that he would not stay long. At least two different groups of faculty members convened explicitly to discuss the question of whether Summers could be ousted. Their discussions went nowhere, as the only people who could fire Summers were the members of the Corporation, and they would never do it—after all, they had chosen him. If anything, Summers' relationship with the Corporation was even stronger now that Bob Rubin had become a fellow.

No, the faculty conversations that imagined Summers losing his job were based on wishful thinking. But there were other conversations among people who thought that Summers himself might *want* to leave—that he could not long tolerate the culture of the university. He was so impatient! In conversation and demeanor, Summers repeatedly made it clear that he thought the pace of change at Harvard was glacial. He seemed bored by some aspects of his job, the way people felt free to ask him about the pettiest details of student life, as if the president didn't have better things to do with his time. When one student told Summers that he thought Harvard should have the world's largest bell, Summers told him to go raise the money for it and then they'd talk. On several occasions he voiced his frustration that no one seemed to want his opinion on the looming war with Iraq.

Plus, Summers seemed so concerned with his image, it was easy to think that he was grooming himself for another job. That fall he hired his own press secretary, Englishwoman Lucie McNeil, an attractive, twenty-something-year-old woman with virtually no knowledge of Harvard. Her job was to promote Larry Summers. It was not always easy. When Summers visited the *Boston Globe* editorial board in the fall, he instructed reporter Patrick Healy, who covered Harvard, to fetch him a Diet Coke. Then Summers said, "It's a pleasure to be here, but I wish that your reporters would pay less attention to me and your editors would pay more attention to your reporters." That wasn't the smoothest way to meet the press.

On McNeil's advice, Summers agreed to cooperate with the *New York Times Magazine* and 60 *Minutes* for profile interviews. Some of his advisers thought that talking to an investigative news program was a bad idea, but ultimately it was decided that the profile segments on 60 *Minutes* were puff pieces, sure to be flattering. Meanwhile, members of the community wondered just what was the point of all this publicity. Did Summers want to run for senator from Massachusetts if the Senate seats held by John Kerry or Ted Kennedy opened up? Or maybe he was angling for the position of Federal Reserve chairman, should Alan Greenspan leave the job?

The rumors spread over cappuccino at Au Bon Pain in the Square . . . among professors who bumped into each other in the Yard . . . between administrators zipping e-mails across campus . . . students hanging out in their rooms. The gossip about Summers was incessant. There was something about his remoteness—even when he was in the same room with you, even when he was *talking* to you, he seemed far away—that made people obsessed with figuring the man out. And even though the rumors were based on mere impressions, insinuations, and inferences, they rankled. Because people who worked for Harvard thought that being its president was just about the best job in the world, and now they had a president who sometimes seemed as if he couldn't wait to leave it.

People wondered if he was happy. For one thing, he never looked relaxed. Even when playing tennis, he radiated intensity; he was not a good loser. And though he had allies, supporters—usually men, often other economists, sometimes professors he had courted, plus the young people on his staff—it was hard to name people whom Summers would consider his friends. Most people didn't want to socialize with him, and in one embarrassing episode, Summers "had an elevator shut in his face by a group of people who were going to an event he should have been invited to," said someone familiar with the incident. "They just didn't want him to come."

Maybe he was lonely. Many weekends, he left campus to visit his children in Washington. (Harvard paid for his travel expenses and a Washington apartment so he could see the kids.) Sometimes the children would come up to Cambridge; once Summers brought them to a lecture he gave at the business school.

In the spring, Summers went out to dinner with a group of economics grad students at a local restaurant called Grafton Street. The students had been asking Summers to dinner for a year, and he'd finally found the time to get it on his schedule. They decided to start with a little joke; they told Summers that they really wanted to talk about how the best printer in the econ department had disappeared. The president looked suddenly weary. "Okay, tell me about it," he said. Seeing his expression, they hastened to assure him that they were kidding. What they were really interested in was economics, so they asked him what economic questions he thought would be interesting to work on.

Summers thought for a few moments and then started talking about the processes of micro-decision-making. Like, for example, why he had decided to go to dinner with them. It was a small decision, yet it had required multiple calculations. Was it worth the time? Did he want to do it? What would he gain from it? What might he lose? So much involved over a simple matter of whether to have dinner with some grad students. Still, the process was important. Summers often talked about the fact that people tended to spend as much time trying to save money when buying a book as they did when buying a car—even though the potential savings on a car purchase were much greater than when buying a book. If those processes of micro-decision-making could be broken down and analyzed, people might learn to use their time much more productively.

Summers recalled that when he was at Treasury, he used to ask Bob Rubin why Rubin had made a particular decision or acted in a particular way. And Rubin would say, I don't know, it just seemed the right thing to do. Invariably it was—but Rubin didn't even have to think about it. His knack for doing the right thing was either instinct or second nature. How did he acquire that gift?

Some people might have been put off by their guest's clinical dissection of his decision to join them for dinner, but these economics students were accustomed to such dispassionate language, and they enjoyed seeing Summers' mind at work. They talked for several hours, and the econ students enjoyed every minute. Summers seemed smart, thoughtful, interested in what they had to say, and, surprisingly, a little vulnerable. He said that he wished he were able to have more conversations like this one, and the students quickly answered, okay, let's do another dinner. Summers laughed glumly. Maybe next fall, he said.

Maybe next spring. He might not have a free night for another year.

To be sure, Lisa New helped make the president's job less lonely. Summers took her to faculty parties, cultural events, and Red Sox games—he got terrific seats—and the two looked happy together. When New was with Summers, there was at least one person capable of making small talk, of performing the little rituals that facilitate pleasant social interaction. New seemed to humanize her boyfriend. But people still frequently received e-mail from Summers late at night—eleven o'clock, midnight—and that didn't seem so romantic. Victoria Perry had complained of just such workaholic tendencies when she was married to Summers.

But not many Harvardians got the chance to see Summers in his less formidable moments, and their predominant attitude toward him was a mixture of dislike and distrust. Though few felt comfortable openly expressing their dislike, discontent surfaced in odd and indirect ways. Someone wrote an allegoric letter to "Ask Dog Lady," a pet-advice column in the *Cambridge Chronicle*, a local weekly. "Dear Dog Lady," the letter began. "Our rottweiler, Larry, has been very confrontational since we moved him to Cambridge from Washington a few summers ago. He's not nice around the kids, and even worse with the staff. He attacks anything that comes near him. . . . He's also developed some bad manners: He slobbers all over the place, and he's messy when he eats. Would castration help?" The letter was signed "Carl."

Columnist Monica Collins responded, "Carl, it sounds like your dog must be a Democrat because his agitation started when he was ousted from Washington. Merely assure him that better things may come in 2004. And yes, Dog Lady heartily recommends castration. . . . Larry is in a chaotic hormonal state and neutering him will surely calm him down." When the apparent meaning of the letter was pointed out to her, Collins insisted that she hadn't picked up on the joke.

Summers may have been in control, but he was inspiring a well of resentment that could rise up against him should he make a misstep. He needed a break, and he got one from an unexpected source—the department of Afro-American studies.

On December 4, 2002, Skip Gates announced that he had turned down a job offer from Princeton and would be staying at Harvard. He explained that rather than leave and see Af-Am crumble, he wanted to stay and rebuild. "This was a gut-wrenching decision for me because of my dear friendship with Anthony Appiah and Cornel West, and never about any financial support for me or the department," Gates said in the *Boston Globe*. He told the *Times* that "any raise in salary would be based on merit and in line with his previous raises."

Gates' answers may have been technically accurate, but they didn't tell the whole truth: He was well rewarded for his decision to stay at Harvard, and his decision to stay was partly contingent upon that reward. It came in the form of a million-dollar donation to the W. E. B. DuBois Institute for Afro-American Research, a Harvard scholarly center of which Gates is the director.

The donor was a Harvard alumnus—one of the university's wealthiest—named Glenn Hutchins. He was a graduate of Harvard College, class of '77, and in 1983 had earned simultaneous degrees from the Harvard business and law schools. After graduation, Hutchins would recount in an essay for his 25th college reunion, "I resisted Wall Street's siren call and set out to be an entrepreneur. Eventually I signed on to help another Harvard grad . . . to build a firm in a neglected backwater of finance known as LBOs," or leveraged buy-outs. "Since the underlying math of the profession has prevented me from doing more harm than good, I am still at it nearly twenty years later," as cofounder of an investment firm called Silver Lake Partners.

Hutchins was unduly modest; he was hugely successful in his field, and by 2002 his personal fortune was estimated to be in the hundreds of millions of dollars. He was also politically active and had served a brief stint as an aide in the Clinton White House in the early 1990s, during which time he'd met Larry Summers. He was also, by several accounts, a good man with a strong social conscience. Hutchins served as a director of CARE, the international relief and development organization, and gave away large sums of money to organizations he considered worthwhile.

One of them was Harvard, and as Hutchins' 25th reunion in June of 2002 approached, he decided that he wanted to pay back the university for all it had done for him with a class gift of one million dollars (one reason why Hutchins was promptly awarded Harvard's "Richard T. Flood '27 Award" for his "exemplary leadership and singular achievements" as a fundraiser).

Sometime after that gift was made, according to sources familiar with it, Larry Summers asked Glenn Hutchins for help. Summers was in a tight spot with Skip Gates. He wanted to do everything he could to keep Gates from leaving, and he knew that Gates was negotiating with Princeton. If Gates left, his departure would be deeply embarrassing to Summers and at least as damaging to the Af-Am department. Would Hutchins mind if Summers directed his generous gift to the DuBois Institute, which Gates essentially ran?

After some consideration, Hutchins decided that he did not mind. If this was what Harvard needed, he was happy to help. Plus, partly through his work with CARE, he had an interest in African-American studies, and wanted to see the department succeed. "Glenn is a very reasonable man," said one Harvardian who knows him. "He gave the million dollars just to Harvard, so it wasn't a big stretch if Larry says to him, 'Do you mind if I apply it here . . . ?'"

And so in the fall of 2002, the DuBois Institute received from Glenn Hutchins a million dollars. The money was earmarked for Skip Gates, along with the already-departed Anthony Appiah, to use to underwrite the costs of editing *Africana: The Encyclopedia of the African and African-American Experience*, a multivolume work to be published by Oxford University Press in the spring of 2004. It certainly wasn't cash that Gates could use to buy a sports car or travel to Paris, but it was money that Gates could use with some leeway in the context of editing an encyclopedia.

Skip Gates denies this account, saying that Hutchins had intended to give his gift to the institute before Larry Summers even became president, and that his decision to stay at Harvard was solely a renewed commitment to his department. "I stayed at Harvard because I had a choice between going to Princeton to work with my two closest friends"—Appiah and Cornel West—"or staying at Harvard to protect this great department that my friends and I have built, particularly at a time of its greatest vulnerability," he said. "And I decided that it mattered that I stay, because I felt that all the work that I had done there could be dismantled, and I'm absolutely convinced that I made the right decision to stay."

Others disagree. "This grant was made in the context of trying to keep Skip at Harvard," said one colleague of Gates'. "There is no question."

More than a year before, Larry Summers had begun his presidency by dressing down of one of Harvard's highest-profile professors. The incident led to that professor's departure and left Summers vulnerable to charges of racism. Skip Gates, who knew something about power himself, had exploited Summers' vulnerability to improve his own professional situation. In the months to come, he fulfilled his part of the bargain by repeatedly and publicly praising Larry Summers, saying that Summers was going to be a great president of Harvard. No one could quite figure out why Gates was saying such nice things about Summers. But the very fact that he was often made people stop and, sometimes, reconsider. Completing the circle, Summers repeatedly and publicly declared how happy he was that Skip Gates had decided to remain at Harvard.

In his ongoing chess match with Larry Summers, Skip Gates appeared to have checkmated his opponent. Yet, as was generally the case with Gates, he had guided the situation so that both sides could claim victory. If you played along with Gates, everyone won.

But though the game appeared to be resolved, it was, in fact, far from over.

7

The Unexpected Exit of Harry Lewis

At about three o'clock in the afternoon of December 6, 2002, a junior in Winthrop House named Marian Smith sat down at her computer to e-mail a friend. A striking young woman, the child of a Dutch father and Somali mother, Smith had curly dark hair, cocoa-colored skin, and laughing, sparkling eyes. She was a well-liked and successful student. Concentrating in anthropology, Smith spoke six languages, but she was also known for her edgy sense of style, dressing in haute couture or in cast-off clothing she found at the Salvation Army. From outward appearances, the nineteen-year-old Smith had everything going for her.

But something was wrong. In the e-mail that she wrote to her friend, another student, Smith confessed that she intended to kill herself. She wasn't bluffing. Soon after hitting the SEND button, she apparently consumed a lethal combination of alcohol and drugs. Less than an hour later, her friend read the e-mail. Quickly contacting the Harvard police, she rushed to Smith's room, but it was too late. The officers, who arrived just before four o'clock, could not save Smith.

Suicide is not an unknown phenomenon on the Harvard campus. Though the university is loath to disclose numbers, Harvard loses a student to suicide a little more than once a year. Because of scarce data on college suicides, it's very hard to make comparisons, but the suicide rate at Harvard appears to be higher than that of most universities. A 2001 *Boston Globe* survey found that, of twelve universities studied, MIT had by far the highest suicide rate, with eleven student suicides since 1990, or about 10.2 per 100,000 students. Harvard came in second, with fifteen suicides since 1990, for a rate of 7.4 suicides per 100,000. (Harvard's enrollment is considerably larger than MIT's, which is why its percentage was lower even though its number of suicides was higher.) By contrast, the University of Michigan, with a student body of nearly forty thousand a year, had a rate of just 2.5 per 100,000. And of course some students at Harvard try to kill themselves but don't succeed (sometimes because they don't want to). Between January 2000 and January 2004, the Harvard police responded to fourteen attempted suicides.

Mental health problems are a challenge for any university, but just how big a challenge is very hard to assess. First, today's greater awareness of mental health issues can make them seem more abundant than in past decades. Whether a college culture can contribute to depression is also difficult to pin down; the average age at which depression first strikes its sufferers is the late teens, which also happens to be the age at which most people go to college. And because of better early diagnosis and treatment, more young people with mental illness are attending college than in previous eras. While colleges benefit from their talents, they also become partly responsible for treating their illnesses. And the terrorist attacks of 9/11 contributed to student depression and anxiety; the world had suddenly become a more stressful place.

Part of the difficulty of determining the scope of Harvard's suicide problem is that the issue is rarely discussed there. Student suicides are, of course, lamented, and the university devotes considerable resources to mental health care. But suicides are also generally accepted as a tragic but inevitable reality. That's because Harvard has long had a sink-or-swim culture. If you are capable enough to get in, the theory goes, you don't need a lot of helping hands once you're there. It's a university stocked with overachievers used to toiling, often in solitude, for their own advancement. The university's advising systems have long been a focus of student complaint; most authority figures at Harvard are either too busy, too important, too self-important, or some combination of all three to spend much time talking to students about their course of study or personal problems. Indeed, from one perspective, the existence of other people lagging behind is merely an indicator of one's own success, proof that, in the race of life at the world's top university, you are pulling ahead. Some students are bound to fall by the wayside.

For their part, people who are struggling don't feel encouraged to ask for help. Intentionally or not, Harvard fosters an environment of rugged individualism in which students feel pressure to cover up perceived or actual weaknesses. It's no coincidence that for years one of the suggested readings for entering freshmen was Ralph Waldo Emerson's prescriptive essay "Self-Reliance."

Only rarely does a death on campus force members of the community to look inward and question themselves. In 1995, a young Ethiopian woman named Sinedu Tadesse murdered her Dunster House roommate, a Vietnamese immigrant named Trang Phuong Ho, by stabbing her forty-five times. As a visiting friend ran screaming for help, Tadesse hanged herself in the bathroom with a noose that she had made beforehand. The incident was so horrific—and, because of both women's immigrant backgrounds, so symbolically charged—that it prompted national headlines. While shocked students tried to figure out what could have gone so wrong, the Harvard administration's response was to try to squelch public discussion of the murder-suicide. University officials refused to disclose basic information, discouraged students and family members from talking to the press, and stonewalled even the most legitimate reporters. It was impossible to judge if they were concerned more with protecting the students or the university.

The 1995 murder-suicide was so bizarre it was almost easy to consider the episode a horrible fluke. The death of Marian Smith, however, seemed to crystallize student concerns about mental health. Because, although Harvard has some things in common with other universities when it comes to dealing with mental health, the university also faces distinctive problems that stem directly from its competitive, achievement-oriented culture—pressures that some thought Larry Summers' vision of the university would only exacerbate. Marian Smith's suicide raised issues of increasing concern to many students and some faculty members as Summers' grip on Harvard began to tighten.

In March 2003, a survey by Harvard's University Health Services found that "nearly half of the Harvard College student body felt depressed during the last academic year and almost ten percent of the undergraduates reported that they had considered suicide," according to the Crimson. That prompted the paper to undertake a four-part series on Harvard's "mental health crisis." Its conclusion? The high demand for mental health care, along with its high cost, had led to a dangerously inadequate "assembly-line approach" to student mental health. As a consequence, "some students' conditions . . . spiral out of control as they fall through the cracks in the system." Explained 2003 class marshal Krishnan Subrahmanian, "There are a lot of unhappy people here. You become so involved with what you're doing that you never stop and take care of yourself. Harvard students rarely sit back. In a world where everyone is running that fast, who's going to stop and say, 'How are you doing?'"

In fact, the trouble begins before students even start at Harvard College. Just the pressure to get in puts them under enormous strain. Today's students don't win acceptance to Harvard merely because their fathers are alumni or they did reasonably well at boarding school; with some 20,000 applicants for roughly 1,600 spots, the competition is so great that aspirants must begin their preparations at earlier and earlier ages. If Harvard wanted to, it could probably fill its classes with only high school valedictorians with perfect scores of 1600 on their SATs. Harvard accepts about two thousand people annually (and the percentage of accepted students who choose to go to Harvard, the "yield rate," is the country's highest); in the 2001–2002 school year, the university received applications from 3,100 high school valedictorians.

Grades alone are not enough. Applicants to Harvard must also be world-class musicians, science prodigies, and star athletes who travel around the world when they're not volunteering at their local hospital, running their student government, or starting their own corporations. "I have the distinct feeling that they've been preparing for their applications since they were nine years old," said one Harvard alumna who interviews prospective applicants for the college. "It's a little sick."

It can certainly make them sick after they get to campus. For many entering students, Harvard is a holy grail toward which they've been striving for most of their self-conscious lives. But when they arrive in Cambridge, several things can shake their faith, not just in the university, but in themselves. They may find that although they were far and away the best student in their high school in Indiana or Missouri or Texas, they are now surrounded by classmates who seem (and often are) far more intelligent and more prepared. "A lot of people have the feeling that 'Everyone at Harvard is smarter than I am,'" said Rohit Chopra, a 2004 graduate who was the Undergraduate Council president during his junior and senior years. "There's a culture of, 'I need to be the best at something or I'm a loser.' But it's very hard to be the best at something here."

FAS dean Bill Kirby tried to address that concern in a speech to incoming freshmen in September of 2003. "Some of you may worry that you're here by mistake; that you cannot do the work; or that you were admitted despite what you wrote on your admissions essay," he said. "I know that this is an unfounded anxiety. I know it because Harvard has the best admissions staff in the business. We simply do not make mistakes. You will prove that to us in four years' time."

The competitive nature of life at Harvard alternately energizes and exhausts its students. Undergraduates feel pitted against each other for grades, honors, fellowships, prizes, scholarships, leadership positions in student organizations, and so on. Just as the university as a whole feels a constant, self-imposed pressure to be number one, the best at everything, so do its students. Many feel that they're losing even when they're not. A small but revealing example: A 2003 study by the University Health Service showed that 49 percent of Harvard students had had vaginal sex. Sixty-one percent, however, thought that the average student had slept with two or more people during the past twelve months. In fact, the actual number of students who fit that description was just 23 percent. In other words, the typical Harvard student doesn't have sex very often or with very many people—but is pretty convinced that everyone else does.

"The feeling that everyone else here is doing great is profound," said Dr. Richard Kadison, Harvard's chief of mental health services. "In surveys, students always say that they think other people are happier, healthier, and getting more sex than they are." This is probably one reason why seniors throw an annual spring bash called, for obvious reasons, the Last Chance Dance. The 2004 dance took place in a Boston nightclub rented out for the occasion, and on the upper level, couples were tucked way in various nooks and crannies, making out and having sex. Not many people were dancing—instead, everyone was trying to play catch-up.

Harvard students lament that their university lacks a sense of community, by which they mean a supportive and collegial—in both meanings of the word—environment. They appreciate the excellence distilled by Harvard's competitive culture, but they wish that there were another, less divisive way to attain it. A startling number of Harvard students will tell you that they don't like their school. They appreciate it. They respect it. They are thankful for the opportunities it provides them. But they don't *like* Harvard. The atmosphere is just too cold, too isolating. (And so is the climate. Gray and bitterly cold, Boston winters routinely last more than half the school year, adding to the mental health problems on campus.)

Because Harvard students are so impressive, the university has a hard time suggesting that they should sublimate themselves to some communal interest, sacrifice individual accomplishment for the good of a larger group. It would, after all, contradict the sorts of activities that gained them acceptance to Harvard in the first place. "Everyone realizes what you have to do to get into Harvard," Krishnan Subrahmanian said. "Compassion is not part of that." Nor is it something you'll find in abundance after you get in. "Being social and humane is completely optional at Harvard," said 2003 graduate Catherine Bass in a Class Day address to an audience of thousands. "Many of us have gotten through Harvard . . . alone, desperate, and bitter." Bass' speech was supposed to be humorous, so the parents on hand laughed nervously. The students, however, laughed knowingly.

For many students who have long carried within them idealized visions of the red-brick university perched on the banks of the Charles, that gap between their expectations and Harvard's reality creates a conundrum. If you've worked and sacrificed to get into Harvard since you were barely old enough to understand what Harvard is, what do you do when you realize that you don't like it?

Some students adapt by changing expectations or finding alternative satisfactions. It's common to hear students say that though they're not fond of the university, they cherish the friendships they've made and value their extracurricular pursuits. Others turn pragmatic, deciding that the point of Harvard is not to enjoy your time there, but simply to acquire skills and make connections for use after graduation. Still others conclude that the reason for their unhappiness couldn't possibly rest with the institution. It must be because, in some mysterious way, *they* have failed, *they* are inadequate. It's these students who may be tempted to emulate Marian Smith.

Student complaints about community often revolve around campus social life. Freshmen, who cannot legally drink alcohol, are on their own. Since they don't become affiliated with the houses until the end of their first year, they have few social connections to upperclassmen. Though students have pushed for one for years, if not decades, there is no student center or pub at which students from all classes and houses can gather. College-wide parties are rare, and some of the ones that do exist betray a longing for a more typical, more *fun* college experience. The recently inaugurated "Harvard State" party, at which participants are invited to "party like you go to a state school," is sometimes criticized for its snobbish implications. But in truth, Harvard State isn't really a reflection of arrogance, but of envy, longing and maybe even a little insecurity. Sometimes, Harvard students just want to have fun the way they imagine students at other colleges do.

For all these reasons, there is a vacuum in the college's social life, and that vacuum is filled by a peculiar Harvard phenomenon known as final clubs.

The tradition of private men's clubs at Harvard dates back to 1791, with the founding of what is still the university's most exclusive club, the Porcellian. Now there are eight clubs, all of them still men-only, with names like the Fly, the Fox, the Phoenix, and the Delphic. Their multistory, elegantly furnished clubhouses are discreetly scattered about Harvard Square on immensely valuable real estate. Collectively, the final clubs are said to be the second-largest property owners in Cambridge. The university would love to buy their land, but it cannot; each club is privately owned by its alumni. For many years, the clubs were connected to the university through utilities such as the electric and phone systems. But in 1984, anxious about the legal ramifications of the clubs' discriminatory policies, Harvard severed its official ties with them. While the university administration probably wouldn't mind if the clubs disappeared altogether, it can't do anything to make that happen, and in some ways it can't afford to. Club alumni are wealthy and powerful—probably more so than Harvard alums who weren't club members—and wouldn't take kindly to hostile actions on the part of their alma mater.

Unlike Yale's secret societies, such as Skull and Bones, which aim to foster an intense but secretive bonding experience among their members, Harvard's final clubs are primarily social organizations.

(They derived their name because they were once the final step in an ascending hierarchy of Harvard clubs.) Every year, the clubs "punch" their new members from the sophomore and, less frequently, junior classes. Punches attend a series of competitive social events during which their numbers are whittled down. The twenty or so men who make the cut at each club become members of a circle that's exclusive even by Harvard standards. "There's a lot of social cachet that comes from being a member of a club," one Phoenix member explained on the condition that his name not be used. (Members are discouraged from talking about their clubs.) After he was admitted, he said, "girls I'd never spoken to would come up to me on the street and say, 'Congratulations.'" Final clubs have another big perk: their alumni networks help members find employment after graduation.

And, of course, members get a key to some of the most luxurious facilities on campus. With libraries, dining rooms, studies, poker rooms, bars, and the like, the clubhouses feel like comfortable upper-crust remnants from a bygone era. Though zoning regulations prohibit residency in the clubs, most have bedrooms that are pressed into service as needed. Private chefs prepare meals for the young men several times a week. It's slightly bizarre to see such extravagant spaces inhabited by such young people, as if the children have taken over the mansion while their parents are out of town. "The clubs," Harvard historian Samuel Eliot Morison once wrote with unintentional understatement, "are not the best preparation for living in a democratic society." But they are not meant to be. Instead, they serve as a bulwark against the encroachment of meritocracy, a means of further solidifying an already privileged position.

On weekends, the clubs throw open their doors and host parties, rowdy, alcohol-fueled bashes that dominate the college's social life, both for those who are invited and for those who aren't. Because the clubs don't open themselves up to just anyone. Students usually need to be on a guest list to gain entry, and as a matter of course, the lists consist of a few male friends of the members and the prettiest girls on campus. (The Phoenix, for example, allows each member to invite seventeen women.) While most students say they find this weeding-out process offensive and contrary to the merit-based methodology by which they gained acceptance to Harvard, the invitees go anyway, because of the lack of other activities and because the clubs serve alcohol. Since most college students are under the legal drinking age of twenty-one, the Cambridge bars regularly ask for proof of age; final clubs do not, not least because that would exclude most of their own members from drinking. Cambridge bars close at 1:00 A.M. The final clubs do not. Some of the parties have particular themes. The Fly has an annual Great Gatsby bash; the Owl slums it with a yearly "Catholic Schoolgirl" party, at which female guests are expected to arrive thematically costumed. At most of the clubs, women can enter only by the back door and are permitted only in certain rooms.

Invariably, final club parties serve as a nexus for students—particularly male students, given the generally high female-to-male ratio—cruising for sex. Equally predictably, they have become a locus for date rape. Every year produces new rumors of another woman raped in some upstairs room late at night after drinking too much. "It is . . . almost a platitude that rape and the conditions for its persistence are found within finals clubs," wrote *Crimson* columnist Madeleine S. Elfenbein in May 2003. If the victim wants to pursue the matter, she can take it before the university's Administrative Board, colloquially known as the Ad Board, which handles student disciplinary matters. (They can also go to the Cambridge police, of course, but few do.) Accusations of date rape are frustratingly hard to prove or disprove, and the college struggles with their resolution. Since Harvard has no control over the final clubs, the university can do little to tackle the problem.

The clubs' most widespread effect, however, is to polarize the campus between those who join them or are invited to their parties, and those who don't get punched and aren't invited. If you're a male junior wandering around campus on a Saturday night wondering where all the cutest girls have gone, they're probably at the final clubs, dancing and drinking with guys who, apparently, rank higher in the social pecking order than you do. Inevitably, the social disparities cause tensions among friends and roommates. The irony is that few involved with the final clubs, neither members nor guests, sound entirely comfortable with their existence. "In my ideal Harvard, I wouldn't have the clubs," said the Phoenix member. "But there aren't many other opportunities for fun."

Everything is competitive at Harvard: applications, academics, extracurricular activities, social life, sex. And while of course this is to some extent true at any college, and in life itself, at Harvard that competition is ramped up. Because, although these students sit atop the educational pyramid, they're still young, still developing the emotional maturity that enhances judgment and helps weather stress. The combination of competition at the highest level and all the psychological and emotional challenges of young adulthood is a potent recipe for unhappiness and, sometimes, worse.

Many students seem to have a love-hate relationship with Harvard. They respect its history, its tradition, its power; students refer to that moment when they tell outsiders where they go to school as "dropping the H-bomb." But they also feel oppressed by the weight of the university's past. They are encouraged to be individuals at an institution whose oft-cited glorious history obliterates individual importance. Sometimes they long to rebel—but rebellion seems foolish when all around them they see the rewards of conformity: the power, wealth, and prestige that come to those who play by Harvard's rules.

The students do, however, have their subversive moments. It's telling to consider the three rituals that, according to campus tradition, every Harvard student endeavors to participate in before graduating. All three protest against Harvard's self-importance, reminding the institution that its hallowed halls ring empty without the sounds of flesh-and-blood human beings.

The first ritual is to have sex in the dimly lit stacks of Widener Library, amid the millions of dusty volumes and the book-lined carrels of solitary, diligent graduate students. This is not easy, as the windows of opportunity during which a couple can escape detection are of short and unpredictable duration. Library employees are constantly re-shelving books, and then there are those midnight oil–burning grad students. Of course, the risks are what make it exciting. So is the sense of bringing crazy, irrational life to a place filled with the august works of the dead. It's a much healthier—and potentially more comical—version of the anti-intellectual impulse that led SDS to threaten to burn the Widener card catalog in the 1960s.

The second ritual is called Primal Scream. Every semester, at midnight on the evening before exams start, hundreds of male and female students run around the interior perimeter of the Yard—stark naked. This is courageous, and not just because hundreds of other students and some faculty members gather to watch, but because fall-term exams take place in January, arguably the coldest month in New England. Wearing only sneakers, yelling and screaming and shivering, the students streak around the Yard, a course of probably five or six hundred yards. It's not a sexual demonstration or an act of physical braggadocio; no one looks good running naked. It is, rather, a wonderfully human outburst, this posse of Harvard students cutting loose in a manner that is inherently unpretentious and deliberately dumb. Primal Scream is that rare thing at Harvard, a *communal* act. Even if for only a few minutes in the thick of the night, it makes people feel that they are part of something both human and humane—like the tent city that sprang up in the Yard during the Mass Hall occupation.

The third ritual involves the bronze statue of John Harvard located in front of University Hall in the Yard. Engraved with the words JOHN HARVARD, FOUNDER, 1638, the 1884 statue is a stopping point for tour groups, whose guides refer to it as "the statue of three lies." John Harvard wasn't the founder of the college but its first large donor. The founding date wasn't 1638, but 1636. And because there are no surviving paintings of John Harvard, sculptor Daniel Chester French had no idea what he looked like, and so he used as his model a comely young graduate named Sherman Hoar, class of 1882. Hence, three lies.

Because it makes a picturesque backdrop for a photo, the statue of John Harvard is probably Harvard's most popular tourist attraction. In fall and spring, it's rare to walk by without seeing visitors snapping pictures of each other standing in front of it. Usually they partake in another ritual—rubbing its left foot for good luck. So many thousands of people have rubbed that foot over the years that its dark bronze color has been polished to a shiny gold, considerably brighter than the rest of the statue.

But there's another reason why that part of the statue is colored gold, one that the tourists don't know. The third rite of passage for Harvard undergrads is to urinate on John Harvard's left foot. The act involves some athleticism, as the statue rests on an elevated base that would require climbing for anyone wishing to relieve him or herself on its foot. But anyone walking through the Yard late on a weekend night can see students gleefully baptizing John Harvard with their urine. Such blasphemy, of course, only happens in the dark. When the sun rises, the rebellions disappear, and the polishing starts anew.

"On Monday mornings, I see all these visitors eagerly rubbing that foot," one tour guide said, "and I wish I could tell them what they're really rubbing. But of course I can't."

The culture of Harvard, and student reactions to it, matter for two reasons. First, because Harvard shapes its students' understanding of the way the world is and ought to be. As Summers said, the students are malleable. For four years, they are instructed that the way to get ahead in life is to compete relentlessly and individually—indeed, that competition is the essence of life. And then, they go out after graduation, some 1,600 strong every year, making their way into leadership positions in banks, law firms, businesses, the media, and governments, and they apply the lessons that Harvard taught them, shaping the world around them as they were shaped. It may not make them happy, and it may not make the world a better place in which to live. But it keeps them on top. And, very frequently, it makes them wealthy—so that they can, in turn, give back to Harvard, and help it stay on top as well.

And second, the culture of Harvard matters because Larry Summers' vision for Harvard's future didn't address or ameliorate the tension between its students' prowess and their discontent, but amplified it.

By the end of 2003, Summers' specific agenda for the university was clear—reforming the curriculum, boosting the sciences, globalizing the university, and launching the massive expansion of the Harvard campus across the Charles River, in Allston. Progress was being made on all fronts. As part of the globalization effort, for example, FAS dean Bill Kirby had taken direct control of the study abroad office. He aimed to facilitate studying in other countries, something Harvard had previously discouraged on the grounds that foreign academic programs did not meet its standards. Kirby was also preparing four different committees to study aspects of the curricular review. And the university was bidding on yet another large chunk of land in Allston.

But gradual progress was too slow for Summers. Always impatient, he wanted things to change faster. The people who worked for him talked about how Summers wanted to create "a legacy." He was already thinking about how he would be remembered in the pantheon of Harvard presidents, possibly already considering what he wanted to do after Harvard. If his next move was already on his mind, then he didn't have much time to effect a legacy. Everything had to happen fast.

The president of Yale, Richard Levin, once wrote that "in Yale Time, the day (at least the weekday) has four parts: classes, extracurricular activities, study, and hanging out, generally in that sequence, although sometimes (I hope not too often) the hanging out part starts early in the evening and displaces the study portion of the day. Each part of this daily cycle is an essential element of the Yale experience."

If he were aware of it, Larry Summers would have questioned the merits of Levin's temporal division. He didn't want his university more relaxed or introspective; he wanted to make it more "rigorous," a word he used like a mantra. Just as globalization meant a quickening of the pace of economic competition and cultural integration, Summers wanted to eradicate from Harvard the old-fashioned, the venerable, and the traditional, replacing it with the faster and the tougher and the more competitive. "The greatest danger for a university is to be complacent and comfortable," Summers explained. "I have tried to resist the idea that the fact we have done things in a certain way is the reason why we should continue to do things the same way."

In practice, what Summers' credo usually meant was that if a thing had traditionally been done one way, Summers was instinctively hostile to it. To lead in the twenty-first century, Harvard would have to move more aggressively than it had in the past. Forget about "hanging out"—Summers already thought the students spent too much time engaged in extracurricular pursuits, like writing for the *Crimson*, or performing in dance and theater productions. He was not much interested in creating well-rounded graduates; he wanted students who excelled within specific fields, who would make new discoveries, reach new heights of accomplishment, and win the highest awards. He was convinced that many students put more effort into their extracurricular activities than into their classwork, and he was probably right—though not everyone would have said that these differing priorities were a bad thing.

Summers' argument was substantive and serious, but his way of expressing it was usually less than diplomatic. At a first-year meeting with house tutors—the administrative heads of the houses—Summers emphasized his desire for students to work harder by saying, "We don't want this place to be Camp Harvard." Reported in the *Crimson*, the comment infuriated students, who spent long hours in libraries and slept less than they should have (another contributing factor to mental health problems). Perhaps the greatest insult one can deliver to Harvard students is to call them slackers. They pride themselves on their ability to balance academics and extracurriculars while doing both at a high level.

Although Summers never changed his mind about Camp Harvard, he did distance himself from the remark. In his second year, a *Crimson* columnist asked him about the incident. Summers equivocated, saying that he was "not aware of having used that phrase, [but] I did once use the phrase 'camp counselor' to refer to some of the functions of House tutors." Nonetheless, the memory of Camp Harvard lingered. In Summers' third year, a student asked him about the remark when the president visited Adams House for pizza and conversation. "I don't recall ever saying that," Summers answered. "It's taken on elements of an urban myth." Others disagree. "Larry denies it now, but I remember him saying that," said one senior administrator who was in the room at the time.

About college athletics, Harvard's largest extracurricular pursuit, Summers was profoundly skeptical. Harvard has forty-one varsity teams, the greatest number of any NCAA Division I school in the country. Some of them are better than others. Men's crew and women's hockey are perennial national leaders, but the Harvard football and basketball teams aren't high-powered programs. Yet regardless of the teams' excellence relative to schools that devote more resources to athletics, Harvard has long considered sports a valuable part of a liberal education. Summers, however, thought that the breadth of Harvard athletics was a waste of money and a poor use of student time. Worse, he was convinced that highly intelligent students were being rejected from Harvard to make room for less smart athletes. In public, he talked up Harvard athletics because he knew that alumni who had played sports at Harvard were among the university's most consistent donors. But in private he pushed a plan ultimately adopted by the Ivy League that lowered the number of football recruits from thirty-five to thirty every year and instituted a mandatory seven-week break from training for all athletes during their off-seasons. Summers wouldn't have minded if the number of athletic recruits fell lower still. Even when he tried to look like he supported Harvard teams, he was less than convincing. When he attended a women's hockey game during the 2002–2003 season, he turned to someone on the bench and asked,

"So, are we any good?" At the time, the team was ranked number one in the nation.

Summers preferred the sciences. At every opportunity, he talked about the need for Harvard students to be more scientifically literate. Harvard had missed out on the Internet gold rush, he said; this time around, it would not miss out on biomedicine. Again and again he spoke about the importance of the human genome and how critical it was that students understand it. For too long, Summers argued, a university graduate could be considered well-educated if he was fluent in a literary tradition, a foreign language, some history—but knew next to nothing about science. The current age of discovery was making such scientific illiteracy irresponsible. In just a few years, Summers predicted, every human being could have his or her genome sequenced for about two thousand dollars. "That has staggering potential for increasing our understanding of disease, for making it possible to find scientifically based cures for disease," he said. ". . . And that is likely over the next quarter century to lead to profound progress. My guess is that the life expectancy of my daughters is probably one hundred, and it's going to keep rising."

Two hundred years from now, Summers asked over and over, what would historians of the future consider most noteworthy about our time? His answer: the scientific revolution in the understanding of human biology. It was imperative, Summers insisted, "to create a culture in which it is as embarrassing to not know the difference between a gene and a chromosome as to not know the names of five plays by Shakespeare."

Summers' passion for science was proportionate to his disinterest in the humanities. He had never studied literature, art, language, history, or philosophy; he admitted that he didn't read serious fiction. He was an applied economist whose litmus test for an academic field was the practical results that it could generate. He did not believe that things should be studied for their own sake, or to preserve and understand the past, and repeatedly questioned the need for the existence of certain small departments and areas of study. Why did there have to be a Department of Slavic Languages and Literatures? What about Sanskrit? Why were there so many German books in Widener Library when no one studied the language any more? Even some of the social sciences weren't exempt from his skepticism. Was there any question that sociology could answer, he wondered aloud, that economics couldn't answer better? His clash with Cornel West exemplified this pattern. Few believed that Summers would have lambasted West if the former had taken Afro-American studies seriously.

"Economics is a hegemonic discipline," said one law school professor who has interacted with Summers on a number of issues. "This informs his vision in a number of ways. He actually believes that there are right and wrong disciplines. So, to him, Cornel West was simply illegitimate."

True, Harvard was not the only institution where humanists felt defensive. The power and status of the humanities had been declining at American universities since World War II showed not just the importance of scientific research, but also its potential for profit. That trend has only become more pronounced in recent years, as government aid has become more uncertain and the payoffs from science have grown. In 2004, for example, Stanford University stood to make hundreds of millions of dollars from the initial public offering of Internet search company Google, because much of the research that had led to Google's creation had taken place under Stanford's auspices. Science can bring not only big profits, but big donations. Wealthy benefactors give tens of millions for new science laboratories. In the humanities, even when a star like Skip Gates hauls in a grant from a massive corporation such as Time-Warner, the numbers are relatively small, maybe a few million dollars. Since the stock market collapse in 2001, talk of that legendary billion-dollar gift, the Holy Grail of university fundraising, had subsided. But someday, a billion-dollar donation *would* happen—and whether at Harvard or anywhere else, it wasn't likely to go to a history department.

Still, Summers' manifest disdain for the humanities unnerved their practitioners at Harvard. It was true that their work did not produce the tangible results that, say, chemistry and biology did. There were few eureka moments in literary criticism. But professors of history, literature, the arts, and the like did not believe that the value of a field was determined by the number of its practical applications. Few humanists thought—and many scientists agreed with them—that the point of a liberal arts education was so limited. Maybe studying the humanities couldn't help you live longer, the way that knowing the breakdown of your genome could, but it could uplift the character and quality of your life. It could add morality and wisdom, introspection and humility. And it could inform the way you approached other citizens of the world—whether you saw them with tolerance and understanding and curiosity, or whether you took a more competitive, hierarchical, imperialistic approach.

Indeed, the fact that Summers had no serious interest in the humanities made some professors question the breadth and nuance of his intelligence. "He is not an intellectual," insisted professor of romance languages Bradley Epps. "He is a statistician; he is a power-broker. But he is not an intellectual, because intellectuals know the power of doubt." Though few others would say so in public, a great many of Harvard's humanists shared this conviction. Summers, they agreed, was clever, even brilliant in some ways. But he was not wise.

Summers would have responded that his vision merely corresponded with the true nature of the world, which was a tough place that needed real answers to life-threatening problems. He spoke frequently of the benefits of economic growth and scientific discovery. Science and economics could lift millions out of poverty, eradicate disease, and extend human longevity. Could anyone seriously argue that the study of the past mattered more than finding solutions to the problems of the present and future?

Those who considered Summers' vision of the future with skepticism made two recurring arguments. First, it seemed that he was simply imposing his own intellectual experience upon Harvard. He was promoting the sciences and downplaying the humanities because that equation reflected his intellectual interests rather than some more objective judgment. He was anti-athletics because he had never been a jock; he had been the kind of kid whom, in high school, the jocks picked on. He was opposed to extracurriculars because, except for his experience on the MIT debate team, he'd never been much for activities outside the classroom. "Larry wants to make Harvard into the kind of school that would have accepted him," one faculty member said—a school where all that mattered was brainpower.

This charge led directly to a second critique, because a school where brainpower was all could already be found just a mile or so down the Charles. Harvard's new president, both faculty and students fretted, wanted to turn Harvard into MIT—a school where sports were insignificant, science and economics were the dominant disciplines, and extracurriculars were clearly subordinate to classwork.

A student named Noah McCormack advocated this point of view in the *Harvard Independent,* a campus weekly. "Harvard is not MIT," McCormack wrote in April 2003. "We don't drink to get dead here. We're not monomaniacal math nerds. . . . We're Harvard. Larry Summers doesn't appear to understand that."

What made Harvard special, McCormack continued, was the diversity of its students and their achievements, many of which occurred outside the classroom. It is those "that provide outlets for us and allow us to make friends (President Summers, largely friendless here at Harvard, should take note). If Larry wants to run a school for greasy-grinds without satisfying lives and/or souls, that's fine. Just walk down the river a little."

In spite of the growing chorus of concern, Summers was growing steadily more powerful. One by one, he was outmaneuvering his opponents. Piece by piece, he was putting in place the foundations of long-term power.

One reason the Harvard presidency had historically been considered weak was that the office was relatively poor. The central administration's share of the endowment (of which the president controls only an undisclosed fraction) was about $2 billion at the end of 2002—less than one-quarter of the almost $9 billion controlled by FAS dean Bill Kirby. The president had less money because, traditionally, his fund-raising role was to aid the various tubs; he was supposed to fundraise for the entire university and only rarely for his own discretionary funds. Moreover, each individual school controlled access to its alumni, but the central administration, of course, had no graduates from whom to solicit. So the president might meet with a wealthy alum of the college to land a contribution for FAS or with a business school graduate to seal a deal for the business school. With his limited ability to fundraise on his own behalf, his ability to fund his own priorities—scholarships, academic initiatives, interdisciplinary programs—was similarly constrained.

To compensate, Harvard tithes contributions. Depending on the school, and sometimes even the department, about three percent of every gift is redirected to the central administration—something alumni donors almost universally don't know. But that wasn't enough for Summers. He wanted more access to alumni money and more control over its disposition. So he convinced Bill Kirby to agree to a subtle but hugely important rule change that weakened the tight relationship between Harvard College and its donors.

As with many colleges, Harvard's fundraising is built around the concept of class loyalty. Undergraduates may not feel an overwhelming, sentimental loyalty to their institution, but they often feel a powerful connection to their academic class. They first feel that group identification as freshmen, when they spend the better part of two semesters together before being assigned to the houses. Then, in the spring of their senior year, they are flooded with class-based activities—tickets to a Red Sox game, special dances, a "senior beach day." The bonding effect is powerful. Harvard students commonly express more affection for their class than they do for the institution as a whole.

Harvard College promotes class spirit largely so that its fundraisers can tap into it. Students are first asked for donations when they are seniors, as designated classmates urge them to contribute to the "senior class gift." No one is expected to give large sums—the point is to get the students in the habit of giving money—so the student fundraisers generally ask for ten dollars. Participation level is most important; every class wants to beat the level set by its predecessors. So, although the class gift is generally in the area of $10, 000 to $20,000, a relative pittance, this is serious business. Bill Kirby gives the fundraisers a pep talk, and recent graduates pass on pointers about how best to wrangle contributions from their classmates.

After graduation, the college continues to promote class loyalty by throwing lavish reunions, replete with parties, dinners, and lectures. Rivers of alcohol flow, and attendees are inundated with Harvard paraphernalia—sweatshirts, mugs, T-shirts, caps, and the like. These are meticulously planned, well-attended parties that more than pay for themselves in subsequent alumni gifts. Then, at the afternoon session on the second day of commencement, an alumni representative proudly reads off the millions given by that year's reunion classes, being sure to use the phrase "a new record" whenever possible. The idea of getting the classes to compete against each other to see who can raise the most money may seem too crude to be effective, but these alumni take competition seriously, and the appeal to give more than the classes before and after resonates with them.

Every year, the college prints the "Harvard College Fund Annual

Report," which lists the names of donors by class and rough donated amount. Just to be listed in the report, alumni have to give a minimum of $1,000. It's the fundraising equivalent of the Social Register, an exclusive roster of people rich enough, successful enough, to give large sums of money to Harvard. One reason that alumni give is so their names get printed in that booklet; they want their classmates to see them.

In the past, if alumni contributed to any other part of Harvard besides the college, their names didn't appear in the "Harvard College Fund Annual Report," and their gifts didn't count toward the class total. The consequences were twofold: First, their classmates wouldn't know of their wealth and generosity. Second, their gift wouldn't help their class beat the fundraising levels of other classes. "If someone's gifts don't count, his classmates can get very upset at him," said one administrator familiar with the process. The threat of that omission helped the college to ensure that its alumni gave money to it, rather than, say, to the president.

So Summers convinced Bill Kirby to sign off on a new rule that changed fundraising policy. Very simply, it said that a Harvard College alum giving $250,000 or more to other parts of the university could still receive class credit. Summers presented the change as a way to encourage donors to give to Harvard's poorer professional schools: the money had to go to the schools of design, divinity, education, government, and public health, which traditionally found fundraising difficult because their alumni were not wealthy. The business, law, and medical schools were excluded. But the change also meant that big-dollar donors could give money to the president and receive class credit for it.

The rule may have seemed arcane, but its impact was huge. Summers already had access to high-level contributors, because people who could give a quarter of a million dollars tended to want to meet with him. And, of course, Summers knew plenty of wealthy people from his days at Treasury. In the past, the president could really only encourage such potential givers to give to the different tubs. Now he could meet with big donors and say, "If you give to my office, your name will still show up with those of your classmates and still count toward your class gift." If the donor was interested in giving to, say, the Kennedy School, instead of the college, he could.

Or Summers could encourage him to give the money to the president's account for disbursal—which meant that, in order to receive the cash, the deans had to come before Summers as supplicants, explaining to him why he should give them the money they hoped for. Summers could give them the money with strings attached, or he could just turn them down. And while gifts of $250,000 might be relatively rare, what mattered was that the principle had been established: The president could raid the college's donors, drain away the college's money, and the donors would still be listed as having given to Harvard College. The level of the dollar amount could always be reduced later, and there were hints that it would be. But for now, Summers would control the kind of discretionary funds no Harvard president had ever possessed.

Inevitably, the rule change meant a loss of power for Bill Kirby. The FAS dean was losing control of his alumni, something no other dean had ceded, so why Kirby had submitted to it was unclear. Perhaps he was simply trying to be a team player, facilitating a shift that would benefit Harvard's poorer schools. "I've always felt that we in the Faculty of Arts and Sciences are part of a broader university," Kirby said at the time. The rule change "simply expands the number of options open to those who wish to give gifts." (That, of course, was the crux of the issue.) However, since the change was quietly made not long after Kirby's appointment, others had a different theory: Summers had demanded that Kirby accept the rule change as a condition for giving him the job in the first place, and Kirby had agreed because he badly wanted to be dean. Whichever the case, the result was predictable: Bill Kirby's power shrank, and Larry Summers' increased.

The power to appoint deans gave Summers that kind of leverage, and during his second year, the number of deanships he filled grew. In addition to Bill Kirby, he had had already named a new dean of the School of Education, a New York University professor named Ellen Condliffe Lagemann. Now Summers appointed a dean of the divinity school, William Graham, a scholar of Islamic religious history, to fill the shoes of the outgoing J. Bryan Hehir, a Catholic priest. At the law school, Summers replaced resigning dean Robert Clark with professor Elena Kagan, a former colleague of his from the Clinton administration. As deputy director of the White House's Domestic Policy Council, Kagan had worked on tobacco-related legislation with Summers. "He was extraordinary," Kagan said of Summers. "It's a great experience working with Larry."

Summers' decanal appointments had several things in common. All were well-qualified candidates, and Kagan in particular was a popular choice, the first female dean in the law school's 186-year history. In every case, Summers set up a process for student and faculty input— and in every case, students and faculty complained that he ignored their suggestions and that the process seemed crafted for public relations purposes. Finally, and most important, each new dean was conferred with less power and autonomy than his or her predecessor had possessed.

Shortly after Kagan's appointment, for example, it was announced that Summers would now be sitting in on law school ad hoc meetings, something no Harvard president had ever before done; the approval of law school tenure nominations had always been the sole prerogative of its dean. A strong, established dean would likely have fought such a lessening of the law school's independence. A new dean, especially one who wanted the job, might well have traded the loss of autonomy in order to be appointed.

And Kagan did have reasons for wanting the job. She still hoped to return to Washington, where her work had been interrupted. President Clinton had nominated Kagan to serve on the U.S. Court of Appeals for the Washington, D.C., circuit, but the nomination had been blocked by Senate Republicans stonewalling Clinton judicial nominees. In the event of a Democratic administration, Harvard law dean Elena Kagan would instantly become a strong candidate for the position of attorney general, or possibly for a place on the Supreme Court.

Not only was Summers' power over the deans growing, so was his influence over the Corporation. Fellow Robert Stone, thought to have been Lee Bollinger's strongest supporter, announced that he would step down at the end of 2003. Harvard class of 1945, Stone was elderly, and his resignation was not attributable to Summers. But it did give the president the opportunity to put someone else close to him on the Corporation, and he did. Stone's replacement was Robert Reischauer, Harvard class of 1963. Reischauer was in some ways a natural fit for the Corporation. He had long-standing ties to the university: His father, Edwin O. Reischauer, had been a Harvard professor of Japanese history for decades. And Robert Reischauer had been a member of the Board of Overseers from 1996 to June 2002.

But Reischauer was an unusual pick in that he was neither immensely wealthy, as Stone and James Richardson Houghton were, nor an academic of great distinction, as Hanna Gray was. Instead, he had other traits Summers found appealing. He was an economics Ph.D. who'd spent the bulk of his professional career in Washington, where he and Summers had overlapped. From 1989 to 1995, Reischauer was director of the Congressional Budget Office. After 1995, he was a fellow of the Brookings Institution, then president of a public policy think tank called the Urban Institute. He lived in Bethesda, Maryland, a mile or so away from where Summers had lived with his wife and children. Robert Reischauer and Larry Summers had much in common.

The Corporation had always been Summers' strongest support at Harvard, but its support had not been absolute. Now, with the appointments of Bob Rubin and Robert Reischauer, Summers was filling that body with men who traveled in the same circles as he and who thought much as he did. The Corporation had always been secretive, lacking in diversity, and accountable to no one. Under Summers, it was becoming even more so.

Piece by piece, Summers was putting his team in place, remaking Harvard in his own image. But there was still one person on campus, maybe the only one in a position of power, who both profoundly disagreed with Larry Summers and was willing to say so.

Harry Roy Lewis, the dean of Harvard College, was a man of medium size and modest disposition, with thinning brown hair, bright blue eyes, and an amiable face. He looked, one of his colleagues said, "like a preppy wizard." He was a casual man, not intense or arresting like Summers, but his relaxed demeanor belied a thoughtful and far-reaching intelligence.

By January 2003, Harry Lewis had been at or around Harvard for most of his fifty-five years. He grew up in Wellesley, Masachusetts, a suburb of Boston. His family were new Americans, a mix of Ukrainians, Russians, and Germans—Lewis liked to joke that his family was "the Lewises of Ellis Island." His maternal grandfather had been a mill worker in Grand Rapids, Michigan, and his paternal grandfather owned a small grocery store in working-class East Boston. Though Lewis' grandparents never attended college, his father was raised with the strong sense that education helped a man become an American; he attended Boston University. It was not his first choice. Once, as an adult, Harry Lewis was digging around in the family basement when he found a file of correspondence between Harvard and his father. The letters were all rejection slips from Harvard. It had taken more than one rejection for Lewis' father to give up his dream.

Still, Harry Lewis' parents made for themselves a good life, certainly a more prosperous life than Harry's grandparents had enjoyed. Both were doctors; Lewis' mother would become the superintendent of a school for retarded children. She and Lewis' father were determined that young Harry would benefit still further from America's opportunities, and he did.

Lewis attended the legendary Roxbury Latin School, which, having been founded in 1645, was almost as old as Harvard. Well known for its academic excellence, the school took its Puritan heritage seriously. In its mission statement, it says, "We seek to help our students identify and address life's deepest questions. We seek to help them find out who they are and what they want to do with their lives. Whether or not the resulting direction and values are recognizably religious, the faculty believes that, in helping students find the meaning and purpose of their lives, it is engaged in what our Puritan forebears meant by 'theological discipline.'" This process of constant questioning, trying to answer life's deepest questions, was something Lewis would always carry within him, and in later life he would return to Roxbury Latin as a member of its board of trustees.

Like Larry Summers, Lewis left high school after the eleventh grade—but unlike Summers, he left to go to Harvard, making a family hope come true. He graduated in 1968 with a summa cum laude degree in applied mathematics. Just days after his graduation, he married fellow student Marlyn McGrath, whom he had met while in high school. McGrath's mother was from Montana, and in later years the two would return as often as possible to visit and relax in the Montanan wilderness. Lewis loved the journey; he loved to drive his 1991 Dodge Caravan across the nation's great expanse, meeting Americans from all walks of life and appreciating that there remained in the United States places of wild and primitive beauty. "I am not sure what moves me so much about these isolated spots with their ghosts," Lewis said in a 1999 Morning Prayers talk. "There is something spiritual I find in them. It is, perhaps, a recognition that I, and each of us, is on a lifelong voyage of discovery of ourselves."

After two years working in the U.S. Public Health Service and a year of travel overseas, Lewis returned to Harvard in 1971 for graduate work. By mid-1974, just three years later, he had earned his doctorate in applied math, making him something of a young turk in an exciting young field: computer science. In 1981, one year before Summers did, Lewis received tenure, a rare event for a junior faculty member. (Marlyn was also working at Harvard, becoming the director of admissions for Harvard College in 1987.) In July 1995, then-FAS dean Jeremy Knowles appointed Lewis the dean of Harvard College, responsible for overseeing the non-academic side of college life, from the house system to extracurricular activities to the Ad Board.

The dean of Harvard College had not traditionally been a powerful position. Past deans had been career administrators, who carried little clout with the faculty. But Lewis was a tenured professor empowered by Knowles to deal with some hot-button issues. Knowles knew that the college needed reform and that a weak dean could not effect it.

The decisions that Dean Lewis made were not always popular. In 1995, he revised the system by which freshmen were assigned to the houses so that they could not choose their houses themselves, but instead received random assignments. With the randomization, Lewis broke up the self-segregation that occurred when students got to pick where they wanted to live—Adams was the artsy house, Mather the jock house, and so on. But in the short term, the move raised an enormous hue and cry from the undergraduates, who liked the old way.

Randomization was hardly Lewis' only controversial decision. In the fall of 2002, he banned students from bringing kegs to the tailgate parties at the Harvard-Yale game, arguing that kegs promoted binge drinking. Furious students responded that, given their intractable intention to drink themselves mindless, better they drink from a keg than pint bottles of vodka. It took longer to quaff a beer than to throw down a shot. The debate prompted dozens of *Crimson* articles and editorials, with headlines such as "Repeal the Keg Ban."

A decision of greater import had come in 2001, when Lewis led a committee that altered the college's sexual assault policy, so that students accusing other students of rape had to show "sufficient corroborating evidence"—a diary entry or a conversation with a roommate about the alleged incident, for example. The change, an attempt to move away from the Scylla and Charybdis of "he said/she said" situations, infuriated some female students, who claimed that it would discourage women from reporting rapes. A subsequent committee, headed by a female professor, decided to tone down the wording and hire a "fact finder" to investigate every single allegation. This soothed student concerns.

Even if students didn't always like Harry Lewis' decisions, they invariably liked him. His dedication to the life of the college was so obvious, the students were a little shocked—they weren't used to that degree of interest from a high-level Harvard administrator. Lewis was committed to improving the system of advising, and he'd get under the skin of department chairs who didn't seem to care much—the economics department, which left advising up to a roster of graduate students, was the worst. "Dean Lewis really cared about students," said John Moore, a member of the class of 2004. "I had an adviser who paid no attention to me, and when I told Dean Lewis, he offered to be my unofficial adviser."

Accessible and responsive, Lewis answered all student e-mails within a day. He liked to joke that because the answer was so often no, the least he could do was answer promptly. And he conducted his business with a transparency that was hard to find in the Harvard administration. If the *Crimson* asked him about something, he'd give the paper an honest answer, on the record. By contrast, Bill Kirby had taken to having his press secretary sit in on meetings with *Crimson* reporters—when, that is, the *Crimson* could actually get a meeting with him. And around the university, professors were growing increasingly nervous about talking to reporters under any circumstances, knowing that saying the wrong thing would draw retribution from the president's office.

Harry Lewis cared about the students, and they knew it. When, in 2000, a student was dying of cancer in March of his senior year, Lewis worked with Jeremy Knowles and Neil Rudenstine to ensure that the student received his diploma early. Two days after receiving the diploma by overnight mail, the young man passed away, but to the grateful parents, the gesture had made a difference in their son's last days.

For Lewis, that kind of effort was standard operating procedure. He believed that the dean of Harvard College wasn't there just to find space for student extracurricular groups or to set policy on the use of fireplaces, but to help guide students from youth into adulthood, from the structure of Harvard College into an unknowable but exciting future. In his office on the first floor of University Hall, Lewis had hung three maps of the United States at different periods. His favorite dated from the year 1750. It showed the eastern coastline with a crude accuracy, and the same for the rivers and settlements across much of the continent. But the part of the map that would come to be known as the Pacific Northwest was labeled "Parts Undiscovered." Lewis loved that metaphor. "That's the right way to think about our souls," he said in another Morning Prayers talk. "As real places that are, temporarily, undiscovered."

Lewis was constantly writing. He wrote talks for Morning Prayers, editorials for the *Crimson,* and lengthy e-mails to deans, professors, and students about issues in college life. Jeremy Knowles later praised Lewis' letters, dryly pointing out that while they "are not short, they are gracefully unambiguous." Unlike Larry Summers, whose experience with The Memo had taught him to avoid committing his real thoughts to paper, Lewis thought that explaining his decisions was a moral obligation. He believed that students would learn from the process, and even if they didn't agree with his decisions, at least they'd understand why those decisions had been made. That, Lewis thought, was how you built consensus, and consensus mattered, because decisions imposed by one man wouldn't take. The community would reject them.

It was inevitable that Harry Lewis and Larry Summers would clash. In some ways, both men were surprisingly similar—opinionated, stubborn, strong leaders. But their similarities only highlighted their points of contention. "The differences between them became apparent very early on," said one of Lewis' co-workers. "Harry would stand up to Larry, and you could tell that wasn't appreciated. At the beginning, we'd be talking about dealings with Mass Hall, and Harry said, 'This is going to be interesting.' I don't think he knew how interesting it was going to be."

They disagreed about the state of college academics. While Summers joined in the cry against grade inflation, Lewis was skeptical that grade inflation existed, or, if it did, that it made very much difference to people interested in hiring Harvard graduates. He had already challenged Harvey Mansfield's view that grade inflation was the result of affirmative action, but in a subsequent Morning Prayers talk he went further, suggesting that grades were just not as important as some people made them out to be; that they were, in fact, a superficial way of judging a Harvard student. "We certify a minimum standard with our diplomas, and our consumers choose among our graduates on criteria other than grades," Lewis said, "because they recognize that for most purposes, course grades at Harvard are not the most important thing differentiating one student from another. Things that Harvard used to talk about—courage, ambition, mental toughness, integrity, compassion, capacity to rebound from reversals, a desire to leave the world a better place than you found it—these are the things that matter in real life. Not insignificant variations in grade point average."

Lewis and Summers also disagreed on the question of globalization and the university. Even as he spoke of the need for Harvard to support ROTC and act patriotically, Summers pushed for the internationalization of Harvard, hoping to steadily increase the number of foreign students enrolled. If there was a tension between making Harvard a "truly global university," as Summers said, and insisting that "The Star Spangled Banner" be played at commencement, Summers either didn't recognize it or didn't acknowledge it. Lewis worried that Summers wanted to reduce the number of American students at Harvard, which was inevitable unless you increased the total student population. He feared that Summers' globalization push was occurring without any meaningful discussion of what it meant to be an American university in a post–9/11 society, particularly in the context of the curricular review. "A review taking place post–Sept. 11 will inevitably have a different character because America's place in the world is so much under discussion today," Lewis wrote. "How will the Harvard faculty balance the reality that the U.S. is one nation among many in an ever smaller and more interconnected world, with a recognition that the particular 'free society' in which Harvard exists is founded on ideals which Americans continue to be proud to defend and preserve?" The *Crimson* editorialized that "Lewis' introduction of American values into a debate that has hardly begun contrasts sharply with the themes emphasized by Summers and Kirby."

The two men disagreed about the tolerance of free speech at the university. After Lewis tried to stick up for commencement speaker Zayed Yasin, Summers told Lewis to say nothing. In a letter to the *Crimson* on September 11, 2002, Lewis reflected about the year after the terrorist attacks in New York and Washington. "I was least proud of our civility during the controversy over the undergraduate Commencement speaker, during which I heard both American Jews and American Muslims referred to as 'those people.'"

Summers' attack on the divestment movement as anti-Semitic also disturbed Lewis. On September 23, 2002, just ten days after Summers gave his anti-Semitism warning, Lewis took his turn at the pulpit of Appleton Chapel. The subject of his talk was the dialectic between the Harvard curricular review and events in American life. He began with a Biblical quotation from the Book of Kings: "It pleased the Lord that Solomon has asked this. And God said to him, 'Because you have asked for this, and have not asked for yourself long life or riches or the life of our enemies, but have asked for yourself understanding to discern what is right, behold. I now do according to your word. Behold, I give you a wise and discerning mind.'"

If any in the audience thought that Lewis might have chosen that Biblical text as a commentary on Harvard's new president, his subsequent words probably confirmed their suspicions. "We have just come through a year in which America has been reminded of her dependence on the rest of the world, and of the fact that her fundamental values of freedom and equality are not accepted universally," Lewis said. "We rely on these freedoms more in this old University than anywhere, especially the freedom to speak and to have a rational argument, an argument in which distinctions are respected and broad labels are avoided."

Lewis did not call the *Crimson* to publicize his talk, but his rebuttal of Summers was clear. Everyone knew to which "broad label" he was referring.

Lewis and Summers disagreed about the importance of extracurriculars, and in particular athletics. Student athletes understood that Harry Lewis supported their efforts. In the winter of 1999, he had even flown to Minnesota to watch the women's hockey team compete for a national championship, and after they won, the team had asked Lewis to pose for pictures with them. But the real object of Harvard athletics, Lewis thought, was not victory, but learning to work with others. "Except for that minority of our graduates who go on to academic careers . . . most students go into careers in which teamwork is more important than individual achievement," Lewis said. In its classrooms, Harvard didn't prepare its students very well for teamwork; in its extracurriculars and athletics, it did. And Lewis didn't hesitate to note that alumni who had played on teams were among the university's most loyal and involved graduates, not to mention its most consistent givers.

"Viewed from the distance of their twenty-fifth reunion, most Harvard graduates remember their friends, a few of their teachers, and their coaches, artistic directors, and other mentors better than they remember what they learned in most of their courses," he said, and he clearly didn't think this was a bad thing. "On many college campuses, athletes are the last group that is safe to stereotype," Lewis said. "We just don't do that here."

Like Summers, Lewis worried about what Harvard students would go on to do with their lives. But when they raised the topic, the two men sounded very different. Summers focused on individual achievement; Lewis emphasized community. In a 2000 Morning Prayers talk, Lewis wrote of Harvard scholar Robert Putnam's book *Bowling Alone*, which argues that Americans have markedly less social engagement with friends and neighbors than they did in the middle decades of the twentieth century. Harvard needed to do its part to redress this problem, said Lewis. "We need to think about how Harvard can produce not just better scholars, better leaders, and better social activists"—Summers would never have wanted Harvard to produce social activists—"but better and more committed ordinary citizens," he said. "We need to think about how to do our part, over the long run, for this country, through the lessons we teach our students about working together with their peers, not simply about excelling as individuals."

Both Lewis and Summers thought of themselves as teachers inside and outside the classroom. Both wanted to influence the development of their charges. But they had profoundly different visions of what the proper influence should be. Nowhere did their clashing perspectives show themselves more starkly than in their disagreement over "slowing down."

Before the beginning of each school year, Lewis sent a lengthy letter to every incoming freshman. Entitled "Slow Down—Getting More out of Harvard by Doing Less," the letter encouraged the new students to consider carefully the pace of their lives at Harvard. Rather than trying to excel at everything, Lewis suggested, students ought to focus their choices. Certainly Harvard wanted them to maintain the excellence for which they had been selected. Nonetheless, "you may balance your life better if you participate in some activities purely for fun, rather than to achieve a leadership role that you hope might be a distinctive credential for postgraduate employment," Lewis said. "College is a transition period; we will certainly give you grades and transcripts attesting to some of the things you have done here, but much of what you do, including many of the most important and rewarding and formative things you do, will be recorded on no piece of paper you take with you, but only as imprints on your mind and soul." Lewis concluded with a simple admonition: "It's your life, even at Harvard," he said. "Enjoy it."

Larry Summers was not a big believer in slowing down, nor was he a big fan of "Slow Down." Summers had always done everything fast—and young. None of his many achievements had come as a result of introspection, reflection, hanging out, slowing down, taking time to smell the roses. And, in thinly veiled autobiographical references, Summers didn't hesitate to point this out.

In his 2002 baccalaureate address to the seniors, given on the Tuesday before Thursday's commencement exercises, Summers gave the imminent graduates his view of life after graduation. Neither community nor self-examination were his emphasis.

"Think about this," Summers encouraged the students. "Newton and Einstein did their main thinking about physics in their twenties, Alexander conquered most of the known world by the time he was thirty, and when he was your age, Mozart had composed all his violin concertos. Of course, when he was my age, he had been dead for fourteen years.

"So take it slowly from Dean Lewis," Summers continued, "but from me: blow off the rest of this week, have a great commencement, and then on Friday, get cracking." That meant the students should get to work the day after they graduated.

Three months later, Summers gave virtually the exact same instructions to the incoming class of 2006. Only the ending was slightly different. "Not to put too much pressure on you—enjoy the rest of Freshman Week and then get cracking," Summers said.

This time, the reference to Harry Lewis was deleted.

Bill Kirby liked to start his speeches with anecdotes about Chinese history, and when he spoke at Morning Prayers in the fall of 2002, he began thusly: "In Chinese history—my area of study—autumn was the time for executions. For us, however, autumn is a time for renaissance."

In Cambridge, apparently, spring was the time for executions.

On the afternoon of March 5, 2003, Kirby informed Harry Lewis that he wanted to make a change. Kirby was restructuring his administration, merging the office of dean of Harvard College with its academic counterpart, the dean of undergraduate education. Lewis was out. After eight years as dean—and with two more years left on his contract—he would have to leave the office by the end of the semester.

Lewis couldn't quite believe it. "Harry was stunned by the way his dismissal was handled," said one administrator familiar with the details. Kirby informed him that his replacement would be the current dean of undergraduate education, a mathematician named Benedict Gross. Kirby had hired Gross at the beginning of the school year, primarily to oversee the upcoming curricular review. Dick Gross, who'd earned his B.A. from Harvard in 1971 and his Ph.D. in 1978, was well respected and well liked—"one of the few mathematicians with social skills," said a math concentrator who took a course with him. And he was ambitious—"the most ambitious man I've ever met," according to a classmate who knew him well.

But perhaps Gross' most important qualification was that he had a friend in a high place: Larry Summers, who had once wanted to be a mathematician himself, not only thought highly of Gross as an intellect, but also played tennis with Gross every couple of weeks. With Gross' appointment, Summers had not only an FAS dean who was under his thumb, but also a friend who was about to become the second most powerful person in the Faculty of Arts and Sciences. And then Summers wouldn't have to worry about Harry Lewis anymore.

For those who knew of Summers' record in Washington, the incident felt like déjà vu. In 1999, Treasury Secretary Larry Summers had apparently engineered the ouster of dissenting economist Joseph Stiglitz from the World Bank, but so skillfully that his fingerprints could never be found. Now it appeared that history had repeated itself. Summers wanted Lewis gone, but he would never admit it and would never take responsibility for it.

Kirby asked Lewis to say nothing until he was ready to announce the change, at which point he wanted to put out a statement saying that Lewis was "stepping down." Lewis refused. Kirby had the right to fire him, but Lewis wouldn't pretend that he was leaving voluntarily. Though the news stayed secret for almost two weeks, administrators in other offices began to suspect that something was amiss when Lewis suddenly couldn't answer their questions and began referring them to Bill Kirby. Then, on March 17, Lewis held a staff meeting at which Kirby delivered the news. The FAS dean talked about how it had been his idea to restructure his administration, but no one believed him. "Bill gave the press release version," said one person present. "But it was obvious that he had become the puppet for Larry. I wanted to ask him, 'What do you *really* think about this?'"

"Lewis Forced Out," read the *Crimson*'s full-page headline on March 18. In a press release, Kirby said, "We will be consulting broadly with students, faculty and staff as we proceed." Gross said that he didn't know if he would take over the newly merged position. Neither statement was true.

Over the next days, follow-up stories, editorials, and letters to the editor contained headlines such as "Colleagues Admire and Respect Dean Lewis," "An Understanding Dean," "[Undergraduate] Council Worries about Future without Dean Lewis," and "Lewis Departure May Mean Shift in College Priorities." Stephen M. Senter, a Harvard parent and alum of the class of '68, wrote, "I think [Lewis] has been an effective advocate for trying to keep student life relatively sane. . . . I am just a bit leery of the tone currently emanating from University Hall, which seems to be pushing for ever greater academic rigor while letting the emotional chips fall where they may."

While Harvard students generally pay little attention to administrative reshufflings, they cared about this one; Harry Lewis was their advocate, and their near-universal reaction to his dismissal was dismay. Being dean of the college was a more than full-time job. To fold into it all the responsibilities of another deanship invariably meant that less attention would be paid to student life. Nor did anyone believe Kirby's claim that he was acting of his own volition. A *Crimson* cartoon showed Summers as a puppeteer, pulling strings attached to Bill Kirby as Kirby gave Harry Lewis a kick in the pants.

Kirby and Summers, meanwhile, were said to be furious that Lewis would not deny that he had been "forced out." Certainly Summers' statement to the *Crimson* was underwhelming. "Dean Lewis has done a great deal for the College during his deanship," Summers said. He did not amplify his remarks.

The president's anger manifested itself in more threatening ways. On Thursday, April 3, and Friday, April 4, the members of the Board of

Overseers came to Harvard to fulfill an annual duty. Together with carefully selected alumni, the Overseers were supposed to write annual reports on the status of specific academic departments and the college itself. Though the process is part of their mandate under the Harvard Charter of 1650, it had in modern years become something of a farce. Members of the "visiting committees" were chosen by the development office and FAS deans with fundraising in mind, and the committees' real purpose was to make potential donors feel privy to the college's inner workings. From the administration's point of view, the trick was to make the Overseers feel as if they were involved—without actually having them *be* involved. Though the committee members did their best to write accurate and useful reports, their evaluations were, metaphorically if not literally, thrown into the circular file.

On April 3, several members of the Board of Oversees and the college Visiting Committee asked Harry Lewis about Bill Kirby's sudden reorganization of the college administration. The party line was that the fusion of the two deanships was in everyone's best interest, but as was his wont, Lewis told them his true opinion. The integration of the two deanships was a big deal, he said, and whether it would work was an open question. One inevitable consequence, he added, was that student concerns would receive less attention from the highest college officials than they had previously.

That Saturday night, the Board of Overseers had a joint dinner with the members of the Corporation, and some of them mentioned their concerns about the reorganization, based on Lewis' remarks. The next day, as was traditional, the Corporation met in Loeb House. And on Monday morning, two of its members, Corning Inc. chair James Houghton and university treasurer D. Ron Daniel, sent Harry Lewis a message: They wanted to meet with him as soon as possible.

That afternoon, Lewis walked from his office in University Hall to meet the two Corporation members in Loeb House. In a letter he later wrote to Houghton and Daniel and distributed to a small cc: list, Lewis described what happened next. "You both advised me to tone down my statements in light of your discomfort with the reports that had reached you from the Visiting Committee meeting," he wrote. Daniel had urged Lewis to say that the reorganization was "something that would work out well in a couple of years." Lewis responded that he found it bizarre that members of one Harvard board would urge him to, if not lie, then at least dissemble to members of another Harvard board. Then Houghton said bluntly that it was "not in [Lewis'] professional best interest" to keep making "noise" about his ouster—a statement Lewis interpreted as a threat. "As I am returning to teach full-time . . ." he wrote, "I remain puzzled as to what professional interests Jamie [Houghton] was hoping to help me protect with this advice."

In addition to Houghton and Daniel, Lewis sent his letter to Larry Summers, because it seemed impossible that the Corporation members were acting of their own volition. Their summons had, after all, come one day after the Corporation meeting at which Summers would have been present, and it was well known that Summers was furious with Lewis for his refusal to get on message. Summers' desire to control the channels of information from the Harvard administration to the university governing boards was near-obsessive. But Lewis never received a response from any of the three men.

A few weeks later, Bill Kirby attended a meeting of the Undergraduate Council. One student asked Kirby about the secrecy regarding his decision to eliminate Lewis' position. "There are certain announcements that have to be made in a certain way," Kirby said. "This change was made possible in part because Dean Lewis had been so successful." The student seemed unconvinced. "There are certain announcements that have to be made in a certain way"? Bill Kirby had picked up his boss' knack for political language.

Undergraduate Council chair Rohit Chopra then said to Kirby, "There's a general impression that there's a lack of independence of the Faculty of Arts and Sciences from Mass Hall."

"It was my decision [to fire Lewis]," Kirby insisted.

On April 4, the Crimson reported that Kirby had named Gross to the new position, which would be called the Dean of Harvard College. "The administration didn't even pretend to ask students," Chopra said.

Throughout the episode, Kirby continued to argue that merging the two deanships would facilitate the curricular review. He claimed that the distinction between academic and non-academic life was illogical, and that it was important to merge the positions before commencing the review. Moreover, he said, the combined workload would not be excessive—students should not fear that they will get the short end of the stick.

On at least one of these questions, Kirby was wrong. Within

months it was clear that Gross was overwhelmed by his new double duties. "I [have] to hire someone to help me divide up this job," Gross admitted. A search was begun to fill a new and newly named post of "deputy dean," which skeptical administrators quickly dubbed "deputy dawg." The position appeared to have all the responsibilities of Harry Lewis' job, but with none of the authority or autonomy—not exactly an enticement for strong candidates. In June 2004, Gross announced that the deputy dean would be a woman named Patricia O'Brien. The dean of the business school at Simmons College, a small women's college in Boston, O'Brien was also the co-master of Currier House; the other co-master was her husband, Joseph Badaracco, Jr., a professor at the Harvard Business School. They had, ironically, been appointed house masters by Harry Lewis.

Kirby's office put out a press release saying that O'Brien would "oversee all aspects of College life." O'Brien announced that she'd be working with associate deans, University Health Services, the registrar, the Freshman Dean's Office, and the Office of Career Services.

"And I hope to be working with students," she added.

8

War

With Harry Lewis gone, few people could directly challenge Larry Summers' muscular grip on Harvard. Certainly there was no one who had both the power and the inclination to confront the president. But there were still those who could challenge him through the example they set and the lessons they taught. One such person was a thirty-two-year-old lecturer on the Committee on Degrees in History and Literature named Timothy Patrick McCarthy.

In the spring of 2002, McCarthy was co-teaching English 176a, "American Protest Literature from Tom Paine to Tupac." His classroom partner was a young associate professor named John Stauffer, a rising star in the English department who shares McCarthy's progressive politics. In Room 202 of Harvard Hall, a 1766 building parallel to Mass Hall, McCarthy and Stauffer lectured to almost two hundred students on what they had dubbed "protest literature." Their syllabus included Tom Paine's *Common Sense*, Harriet Beecher Stowe's *Uncle Tom's Cabin*, Upton Sinclair's *The Jungle*, John Steinbeck's *The Grapes of Wrath*, and yes, the music of murdered rapper Tupac Shakur. But at 2:00 in the afternoon of March 18, 2003, McCarthy and Stauffer were talking about current events. They did that sometimes, but at this class they had a special urgency. The day before, President George W. Bush had delivered an ultimatum to Saddam Hussein: leave Iraq within forty-eight hours, or war will come.

Stauffer began. "The lessons of the course can be applied to this situation," he said. John Brown, Stowe, Martin Luther King, Jr.—all had tried to change the world without having any idea what the consequences of their work might be. Activism is not science, "and it's impossible to predict the results of protest." But fear of the unknown—or of failure—should not stop anyone from acting on his or her conscience.

Stauffer and McCarthy stood on a slightly elevated stage in front of long rows of wooden chairs, most of them filled—the students liked these lectures and rarely skipped class. To the audience's left, Stauffer was standing almost completely still behind a podium. Dark-haired and bespectacled, he was McCarthy's physical opposite. McCarthy's energy overflowed in physical restlessness—at the moment, he was pacing back and forth, staring at the carpeted floor; Stauffer's intensity seemed self-consuming, like a slow-burning fire. His body was alarmingly thin and his cheeks had a gaunt, hollowed-out look, like the subject of his second book, abolitionist John Brown. It was a little hard to believe that, while a student at Duke University, Stauffer had been a nationally ranked tennis player. Larry Summers had asked him to play, but even though Stauffer would be considered for tenure in 2003, he had declined to play with the president. Something about the idea didn't sit right with him. Still, he felt more constrained than McCarthy in articulating his political opinions; young scholars known for their activism tended not to get tenure at Harvard.

McCarthy moved behind his own podium, in the center of the stage. He took over from Stauffer like a football player taking a handoff. "One of the themes of this course is passion," he said. "Another is faith. Another is courage. The people who wrote the texts we read in the course had courage."

If war with Iraq breaks out, Stauffer announced, there will be a campus-wide walkout. Students could leave their classes and gather at a protest in front of the statue of John Harvard. He and McCarthy would not teach that day. They'd make up the material later. But it was important to show how they felt.

With war coming, McCarthy said, it was time for students to have the courage of their convictions. "Once we start bombing Baghdad, the world will change and people will die," he said, pacing back and forth across the stage while Stauffer leaned on his podium. "We have to figure out if we are okay with that. I'm not going to tell you what to do. You're all individuals. You are all children of God."

McCarthy paused a moment, as if he wasn't sure that he should say what he was about to say. Then he began to tell a story. He and some friends had been out at a bar the night before, he said, when he had been accosted by a nasty drunk. "You're a faggot, aren't you?" the man said—which was a little weird, because McCarthy didn't fit any physical stereotypes of a gay man. He was big and strong and dressed like a preppy college student, with inexpensive clothing from the Gap and Banana Republic. He kept his brown hair cut short like a young Mickey Mantle. But somehow the drunk knew. "I want to kill you, you faggot," the guy said to McCarthy. "Just like we're going to kill those motherfuckers in Iraq."

McCarthy told the students that he'd tried to talk to the guy, to calm him down. But the man kept saying it—that word. *Faggot. Faggot. Faggot.* He must have said it forty times. McCarthy and his friends left the bar, and the man followed them outside, taunting McCarthy and getting in his face. "I'm not going to fight you because your blood will give me AIDS," he said.

"I wanted to fight him," McCarthy said, "but that would only continue the cycle of violence." There was so much violence in the world, he continued. From an incident at a bar to imminent slaughter in Iraq. What was the point of it all? What was it accomplishing?

"I just wanted to share that today because I'm not doing well," McCarthy said, his face grim. "Today I'm not doing well at all."

There was dead silence in the lecture hall. It lasted for ten or maybe fifteen seconds, which felt like a long time after what McCarthy had confessed. Then a young woman in the middle of the room called out, "We love you, Tim," and someone started to clap, and then everyone was clapping—a long, cathartic burst of applause that was consolation to McCarthy but also something more, a wave of emotion that said, *We're in this together.*

"Thank you," McCarthy said, choking up. "I love you, too."

And without further ado, he and John Stauffer began their lecture on James Agee and Walker Evans' classic work, *Let Us Now Praise Famous Men.* That was how it worked in their classroom. You taught the past and you taught the present, because to believe that the two could be separated—well, that was a fallacy. To think that you could ever keep politics out of the classroom was a politics of its own.

Tim McCarthy is a student of the past with a very modern personal history. The adopted son of middle-class parents, he is a Harvard graduate, class of 1993, with a doctorate in American history from Columbia. A former high school jock, at 6'4" and two hundred–plus pounds, he now struggles slightly with his weight. He dated women in high school, college, and after, but came out of the closet during graduate school. He has the clean-cut look of a Little Leaguer, but he likes to smoke Parliament Lights when he's writing, drinking, or driving long distances. An intensely serious man, McCarthy is passionate about civil rights and social justice, yet he loves to laugh and does so loudly and often—a deep, joyous yelp that rises up from his stomach. And he is the kind of teacher who—for better or worse, and there are people on both sides of the question—is rare at Harvard. Intense, committed, learned, and yet vulnerable, McCarthy never hesitates to connect the past and the present. In his classroom, the lines between the intellectual, the personal, and the political are frequently blurred. Intellectual purists—scholars who feel that their emotions and political opinions don't belong in the classroom—did not approve of his style, but many students did. They loved McCarthy. During his time at Harvard, he won four college prizes for teaching and advising. Walking across the Yard with him was not unlike walking with Cornel West; a five-minute jaunt could take half an hour, so many students called out to McCarthy.

He was, he will admit, a troublemaker from an early age.

McCarthy grew up near Albany, New York, the adopted son of Tom and Michelle McCarthy, a basketball coach and a public school teacher. He never knew his biological parents and never wanted to; Tom and Michelle loved Tim as if he were their own, and that was good enough for him. Still, McCarthy's conception of family was shaped by his early awareness that he was adopted. Once, in kindergarten, he and his classmates were asked to draw a picture of their birthday party. "I basically drew a picture of everybody I knew," McCarthy said. "Of this woman in a car bringing me to my parents, the guy at the candy store, my teacher, friends, grandparents. My dog and cat." Even then, McCarthy said, his conception of family wasn't about biology, but about community.

Anyway, Tom and Michelle were all the parents anyone could ask for. Tom came from Irish stock, and Michelle was of Italian descent.

Politically they were FDR and JFK people—bread-and-butter, middle-class Democrats. Both were devout Catholics but low-key about their faith, more prone to doing good works than talking about them. They never liked ostentatious public displays of piety, such as when a football player on TV thanked Jesus for a touchdown. Michelle was a third-grade teacher, quiet and patient; she spent the last fifteen years of her career in the same classroom where Tim had attended third grade. Tom was a basketball coach and athletic director at Guilderland High School. Tim went to Guilderland and played basketball for his father, and "there would be teammates who couldn't afford shoes or basketball camp, but they'd always seem to have shoes or go to camp," McCarthy said. "I learned later that my father was taking care of those things." Every Christmas, Tom McCarthy drove to the local liquor store and bought a bottle for the school custodians and bus drivers, because he thought those were the guys who really kept the school going. "And at my high school graduation party," Tim said, "there were all these janitors and school bus drivers."

The McCarthys took so many people into their home—foreign exchange students, foster children from China, a friend who'd lost his job—that Tim's classmates dubbed his house "Hotel McCarthy." But for Tim, the most important visitor was John Cottingham, an African American kid from a tough section of Brooklyn, New York. John had come to the McCarthys through the Fresh Air Fund, the charity that arranges for inner-city kids to spend time with host families in rural areas. "I was six when he first started coming, for a week or two at first and then a month, and for a long time John was my best friend," McCarthy remembered. "John would tell me stories about New York, and he was a Yankees fan, and he told me when he lost his virginity—I was about twelve." There weren't many black kids in Duanesburg, New York—"the middle of nowhere," McCarthy calls it—or many people of color, period. Its population of about 5,800 is now 97.2 percent white, 1 percent American Indian, 0.8 of a percent Hispanic, and 1 percent "mixed race." But McCarthy never felt that John's presence was unusual. "My parents had invited him into our home, which made our relationship seem normal for me. It was only in retrospect that I realized how extraordinary this was," he said.

Young Tim was a troublemaker both in and out of class. "There were constant parent-teacher conferences," he said. "I was rebellious. I

wanted attention. If I was in trouble, it meant I was relevant." In second grade, McCarthy got all As on his report card, but his teacher
wrote in the comment section that "Timothy talks too much." His
father wrote back, "You're telling us." Tom liked to joke that Tim was
vaccinated with a phonograph needle. At age nine, shortly after his
class had practiced a nuclear fallout drill, Tim wrote a letter to President Reagan advocating a nuclear freeze. Someone at the White
House sent him a letter back, with the president's signature on it and
an autographed photo attached. It didn't make much difference. A few
days later, McCarthy's school held a mock presidential election and
young Tim organized the students to vote against Reagan.

The assignment gave McCarthy a sense of purpose that the other

It was around then that McCarthy's teacher came up with the idea
of pairing Tim with Shawn Page. Shawn was a boy with Down's syndrome, a chromosomal irregularity that impedes physical and intellectual development, but because of the way the schools worked back
then, he and Tim were in the same class. Tim agreed to hang out with
Shawn, helping him with his homework and looking out for him
whenever possible. McCarthy didn't have any brothers or sisters, but
he would have Shawn.

The assignment gave McCarthy a sense of purpose that the other
kids didn't, and he rose to the responsibility. He tried to help Shawn
learn to read; he always picked Shawn for his kickball team; he went to
Shawn's birthday party, noticing that there weren't many other kids
there, that it was mostly parents in attendance. Shawn's mother
thanked Tim effusively for coming, but McCarthy didn't think he
deserved any special thanks. He may have been helping Shawn, but
Shawn was also helping him. Working with Shawn calmed him down.

In junior high, Shawn was placed in a special education classroom,
and the two boys lost touch. McCarthy went on to be a top-notch student and one of the most popular kids at Guilderland. He was also an
athlete whose skills at basketball, football, and track had led Dartmouth and Harvard to express interest in him. Even though McCarthy
never expected it, Harvard accepted him. He started there in the fall
of 1989.

In one sense, everything seemed perfect for Tim McCarthy. He was
succeeding in high school by every standard measure. He was smart
and popular and had a girlfriend, and in their senior year she was voted
Classiest and Best-looking and he was voted Most School Spirit and

Most Likely to Succeed. But McCarthy's life was not as simple as appearances suggested. Back in ninth grade, he'd had a homosexual encounter with one of his best friends. Neither spoke about it much; both were popular athletes whose social personae conflicted with their real identities. But their sexual relationship would continue on and off for almost a decade, during which time McCarthy would continue to date women yet occasionally have clandestine flings with men.

Harvard was a new world for McCarthy. He went there fearing that he wouldn't fit in, that somewhere, sometime, someone was going to tap him on the shoulder and tell him, sorry, there'd been a mistake, the admissions office meant to send its acceptance letter to some other Timothy McCarthy. That didn't happen, of course, and McCarthy continued along much the same path that he had in high school. He was gregarious, well liked, and busy, reveling in all that Harvard had to offer. He even joined a final club, the Phoenix. He'd be a little embarrassed about that later, because he wasn't comfortable with the politics of the exclusive clubs, but he did agitate for the Phoenix to admit women—not that it made any difference. And, yes, he had to admit, it was flattering for a kid from upstate New York to be "punched." The guy who wasn't even sure he belonged at Harvard was moving in its innermost circles, and he loved it. The professors, his classmates, the academic opportunities, the social life—McCarthy drank deep from all that Harvard had to offer. When he graduated, he was asked to serve as the secretary for his class, a lifelong post which kept him in touch with official Harvard.

He did not, however, forget where he had come from or what he believed in. At the end of his sophomore year, McCarthy returned to Guilderland to see a friend graduate. As the names of the graduates were read off, McCarthy suddenly heard the words "Shawn Page," and saw his old friend walk across the commencement stage, all decked out in cap and gown. Before he could catch himself, McCarthy felt tears roll down his face, and he thought, *I helped teach him to read.*

As a junior in Quincy House, McCarthy volunteered for a Head Start program in which he mentored a four-year-old African American boy named Malcolm Green. The boy's father wasn't around much, so Malcolm quickly connected with McCarthy, and vice versa. Over the following years, the two grew close as brothers; for two people who appeared to have little in common, they actually had a lot in common.

"Malcolm and I don't share an ounce of blood, but we finish each other's sentences," McCarthy said. They liked to joke that they could understand each other so well, they could read each other's minds. When Nelson Mandela spoke at Harvard in 1998, McCarthy brought Malcolm and they sat in the eighth row. Afterward, he asked the boy if he understood how important the day had been, what miracles Nelson Mandela and the liberation of South Africa were. Malcolm responded, "I'm not sure I understand everything, but I do know that democracy is a good thing, right?"

McCarthy did his best to keep Malcolm out of trouble and help him with his schoolwork, and whenever a major decision needed to be made, McCarthy would sit with Malcolm's mother and they would talk about what was best for the boy. Their relationship continued even when McCarthy graduated in 1993, heading to New York City and Columbia to study American and African American history with Eric Foner and Manning Marable, two of the most distinguished figures in their fields.

Graduate school was a struggle. McCarthy didn't get any grant money from Columbia, so he was constantly broke. For fun, he'd cheer on the Yankees from the cheap seats in the right-field bleachers. It helped him get perspective on the frustrating internal politics of the academic world, the way graduate students fought over teaching positions, competed for grant money, sucked up to professors, and sniped about one another. He was in a serious relationship with a woman, a former tennis star now working in international development, who showed every sign of wanting to marry him. He loved her and told himself that he should be happy, but at the same time he wondered whether, if they did get married, he'd one day become "that guy"—the happily married man who gets caught in the sack with another guy. Increasingly depressed, desperate for a change of scene, he called up Harvard English department chair Larry Buell, whom he'd known as an undergrad, and asked if there was any way he could teach at Harvard. There was. In the fall of 1998, before he had even completed his dissertation, Tim McCarthy returned to Harvard to teach in the Department of History and Literature.

That helped. But McCarthy's sexual problems were still unresolved. His girlfriend moved from Washington to Boston to be with him, and finally McCarthy broke up with her. It was a messy, dishonest breakup, one of the great regrets of his life: he told her that it was because she didn't get along with Malcolm well enough. Afterward, he exercised too little and drank too much. Still in the closet and deeply unhappy, he rationalized reasons to hide his homosexuality. Malcolm was thirteen now, a student at Cambridge Rindge and Latin School, and McCarthy thought he needed to set an example for the boy he considered his younger brother. The two went to church together every week; McCarthy doubted that the predominantly black congregation would feel comfortable with a gay white guy hanging around young Malcolm. So, instead of dealing with the problem, he poured himself heart and soul into his teaching. It was the only thing that kept him going. On the other hand, his dissertation-writing stopped entirely.

It was Malcolm who helped him break out of his depression. One day after school, he came to Quincy House, where McCarthy was living again, to work on his homework and spend the night in McCarthy's suite. That day, Cambridge Rindge and Latin had hosted a guest speaker, a civil rights lawyer who happened to be gay. He'd reminded Malcolm of Tim. And so, while McCarthy was checking his e-mail, his thirteen-year-old brother turned to him and said, "Tim, are you gay?" McCarthy hemmed and hawed. Finally Malcolm said, "Tim, it's a simple question. If you asked me if I'm black, I'd say 'yes.'"

And that was it. McCarthy told him the truth, and the next morning he woke up with a feeling of lightness and liberation. He started to tell those friends who hadn't already figured out the truth. He told his students, because he saw so many of them, both in and out of the closet, who were struggling with their sexuality. Harvard doesn't have many openly gay faculty members, and McCarthy thought that he could help the students. There were a lot of kids at Harvard who came from backgrounds where being homosexual was a particular stigma—working-class kids, Catholic students, athletes, black kids. McCarthy had had experience with all of those.

Telling his parents was the hardest thing. He had always been the success story, the adopted kid who'd made good. Now he feared that he would disappoint them. He couldn't tell them for years, and even then he needed a shove: McCarthy was so enraged by the Bush administration's push for a constitutional amendment banning gay marriage that he grew ashamed of his reticence with his own family. But when he finally sat down with Tom and Michelle in the spring of 2004, they amazed him again, just as they always had. There was no disapproval, only support. "Well, I had a feeling," his mother said.

After the conversation with Malcolm, McCarthy's life started to fall into place. He resumed writing his dissertation. Along with graduate student John McMillian, he began work on a collection called *The Radical Reader: A Documentary History of the American Radical Tradition*. He began teaching a class for low-income adults in Dorchester, a poor section of Boston. Beginning in 2001, he led a group of students on what he called his "alternative spring break." McCarthy had grown interested in the widespread incidence of arson suffered by African American churches in the South; while other students were off in Jamaica or the Bahamas, McCarthy and fifteen or twenty students traveled down to Alabama and North Carolina, where they'd work on a church that some coward had tried to burn down. McCarthy was making $42,000 a year, with no savings or investment, and "in debt up to my ass," as he put it. Until recently, he qualified for food stamps. But he was getting paid to teach at Harvard, and that was a fantastic thing.

And McCarthy grew increasingly politically active. He got involved with the living wage movement, which was why he had met with Larry Summers in August 2001. That meeting, at which Summers had humiliated the sophomore who got a fact wrong, until McCarthy intervened, left McCarthy worried. On the one hand, he appreciated that Summers had taken an hour from his day to meet with the group of living wage supporters. But Summers' tone, the hostility he'd shown to the kid who dared to challenge him, were alarming. "I found his behavior in that meeting to be really unsavory," McCarthy said.

Though McCarthy thought that Neil Rudenstine had erred by not supporting the living-wage movement, he had always liked and admired the former president. He'd once written Rudenstine a letter reflecting upon the importance of ethnic diversity at Harvard, and gotten a two-page, handwritten response back. "I appreciate more than anything your own description of what the experience of diversity at Harvard meant to you and your roommate," Rudenstine said, "and how the experience turned into such a rich and lasting friendship. These are exactly the kinds of experiences that will be lost if we don't somehow change the mood of the courts, legislatures and others."

When it was announced that Larry Summers had been chosen to

replace Rudenstine, everyone said that he'd been picked to "shake up" Harvard. Tim McCarthy hoped that support for affirmative action would not be a casualty of the shake-up.

Then came the Cornel West matter, and that more than worried McCarthy—it infuriated him. He knew West only slightly, but admired him immensely. And he owed him. When McCarthy and McMillian were trying to land a contract for their collection of documents, West had picked up the phone and called a publisher on their behalf, and his recommendation had probably sealed the deal. Not many professors would expend capital in the publishing world to help out a couple of junior scholars. For Summers to attack a man who did so much for the Harvard community—no, who did his best to *make* Harvard a community—seemed inexplicable. McCarthy could think of only one rationale that seemed to fully explain Summers' actions— racism. But he hoped he was wrong; he did not want to believe that of Harvard's new president.

McCarthy was also uncomfortable with Summers' notion of patriotism. McCarthy did not believe that it was the work of a university to rally around the government, but to analyze and question the actions of that government. This was particularly true after September 11, when the White House was using the terrorist attacks to justify all sorts of far-reaching policies. At a peace rally on September 20, 2001, McCarthy decried the rush to war. "I deplore those who are deploying rhetoric and deploying troops without thinking before they speak," McCarthy said. He argued that the Bush administration was exploiting the aftermath of 9/11 "to further its imperial intentions."

Shortly after that, McCarthy's name landed on a list of one hundred and seventeen unpatriotic academics compiled by the American Council of Trustees and Alumni, a conservative think tank founded by Lynne Cheney, wife of Vice-President Dick Cheney. Mrs. Cheney's group had published a report called "Defending Civilization: How Our Universities Are Failing America and What Can Be Done about It." The report argued that "the events of September 11 underscored a deep divide between mainstream public reaction and that of our intellectual elites." Rather than rallying behind President Bush, "many faculty demurred. Some refused to make judgments. Many invoked tolerance and diversity as antidotes to evil." The report concluded that "moral relativism has become a staple of academic life in this country."

The words were only slightly to the right of the rhetoric that Larry Summers was then employing. But McCarthy couldn't agree with the sentiments, whether they came from the president of Harvard or a vice-president's wife. He didn't think of himself as an intellectual elite; he was the son of public school teachers. And he certainly was no moral relativist. He believed in right and wrong. He was a religious man, deeply involved in social work and social activism, with passionately held moral convictions. They just weren't those of Lynne Cheney or Larry Summers.

As Summers' presidency continued, McCarthy grew increasingly skeptical of the tone Summers was establishing. Harvard, he thought, did not need a president who would make it a still more competitive, more individualistic place, but rather a more humane and spiritual community. The suicide of Marian Smith helped crystallize his concerns. Just a few days after her death, McCarthy was taking a group of students from Quincy House to see the Michael Moore documentary *Bowling for Columbine*. The subject of Smith's death came up, and McCarthy noticed that even though the university had said nothing official about her suicide—hadn't even told the students what was really going on—everyone in the group knew what had happened and was deeply upset by the tragedy. Some of them had known Smith and were on the verge of tears as they remembered their late friend.

"I started talking to them about 'Why do you think she did it?'" McCarthy remembered. "One student said that she could understand how Marian Smith could seem so happy outside and be so depressed inside. And I said, 'Do the rest of you feel that way?' And their answer was, 'Yeah, maybe not that bad, but Harvard's a place where you always have to look happy, always on the go.'"

So, after the movie, McCarthy sat down at his computer and composed an e-mail to Larry Summers. It said something like, "I know you've got a lot on your plate, but someone high in the administration should send out a message about Marian Smith, just to say that it's always tragic when something like this happens, what a vivacious person she was—that kind of thing. Just so the students know that someone up there cares."

McCarthy knew that Summers responded to e-mailed suggestions that he liked. He was disappointed but not surprised when he got no response to this one. Certainly the suggestion was never acted upon.

The lack of a response didn't deter him, though. McCarthy had come to see himself as an advocate for students, who had so few advocates on campus—and now even fewer, with Harry Lewis leaving. McCarthy knew how messy, how complicated, a life can be, and the students saw that he knew, and they asked him for help. Like the time when one junior called McCarthy late at night, distraught over a family problem. Things were so bad that the kid was considering dropping out of Harvard. But by the end of his conversation with McCarthy, the student felt a little better, a little stronger. In the end, he would make it through—and he gave McCarthy much of the credit.

"That kind of thing, it's not the kind of thing that I could put on my CV, and it's not going to get me tenure," McCarthy said. "But how could I not do it? They're clearly unhappy, these kids, and that's become something of an obsession for me.

"I know that I don't quite belong here at Harvard," he said. He loved his alma mater, but he was afraid of staying too long, of growing bitter about his inability to change an institution that seemed not to care about its students. If he became pessimistic or cynical, what kind of message would that send to the students? So McCarthy made a painful decision. The University of North Carolina at Chapel Hill had offered him an office and a telephone to work on a book about the burnings of African American churches, and McCarthy accepted the offer. He was going to leave Harvard at the end of the semester, a year before his contract was up. Harvard was going in a direction Tim McCarthy didn't like, and he could try to change it only so much before getting jaded. It was time to move on.

"I don't think that Larry Summers spends a minute thinking about me, but if he did, he would prefer not to have me here," McCarthy said. "I would just hope that if Larry really knew what I did, that he'd have an appreciation for that."

It was not, he admitted, a hope in which he placed much confidence.

In mid-February, Harvard and six other universities filed an amicus curiae brief with the Supreme Court supporting the University of Michigan's defense of affirmative action. The brief argued that the point of affirmative action was to promote diversity on campuses. "Academically selective universities have a compelling interest in ensuring that their student bodies incorporate the experiences and talents of the wide spectrum of racial and ethnic groups that make up our society," it stated. Universities couldn't adequately prepare their students for a globalized world if they didn't attend school with students of different origins. "By creating a broadly diverse class, [the universities'] admissions policies help to assure that their graduates are well prepared to succeed in an increasingly complex and multi-racial society."

In the past, proponents of affirmative action had argued that its purpose was to remedy prior discrimination, mostly against African Americans. But over time the argument had shifted to claim that, because diversity was inherently educational, affirmative action benefited everyone, not just its direct recipients. Affirmative action was no longer so much about fixing the past as about shaping the future. It was impossible to tell whether supporters really believed the new position or simply felt that, in the current political climate, the idea of reaching out to African Americans at the expense of whites would not be broadly supported. Indeed, almost unanimously, polls showed that most Americans agreed with the White House's opposition to affirmative action, despite the fact that they also believed that the country had not eliminated discrimination based on race.

Larry Summers' position on the issue had changed as well. In his early meeting with African American professors, Summers had sounded skeptical about, if not hostile to, affirmative action. Now he signed off on the friend-of-the-court brief, and in March he and constitutional law professor Laurence Tribe published a *New York Times* op-ed piece headlined "Race Is Never Neutral." Mostly written by Tribe, the editorial repeated the argument that diversity helped prepare students "to live and work in a global economy and a multiracial world."

This was an argument that Summers could support, but whether he actually supported affirmative action as a means to the end of diversity was still in doubt. Charles Ogletree, the law professor who had clashed with Summers at a meeting in the summer of 2001, felt that Summers had genuinely come around—thanks in large part to Ogletree. After the departure of Cornel West, Ogletree met with Summers several times to push him on the issue. "He and I spent more than a year in some intense but very productive meetings, talking about [the Michigan cases] and the future of diversity, and we went from being very far apart to coming to a meeting of the minds," Ogletree said. "Larry was a new president and he made a number of terrible errors.

But he's moved miles away from rigid thinking to a much more nuanced sense" of the value of affirmative action.

Not everyone agreed. Two sources familiar with Summer's thinking on the issue suggested that Summers had, in fact, not changed his mind about affirmative action one bit—he'd only adjusted his public position. His defense of the policy, they said, had more to do with affirming Harvard's independence—its power to admit whom it wanted, how it wanted, with no government interference. Moreover, opposing affirmative action would break with the tradition of both Derek Bok and Neil Rudenstine. Summers was loathe to reverse a thirty-year tradition advocated by two past, but still living, presidents. And, of course, after Cornel West, Summers was hyper-sensitive to any suggestion that he was hostile to the presence of African Americans at Harvard.

"In his heart and soul, Summers has some real doubts about anything that is not merit-based," said one professor who has discussed the issue with him. "But he can't come out against affirmative action. It's established policy at Harvard. And especially not after Cornel West."

On occasion, though, Summers showed glimpses of his true feelings. At one meeting with agents of the Harvard Alumni Association, in the spring of 2003, the subject of a commencement speaker for 2004 arose. One person suggested then National Security Advisor Condoleezza Rice. Summers reacted quickly and angrily. "I will not select my commencement speaker based on affirmative action," he snapped.

Nor did Summers feel the need for affirmative action—or even simple desegregation—within Harvard's upper echelons: He did not speak at all about the importance of diversity on the faculty. By the end of his first three years in office, the percentage of tenure appointments who were women had dropped from 36 percent in Neil Rudenstine's last year to 13 percent. This wasn't entirely Summers' fault—tenure nominations came first from the departments—but it did reflect the fact that Summers never mentioned the issue, and department chairs clearly did not think he cared about it. On this issue, Summers chose not to use his bully pulpit.

Moreover, after his first three years as president, Summers had not appointed a single African American to a high-level university position. His mostly male administration was glaringly white. (One exception was aide Colleen Richards Powell, the woman who took notes while students met with Summers.) While Summers grudgingly conceded the need for affirmative action to promote diversity within Harvard's student body, he did not appear to believe that the same approach applied to his own administration. He had worked with homogeneous groups in the Harvard economics department and at Treasury, and as Harvard president would repeat the pattern.

In the spring of 2004, Summers spoke at a Harvard Club luncheon, and one alum asked him how he felt about affirmative action. "I do believe in affirmative action," he responded. "The reasons for my belief are stated in the brief Harvard filed. . . . But the really important issue for the future is not affirmative action in college admissions today, but what are we going to do about the continuing achievement gap in American education?"

Which was his way of saying that he would tolerate affirmative action, but he preferred to change the subject from race to class. Summers was more interested in the relationship between income and education, which was, to be sure, an important area to investigate. Poor students of any color had a harder time getting into Harvard than did more affluent students, because they lacked access to good schools and other educational opportunities—music lessons, travel abroad, and so on. The problem was that reaching out to such students almost always necessitated a lowering of standards—they lacked the training and resources to match up with more affluent students—and that was something Summers was loath to do. He hoped that if the university looked hard enough, Harvard could find poor students who were academically gifted and tough enough to survive there.

The president's public support for affirmative action, then, was carefully crafted but not entirely honest. In truth, he would put Harvard's weight in defense of affirmative action because that was his only realistic option. At the same time, he would push the institution to worry less about racial discrimination and more about the inequities of class in America.

In his first year as president, Summers had spoken his mind more freely. He'd learned, however, that sometimes it was better to keep his opinions to himself—or at least largely to himself, because he could not entirely contain his true feelings and they inevitably spilled out one way or another. He had also learned that you could say one thing in public and another in private and usually get away with the contradiction. Like when the *New York Times* called for input on an article about how pragmatic and career-focused modern students are, and Summers gave them this quote: "I do worry. I do somehow wish that students would smell the roses a little more." Suggesting that his students "smell the roses" contradicted virtually every message, spoken or otherwise, he had delivered to his campus—this was the president who repeatedly urged his students to "get cracking"—yet the *Times* ran the quote without question or context. It was understandable that Summers thought the press could be manipulated.

He still chafed, though, at the idea of restricting his public commentary to those issues that had direct relevance only to Harvard. Summers was strongly in favor of the coming war—he believed that Iraq posed a genuine danger to the United States and that preemptive military action was justified—but there was no particular reason for the Harvard president to say so publicly, and he was frustrated that few campus questioners seemed to want his opinion on the matter. He lamented that students were more interested in talking to him about the pre-registration debate—a failed attempt by Bill Kirby to curtail the time in which students could choose courses—than about his position on the war.

There was, of course, one issue on which Summers had taken a very public position—anti-Semitism. That he had done so was about to make his life extremely awkward.

There were, of course, many on the Harvard campus who strongly agreed with Larry Summers' attack on the advocates of divestment from Israel. One of them, a young Jewish woman named Rachel Fish, was inspired enough to act on Summers' words. Fish, a second-year student at the Harvard Divinity School, was convinced that the left-wing anti-Semitism Summers was talking about was prevalent at HDS. "The school is very sensitive about race, gender, and women's rights," she said. "Yet it seems to be lacking any sensitivity to anti-Jewish sentiment."

Certainly the Harvard Divinity School has a long-standing reputation for political radicalism; that was a big reason Summers didn't like it. He considered the place a hotbed for students more interested in activism than academia. Another possibility is that many students interested in theology and spirituality are interested in promoting social justice, and vice versa. But whichever the case, there's no question that the divinity school tilts to the left. A not-atypical 2002 conference at the school included sessions on the following topics: "Woman's Inhumanity to Woman," "Seeds of Violence in Religion," "The Legacy of Patriarchy: Unraveling the Gender Knot," and "Is Violence in Humans Inevitable?"

While the divinity school's primary purpose has always been to train Christian ministers, it welcomes students of all faiths, many of whom never enter the ministry but go into social work or political activism on behalf of women, gays, children, and other oppressed groups. Some, perhaps many, divinity school students would include Palestinians among the ranks of the oppressed.

Rachel Fish was convinced that some of that pro-Palestinian sentiment crossed a line into anti-Semitism. She had already helped to organize a group called the Harvard University Graduate Student Friends of Israel. Her next act, in December 2002, was to stage a conference about global anti-Semitism. She invited some experts on the subject for a panel discussion, moderated by professor Ruth Wisse, in a divinity school classroom. The conference took place on a bitterly cold night, but some forty people showed up, which Fish considered a pretty good turnout. She was distressed, though, by something she learned from one of the speakers that night.

In the summer of 2000, the divinity school had received a $2.5-million donation to endow a chair in Islamic Studies. Two and a half million dollars is a lot of money for that school, which has always been one of Harvard's poorest tubs. (Its endowment of around $350 million is about two percent of Harvard's total.) This gift came from a potentially huge source of future contributions, but one that was also morally problematic: Sheikh Zayed bin Sultan Al Nayan of the United Arab Emirates. Born in 1918, Sheik Zayed had been that country's unelected "president" since 1971, and, though well into his 80s in 2003, he was still an immensely powerful figure in the Middle East. Fish learned that while Sheik Zayed was giving money to Harvard to promote the study of Arab culture, in his own country he was using his immense wealth to promote anti-Semitism. And that made Fish wonder: how could a university whose president denounced anti-Semitism accept millions from a man who funded it?

Rachel Lea Fish does not particularly look like a fighter. Born in

1979, she is a pretty, petite woman with blonde hair and brown eyes. She speaks so quietly it's possible not to hear the grit in her voice. But her upbringing gave her a passion and a courage to stick up for her convictions. Fish is the daughter of a pediatrician and a homemaker who settled in Johnson City, Tennessee, after her father's military service during Vietnam. Johnson City is a medium-size town of about fifty thousand people, very few of whom were like the Fish family. "In that town and the six surrounding it, there were only about 60 Jewish families," Fish said. "We all knew each other."

Folks in Johnson City took it for granted that their neighbors were Christian. When Fish started grade school, each day would begin with Christian prayer, and Fish sat outside her classroom while the other students bowed their heads. When she told her parents, they met with the teachers and the school board, and eventually the prayer was dropped. Of course, virtually everyone in school soon knew what had happened, and some of Fish's classmates decided that the appropriate response was to try to convert her to Christianity. "It wasn't malicious," she said. "Just ignorant."

Some behavior was especially ignorant. In sixth grade, a classmate scratched a swastika onto the front of her locker. Her teacher wanted to suspend the boy, but Fish thought that would only make the problem worse. He didn't come from much of a family, this kid. Even though he was in sixth grade, he was illiterate. Suspending him from school would only make things worse. So Fish proposed another option: after school every day, she'd teach the boy to read. "Because if he knew what the swastikas meant, he probably wouldn't have done it." And for four months, she did just that. "I didn't understand how he couldn't know how to read," Fish said. "He taught me about that, and how his family didn't support him."

After high school Fish attended George Washington University in Washington, D.C., where she double-majored in Judaic studies and Middle Eastern studies. She spent her junior year abroad at Hebrew University, in Jerusalem. Her identity as a Jew was important to her, and after college Fish wanted to pursue the study of the religions of the Middle East. The Harvard Divinity School seemed a natural choice. Graduates included such inspiring figures as Ralph Waldo Emerson and Transcendentalist minister Theodore Parker. "Harvard is *the* university," she explained. "It's the place where people go to make something of themselves." Fish liked that the divinity school application said that the school was seeking people who could create change in the world. "The notion of 'veritas' seduces you," she said.

When Fish took a closer look into what else Sheik Zayed did with his money, what she found was disturbing. In 1998 the sheik's wife donated $50,000 to support Roger Garaudy, a French writer whose book *The Founding Myths of Israeli Politics* argued that the Holocaust had not happened, but that Jews had died of disease and starvation during World War II. And in 1999, Sheik Zayed founded the Zayed Centre for Coordination and Follow-up, intended to be the official think tank of the twenty-two–nation Arab League. Sheik Zayed's son, the deputy prime minister of the United Arab Emirates, was the center's director.

Over the next few years, the Zayed Centre hosted a number of foreign dignitaries, including Jimmy Carter, Al Gore, and former secretary of state James Baker. But it also engaged in some less savory activity, including the publication of anti-Semitic literature charging that Israel is the tool of "forces of world hegemony." The center offered programs on topics such as "the Jewish control of the American government and media"; its director announced at one conference that "Jews are the enemy of all nations." One guest lecturer, Saudi professor Umayma Jalahma, declared that "the Jewish people must obtain human blood so that their clerics can prepare holiday pastries." And the center had published a translation of French writer Thierry Meyssan's crackpot book, *The Horrifying Fraud*, which charged that the United States attacked itself on September 11, flying planes into the World Trade Center by remote control in order to justify imperial war against Afghanistan and Iraq. Reading the Zayed Centre's literature, Fish said, "was like reading history written by the Nazis."

Here was a new challenge of globalization. As Harvard extended its presence around the globe, it also searched for donors worldwide. The idea made perfect sense. In many countries, the Harvard name is even more revered than it is in the United States, and for wealthy foreigners, the idea of linking themselves to the Harvard brand holds enormous appeal. The problem for Harvard is that it's considerably more difficult to investigate how foreign donors make and spend their money than it is to conduct background checks on Americans. In 1993 and 1994, for example, Saudi Arabia's Bin Laden Group contributed

$2 million to the law and design schools. After 9/11, the bin Laden contributions became an issue, but Harvard officials insisted that the business had no connection to Osama bin Laden, and that if anyone could show that the money was tainted, Harvard would return it. Of course, trying to disentangle the finances of the bin Laden family is a task that the FBI and the Justice Department have found challenging, and Harvard didn't appear to be trying very hard to do it. Its only public action was to delete details of the bin Laden gift from the university website. And if a connection could be found, a common argument made at Harvard (and, to be sure, at plenty of other universities) is that it's better for crooks, tyrants, and killers to give their cash to a university than to spend it on nefarious evildoing. At least a university would put it to good use.

Rachel Fish did not agree. She took all that rhetoric about truth seriously. What did the Harvard name stand for if it could be rented out to any bidder, no matter how unsavory? "Harvard sets the tone for so many universities," she said. "It sets the precedent." On March 19, Fish met with divinity school dean William Graham to argue that Harvard should return Sheik Zayed's money. After all, Larry Summers had taken to the pulpit of Memorial Church to denounce anti-Semitism. The president of Harvard, she was sure, would be on her side.

Fish's due diligence put Graham in an extremely awkward position. A scholar of Middle Eastern religious history, Graham is an affable North Carolinian who has been a member of the Harvard faculty since 1973. Though he had served as acting dean since January 2002, when Father J. Bryan Hehir resigned the position, Graham did not want to run the divinity school. He had apparently been a candidate for deanships at Georgetown University and the University of North Carolina at Chapel Hill, but was not offered either job. Now he was interested in an FAS position. For years he had paid his dues in the Faculty of Arts and Sciences by volunteering for soporific committees and thankless administrative positions. He had been a dedicated master of Currier House, well known for his support of the students. But the head of the divinity school presided over a lackluster endowment, a fractious faculty, and a politicized student body. Graham wanted something better.

Such a post was not in the offing, however, and so Graham accepted Summers' imprecations to take the divinity school job. "Bill probably figured that he had the opportunity to turn the divinity school into a truly secular, intellectual institution," said a colleague who knows him well. The appointment was greeted with suspicion in some quarters; Graham would be the divinity school's first dean who was not an ordained minister or priest, fueling the theory that Summers wanted to make the divinity school less of a training ground for ministers and more a center for scholars of religion. As Summers had said, somewhat obliquely, in a September 2002 speech at the school, "In what ways should Christianity be privileged and not be privileged, recognizing the school's traditions, strengths, and need for focus, and also taking into account growing religious pluralism?" His audience could read between the lines.

Graham also had another question mark hovering over his deanship. In the spring of 2002, he had signed the petition to divest from Israel. A week or so later, he changed his mind and asked that his name be removed, which it was. "I took my name off when I discovered that [the petition organizers] were putting the petition online," Graham said. According to Graham, the divestment website contained links to "at least" one website that he considered anti-Semitic. (Petition organizers deny the accusation.)

Inevitably, Graham's change of heart convinced no one. When Summers announced that Graham was his choice to be the divinity school dean, both opponents and supporters of divestment instantly suspected that Graham had taken his name off the petition because Summers had demanded that Graham renounce the petition as a condition of being appointed. Graham denied the charge, saying, "You'll have to ask Larry about that. He appointed me. He knew very well that I had signed [the petition]. I told him I had signed it."

Though he officially became dean in August 2002, almost two years after the Sheik Zayed donation was made, Graham had welcomed the money when it was given. "This endowment is a most welcome gift," he told the *Harvard Gazette*. But when Rachel Fish informed him of Sheik Zayed's extracurricular activities, Graham was concerned. He promised to investigate the matter, and he subsequently told reporters that if the charges were true, the divinity school would give back the money. But when Fish mentioned that she was sending a copy of all her research to President Summers, Graham insisted she needn't do that. "He said, 'I'll keep [Larry] informed,'" Fish said.

Fish responded that she would send her research to Summers anyway. "I'm giving you the chance to reclaim the moral authority of the divinity school," she said.

It was a tense meeting at an already tense time on campus. At 10:30 that night—5:30 A.M., March 20, Bagdad time—United States aircraft began dropping bombs on Iraq. The war had begun.

The peace rally commenced at 12:30 the next afternoon, when some one thousand students, faculty, and Cambridge locals gathered in front of the statue of John Harvard. It was a miserable day, cold and wet and gray. The winter snow had melted—more would fall soon enough—leaving the Yard so muddy that it resembled the pig pen it had been during the seventeenth century. The protesters walked gingerly lest the mud suck the shoes off their feet. Some people stood on the cardboard signs that they had intended to wave.

As Harvard police cars quietly cruised along the Yard's paved paths and parked in its corners, a group of protesters chanted, "No war on Iraq / Bill of rights / Take it back!" Near them a man carried a sign that said DRAFT BEER NOT BOYS. One student waved a sign saying HARVARD STUDENTS WANT PEACE, the words scrawled on the back of an Amazon.com box. Members of a local church were passing out granola bars.

There were counterprotesters too, a group of young men with shaved heads dressed up in military fatigues. Their signs read, I LOVE BUSH AND RUMSFELD, and IF YOU WANT TO PROTEST, GO TO FRANCE. They looked too young to be Harvard students, and they hung out on the fringe of the protest. About half the crowd, though, just seemed curious, milling around and talking. In fact, there was no consensus at Harvard about the war. Most of those who supported it did so with reservations; most of those who opposed it admitted that they might be wrong. The anti-war certitude of 1969 was ancient history.

A couple of hundred yards away, in Memorial Hall, the freshmen were receiving their housing assignments for sophomore year. Whooping and hollering, they made so much noise that one local news crew would air footage of them, mistaking the rambunctious freshmen for anti-war protesters. Almost directly opposite John Harvard, on the other side of the Yard, a burly police officer stationed himself outside the front door of Massachusetts Hall. No one had threatened the president's office, but Harvard was taking no chances. Everyone knew how Summers felt about protesters.

A student named Michael Getlin stood before the microphone. Just days before, Getlin told the crowd, he had withdrawn his application to join the Marines. It was not an easy decision, Getlin said. Both his father and uncle had fought in Vietnam; their family took military service very seriously. But the war, Getlin said, "represents a trajectory for our foreign policy of which I will take no part. It is an effort that will alienate our country from the global community that we have worked so hard to create." Getlin looked distraught and a little lost.

After Getlin came a lecturer in the Department of Religion named Brian Palmer, a thin, wispy thirty-eight-year-old with a shock of dark hair, thick glasses, and a voice so fragile it sounded as if he were struggling for breath. Palmer taught one of Harvard's most popular courses, Personal Choice and Global Transformation, which had some five hundred students that semester. Like Tim McCarthy, Palmer knew that, as an untenured professor, his political activities would not help his chances of staying employed at Harvard—but he also knew that many students were desperate to hear professors who connected the classroom to the real world. "The press won't tell the truth about this war," Palmer declared. "CNN will show Iraqis dancing in the streets, but it won't show burned and crushed and obliterated bodies." The line brought an approving cheer.

Behind him and to the right was Tim McCarthy, wearing khakis and a black windbreaker with a white armband on his left arm. He kept striding back and forth in front of John Harvard. McCarthy looked impatient, as if he had something to get off his chest and couldn't wait much longer. He would not have to. Palmer finished, and McCarthy took the megaphone from him. The crowd applauded just to see him. Many of these people seemed to know McCarthy, and not only because there was a large contingent from the Protest Lit class on hand.

McCarthy began intensely but almost quietly, so the crowd had to hush to hear him. "I came here today to talk about two things: dissent and God," McCarthy said. "We live in a truly historic moment . . . where dissent is vilified and where God is invoked to justify the most sinful impulses of our humanity. Our leaders tell us that dissent is actually 'un-American' and that God loves the United States more than any other nation on earth. We are expected to shut up and pray that God continue to bless America. But I am here today to speak out against this war, and to pray for peace."

Throughout the crowd, heads began to nod.

"Today we have walked out of classes, out of work, to show our opposition to the Bush administration's war on Iraq," McCarthy continued. "We have decided to encourage our students to walk out with us, because we are not content to simply read and study American protest writings. We are not content with confining our work to classroom discussions. . . . We believe that education means nothing if we, your teachers, do not practice what we teach.

"We are at war," McCarthy said. "We must articulate—as clearly and loudly as possible—our grievances with those currently in power. The Bush administration has made the case for war against Iraq. . . . They would have us believe that there is a connection between the terrorist attacks of September 11 and the country of Iraq.

"*There is not.*

"They would have us believe that there is a connection between Osama bin Laden and Saddam Hussein.

"*There is not.*

"They would have us believe that Saddam Hussein poses a clear and present threat to the security of the United States.

"*He does not.*"

McCarthy knew what he was doing, appropriating the rhythm and repetition of orators such as Jesse Jackson and Martin Luther King, Jr., the call and response of African American music and prayer. The crowd murmured its approval. McCarthy was so focused, his cheeks were turning red. His voice had increased in volume until he was almost shouting. He was connecting with this audience, firing them up, making them believe, at a moment when they felt demoralized and helpless, that they were neither.

"I can't help but think that God is not happy with the world right now," McCarthy continued. "He cannot be pleased with our greed and arrogance and violent disregard for His children. But we can still save our world. As Abraham Lincoln urged his fellow countrymen to do during another time of great national crisis, we must embrace 'the better angels of our nature.'

"We are at war, my brothers and sisters. This great crisis will be the first test of our generation. May we find the moral courage to resist this unjust war. May we find the strength to be prophets of peace. And may the God we all share bless those of us in America and across the globe who are engaged in the work of peace, so that we can save our souls before it's too late."

McCarthy was done and the crowd cheered its appreciation, and then the demonstration shifted to march down Massachusetts Avenue, toward MIT and Boston. In front of Mass Hall, immobile and unresponsive, the police officer looked on, his hands clasped behind his back.

About a week after she met with Dean Graham, Rachel Fish sent her research on Sheik Zayed to Larry Summers' office. When she didn't hear from him after a few days, she called to confirm that he'd received it. Clayton Spencer, a presidential aide, assured Fish that he had and that she shouldn't "panic." President Summers was well aware of the issue, but he expected Dean Graham to handle it.

In the meantime, Graham had hired a graduate student to look into Fish's accusations, saying he'd report back to her in four to six weeks. Fish was skeptical. "He was very polite," she said. "I think he probably thought that I would go away." After all, time was on Graham's side; Fish would graduate in early June, and after graduation, students tended to let such issues fall by the wayside. They moved away. They got jobs. Things that seemed important on campus were relegated to the back burner, then gradually abandoned.

Weeks passed, and Fish didn't hear anything, but she was far from idle. She was working with other Jewish students and Jewish organizations on campus to spread the word about the Zayed gift, so that they could bring pressure to bear if Harvard did not address the issue. At the same time, Bill Graham was doing his best to investigate her claims. He was in contact with the U.S. ambassador to the United Arab Emirates and a former UAE ambassador to the United States. "We were all appalled when we heard about this center," Graham said. "But it's very difficult to find out who's running what and who's paying attention to what in a situation like that. There are thousands of things named Zayed in the UAE. I mean, you can find Taco Bells with Sheik Zayed's name on them." Graham certainly agreed with Fish's estimation of the Zayed Centre. "This was producing very ugly anti-Semitic stuff," he said. "Stuff that we wanted to have no part of whatsoever."

The situation was delicate not just for Harvard, but also for the United States government. Even considering the work of the Zayed

Centre, the UAE is one of the most moderate, pro-Western countries in the Middle East, and it has made itself into a locus for international business. Companies such as CNN and Microsoft have regional head-quarters there. And it is an important U.S. ally; the UAE is the only Middle Eastern country with a port large enough to dock an aircraft carrier, and it allows the United States to do so. For Harvard to return Sheik Zayed's money could spark an international incident that would damage U.S.-UAE relations at a time when the United States needed every Middle Eastern ally it could get.

Harvard was also building a relationship with the UAE, of which the divinity school gift was probably the least important part. In April, officials from that country attended a conference at the Harvard Grad-uate School of Design. GSD dean Peter Rowe lauded Dubai, one of the seven "micro-kingdoms" that constitute the UAE, as "a very important . . . connecting link between the East and the West." Meanwhile, rep-resentatives from the Harvard Medical School were meeting with offi-cials in Dubai to discuss a joint venture between the medical school and a UAE complex called Dubai Health Care City, in which Harvard would set up a medical education program. One Harvard medical con-ference there had expected 300 attendees and instead hosted 1,300.

A strong relationship between Harvard and the United Arab Emi-rates would further Larry Summers' goal of globalizing the university and could also prove immensely lucrative. If, on the other hand, Har-vard returned Sheik Zayed's money, it could damage the university's relationship not only with Sheik Zayed, but any number of Arab lead-ers who might not appreciate the idea of an American university insulting an Arab head of state—thus alienating a pool of potential donors with almost infinite wealth.

After eight weeks with still no word from Dean Graham, on Fri-day, May 10, Fish got a phone call from a *Boston Globe* reporter who'd heard about the controversy. She e-mailed Graham that she wanted to meet again, but that she planned to talk to the reporter. The next day, an angry Graham wrote back. "Dear Rachel, I was about to write to you just now to set up a time [to meet] when I got a call [from the *Globe*] indicating that you have already been talking to the media," Graham said. "If that is true, I don't think I can be of much help to you or meet with you. . . . This kind of irresponsibility and unwillingness on your part to act in good faith when that is how I have dealt with you does not make me feel able to take this matter up with you in the detail that I wanted to. . . . I expect to have a full report for the community before the end of May, and I think you might as well wait for that with everyone else. Sincerely, William Graham."

Fish would not simply "wait for that." The *Globe* ran its story on May 11; it prompted an explosion of media interest. NPR, the *CBS Evening News*, the *Los Angeles Times*, and other news organizations all ran features on the controversy. Convinced that working within the system was doing no good, Fish granted interviews, appeared on talk shows, and wrote an op-ed piece in the *Crimson*. "I honestly thought—and this may have been naïve—that once the issue was brought to [Dean Graham's] attention, he would contact the president of the UAE and say, 'I disassociate myself with this,'" she said. "What made me question his intent was that he'd been dragging his feet, and that made me nervous."

What Fish later found out was that, around mid-May, Larry Summers had taken the decision out of Bill Graham's hands. He had come to the conclusion that the matter was too sensitive, the stakes too high, for him not to take control. But Fish couldn't have known that from press accounts; Summers refused to speak about the issue, either not returning reporters' phone calls or letting spokeswoman Lucie McNeil proffer a vague comment. The stonewalling typified Summers' approach to the media: If something good happened, he wanted credit. If a controversy arose, he let an underling take the hit. In this case, he had no intention of being tarred by what seemed a no-win controversy over a gift made before he became president to a school that he didn't respect. That approach to press management was business as usual in Washington, but to the growing number of people around campus who noted their president's chronic invisibility on matters where his reputation might be even slightly nicked, it suggested that Summers was more concerned with his image than with Harvard's.

But Summers never made it clear that the Sheik Zayed matter was now in his hands and not Bill Graham's, which meant that Graham had no power to fix the problem even though he was the figure publicly associated with it. "Summers hung Graham out to dry," said one professor familiar with the interaction between the dean and the president. "Like an officer letting his troops take the blame."

Though she rightly suspected that the media attention was having an impact, Rachel Fish never heard back from Larry Summers' office and didn't know what was going on behind the scenes in Mass Hall, or at her own divinity school. She was growing disillusioned with the university she had selected because she believed in its motto—or rather, she believed that *Harvard* believed its motto. Even if the proper response to the gift was complicated, couldn't Harvard at least issue a statement deploring anti-Semitism? Wasn't that the kind of moral act a great university was supposed to do? How could Larry Summers hide behind surrogates when he'd given such a principled speech about anti-Semitism?

Fish was saddened by Harvard's moral obfuscation and disappointed by the president whose words had inspired her to action. Still, she was a stubborn woman when she had to be. At twenty-three years old, she hadn't given up on the idea that one person with idealism and persistence could change the world—or at least Harvard. With neither Bill Graham nor Larry Summers talking to her, and the sneaking suspicion that Harvard just wanted her to go away, she began to plan a commencement protest.

The last Protest Lit class of the semester, the last class of Tim McCarthy's Harvard career, was titled "The Costs of American Dreaming." On May 1, John Stauffer began by talking about American wealth and globalization. Both subjects had been themes of the course—the students were now reading Barbara Ehrenreich's *Nickel and Dimed*, about the reality of minimum-wage jobs, and Kevin Bales' *Disposable People*, an investigation of modern-day slavery. As the class moved from the past to the present, the subjects of American economic inequity and globalization inevitably converged.

"One percent of the United States owns fifty percent of its wealth," Stauffer announced, holding onto his podium. "The top five percent owns ninety percent of the country's wealth." That consolidation of wealth had an impact beyond American borders. "United States' wealth leads to people in other parts of the world being poorer than ever," Stauffer said, looking even more intense than usual.

McCarthy segued into his subject for the day: hip-hop music as protest literature. McCarthy and Stauffer each had areas where one or the other felt more comfortable, and this was McCarthy's turf. "We can't understand hip-hop without linking it to globalization, the increasingly rapid flow of money, culture, and information between countries," he said. He talked for a few minutes about the female hip-hop group Salt 'n' Pepa, whose frankness about sex and AIDS during the 1980s promoted ties between gays, blacks, AIDS advocates, and the public health community. And McCarthy mentioned how, a decade before, Skip Gates had testified at the obscenity trial of rap group 2 Live Crew. Chuckling a little, McCarthy said, "We won't tell Larry Summers about that because we don't need any more people going to Princeton."

In the back of the room, McCarthy's father, Tom, an older man with eagle-white hair, wearing slacks and a coat and tie, sat in a corner chair listening intently. Malcom was there, too. McCarthy's mother, Michelle, couldn't come because she had to work that day.

Before taking over, Stauffer said, he had to digress for a moment. "The problem of being a complete outsider is that you have no power," he said. "But you have a certain sort of freedom as well. . . . Effective protest is not about being hip, cool, or trendy, but about principles, about action based in deep-seated belief. To quote James Baldwin, 'I love America more than any other country in the world, and for this reason I reserve the right to criticize her perpetually.'"

He paused and cleared his throat and said, "No one I know embodies those ideals better than Tim McCarthy."

The class, which knew the import of this occasion, jumped to its feet and applauded, while the course teaching fellows—a white English woman, a black woman, a black man, and an Asian man—approached the stage and hugged McCarthy, who looked a little overwhelmed. "Tim has been a beacon, a source of inspiration, a very close friend," Stauffer said. "We are, in many respects, very different, but we usually end up at the same point. My Harvard is going to be different from now on. My Harvard has been enjoyable in large part owing to Tim McCarthy."

Stauffer stepped back from his podium, looking like he didn't trust himself to keep talking.

McCarthy gathered his breath. In a few weeks, he would be heading to North Carolina to start writing his book on church burnings. Dressed in khaki pants, a blue shirt and brightly colored tie, and a seersucker jacket, he looked more suited for preppy Chapel Hill than he did for a class on protest literature.

He asked the students if they could just listen to something before he started, and punched a button on the classroom's rack of audiovisual equipment. The music that filled the room was a Tupac Shakur song called "Changes." Rapping over a drumbeat and the sampled piano melody from Bruce Hornsby's "The Way It Is," Shakur laments the state of race relations in America. "Wake up in the morning / And I ask myself / Is life worth living? / Should I blast myself? . . . Cops give a damn about a negro? / Pull the trigger / Kill a nigga / He's a hero . . ."

Then, at the chorus, Shakur lifts the song from desperation to hope. "We gotta make a change," he sings. "Let's change the way we live / And let's change the way we treat each other."

McCarthy stood on the stage, head down, collecting his thoughts. When "Changes" was over, he made a visible effort to pull himself together.

"I would like just for a second to respond to Tupac," he said slowly. "After 9/11, after those towers came down, we were better for a couple of hours, a couple of days. Our immediate impulse was to reach out and embrace firefighters, working people. . . . People came together, regardless of faith and background, to help each other.

"After that set in the culture of fear that we now live in. By playing to our worst fears and prejudices and ignorance, the president has constructed a republic of fear to keep us subdued. A republic of fear which has led to silence or complicit acceptance of Bush's policies.

"There are similar kinds of fears at Harvard," McCarthy said. "We too often accept what happens in our own backyard as well. I'm worried about the complacency. We have some things that are wrong here. We still have people who don't make enough money at Harvard to feed their children. We have a president who is interested in a consolidation of power. We need to question why people like Cornel West have to leave Harvard. We need to question why the university did not respond to the suicide of a young woman. We need to ask, 'Why are people at Harvard not happy? Why are we not more accountable for our teaching?' You all need to hold your teachers accountable. Because you want to learn. Because you love knowledge."

The students knew that this was a moment they would not forget. For many of them, it was just such such idealism that had brought them to Harvard in the first place. They might not have found *veritas* where they expected to, in the tenured giants of the faculty or in the president of Harvard. But they recognized the passion of a thirty-one-year-old untenured lecturer. And they also knew the bitter irony that the very things they cherished in McCarthy—his commitment to teaching and to their well-being even at the expense of his own scholarship—would ensure that he could never stay at Harvard. Teachers who cared about the students more than they cared about their own success—the institution used them up and spat them out. That was why McCarthy was leaving early, so he would never reach the point where he stopped loving his alma mater.

"I have been very grateful for my time at Harvard," McCarthy said, and he was starting to choke up now. "Harvard has taken me from humble roots and given me the world. So when I criticize Harvard, I do so because I love Harvard."

Around the room, students were starting to cry, not even trying to hold back their tears. And not just a few, an isolated sniffle here or there, but *dozens* of students. Others were taking pictures.

"With the enormous privilege that we have here, we cannot afford to be afraid," McCarthy continued. "We must confront the fear and the complacency that threatens to kill us in a moral sense. . . . So remember in these times of loneliness to read James Baldwin, read the Declaration of Independence, read Martin Luther King and Betty Friedan. And realize that you will never be alone."

McCarthy was losing it now too, biting his upper lip to try to contain his emotion, speechless, but that was okay, because the students saw that he needed help and they were standing and applauding and they would not stop.

In the spring of 2004, almost a year after McCarthy departed Cambridge, one of the students from that class would visit Larry Summers during his office hours to discuss the problem of teaching at Harvard. They sat in his office, the student on the couch, Summers in one of the leather chairs with his feet up on the glass coffee table. Next to his feet was a small box containing three multicolored stress balls, the kind you squeeze to alleviate tension. (And Summers did squeeze them: during a previous meeting with another student, living-wage supporter Emma MacKinnon, class of 2005, Summers actually popped one.)

The student told Summers that he was disappointed by how little contact he'd had with most of his professors, and wondered why there couldn't be more people like Tim McCarthy at the university—professors who really engaged with their students, who were passionate about their material *and* about teaching it.

When Summers heard McCarthy's name, "his face got a little contorted, he put his hand up to the side of his mouth, nodded and looked away," the student remembered.

"He basically said that at Harvard, we choose to go only for the best scholars, and that if you wanted somewhere that focused on undergraduate teaching, you should go to a place like Amherst or Swarthmore," two excellent but considerably smaller colleges. Harvard had to hire the "best physicist" or "the best Shakespeare scholar," even if they weren't the best teachers. Even if they were mediocre teachers.

But Harvard could change, the student protested, startled by Summers' admission. If we actually wanted things to be different . . .

"No," Summers said. "No, we can't."

For a second, he sounded almost wistful.

"This has been a good year for the university," Summers told an audience of about thirty thousand on the afternoon of June 5. It was the first line of his commencement address, and he certainly had reason to be satisfied. The 2002–2003 school year had indeed been a good one for him.

Granted, his second year as president had not been entirely free of turbulence. There was the controversy over his anti-Semitism speech, the Tom Paulin brouhaha, and the flap over the ouster of Harry Lewis. But none of those controversies had threatened Summers' viability as the Cornel West matter had done during his first year, and that fiasco was now fading into the distance. Every graduating class meant one less group familiar with the incident. That Summers had come out in defense of affirmative action also eased the sting of the West fiasco— particularly when, on June 23, the Court released its ruling in the Michigan cases and largely upheld university admissions policies that included affirmative action.

The Skip Gates matter also seemed largely resolved. Largely, but not entirely—there was still a whisper of doubt about Gates' future at Harvard. This was true even though Gates had leveraged his position after West's departure to make gains not just for himself, but also for his department. In May, the faculty had voted to enlarge Afro-American Studies, making it the Department of African and African American

Studies—a huge victory for Gates. By explicitly adding the continent of Africa to the department's purview, Gates had globalized Af-Am, expanding its scope far beyond the traditional study of black American history and literature. Now there would be instruction in African languages, bridge-building with African scholars and universities, vast new areas of research, more funding, more travel, more professorships—and, ultimately, more power for Gates and the department. The move had come with Summers' strong support, and at the May 20 faculty meeting where it was formalized, Gates and Summers had extravagantly praised each other's virtues.

Even so, Gates kept people wondering. Earlier in the month, he had announced that he would be taking a sabbatical during the 2003–2004 school year. The sabbatical had been long planned, but the destination came as a surprise to many: Gates would spend his year off at the Institute for Advanced Study, a scholarly center on Einstein Drive in . . . Princeton, New Jersey. Though the institute is independent, it has close ties to the local university, the new home of Cornel West and Anthony Appiah and a place that had already voted, in 1990, to offer Gates tenure. (News of Gates' sabbatical was promptly reported in the National section of the *Times*, prompting one bemused colleague to crack, "Skip Gates could wake up tomorrow and take a really good shit, and the *New York Times* would write it up.")

The decision to go to New Jersey provoked speculation that Gates was initiating a new courtship, inviting Princeton onto the dance floor. Gates insisted otherwise, but few believed him. Especially when, on May 28, he announced that he had donated the manuscript of *The Bondwoman's Narrative*, the first novel written by a female slave, to Yale's Beinecke Rare Book and Manuscript Library. Gates explained that Yale had given him his start in academia, and this was his way of saying thank you. But there were other interpretations. One was that Gates' move was a shot across the bow to Summers, who had been pressuring the Harvard libraries to cut their budgets, resulting in reduced hours, closed entrances, and librarian layoffs. Another, more likely, possibility was that Skip Gates did not want to be taken for granted.

And there were lingering rumbles of discontent throughout the faculty and amidst those administrators who still aspired for a measure of independence. At a May 29 party celebrating Harry Lewis, Peter

Gomes rose to toast the outgoing dean. In his sonorous baritone, Gomes spoke of how Lewis believed deeply that history and tradition mattered at Harvard more than the aggrandizement of any individual. "Harry by and large trusted the system," Gomes said. "He was a child of the system." Gomes compared Lewis to Charlemagne, the eighth-century emperor of Western Europe, and spoke of the marauding pagans and barbarians who had threatened Charlemagne's enlightened rule. After his death in 814, Gomes explained slyly, Charlemagne had been followed by bumbling successors with names such as "Charles the Fat." To laughter from the seventy-five people in attendance, Gomes said, "I think of Harry as our Charlemagne, and I worry for the future of Europe."

Still, Summers had worked to improve his image, and at least in the media he had done so. In his first year, he had acquired a reputation as a "bull in a china shop," and while many people outside of Harvard liked that trope—and some, but fewer, inside Harvard did as well—it was not the image Summers wanted to define him. Now, in a year-end interview with the Crimson, Summers was asked "why he had received less negative press this year than last." The president replied that he didn't know, but that "different people have different views on different things. I think my job is just to pull the high academic standards to make the university as great a place as I possibly can."

Though the response did not explicitly answer the student's question, it did suggest one possibility: that Summers had learned that one way to avoid bad press was to issue bland and content-free statements to the media. As he had been advised more than once, just because he had opinions on everything did not mean he always had to give them.

Nor had there been any full-fledged commencement controversy, like the "American jihad" speech. The student orations at this commencement were safe and sanitized; Summers had made sure of that. The afternoon speaker at commencement would be Ernesto Zedillo, who had been president of Mexico when Summers and Bob Rubin had organized the U.S. bailout of that country. Zedillo was ensconced in New Haven now, heading the Yale Center for the Study of Globalization. Although Zedillo's talk would prove less than scintillating, Summers' choice honored an old ally while promoting one of his favorite subjects.

In addition to the commencement exercises, Summers' hold over the university had tightened in other respects. By the end of his second year, he had installed new deans at FAS, the law school, the education school, and the divinity school, all of whom, and particularly Bill Kirby, seemed willing to cede some degree of autonomy in exchange for the job. Summers had also diminished the power of the most powerful deans by boosting his own access to alumni cash; he could now tap into alumni donors through the rule change that allowed those who funneled money through the president's office to receive class credit.

He was also starting to shape the professoriat by hiring scholars whom he admired—and rejecting those he didn't. Summers didn't hesitate to veto candidates because he thought they weren't good enough, or because they didn't fill the niches he considered important. After he rejected two tenure candidates proposed by the government department, "We had a department meeting for almost two hours, everyone talking about Summers," Professor Harvey Mansfield remembered. "If he had known that—and probably someone told him—I think he would have been quite pleased. He'd gotten everyone's attention."

Summers also recruited scholars he'd decided should be at Harvard, whether or not the relevant departments wanted them. Notable among these figures were MIT's Steven Pinker, an interdisciplinary psychologist who studied development of the brain, and Louis Menand, a Pulitzer Prize–winning literary historian at New York University who also wrote for the *New Yorker*. A few months later, Summers would complete the wooing of New York University historian Niall Ferguson, whose writing about the British empire was widely acclaimed. Although some critics thought that Ferguson overstated the benevolence of twentieth-century British imperialism, that criticism was not a concern for Summers.

In a marked break with precedent, Bill Kirby had little to no input in these faculty hires. It was traditionally the FAS dean who recruited new professors; Skip Gates, for example, had been wooed primarily by Henry Rosovsky, not Derek Bok. Now Summers had taken it upon himself to recruit academic celebrities and offer them up to specific departments. If the department chairs declined to accept the candidates, they would lose the professorship Summers was dangling. Most department chairs accepted, even though it meant sacrificing their ability to fill the intellectual vacancies that they deemed important, rather than those that interested the president. This is not to say that the professors Summers recruited were sub-par; almost all were top names in their fields. But rejecting them, for any reason, might anger the president. Summers could give, and he could also take away.

Especially with the curricular review foremost on Summers' agenda. The review was to begin in earnest during his third year, and in his commencement speech he wanted to lay out what he expected from it. For two reasons: one, because he had strong opinions about how the Harvard College curriculum needed to be reformed; and two, because a fund-raising drive with the review as its centerpiece was just beginning. Donors would be urged to contribute toward new programs, more professors, new classrooms, and so on. Summers wanted to use commencement as a sort of fund-raising kickoff.

For half an hour or so, on this damp and chilly June day, Summers spoke about what he expected from the new curriculum. He wanted students to be as satisfied with their academic experience as with their "outside activities." Students should be able to compose a literate essay; interpret a great text; connect history to the present; and "all of our students should know—they should genuinely understand at some basic level—how unraveling the mysteries of the genome is transforming the nature of science, and how empirical methods can sharpen our analysis of complex problems facing the world."

The audience seemed to like Summers' speech; indeed, the outside community always liked it when the Harvard president spoke of making a Harvard education *even better*. But FAS administrators were uneasy. Ostensibly, the curricular review was Bill Kirby's domain. In front of tens of thousands of people, Summers was dictating to Kirby what he wanted.

The president concluded with a call to arms. "At one level, revising a curriculum is about endless committees, the structure of requirements, and the ways in which bureaucracies will function," he said. ". . . On another level, very few things are more important. The world is shaped by what its leaders think, and they develop their beliefs, their attitudes and their capacities at places like this one. Harvard College has served this world for fifteen generations. We will do our part in the next generation."

Outside the walls of the Yard, local high school students recruited by Rachel Fish were handing out fliers describing Sheik Zayed and the Zayed Centre. At lunchtime, under a tent on the divinity school lawn,

Rachel Fish had received her diploma from William Graham. As he handed her a scroll, she handed him 130 pages of documentation and a petition, signed by 1,500 people, that called on the divinity school to return Sheik Zayed's gift. Fish received a smattering of extra applause from her classmates and a cheer of "Go, Rachel!" Graham did not react, except to accept the papers and place them on a table. Later that afternoon, Fish delivered the same material to Mass Hall.

As Harvard prepared for the third year of Larry Summers' presidency, the voices of dissent appeared to be growing quiet while the president appeared to be growing steadily more confident. What was uncertain was whether Summers had crushed the opposition to his presidency or if it was merely simmering underground, waiting to erupt.

9

Silent Campus

On Sunday, August 24, 2003, readers of the *New York Times* awoke to find Larry Summers' visage staring at them from the cover of the *Times'* weekly magazine. "Campus Agitator," shouted the cover blurb. The photo was a tight, merciless shot of the Harvard president, whose head dominated about three-quarters of the page. It was an arresting, uncomfortable image. Summers would turn forty-nine in November and his skin, mottled and increasingly furrowed around the mouth and eyes, was showing signs of age. His closely cropped hair was turning a Brillo-like gray on the sides. A small scar ran from his lower left chin to about half an inch below his lower lip. His lips were pursed as if in wary skepticism or judgment, and his chin and Adam's apple were sprinkled with a five-o'clock shadow. But Summers' eyes, staring directly at the reader, were clear and blue and focused. You could see his intensity in those eyes; they demanded that one return their gaze.

Written by reporter James Traub, the ensuing article was called "Harvard Radical," and it was part of Summers' campaign to advance his agenda through the press. The *60 Minutes* television profile had fallen by the wayside after the war with Iraq had broken out, but this article, the better part of a year in the works, had finally panned out. Arguing that Harvard's president was "trying to revolutionize a powerful elite institution," Traub traced Summers' time at Harvard from his selection through some of the early fights, including a portrayal of the Cornel West affair heavily sympathetic to Summers' side of things. The president's opening line in the story was one of his favorites: "The idea that we should be open to all ideas," he told Traub, "is very differ-ent from the supposition that all ideas are equally valid." Members of the Corporation, including D. Ron Daniel, Bob Rubin, and Hanna Gray, spoke out on Summers' behalf. "We agreed that we needed some-body more aggressive, more pushy, bolder" than Neil Rudenstine, Daniel said.

It was strange—the way they ran down the institution, Summers and the Corporation members sounded as if they didn't much respect their university. Readers could have been forgiven for wondering if Harvard was suffering from an autoimmune disorder in which its pur-ported defenders had instead turned upon the university. Summers' argument about not all ideas being equally valid was a good example. It was a pithy line, the kind of tough-talking red meat that plays into the expectations of conservatives who consider Harvard a bastion of moral relativity in which—sexually, politically, intellectually—anything goes and nothing is judged (except, perhaps, for conservatives). Summers' axiom, which he had first delivered at his inauguration and used repeatedly thereafter, implied that such moral relativism ran rampant within the wacky world of Harvard Yard.

But of course, the reality was otherwise. One would have been hard-pressed to find even one professor at Harvard who considered all ideas equally valid. Such relativism was a concept straight out of the sixties, and even then, if it was held by anyone, it was a distinctly minority view. The president had deftly created a straw man, a carica-ture based on lingering memories of a painful past, that he marketed to outsiders as a realistic view of Harvard—and the outsiders bought it, because it fulfilled the preconceived notions they held of the univer-sity as the last stronghold of sixties radicalism. Hence the *Times'* descriptions of Summers as a modern-day "campus agitator" and "radi-cal." The return to standards was, ostensibly, the new radicalism. Larry Summers was throwing out the aging hippies, the intellectually flaccid, the promoters of high grades and low expectations. Or so he implied.

Also curious was the fact that the members of the Corporation had spoken—as a general rule, Corporation members never spoke to the press—and done so in a way that slighted Neil Rudenstine. *They wanted someone bolder.* By implication, Neil Rudenstine had been less than bold. Ever since Summers was chosen, Rudenstine had made it a point never to comment on his successor. At dinner parties, said people who knew him, he would listen to angry criticisms of Summers, colorful descriptions of behavior previously unheard of for a Harvard president, and say nothing, offering only the occasional raised eyebrow. For members of the Harvard Corporation to discuss Summers in a way that belittled Rudenstine struck many Harvard readers as singularly ungracious—if, perhaps, reflecting a hint of defensiveness about their choice of Summers.

Critics of Summers were notably absent from the *Times* piece—Traub explained that they had refused to go on the record—with just one exception. Political philosopher Michael Sandel said, "By training and temperament, economists are intellectual imperialists. They believe their models of rational choice can explain all human behavior. The question is whether Larry can rise above this prejudice and develop the broader intellectual sympathies he needs to be a great Harvard president." A legitimate point—but then, if anyone could safely scrutinize Summers, it was Sandel. A tenured professor, Sandel taught "Moral Reasoning 22: Justice," one of the college's most consistently popular courses. Moreover, his chair was about to be endowed by an estimated $4-million gift from Robert and Anne Bass of the Texas oil family, one of higher education's largest donors. Sandel had cover.

Other professors either refused to speak about Summers, refused to speak on the record, or uttered words of praise that they could never have imagined saying some months before. Continuing his pro-Summers diplomacy, Skip Gates declared that Summers "is not intimidated by the job. He's tremendously self-confident intellectually. He's going to make a great president."

If Traub had one concern about Summers, it was whether the new president had to be quite so confrontational. (Traub was Harvard class of '76, though that fact was undisclosed in the article.) His story ends with an awkward moment in which he tells Summers that "I had been surprised by how intensely people disliked him." Summers' explanation: people resisted change. This was the paradigm into which he had consistently put his detractors—not people who disagreed with his style or his ideas about what kind of change was needed, but an old guard fighting to retain the status quo. Traub pushes back, saying, no, it was Summers whom people didn't like. "I'm sorry to hear that," Summers says "quietly." But "I have an aggressive and challenging approach. And it may be there are times when I have done that in a way that people haven't felt respected. That's certainly never been my intent." Then again, Summers says, "I don't think of leadership as a popularity contest."

As Traub relates the story, it is hard not to feel some sympathy for Summers; few people enjoy being told that they are disliked. But at the same time, Summers' response is another constructed dichotomy, as if the choice were only between intense dislike and a "popularity contest." If anything, the anecdote shows another side of Summers' quick-response intelligence. Even about something so deeply personal, he can instantly employ a rhetorical device to frame the issue in a more favorable light.

Two weeks later, the *New York Times Magazine* ran five reader letters regarding Traub's profile. None was from Cambridge; all were admiring of Summers. Typical was the man—not a Harvard graduate—who wrote, "Thank goodness someone has finally rattled the cage at Harvard. Lawrence Summers may not win the award for Mr. Congeniality, but at least he is willing to shake the tree of conventional knowledge at an institution so vaunted." Elsewhere, the reaction was more mixed. Summers' mother told acquaintances that she thought the story, and particularly the last exchange, had been hard on her son. Summers himself was pleased with the article, but he noted dryly the complete lack of letters from Cambridge's 02138 zip code. Nonetheless, his supporters were delighted. "The *Times* piece was a triumph," said Martin Peretz. "All the people who were critical of him were anonymous." Peretz meant that the opposition to Summers had grown weaker and more afraid to declare itself.

And this was true. Among the faculty, the *Times* article caused a subtle but distinct reaction, a greater caution about challenging Summers based on a deeper awareness of how he was perceived beyond Cambridge. Summers, they saw, had a public stage that they did not, access to the media that they did not, and a national audience that eagerly consumed the storyline he had created for himself and sold to the reporters who dropped in on campus. Harvard was not the subject of the article, but its antagonist. Its president had created a paradox in which the faculty found themselves emasculated. On the one hand, his remarks fueled a long-standing strain of American anti-intellectualism. When Summers spoke of moral relativism on campus or implied that the university was unpatriotic, he confirmed the anti-elitism and mistrust of Harvard felt by some conservative Americans, particularly in a time of war and terrorism. On the other hand, Summers had commandeered the language of standards, of "excellence." Having caricatured his opponents, he now held out a solution—his solution. It was like beating up a man and then offering to sell him health insurance.

This one-two punch was a strangely anti-intellectual device, the kind of maneuver Summers might have learned during his days on the MIT debate team or from his time in Washington politics. If its goal was to squelch dissent and help advance his agenda, it worked. With the exception of Skip Gates and a few others, Harvard professors weren't practiced at speaking through the media; scholars are not good with sound bites. Summers had established the terms of the debate, so whenever they protested his plans, they sounded as if they were protesting excellence. Those who were skilled at working with the press and interested in accommodation with power soon realized that it was better to play ball with Summers than to confront him in an arena where he had a distinct advantage. Several advantages, really—a press secretary, longtime experience with the media, the aura of the office, powerful people willing to speak on his behalf, the lazy but ubiquitous assumption that he, not the faculty, was Harvard's avatar. A single faculty member versus the president of Harvard was not a fair fight.

And so the faculty—most of it, anyway—fell silent.

They were not, by nature, a group that wanted to spend its time publicly debating the future of Harvard. They preferred to conduct their research and write their books. Many were less committed to the institution than professors in past eras had been, especially now that they had less and less say in its operation. Moreover, they saw how critics of the president were punished, while those who made the president look good were rewarded. Skip Gates was getting new money and new territory for his department because he had made his peace with the new president. (A fact that, though little known, was widely assumed.) Later in the year, Summers would name Laurence Tribe, who had co-written the affirmative action op-ed with the president, to the position of University Professor—Harvard's highest faculty honor, the title that Cornel West had once held. New Summers recruits such as Steven Pinker and Niall Ferguson were showcased at university events and overseas alumni gatherings.

In some ways, it had been an eventful summer. In late August the United Arab Emirates announced that it would close the Zayed Centre for good. Harvard then disclosed that it would postpone until August 2004 a decision on whether to keep Sheik Zayed's money. The university "has decided to put the gift on hold during the coming academic year," said Lucie McNeil, although Harvard would continue the search for a candidate to fill the professorship. The announcement, coming as it did in the dead of summer, defused the controversy for twelve more months, after which the number of people paying attention would have further declined. "All that means," insisted Rachel Fish, "is that in a year, when things quiet down, they can accept the money without having to make an issue of it publicly." Like Zayed Yasin, another student caught up in controversy with Mass Hall, Fish never heard a word from Summers. Nor could Summers' name be found in any Harvard statement regarding the future of the Zayed gift. Nor, as Fish would have liked, was there any statement decrying anti-Semitism in the UAE. The closing of the Zayed Centre was progress. But you couldn't exactly say that Harvard was taking a moral stand.

Instead, Summers was promoting the founding of a new and different center, the Broad Institute, which was announced in late June. A partnership between Harvard, MIT, and the nearby Whitehead Institute for Biomedical Research, the Broad Institute would focus on turning information about the human genome into medical applications. Summers could not talk enough about his support for the new science center. After two years of his presidency, one of his priorities was coming to life in tangible form.

Summers was pleased with life in other, more personal ways. His relationship with Lisa New was strong and invigorating. The president was more relaxed when New was around, less confrontational, better company. People who spent time with the couple said that they were in love. To her friends, New described Summers as a big teddy bear, a vulnerable creature slightly incapable of taking care of himself. The English professor was spending more and more time at Elmwood, the president's mansion. When Summers' children came from Washington to visit, they would play with New's girls. New told friends that she was trying to learn economics, while Summers, even though he "doesn't have a metronomic bone in his body," was trying to appreciate poetry.

New's influence extended beyond the intellectual. She and a servant employed at Elmwood would pick out Summers' clothing and set it out for him to wear, and their sartorial support made a difference. While his table manners didn't improve much, Summers did start tucking in and buttoning his shirts, and those shirts and his ties tended to go with his suits rather better than they had in the past. With New's encouragement, Summers was also trying to lose weight; he went on the Atkins diet, and the results were plain to see. As Summers lost weight, his face came into relief, looking longer and less boxy. His chest and stomach shrank so that his suits not only matched better, they fit better. Soon Summers replaced his original web page photo with a new head shot of a more svelte president.

Summers had learned in Washington that there was a time to play the bad cop, and a time to soften one's image. That didn't mean that his agenda, or the way in which he pursued it, had changed.

Harvard's longtime dean of students, Archie Epps, died suddenly on Thursday, August 21. The sixty-six-year-old Epps, who was diabetic, had gone into the hospital for surgery after developing an aneurysm in his aorta. The surgery seemed to go well, but two days later, Epps died of liver failure.

Few of the current students would have known the name of Archibald Calvin Epps III, but the pathbreaking black administrator had led a fascinating life. He was a graduate of Alabama's Talladega College, a small school founded by freed slaves in 1865, and the Harvard Divinity School. In 1964 Epps was named an assistant dean, and he stayed a member of the FAS administration until he retired in 2001. For all those years he was the highest-ranking black man in the Harvard administration. The position could be awkward for Epps, who was often torn between his official responsibilities, the expectations of black students, and the tendency of the Harvard administration to trot him out whenever a racially sensitive issue arose—a tension embodied in one of Epps' publications, a collection called *Malcolm X: Speeches at Harvard*. Like Skip Gates, Epps wanted to be an insider at a powerful institution where black people had always been outsiders. It was not easy. In the 1960s Epps sang with the Harvard Glee Club. More than once, when the glee club traveled to southern states, white racists pressured the group not to sing with its sole black member—and the club succumbed to that pressure and performed without him, a fact that caused Epps enormous pain. At the same time, he loved Harvard and refused to indict the entire institution for the mistakes it sometimes made. Reflecting on his career in 1999, Epps said, "The question to be asked now is, what good did I do? Because you either climb the ladder and pull it up after you, so no one else can follow. Or you put it down so others can climb up too." Epps always tried to extend the ladder, and he did not bear grudges. Gifts in his memory could be given to, among others, Talladega College and the Harvard Glee Club.

His funeral was held in Memorial Church at eleven o'clock on the morning of Thursday, September 4, a cloudy, intermittently rainy day. Some two hundred people filled the church that morning, including far more African Americans than one normally saw at a typical Harvard event. It was also a crowd filled with Harvard history and the custodians of it. Pallbearers included James R. Pusey, the son of former Harvard president Nathan Marsh Pusey. Harry Lewis was an usher. (Skip Gates was listed as one on the funeral program, but he didn't show.) Five rows back from the altar, on the left-hand side, sat Cornel West, who had come up from Princeton for the funeral. West was surrounded by friends who nodded and whispered their greetings as they filled the pews around him. Just as the service was about to start, a solo Larry Summers bustled into the church. Harry Lewis sat him next to Jeremy Knowles, in the fourth row on the right, just across from where West was sitting. Other than Knowles, his wife, and Summers, the row was empty.

As organ music filled the church, pallbearers carried Epps' coffin down the center aisle toward a table in front of the altar. It was not the first time Epps had been carried within a Harvard building. Thirty-four years before, during the 1969 student takeover of University Hall, Epps had refused to leave his office; he would not abandon his Harvard, even if, on occasion, it had abandoned him. And so angry students had unceremoniously hoisted the dean and carried him out the doors of University Hall, dumping him on the ground outside. Now he was being carried again, to a more final resting place, lifted up by a crowd whose emotion was not anger but sorrow and regret. Could there be a more definitive sign that the 1960s were truly gone?

"He served Harvard better than Harvard served him," Peter Gomes said in his eulogy, a bittersweet mixture of love, admiration, and regret. "We all know that, and even he knew that, but it did not trouble him for he, unlike so many of his contemporaries, saw that Harvard was never the present moment, or the present administration, or the present crisis. Archie declined to define his Harvard by its crises, but rather he preferred to embrace the ideal of Harvard as the 'City set on a Hill'; and even though that city did not always live up to its ideal, the ideal for Archie was worth his aspiration and his cherishing."

It was a funeral, and so present conflicts were not spoken of, except perhaps by implication. But at the end of the service, there was an awkward moment. As the crowd filed out of the church, groups of mourners clustered on its steps, hugging, shaking hands, and talking quietly. On the right-hand side of the steps, Larry Summers was greeting those who approached him, stiffly shaking their hands, as if the emotion, the humanity, that surfaces on such occasions made him uncomfortable. On the left-hand side of the steps, Cornel West was warmly hugging friends whom he hadn't seen since leaving Harvard, and there were smiles and gentle laughter among them. Granted, it was not the funeral of an economist; this was not Larry Summers' milieu. But it was impossible not to notice that, both white and black, the crowd around Cornel West was several times larger and considerably more relaxed than the grouping around Larry Summers. People were saying hello to Summers because it was appropriate. The rest were welcoming back their friend.

What did not come naturally for Summers, though, he worked at. Tirelessly, repetitively, and until he improved. Summers would not give up on bettering his relationships with the Memorial Church and African American communities, and in time, his efforts would pay off.

On September 15, the president followed a prayer by Peter Gomes to deliver his now-annual Morning Prayers talk. The previous spring, he'd been stung by Gomes' remarks about "Charles the Fat" at Harry Lewis' going-away party, but now he went out of his way to praise the minister. "Any time Peter Gomes ascends the pulpit, the community assembled is fortunate," Summers said. ". . . While it is best for the community that he continues to be as remarkable as he is, it makes it harder for me to speak after he does."

It is rarely ineffective to flatter a minister from the pulpit of his own church, and Gomes did not look displeased with the remarks.

Summers then began a talk about the relationship between economics and morality. As he spoke, it became clear that his remarks were an implicit response to all those who questioned his compassion, his empathy, his moral character itself—from those who'd protested the World Bank memo to those who charged that economists were more interested in hegemony than humanity.

"Economists like me rarely appear in places like this," Summers said. ". . . Many economists are uncomfortable with moral, let alone spiritual, discourse." That didn't mean, Summers continued, that economists did not think about moral questions, or that the field of economics lacked any means of addressing such concerns. Economists approach the world with respect for the needs and wants of individuals, he said. They did not try to impose their values on others. So, for example, when students criticized sweatshops and called for their boycott, an economist might respond that "there is surely some moral force to the concern that as long as the workers are voluntarily employed, they have chosen to work because they are working to their best alternative. Is narrowing an individual's set of choices an act of respect, of charity, even of concern? From this perspective the morality of restrictions on imports or boycotts advocated by many is less than entirely transparent."

People often charged that economists were "selfish" or coldly rational, Summers said. (He didn't need to add that these were exactly the criticisms his detractors leveled at him.) But the critics were wrong. "The highest morality is respecting the choices and views of people who we all want to help."

Summers' talk received mixed reviews. Some listeners thought that the president had mischaracterized the remedies advocated by critics of sweatshops, who understood very well that people had to work and so pressured the importers of sweatshop-made goods to contract for better working conditions. Moreover, Summers had essentially said that, given the choice between working in a sweatshop and starving to death, most people would choose the former, and critics of sweatshops ought to respect their decision. But some listeners considered this a ludicrous dichotomy. If it was a choice, it wasn't a very palatable one, and only in the most technical sense could one say that it was voluntary. To argue that employees in Asian sweatshops "have chosen to work" was at best a naïve way of describing the situation, at worst a callous misrepresentation of a Hobson's choice as an act of free will.

Yet others appreciated that Summers was discussing moral issues and respected his assertion that, even though he might not always sound like it, these concerns did weigh on him. As he spoke at Harvard about fighting cancer, about addressing the problem of AIDS in Africa, and about trying to extend higher education to students from all income levels, it was difficult to charge that Summers lacked a conscience. People might disagree with his methods or his leadership style, but it was unfair to say that he had no heart. His defenders argued that he just had a different way of showing it—but that, in the end, the president might do more good for the poor and diseased than many of his more emotionally expressive critics.

Then, in the first weekend of October, Summers addressed a gathering of black alumni organized by the college's Black Students Association. On Saturday morning, Summers rose before an audience of several hundred in an enormous classroom known as Science Center B. It was a delicate moment; in the weeks and months after the Cornel West incident, Summers probably wouldn't have been invited to address such a gathering. But he had much improved his standing with Harvard's black community by supporting Harvard's affirmative action brief, and the outcome of that Supreme Court case was ultimately far more important to African Americans than his altercation with West. It didn't mean that they had forgotten the incident, just that they were pragmatists.

Plus, Skip Gates was working the floor on Summers' behalf. Gates was spending most of his time in New York now, living at an apartment provided to him by New York University and keeping a frenetic schedule. In his year off, he researched a new book, popped up in television ads for IBM, consulted on a Showtime reality series about a search for a homegrown presidential candidate, cooperated with articles in both the *New York Times* and the *Boston Globe* on the reinvigoration of his department, wrote guest op-eds for the *New York Times*, served on the Pulitzer Prize committee, publicized the fiftieth anniversary of *Brown v. Board of Education*, made an appearance on Dennis Miller's CNBC talk show, traveled to Russia, and promoted a new encyclopedia he had co-edited called *African American Lives*. Among other things. But Gates would not miss this meeting of Larry Summers and Harvard's black alumni, and everyone knew that he was now doing his best to help Summers.

"Welcome home," Summers told the crowd. "This is your university. This is your science center. . . . It is your stadium that you will visit this afternoon. And let me tell you, we are a far greater university for it."

Summers' speech was a hit. As he spoke of the importance of African Americans to Harvard, he was interrupted twelve times by applause and received two standing ovations. The president was flattering his audience, but he also sent the message that he took them seriously—that they were people he *should* flatter. The alumni appreciated that the president of Harvard had come out on a Saturday morning to speak to them, knowing that the audience he would face was potentially hostile. Many of them came away from the weekend thinking that this president was a very different man, a more humble man, than the one who had berated Cornel West.

But after the alumni departed, many of those who remained on campus were unconvinced. People who lived and worked with Summers day in and day out felt that, however much his public relations management had improved, Larry Summers hadn't changed at all. Among them were the members of another minority group at Harvard, gay and lesbian students. Many gay members of the Harvard community had felt uncomfortable with Summers ever since his campaign of rhetoric to restore ROTC to the Harvard campus, which diminished the concerns of students forbidden to serve in the military. In the fall of 2003, Summers had another chance to show his humanitarian side by positioning the university to take a moral stance against anti-gay discrimination. Once more, as with the Sheik Zayed controversy, he declined.

The controversy began, in a way, with a war—but not the one in Iraq.

Gerald Solomon was a former Marine, a veteran of the Korean War, and a conservative Republican who became a congressman from northeast New York in 1978. Fervently patriotic, Solomon was a passionate advocate of a constitutional amendment to ban flag-burning and a vociferous critic of the United Nations; he once suggested that UN head Kofi Annan should be "horsewhipped." He might also have said "pistol-whipped," because Solomon hated gun control even more than he hated the UN. During one 1996 debate on the floor of the House of Representatives, he flew into a rage when Rhode Island congressman Patrick Kennedy mentioned the toll that gun violence had taken on his family. "My wife lives alone in a rural area in upstate New York," Solomon fumed. "She has a right to defend herself when I'm not there, *son*. And don't you forget it." Solomon asked Kennedy if he would like to "step outside" to settle their differences. (Kennedy declined the invitation.)

Before his retirement from Congress in 1998, Solomon, who died in 2001, was known primarily for two legislative pursuits: his mission-ary-like advocacy for General Electric, which had manufacturing plants in his district, for which Solomon earned the nickname "the congressman from General Electric"; and his repeated legislative attempts to force universities that received federal aid to facilitate mil-itary recruiting. Beginning in 1983, Solomon made a concerted effort to make students register for the draft or lose their federal financial aid. In later years he extended that principle to universities as a whole, and in 1996 he authored an amendment to a military appropriations bill that compelled universities that received federal money to permit mil-itary recruiting on campus. If a university prohibited such recruiting, the federal government could terminate all of its aid to that school, regardless of whether the money had any connection to the military.

The Clinton administration never enforced the Solomon Amend-ment, partly because it did not like the military's ban on homosexuals and partly because the amendment seemed to connect unrelated poli-cies. (After all, many Americans receive government benefits, such as Medicaid, welfare, and Social Security, without having to prove that they have registered for the draft.) But when the Bush administration took office in 2001, and especially after the terrorist attacks of Septem-ber 11, the Pentagon stepped up its enforcement of the Solomon Amendment. One big reason was that the military needed lawyers for its Judge Advocate General (JAG) program, and most prominent law schools did not permit military recruiting. That was less a byproduct of 1960s' protest than a function of the more modern concern over dis-crimination against gays. Harvard and most other law schools, deeply concerned over civil rights, did not allow employers that practiced dis-criminatory policies—any employers, not just the military—to use their employment offices to recruit students.

The Pentagon wanted to change that policy, and with the Solomon Amendment, it had a powerful lever with which to do so. In the spring of 2002, the Pentagon notified then-dean Robert Clark of the Harvard Law School that HLS was in violation of the law. If the school would not allow the military to recruit lawyers from among its students, Harvard could lose every single dollar the university received from the government—some $412 million in the 2002–2003 fiscal year, the vast majority targeted for scientific and medical research. In May, Clark issued a press release saying that the law school had no choice but to reverse its policy, and would now allow military recruiters to interview on campus. Clark explained that the law school could not afford to jeopardize funding for the entire university because of its own principled position.

Straight and gay alike, many HLS students were furious that their school had buckled under with barely a peep of protest. Certainly there was a huge amount of money at stake. Were there no legal options the school could pursue? With Clark leaving and new dean Elena Kagan coming in, however, the law school administration chose not to pick a fight with the government. At a "meet the dean" forum in April 2003, when one student asked Kagan about whether HLS had any plans to file suit to block enforcement of the Solomon Amendment, Kagan demurred. "We have no plans to reopen the issue that I know of," she said. "My own view is essentially congruent with that of Dean Clark's—[the Solomon Amendment] is immoral policy, but when university funding is at risk . . ."

"But are we considering litigation?" the student asked. "It looks really bad when the government just says, 'This is the law and this is what you have to do,' and the law school says, 'Well, okay.'"

"That depends on the merit of the legal argument" against the Solomon Amendment, Kagan answered, and confessed that she was not well versed enough in the matter to give an opinion. The subject was changed when the next student questioner complained that the business school did a better job of branding itself than the law school.

Harvard wasn't the only university affected by the Pentagon's crackdown, and by the fall of 2003, a number of other schools were ready to fight the Solomon Amendment. In late September, a coalition of law schools and law professors called the Forum for Academic and Institutional Rights, or FAIR, filed suit against the Pentagon, charging that the Solomon Amendment was discriminatory and unconstitutional. Harvard was not a member of FAIR; Elena Kagan explained that joining the coalition would reduce the university's flexibility. But a number of HLS students and professors thought that Kagan was simply stuck in a hard place—a new dean trying to balance her personal opposition to the Solomon Amendment versus the opinion of the president who not only had appointed her, but was widely believed to disagree with her on this issue. Two weeks later two student groups at Yale Law School filed a similar suit against the Department of Defense. Members of HLS Lambda, the law school gay students' organization, were frustrated that Harvard was lagging behind. One in particular decided she had to prod the university in any way she could.

Her name was Amanda Goad, she was from Richmond, Virginia, and she was in her second year at Harvard Law School. She was petite and quiet, almost shy, with dirty-blonde hair and wire-framed glasses—and tougher than she looked. Part of that toughness came from her parents, who grew up "dirt poor" working on tobacco farms in Kentucky and sometimes, Goad said, had "an irrational objection to being told what to do." Her parents preached the value of education, and Goad was a bookish kid; in 1992, at the age of thirteen, she won the National Spelling Bee. (The winning word was *lyceum*.) *That* was pressure. But Goad knew how to stick up for herself. Her mother was a news junkie, and dinners at the Goad household abounded with arguments about politics and current events. "There's something liberating about being a nerdish kid," Goad said. "It allows you to be argumentative. And smart."

For a girl in a conservative southern city who was beginning to realize that she was gay, Goad was also confident. That same year she went to summer camp and kissed her first girl. As it turned out, the girl was straight, but Goad and she would always remain friends. At age seventeen, she came out to her parents. It wasn't easy, but on the whole, they were supportive of their daughter.

Still, red-state Virginia was not an easy place to be gay. Throughout Goad's adolescence, the case of Sharon Bottoms was constantly in the local and national news. Bottoms was a Virginia woman, a lesbian, who lost custody of her biological son after a series of state courts ruled—in a lawsuit brought by Bottoms' mother—that lesbians are unfit parents. The case was a constant subject of conversation, and when it came to Richmond to be argued in the state supreme court, Goad remembered her ninth-grade teachers talking about "those faggot lawyers coming to town." The ruling was upheld, and Bottoms has never regained custody of her son. Faced with that kind of hate, Goad had to be tough.

As an undergrad at Rice University, in Texas, Goad had participated in a successful movement to win domestic partner benefits for the faculty. Now, at Harvard, she geared up to fight the Solomon Amendment. Among other things, she helped organize students to participate in mock interviews with the military recruiters. The students would sign up to meet with the recruiters and show up, bright-eyed and well dressed, for their appointments. Then, as the interviews were ending and the recruiters were expressing their interest—these were Harvard students, after all; they were impressive—the students would announce that, by the way, they were gay. Which was sometimes true and sometimes not—but the students wanted to show the military that not only did it want to hire smart, talented people who happened to be gay, but it also couldn't even *tell* they were gay.

In the spring of 2003, Summers came to a town hall meeting at the law school, and students asked him whether the university would consider a legal fight against the Solomon Amendment. According to Goad, Summers answered that his lawyers had informed him that Harvard didn't have a case, but that if the students researched the matter and determined that there was a case, "come back to me."

Goad was skeptical. "We knew that, because of his politics, he wasn't interested," she said. "This was around the time that the ROTC video [in which Summers appeared] came out." A president who was appearing in advertisements for the military probably wouldn't have much interest in suing the Pentagon.

In the fall of 2003, Goad helped to circulate a petition urging Summers to file or join litigation against the Solomon Amendment. By the time she sent it to Summers in early November, almost 1,100 members of the Harvard community had signed it. She also helped distribute a similar letter among the faculty. Forty-seven out of eighty-one law school professors put their names on it, which was more impressive than it might sound—Harvard law professors do not quickly sign on to activist petitions, and getting forty-seven of them to agree on anything was an accomplishment. Moreover, "some people were afraid to sign because of Summers," Goad said. Particularly on the part of the junior faculty, "there was a fear of retribution." After all, Summers was now taking an active role in law school tenure nominations, and he'd already shown in the

Cornel West situation that he did not approve of professors getting involved in politics. Or at least politics that conflicted with his own.

Goad and the other members of HLS Lambda sent the letter to Summers on October 22. His response, a letter back, was dated November 21. "Let me be clear that I regard the Solomon Amendment, as it has recently been interpreted and applied, as unsound and corrosive public policy," Summers said, adding that it "offends ideals of nondiscrimination and individual dignity. By raising the specter of a devastating loss of federal funds for universities . . . it invokes a form of sanction whose severity and coercive quality seem draconian.

"At the same time, having weighed the circumstances, I do not believe it would serve the best interests of the University to enter into a lawsuit challenging the Solomon Amendment. Particularly in light of the highly constructive partnership that exists between higher education and the federal government in a great many areas, the University must exercise considerable restraint when it comes to the prospect of confronting the government through the quintessentially adversarial act of filing a lawsuit."

His private response was more specific. A week before he wrote to Goad, Summers met with a delegation of law school professors. While he was opposed to discrimination, he told them, he just didn't think taking on the Solomon Amendment was a winning fight at a time when Republicans controlled both the White House and the Congress. There had been no great wave of opposition to the military's "don't ask-don't tell" policy regarding gay servicemen and -women. Maybe if opposition to the policy had reached a critical mass, he might support an official challenge by Harvard. But he didn't see that developing anytime soon. Instead, Summers said, university officials would work behind the scenes, negotiating privately with Pentagon officials. Summers had said the same thing at a faculty meeting some months before, when professors asked about Harvard's response to the Patriot Act, the anti-terrorism law that allowed the FBI to monitor library users. We'll take it up with the feds, Summers had said. But if indeed Harvard's Washington lobbyists had done so, nothing had come of their conversations, and professors wondered if Summers' line hadn't been just a way of shutting them up.

When the law professors suggested to Summers that Harvard's involvement could accelerate a shift in public opinion regarding anti-gay discrimination, that Harvard could serve as a leader in the fight, he remained unmoved. "He didn't mind faculty suing [the Pentagon] individually," said one of the professors in attendance. "It takes the pressure off him. But he doesn't see this as something worth fighting."

Granted, Summers was hardly the only university president reluctant to challenge the government; none of the presidents whose law schools were involved in litigation chose to throw the weight of their university behind it. Summers' letter, vague and legalistic though it was, laid bare a new reality for America's most prestigious universities: They had become so dependent on federal aid, so addicted to it, that they simply could not afford to challenge a federal mandate on a matter of principle. This was particularly true at Harvard, which year in and year out ranked as one of the top academic recipients of government largesse. That was what Summers meant by the "highly constructive partnership" between universities and the government "in a great many areas." The unfortunate result was that Harvard, the world's richest, most influential university, was willing to abandon an official policy of nondiscrimination because it refused to jeopardize federal money. *Veritas* was not worth $400 million.

Anyway, most of those areas of "constructive partnership" involved scientific research that Summers cared about more than he did the issue of gays in the military, one reason why his language sounded curiously antiseptic. The Solomon Amendment wasn't "unsound and corrosive public policy"; the amendment *"as it has recently been interpreted"* was unsound and corrosive. Rather than being offensive and discriminatory, the policy "offends *ideals* of nondiscrimination and individual dignity." The distinctions were subtle, but Summers' words gave the impression that he was more afraid of offending Republicans than he was upset by discrimination.

While no one would say that Summers supported discrimination, the issue clearly did not stir his moral passions—not even by the cool-headed standards of an economist. He very much supported students who wanted to participate in ROTC, but he did not particularly worry about gay students who wanted to serve but couldn't. Summers respected power, and gays simply did not have enough of it to force the issue to the front of his agenda. He would not jeopardize the pursuit of scientific discoveries by challenging the government on a policy he considered of marginal importance.

And, possibly, Summers had a point. Maybe, in the grand scheme of things, the Solomon Amendment *was* of marginal importance. After all, as he often said, what would historians remember about our era two hundred years from now? His answer: the scientific revolution in our understanding of human biology. In all likelihood, the number of gay people who cared about serving in the military, or even cared about being discriminated against by the military, was fewer than the number of people who could be helped by scientific discoveries coming out of Harvard labs. Perhaps saving lives *was* more important than protecting them from indignity and discrimination.

But was the choice really so stark? If Summers cared about the issue, couldn't he have found a way to speak out about it? To do more than writing a carefully hedged letter? He needn't have been antagonistic; he need only have led. After all, he had one of the most visible podiums in the country, if not in the world. On the question of anti-Semitism, he'd shown his willingness to use that podium for something he considered important. Why not stand up for another minority group feeling the pain of prejudice?

Summers' position was "more than a little frustrating," Goad said. "Harvard's involvement would have a huge impact; nothing gets press coverage like Harvard. It said to me that Harvard has lagged behind the other schools. It said that Harvard is not a progressive institution. That it is a follower rather than a leader."

On January 12, 2004, HLS Lambda filed a friend-of-the-court brief in the FAIR lawsuit. The very next day, fifty-four law school professors, including Dean Elena Kagan, submitted an amicus curiae brief of their own. But the law students were still frustrated. It was possible, Goad said, that in the 2004–2005 school year they might file suit against the university itself. Incoming students, she argued, had come to Harvard with an implicit contractual understanding that they would not be discriminated against. If Harvard would not even try to preserve that right, those students might wind up taking the university to court.

Some months later, Summers showed that he was indeed willing to take on the White House. This time, however, it was regarding an issue he did care deeply about—science. In the spring of 2004, Summers announced that Harvard would create a multimillion dollar center, the Stem Cell Institute, to pursue the therapeutic applications of fetal stem cells. He made the announcement at the Harvard Club of

New York on March 2. "There has been an abdication of national responsibility in this area," Summers said.

Because foes of abortion charged that stem cell research would lead to an increase in abortions, politics had intruded on science: in 2001, President Bush announced that the federal government would fund only research into existing stem cell lines. But most scientists in the field considered those cell lines inadequate, and the restrictions were impeding research that could make a huge difference in the lives of adults suffering from diseases such as Alzheimer's and Parkinson's, as well as children suffering from neurological damage such as cerebral palsy. "We have a set of policies in place that will not permit stem cell research to be carried on through the traditional channels," Summers explained. "Given those policies, if this research is to be carried out, there is no alternative to strong and decisive efforts by institutions like Harvard." The board of this new institute would include professor Michael Sandel, Summers' erstwhile critic, and Dr. David Scadden, who, twenty years before, had treated Larry Summers for cancer and very probably saved his life. For Summers, this was a very personal matter indeed.

The decision to open the Stem Cell Institute did not directly jeopardize federal money, and in fact it would bring new money into Harvard from private-sector donors. Nevertheless, it was a calculated and highly public rebuke of the Bush administration that entirely contradicted Summers' public rationale for not fighting the Solomon Amendment—that "the question is heavily a political one in terms of the Congress and executive branch." As Summers himself said in a March 20 luncheon at the Harvard Club of New York, "By supporting stem cell research, we are going to take up the slack where our government decided—in my view, mistakenly—not to go." (The line received a healthy round of applause, which may have suggested that, unlike with "don't ask–don't tell," there was a growing and positive consensus regarding stem cell research.) Inevitably, though, the Stem Cell Institute risked angering conservatives in the White House and Congress, which could certainly have resulted in cutbacks in federal aid to Harvard. Summers was willing to take that chance.

It could not be said that Larry Summers would not fight for things he believed in. But there was ample evidence that he would not fight for things other members of the Harvard community believed in, principles to which the university had once been committed. If the president of Harvard was going to place his university in opposition to the government, it had to be for a purpose in which he himself had a personal stake. After all, he *was* Harvard.

Halfway through his third year as president, Summers had imposed an unprecedented level of control over the amount of information that flowed out of the university. Press releases from around Harvard had to be approved—and sometimes rewritten—by Mass Hall. Fewer and fewer members of the faculty spoke to the press about much of anything, because they did not consider it worth the risk of angering Summers. "There is a sense of resignation, of faculty passivity," said professor Bradley Epps, who had already clashed with Summers and didn't much mind if he did it again. Only a few professors, such as history of science professor Everett Mendelsohn, dared to question Summers at faculty meetings, which had taken on a Soviet feel; deviations from the script were not allowed. As a young scholar, Mendelsohn had been accused of being a communist by Joseph McCarthy; having survived that, he was not afraid to dissent. "There is a feeling in the faculty that important decisions which may or may not be good are being made with insufficient consultation," Mendelson said. The professor was a gentleman; he understated the problem.

Most professors, however, buttoned their lips and hunkered down. During the Cornel West affair, Summers had seemed vulnerable, his future uncertain. Now it was clear that not only was he not going anywhere, but that he would brook little dissent. If the professors were going to rise in opposition, they would have to wait for Summers to make a mistake. Until then, they held their tongues.

The university publications marched in lockstep with Summers' agenda. *Harvard Magazine*, once relatively independent by the standards of university alumni magazines, had taken a deep interest in all things scientific, and month after month ran cover articles on scientific issues that curiously paralleled Summers' own interests, while downplaying the abundant signs of campus discontent. Longtime readers of the *Harvard Gazette* noticed that the weekly bulletin had become increasingly *Pravda*-like, featuring a steady stream of flattering photographs of its new president. Summers had instituted an unwritten rule: he would allow his picture to be taken only by photographers of whom he approved. And he cooperated with print journalists only when he appeared to expect gentle treatment from them. As the year progressed, he granted interviews to John Cloud of *Time* and Daniel Goldin of the *Wall Street Journal*. Both were graduates of Harvard College—class of '93 and '78, respectively—though only Cloud disclosed that fact in his piece on Summers. The interviews contained less-than-formidable questioning, as when Goldin asked Summers, "What would you cite as your biggest successes at Harvard so far?"

In the meantime, Summers stiff-armed those journalists who followed his activities more closely, the reporters and editors of the *Harvard Crimson*. His obstructionist attitude toward the student newspaper was not justified by any irresponsible or confrontational reporting. *Crimson* writers and editors report on an institution of which they are a part, and so they err on the side of caution. Though Harvard administrators may sometimes consider the *Crimson* a thorn in their side, they generally concede its professionalism and value to the campus.

On February 20, 2004, however, the *Crimson* ran an astonishing editorial that reflected its frustration with Summers' hostility to the open flow of information. "Ask undergraduates what they think of University President Lawrence H. Summers, and their replies will range from unfettered vitriol to fawning praise, with all possible stops in between," the editorial said. "Still, though every student can be counted on to have an opinion of our University's head, many of them would be at a loss to back up their judgments with specifics—for as Summers has consolidated his hold on Harvard, his administration has demonstrated an unsettling penchant for secrecy and centralized decision-making rather than the proper level of transparency and consultation.

"Summers' tactics . . . hint at contempt for students and faculty," the editorial concluded. "Why does the ivory tower seem to have been occupied by sentries?"

The answer was that Summers did not want to involve the community in his decision-making. That had never been his style. At the World Bank and Treasury, Summers hadn't been a consensus-builder; he made decisions by consulting with a small, select group of wise men, then imposed those decisions on people, even nations, who weren't in a position to protest. (And if they did, he took steps to squelch that protest.) Convinced of the superiority of his own ideas, Summers placed small value on democratic processes, and his leadership style made little accommodation to them. In his favorite story of his past career, the Mexico bailout, he repeatedly emphasized how a majority of Americans opposed the bailout, and members of Congress lacked the spine to do the right thing. He implied that the Harvard community could not help solve problems because the community *was* the problem. Sure that the solutions he advocated were correct, he had little patience for those who disagreed. To palliate them, he went through the motions of process, appointing committees and soliciting advice that, for the most part, he then ignored. "The theater of democracy," one professor called it. Summers didn't need the student press—he had an in-house press and friendly national journalists to promote his agenda, stroke alumni, and raise his national and international profile. And he made sure that those who worked for him—and wanted to keep working for him—employed the same tactics.

None did so better or more faithfully than Bill Kirby.

Two weeks before, the *Crimson* had run another editorial decrying the level of secrecy in Kirby's University Hall. "No journalist is ever satisfied with the level of access and information provided to him or her . . ." wrote outgoing editors David H. Gellis and Kate L. Rakoczy. "Yet over the course of the last year . . . we saw a level of secrecy enshroud the governance process of the Faculty of Arts and Sciences like none we had witnessed before. Information control has become a preoccupation within the Harvard administration, one that threatens to seriously stifle meaningful discussion and debate over the policy decisions that shape this university." *Crimson* reporters were denied routine information they had once been given as a matter of course, such as a list of tenure appointments in the 2002–2003 academic year. Where previously reporters could simply call members of the administration for comment, now they had to go through press secretaries, who stonewalled. Attempts to schedule interviews with members of the FAS administration were either rejected or simply ignored. More and more, the only person permitted to speak to the *Crimson* was FAS press secretary Robert Mitchell, who would provide the students with background briefings that were less than helpful. It was, the *Crimson* warned, "a climate of secrecy being imposed from the top down" that has "made it seem like the administration is trying to control information for the sake of control alone." Perhaps most unnerving were the anxious reactions the reporters received if they did get through to a potential source. "It used to be that you'd call anyone you wanted to," explained editor Kate Rakoczy in a subsequent interview. "Now the people who work with Larry are scared to death" when the *Crimson* calls.

It wasn't only the *Crimson* that noticed the information crackdown. In a Morning Prayers talk on February 13, outgoing Undergraduate Council president Rohit Chopra lamented the university's increasing preference for public relations over honest debate. "Never before has Harvard seen so many communications directors, spokespersons, and other public relations experts to lend a helping hand," Chopra said. ". . . Instead of quietly announcing bad news, too often it is wrapped in a beautiful package with the hope that we will think it is a gift. But a wise friend once said to me, 'Don't eat moldy cheese even if it's on a silver plate, because it will make you sick.'"

One small but symptomatic example was the case of the Korean prostitutes. In talking about the positive effects of globalization and economic growth, Summers often cited an astonishing statistic. In 1970, he liked to say, there were one million child prostitutes in Seoul, South Korea—a horrific number. But today, after decades of economic growth, there are "almost none." He'd been using the anecdote with audiences to great effect since at least the summer of 2003. But in July of 2004, Summers used the line in a speech with a group of summer students, one of whom, apparently, was from South Korea and knew better. It turned out that in 1970 the *total* population of girls between the ages of ten and nineteen in Seoul was about 680,000—or about 320,000 fewer than Summers' number of child prostitutes alone. South Koreans were understandably miffed; the gaffe was reported in several South Korean papers and the country's minister of health publicly criticized Summers, saying that the comment was "regrettable and, frankly speaking, displeasing."

It was an honest mistake, employed in an argument to show that South Korea had undergone impressive economic expansion and that such growth had invariably improved social conditions. More telling was Summers' reaction after his misstatement was pointed out. "Head of Harvard apologizes to Korea," read the headline in *Joong Ang Daily*, an English-language Korean paper. But that was not quite true. Summers had a spokesperson write and release a three-sentence statement that said in part, "President Summers acknowledges that he misremembered a statistic outlining the number of child prostitutes in Seoul in 1970. . . . He would like to apologize for any offense caused." Never using the first person—as in "*I* apologize . . ."—this was an apology via proxy. For Summers, even a simple, clearly deserved apology had first to be neutered and then transmitted by a press secretary. This may have been standard operating procedure in Washington, designed to minimize embarrassment to the person at fault. But at Harvard, people expected precision and honesty in language, which, after all, was critical to how many of them made their living.

The combination of pressure and intimidation, as well as the chill on free speech and exclusion from decision-making, left professors and administrators disheartened and demoralized. "The first question people always ask when making a decision is, 'How does this make Larry look?'" said one high-level administrator. From secretaries to deans, everyone knew that any decision that did not put Summers in a positive light put their jobs at risk: Rick Hunt, Harry Lewis, and others could testify to that. In the spring of 2004, Barry Bloom, dean of the School of Public Health, infuriated Summers by announcing that the school had received a $100-million grant from the federal government without first informing Summers or including the president's name in the relevant press release. According to several sources familiar with the incident, Summers was so enraged that, at a subsequent dinner attended by both Bloom and him, the president insisted on being seated somewhere he could not see the dean. (Asked for comment, Bloom said, "I have the greatest respect for President Summers.")

"I've never been in a place with the combination of low morale and bunker mentality that now exists at Harvard," said an administrator who has worked for several universities. And that included people who were members of Summers' inner circle. Even provost Steve Hyman and dean Bill Kirby engaged in half-serious discussions about who had the worse job. "There's a sense of insecurity" among non-tenured employees, said one mid-level administrator. "You don't know what's coming next. People who you used to know would be loyal to you, you can't depend on anymore. Now people are only valued according to the success of the last project they did."

Often it seemed that the only people free to speak their minds were those who were leaving, those with the least power at the university, or those who were both powerless and leaving. With little to lose, they could fight for their principles. One such person was a lecturer on the Committee on the Study of Religion named Brian Palmer. Perhaps no individual at Harvard represented the antithesis of everything that Larry Summers stood for more than Palmer did, and during the spring of 2004, Palmer and Summers would finally get to express their differences—in front of each other, and a crowd of six hundred people.

The first thing one noticed about thiry-nine-year-old Brian Palmer was his physical fragility. He was five foot eleven and weighed maybe a hundred forty pounds after a big meal. His skin was chalk white and he had inky black, spiky hair that often made him look as if he'd just pulled an all-nighter. He wore thick glasses and spoke in a breathy, hesitant voice that barely crossed the distance between two people. Even when Palmer used a microphone, such as when he spoke at the anti-war rally in the spring of 2003, his voice drifted gently across the crowd like a helium balloon losing its lift. Like a singer in a geek rock band, he was not charismatic, he was anti-charismatic. Clearly, it was not the projected force of Palmer's personality that made him a prominent figure at Harvard. It was instead the power of his ideas, the depth of his convictions, and his willingness to speak his mind that turned the lecturer into a nerd hero for hundreds of Harvard students.

Palmer grew up in Brooklyn, New York, where his father was a clinical psychologist and his mother a career counselor. His paternal grandparents had been Methodist schoolteachers in the Philippines, while his mother came from a Jewish family in Prague. During World War II, she was saved from the Holocaust by British Quakers, and later converted to Quakerism in gratitude; Palmer was raised with that sect's strong moral and pacifist sensibilities. He also had an activist bent. As a Harvard undergraduate from 1982 to 1986—smack in the middle of the Reagan years— he had helped found a muckraking magazine called the *Harvard Citizen*.

During his summers, Palmer worked for Ralph Nader, and after completing his doctorate in anthropology and religious studies at Harvard in 2000, he landed a position as a lecturer there. He wanted to teach classes about ethics, globalization, and "the urgent problems of our time"— nuclear weapons, global warming, and the widening gap between rich and poor. There were, Palmer noticed, lots of courses at Harvard about race and gender, but very few about class. He'd read that at one point Microsoft executives Bill Gates and Steven Ballmer possessed more wealth than the entire population of Africa. So he proposed a course on capitalism as a religion, but the department rejected it.

Instead, Palmer taught a course called "Religion 1529: Personal Choice and Global Transformation." But "taught" wasn't exactly what Palmer did—at least, not in the traditional sense of the word. "Hosted" would have been more accurate. Palmer rarely lectured to his classes. He thought that the large lecture format made students listless and passive recipients of "knowledge," and he wanted his classes to be interactive. So he invited guests from the fields of academia, activism, and politics to visit his twice-weekly course meetings. And then, after a brief introduction, he simply opened the floor to questions. As Palmer scooted up and down the aisles of Science Center C with a microphone, the students would stand, introduce themselves, and ask their questions. The first ten questioners were preselected with only one criterion: that they would be of alternating gender, so that women, who often felt reluctant to speak out in large classrooms, were encouraged to do so.

Almost without exception, Palmer's guests were liberal. In 2002 and 2003, they included theologian Harvey Cox, philosopher Sissela Bok (Derek Bok's wife), and Adam Yauch, the Beastie Boys singer and pro-Tibet activist. Robert Reich was so fired up by his 2001 appearance at Palmer's class that he decided to run for governor of Massachusetts in 2002. "I just left that class thinking to myself, this state is a mess and I need to run for governor," he said at the time.

Even if his students tended to agree with the questioners, Palmer wanted them to ask tough questions, to get in the habit of considering all authority figures with skepticism. "The students are not shy about questioning celebrity guests," Palmer explained, "but they do have trouble questioning authority in general." He believed that all scholarship was in some measure political and could not help but reflect the values and biases of its authors. (Which did not mean that Palmer considered "all ideas equally valid.") As a result, he wanted his students to question everything, not just accept something as true because a professor with a microphone had told them it was.

Much of Palmer's more direct teaching took place outside the classroom, where he was constantly on call for his students. At least once a week, he hosted a dinner where students discussed the issues raised by that week's speakers. At Harvard, the term "office hours" is usually a

misnomer for a single hour or perhaps ninety minutes of faculty avail-
ability, but Palmer's office hours did, in fact, last for hours, as long as
there were students waiting to see him. He responded to every e-mail he
received, and he received hundreds; in the spring of 2003, his course
had some five hundred students. Correspondents frequently received
return e-mails from Palmer at one, two, three o'clock in the morning.

And then there were activities not technically related to the
course but that Palmer considered philosophically important, like serving as an advisor to any student organization that asked, or speaking
out at a rally for laid-off janitors—the only faculty member to do so. It
was, Palmer thought, part of the responsibility of being a member of a
community. During the takeover of Massachusetts Hall, Palmer would
look out his office window well after midnight and see the tents that
had sprung up in the Yard, hear the sounds of students staying up late
and talking. "There were people out there, undergraduates, graduate
students, just enjoying the fact of being alive," he said. It was amazing
to him how little Harvard students enjoyed such simple but profound
pleasures. Most of the time, they were too busy to appreciate life.

Palmer claimed that he invited conservative speakers to his class,
but it was clear, his heart wasn't really in those invitations, and few
recipients took him up on the offer. He thought that Harvard students
were already surrounded by conservatism—that much of the faculty,
most of the administration, and virtually all of the Harvard ethos were
deeply conservative. Not in the sense that professors would vote for
George W. Bush or opposed abortion; few Harvard professors, except
maybe at the business school, were Republican. But they were conservative in that they embraced the status quo, taught their students to
revere power, authority, and money, and rarely challenged students to
question the values that Harvard transmitted to them. Palmer wanted
his students to know that life contained options beyond what Harvard
preached. It wasn't just about competition, fame, professional achievement, individualism, and material gain—the values, essentially, of
American capitalism. Success could be defined differently. Harvard
could, if it wanted to, prioritize family, community, friendship, social
responsibility, the interdependence of the individual and the larger
world. Imagine, Palmer thought, how different the world could be if
Harvard graduates left Cambridge thus inspired—as opposed to, say,

being urged by the university's president to follow the example of Alexander the Great.

As a lecturer, Palmer had a three-year contract that expired after the 2003–2004 school year. He knew that the provocative nature of his course, his own political activities, and the fact that he had spent far more time teaching than pursuing scholarship would doom his future at Harvard, no matter how popular his courses were. Certainly many professors looked down on Palmer's pedagogy. They were suspicious of a classroom in which there were not lectures, but conversations; in which the professor was not the traditional authority figure, but a sort of moderator, deferring to both students and invited guests; in which the subject was not the world of scholarship but the world *beyond* scholarship. Others speculated that the class was popular simply because it was considered a gut, an easy A, and although the grades in the course weren't actually higher than anywhere else in the Harvard humanities, it was probably true that some students took the class because they found it less demanding than the rest of their course load. It was also true that Palmer wasn't very interested in grades. He thought their primary function was to classify students for entry into the labor market, and that "if you grade someone for something, they'll stop loving the quality of the work and focus on the tangible reward."

The idea, impossible to implement at Harvard, that students might actually learn more without grades was certainly unorthodox. That unorthodoxy, the very thing that students so appreciated about Palmer, was also what would ensure that he had no future at Harvard. "Sooner or later," he said, "the university will spit me out like a used piece of chewing gum." Palmer thought that might be good for him; he'd spent virtually his entire adult life at Harvard. But he knew that he would miss the place. You would never find smarter, nicer, more committed students. And since after graduation these students were likely to lead in everything they did, teaching them alternative ways of defining and valuing life seemed particularly urgent.

That spring, Palmer had one class meeting he was particularly looking forward to. In each of Larry Summers' first two years as president, Palmer had invited the president to address his class, and each time Summers had declined, citing scheduling conflicts. The third time, evidently, was the charm. Whether it was because Summers was more confident about confronting a potentially skeptical audience, or because he'd grown curious about what was now, with 613 students, the second most popular class in Harvard College, or just because Summers had a free hour, Palmer would never know. But Larry Summers agreed to be the guest speaker at Palmer's course at three o'clock on the afternoon of March 17, 2004.

Summers surely knew what he was getting into. The syllabus would have told him that "this is a course for students who seek to have an impact as ethically serious global citizens. How do personal choices about consumption, careers, and child-rearing affect a wider world? What are the possibilities for women and men to 'make a difference?'" Listed speakers included Dan Matthews, the head of People for the Ethical Treatment of Animals (who never actually made it to the class because he had staged a nude protest in Harvard Square and been arrested); Jamie Johnson, an heir to the Johnson & Johnson fortune and maker of *Born Rich*, a documentary exposing the shallow lives of the super wealthy; Ani Choying Drolma, a Tibetan Buddhist nun; and "Larry Summers, Economist." Palmer himself was giving one lecture, entitled "Harvard and the Cult of the Winner." If, as Summers had argued at Morning Prayers, economists like him really did analyze the world's problems from a moral perspective, this would be a perfect opportunity to elaborate.

On the prescribed day, Summers arrived only a few minutes late, which was early for him. He wore a dark suit, a light blue shirt, and a slightly darker blue tie. As the year had progressed, Summers had regained some of the weight he'd lost in the previous summer and fall, but he still looked thinner than in his early days as president. Standing on the stage before a packed room—the students were eagerly anticipating this class—he also looked supremely confident. Summers loved the question-and-answer format. Even more than prepared speaking, it was his strength, his virtuosity. Answering questions was like playing tennis; he could pick his shots, play the angles, run his opponents around a little. A game of strategy. Summers loved it.

Palmer briefly introduced Summers, and then the first student rose to question him. "What personal sacrifices have you made to become as successful and accomplished as much as you have, and do you have any regrets?"

Summers looked mildly surprised. He'd attended dozens of question-and-answer sessions at Harvard since becoming president, but this may have been the first time that he'd been asked to speak about the downside of success.

Maybe because Summers was caught off guard, his answer meandered. He spoke about how people's lives never went quite as planned, and "there's a tendency when you look at people's careers or read biographies . . . to assume that there was a plan or a strategy." But that hadn't been the case with him—he'd benefited from good luck and fortuitous timing. "It's terribly, terribly important in life to try to take what you do seriously but not to take yourself too seriously," Summers added. "Do I have regrets? Anyone in a position like I have now is in a position to make lots of decisions, and if you make eighty percent of them right, you're doing well. If you can bet on a roll of the dice, and you're given the choice between betting on one through four or [betting on] five and six, you're going to bet on one through four. But you're still going to be wrong a third of the time.

"Speaking more personally," Summers concluded, "I'm really very happy with how my life has turned out."

The next questioner, a woman, stood up. She asked Summers, "As a father of three, what kinds of fatherly influences transfer to your current line of work?"

Summers looked still more confused; the possibility that being a father was relevant to his current line of work did not seem to have occurred to him. He answered that he was a father of three children, two thirteen-year-old daughters and a ten-year-old son. "I hope they're going to grow up to be fulfilled, happy people," he said. But "as president of the university . . . it is my task to focus more on your academic and professional development than I do on your personal development." Then Summers said something about how he hoped Harvard was a place where students were able to grow emotionally. "I hope that we as a university are a model of openness and tolerance . . . in which it is the power of ideas rather than the idea of power that matters."

Summers had used the line before, and this time it did not appear to go over well, partly because it sounded out of context and partly because many in the room seemed unconvinced that, in Summers' presidency, it was the "power of ideas" and not the "idea of power" that carried the day.

Then it was Palmer's turn to ask a question, a prerogative he sometimes took advantage of. He began by referencing the *New York Times Magazine* profile, the part in which author James Traub asks Summers why so many people dislike him and Summers responds that leadership is not a popularity contest. Before Palmer could get to that line, Summers interrupted, joking that "I have a passing familiarity with its content." He began swinging his microphone up and down like a nightstick. Palmer continued, saying that there were different kinds of leadership—Gandhian leadership, in which people followed the example of an inspiring leader, or leadership as described by social theorist Max Weber, in which followers could be compelled to act by virtue of the authority invested in a strong leader. Could Summers describe any instances where he had exercised Gandhian leadership?

Summers looked a little irritated now; the question implied that his leadership was based on compulsion rather than inspiration. "This is unlike any experience I've had at Harvard," he said.

"Well, this will be my last experience like this at Harvard," Palmer said, and the crowd burst into supportive applause.

"Maybe exposing myself to this questioning is the Gandhian experience you asked about," Summers shot back. "I'm not sure I can answer the question in the terms you put it," he continued. He then launched into the story of the Mexican bailout, which took about ten minutes of class time. The students seemed interested, but unsure how it answered the question.

When Summers was done, a freshman named Ellen Quigley stood up to question him. Quigley knew Summers, and vice versa. In the fall, she had taken the sixteen-person freshman seminar on globalization Summers had taught, his first time teaching a course while president. She had proved such a fearless questioner in the class, challenging Summers on subjects such as sweatshops, the economies of socialist countries, and the virtues of free trade, that she'd earned the nickname the "anti-Summers."

That was a badge of honor for Quigley, because though Summers did try to get the students to relax, questioning him wasn't always easy. For one thing, he himself wasn't always relaxed. Plus, the group met on Monday nights in a conference room in Mass Hall, upstairs from the president's office. That was a little intimidating. So was the fact that Summers would sometimes have the students watch video of him at public events. When one student disputed Summers' interpretation of a week's reading,

Summers replied, "It's a good state of affairs when a student can criticize the president of Harvard University—but you're wrong."

When Quigley stood now to take the microphone from Palmer, Summers smiled a little, anticipating a tough question. After their last seminar meeting in Mass Hall, Summers had said to Quigley, "Thank you for being in the class—you keep us human." But even knowing Quigley, he looked surprised by just how tough her question was.

"President Summers, you've made your views on scholarship and teaching fairly clear during your time as president," she said. "Frankly, this class doesn't seem like something you'd like. It emphasizes compassion over cash and social concerns over hard data. What has changed during the last couple of years for you to agree to come to this class now, but not accept previous invitations? As a follow-up: This class is not going to be offered next year, and I'm sure the other 612 students in this room are as disappointed as I am about that. Can Harvard really go without classes like this one?"

Summers was starting to look like he was trapped on the set of a reality television show he'd never signed up for. Still swinging his mike, he strolled around the stage for a few seconds as if looking for an exit, then turned back to the audience and said, "Someone in my position has to have two different ways of seeing the world—personal views versus what types of activities are valuable to the university.

"It's true," Summers admitted, "that I think that a certain number of views expressed by some of the speakers in this course are silly, and not supported by evidence. A question like whether a course like this should exist doesn't have to do with my views. The views that Brian has on a number of questions are views that I disagree with, but that isn't any reason for me not to participate."

He hadn't come in the past, he said, because he received more invitations than there was time in the day. He then launched into a discussion of whether Harvard should be, in his phrase, "a political institution."

"It's my belief that Harvard will make a grave mistake if we become a political action institute," he said. Citing past anti-Semitism and less-than-universal opposition to McCarthyism, Summers added, "Frankly, Harvard's record as a political institution is not one that we can be terribly proud of. We exist independent of the society precisely because we do not become a political institution. It is not for Harvard to have an opinion on the merits of the Iraq war. It is not for Harvard to have an opinion on the right to choose or the right to life. The idea urged by some that we should be a great social action foundation supported by a huge endowment . . . would greatly compromise us as an institution."

Quigley sat down, frustrated. She had said nothing about Harvard becoming a political action institute or social action foundation. Summers' answer set up a straw man that he then easily demolished, but Quigley herself wouldn't have supported that straw man. She'd hoped that Summers would really talk about the need for at least one Harvard course to consider critically the ways in which the university shaped its students.

Summers next took a question about the Mass Hall sit-in of 2001. "Was it justified," a student named Michael Heinz wanted to know, "and is civil disobedience ever legitimate?"

"I don't see how anybody who looks at the history of the world can possibly take a position that civil disobedience is wrong," Summers said. ". . . [But] if you read Gandhi or have seen the movie, or if you read Martin Luther King . . . they will all tell you that the punishment of the civil disobedient is integral to the concept of civil disobedience. . . . So the position that's been taken by some in this community that civil disobedience is so noble that it shouldn't be punished seems to me a misleading proposition."

After one more question about the merits of accepting legacies into the college, the class was over. The students gave Summers a healthy round of applause, and Palmer walked him back to Mass Hall. Afterward, the students were asked to post their reactions to Summers' visit on the course web page. Palmer encouraged them to consider the question of President Summers' leadership style. The president had said on many occasions that Harvard would train the next generation of leaders, and that all the leaders he knew in Washington were most shaped by what they had learned in school, particularly college. What lessons in leadership had Larry Summers passed on to them?

Some students responded favorably to the president. They recognized that he had been the subject of aggressive questioning. They thought he had handled the situation well and answered the questions directly, and they respected him for toughing it out. Some of their comments—anonymous here because they were not meant for public distribution—reflected that respect:

— "While Larry Summers may not be my favorite person, given his somewhat callous way of dealing with sensitive issues, I have to admit that I liked some of his answers today . . ."

— "I think that Summers' confidence in speaking to us came from his personal confidence in what he believes. I think he does have a lot more social responsibility than he is usually given credit for. Is he somewhat closed-minded? Perhaps. But he seems to give himself plenty of opportunities to be disproved by students or faculty . . ."

— "Summers' most valuable lesson about leadership was that sometimes you must go against what everyone else thinks is right in order to make the right choice. In a democracy, 'the people' can sometimes make the wrong decision. Part of being a good leader is knowing when to disregard what the people you're representing want . . ."

Other students strongly disagreed with Summers' answers, particularly regarding the politics of Harvard, the nature of civil disobedience, and the relationship of the president to the students' well-being. For example:

— "I absolutely do not deny that 'the punishment of the civilly disobedient is integral to the movement' of whatever is being civilly disobeyed. [But] my heart seemed to translate his comments in a terrifying way; he seemed to be saying, 'It's my job to arrest King, to beat Gandhi, and I accept that role . . . I'll be waiting and ready to punish them.' Those comments made me fear ever exercising any kind of power. I do not think sacrificing my sense of right and wrong is worth the accolades that come with high leadership positions. I think I'll leave the punishing to President Summers . . ."

— "The question isn't whether the university SHOULD be a political institution. The university IS one. The university makes political choices because it makes economic choices. The university hires and fires and spends and saves, and economic decisions are political decisions about distribution and values . . ."

— "Larry Summers has no idea what is going on with the students he supposedly values so much. He has refused to take action on the mental health crisis this college is facing, and he is moving the college towards a more competitive and stressful environment. The students, while possibly still functioning at a high level, are not happy and enjoying life. How can you be a good leader while reducing people to the value of the work they produce?"

Probably the largest group of students questioned Summers' candor. They felt that he dodged the questions, answered questions that had not been asked, and generally sounded more like a politician than the president of Harvard.

— "It seemed to me that he had pre-set answers for the questions and somehow managed to evade all the tough inquiries. I felt like his answers were insincere and he was trying to weasel his way out of the truth . . ."
— "Summers skirted some questions with answers that were crafted in an intentionally vague or generalizing way. He would use phrases like 'when you look at the history of the world . . .' or 'I don't think anyone would disagree that . . .', even when asked about some very specific matters. Granted, some of the questions put him in a tough spot, but it was still frustrating to see him dance around the answers. This skill, however, is a major lesson in leadership . . ."
— "What Larry Summers showed us today is that an ability to frame a question and answer selectively is a great way to talk to others from one's strength. . . . It is about the strength and power to make people think that they came to their own conclusions, when really things are framed in such a way as to make those conclusions inevitable."

And a final judgment:

— "What I really took from Summers' practice of leadership is the importance of pursuing a path that interests you and you know you are good at—politics and economics for him—and fine-tuning your best qualities to earn influential positions."

It was true, then, that Larry Summers was indeed helping to shape the next generation of leaders, although perhaps not in the ways that he had expected. Certainly there were students who admired him enormously, who valued his fame and power and respected his intelligence. They were the students who still asked Summers to sign their dollar bills, and they liked the idea that Harvard was led by a man who occupied such a high position, straddling the worlds of power, politics, education, and money.

But many students who had a more in-depth experience with Summers came away with different lessons: that conversations were competitions; that the way to win such competitions was to dissemble, to use your powers to boost your case while stifling even legitimate opposition, to conquer by picking only fights that played into your strengths. And maybe something more: that life consisted of battles, and they always had to be won.

For many of Brian Palmer's students, that was not a life, nor a way of living, that they would choose.

For all the ways in which Larry Summers had changed Harvard during his first years as president, in the spring of 2004 there still remained a lack of tangible results, clearly defined accomplishments by which to judge the Summers presidency. The Broad Institute and the Stem Cell Institute existed only on paper; the Allston planning was moving ahead slowly, as one might expect given the enormity of the project. No one was more aware of this lacuna than Summers himself, and his impatience with the pace of change was a source of ongoing stress to those who worked for him. But in the spring of 2004, that state of affairs changed as the work of the curricular review was introduced to the Harvard community. The review mattered for two reasons: It would affect every undergraduate at Harvard College, and it would be a real measure of the results of Summers' leadership style. As he and his supporters had often suggested, he may have been a bull in a china shop, but if that was what was required to change Harvard, and if that leadership style produced successful results, real improvements, then being a bull was not only justified, it was also necessary. It was *essential*.

In one sense, the Harvard College curriculum was a simple matter. It dictated what students had to do to graduate from Harvard: how many courses they had to take, what requirements they had to fulfill, whether they had to study a foreign language or pass a rudimentary writing course. But for those who believed that Harvard had a great influence on its students—which was to say, virtually everyone who had ever worked or studied there—the curriculum meant much more.

It reflected the university's values, priorities, and mission. Harvard told its students that it wanted them to lead the world, and the curriculum was the official blueprint for their construction as leaders. The curriculum was, in a sense, the matrix in which Harvard students were grown. That was why people cared so much about what it contained, what it encouraged. It was no coincidence that Cornel West had appeared in two of the *Matrix* films; for a man who wanted to liberate students from the addiction of passively received knowledge, the coma of intellectual apathy, such a role made perfect sense.

As times had changed over the twentieth century, Harvard changed its curriculum so that its students would never be unprepared for the world beyond its walls. But that had not always been the case. For the first two centuries of its existence, Harvard had put its students through an inflexible course of study in which they essentially memorized books—Greek, Latin, religious works—then recited the texts back to professors. Change did not come until the presidency of Charles W. Eliot, from 1869 to 1909. Eliot abolished the prescribed curriculum and instituted a program of elective study similar to those at European universities. His successor, Abbott Lawrence Lowell, tacked backwards. Convinced that students had too much freedom under Eliot's system, Lowell imposed the system of concentrations that still exists at Harvard nearly a century later. While the details have changed, the principle is consistent: Harvard students should be exposed to broad areas of study, but it is imperative that they specialize in one area, so that they not be intellectual dilettantes whose four-year education amounts to no more than a hop, skip, and a jump through the course catalogue.

The tension between a general education, in which all students had some common intellectual experience, and academic specialization would remain constant at Harvard throughout the twentieth century. During World War II, James Bryant Conant pushed back in the direction of generalization. His decision to reevaluate the curriculum was very much a product of the time. The United States was at war with fascism, and Harvard was considering how it could best train both soldiers and citizens. In 1943 Conant established a committee of fourteen professors, led by FAS dean Paul Buck, to study the role of education in securing and promoting democracy. "Our purpose," Conant announced, "is to cultivate in the largest number of our future citizens an appreciation of both the responsibilities and the benefits which come to them because they are Americans and are free." Conant thought that Harvard students should have curricular choice. But he also wanted to teach them things that would bind them together, not just as products of Harvard but as Americans. That meant courses that *everyone* took, courses that would transmit the classic works and ideals of Western democratic thought. "There was a feeling [after the war] that we'd had a very close call, that the university had a stake in a particular kind of society and it couldn't just go on its merry way," said professor Samuel Beer at the time.

The unifying power of the Harvard curriculum was especially urgent to Conant because he was pushing the university to open itself to students from all over the United States, from previously untapped minority groups and social classes. How could Harvard take students from all walks of life and provide them with a common and unifying intellectual bond? What did it mean to be an American when one college was filled with upper-crust whites from Massachusetts prep schools, the Jewish children of Eastern European immigrants, G.I.s returning from the war, farm boys from Kansas, and (a very few) black students from northern cities? Americans had to have more in common than simply how different from one another they could be.

In 1945, Buck's committee published a report called *General Education in a Free Society*, often called "the Red Book" because of the color of its cover. "There has been . . . no very substantial intellectual experience common to all Harvard students," the Red Book announced. In Eliot's or Lowell's era, that didn't much matter; now, it was a serious shortcoming. "The undergraduate . . . should be able to talk with his fellows in other fields above the level of casual conversation." While some colleges, such as Columbia and the University of Chicago, had adopted general education curricula that required all students to take specific classes, Harvard would not go that route. The Red Book recommended that students be required to take classes in three areas—sciences, social sciences, and humanities—before continuing on to electives. Which classes, it did not specify. Instead, the faculty created about a dozen courses from which undergraduates could choose. An imperfect solution, it nonetheless achieved much, maybe even most, of what it set out to do: to ground Harvard students in a common intellectual foundation.

Over the decades, though, the program of general education deteriorated. Like a house in need of renovation, it tilted a little as it settled into its foundation, and then started to collapse. Teaching science to non-science concentrators was always a problem. The scientists never liked teaching students who weren't interested in their subjects and who lacked grounding in them; it was far more rewarding to teach those who aspired to become scientists themselves. And some scientists, then as now at Harvard, did not particularly want to teach at all, but saw classes primarily as a conduit for assistants to help them do their laboratory research.

Anyway, as it turned out, many professors in both the sciences and the humanities did not want to teach general education courses. Specialization was all the rage in academia in the postwar years, and Harvard professors wanted to teach courses that reflected their specific interests, or, even better, the books they were working on at the moment. As a result, the classes they did teach became increasingly specialized. At the same time, the number of general education classes swelled, diluting the students' common intellectual experience. Smaller departments had realized that by creating courses that qualified for the Gen Ed program, they could attract more students, thus boosting their own importance—and budgets. On top of those trends, the free-spirited 1960s led to a certain looseness in the creation of courses. Thus, by the early 1970s, Harvard students could take less-than-scholarly classes such as "Auto Mechanics," "Athletic Department Management," and "Scuba Diving." Harvard even offered a class on football's "multiflex offense," which happened to be taught by the quarterback of the team. As it became increasingly apparent that the era of the Red Book was stumbling toward its finish line, the words of former University of Chicago president Robert Maynard Hutchins, spoken about a different era but a similar context, seemed appropriate: "The degree [the university] offers seems to certify that the student has passed an uneventful period without violating any local, state, or federal law, and that he has a fair, if temporary recollection of what his teachers have said to him." Except that by the early 1970s, even the lawbreaking part might not have been true.

Derek Bok took over from Nathan Pusey in 1971, marking the beginning of an era of healing and regeneration at Harvard. In 1974, his new dean, Henry Rosovsky, decided that it was time to initiate another curricular evaluation—a curricular "reform," it was called, in the spirit of the age. Rosovsky did not ask Bok's permission before he started the review; the every-tub-on-its-own-bottom system was strong then, and the FAS dean didn't require the president's permission before reexamining the undergraduate curriculum.

Rosovsky's ambitious curricular reform had several agendas. Of course, it aimed to revamp a sagging curriculum. But Rosovsky also wanted to reenergize the faculty after the conflict and division of the Vietnam years; to say, let us put politics aside for the moment and rededicate ourselves to the primary mission of the university, teaching and learning. His initial letter to the faculty called upon it to embrace curricular reform as a means "to recapture the spirit of its common enterprise."

It was not just the university that Rosovsky wanted the faculty to reconnect with, but the undergraduates. In the decades after World War II, a period of enormous growth among universities and huge sums of money flowing from the federal government, professors at Harvard (and numerous other universities) lost their sense that teaching undergraduates was the center of their professional self-definition. It may, in fact, have been the least of their priorities.

And it was not just the professors that Rosovsky was targeting. He hoped that a process of curricular reform, and then a new and inspiring curriculum, could dampen the antagonism between students and the university. He also wanted to rein in the spirit of academic improvisation that had prevailed during the sixties. "Our curriculum at the moment resembles too much a Chinese menu," Rosovsky said. "A very good menu—but I think that a Chinese menu in the hands of a novice can result in less than a perfect meal. I would like to supply a few waiters." The line was classic Rosovsky—a criticism, but one that was constructive, diplomatic, even elegant.

If Rosovsky's reform was really going to effect such laudatory but ambitious goals, the process by which it was carried out would be critical. And so Rosovsky deliberately involved as many professors as he could. (Though not many students; at the time, there was already an excess of student input into the university.) Rosovsky knew that, in a contentious era, he could not impose reform from the top down, and that was not his style anyway. As Phyllis Keller would write in a history of the curricular reform, Rosovsky "saw his role as engaging the largest possible number of his colleagues. . . . He took the position that the only workable solution would be one that emerged from the faculty itself." It was like the difference between trying to illuminate a room with a flashlight and turning on a chandelier.

In addition to broad participation, Rosovsky enlisted academic heavyweights. Much of the actual theorizing was done by political scientist James Q. Wilson and historian Bernard Bailyn, giants in their fields. If the faculty was going to buy into his curricular reform, Rosovsky thought, it had to have the utmost respect for its intellectual parents. After four years of hard work and patient negotiation, in the fall of 1978 Rosovsky released a report advocating a new "core curriculum," a dramatic departure from any course of study Harvard had previously mandated.

Perhaps the first thing to say about the core was that it rejected a fundamental principle of general education; it did not advocate a common foundation of knowledge for the entire student body. After the explosion of scholarship in the past decades, Rosovsky argued, it was simply no longer possible to define a body of knowledge that everyone would agree was the sine qua non of the educated citizen. The day had passed when one could simply announce that the Greek and Latin classics were more vital than those of the Muslim world, or declare that the history of England was objectively more important than the study of China. And of all the sciences that one should know, how could it be said that biology was invariably more important than, say, chemistry or physics? Even to try to debate these questions could provoke years of heated and divisive discussion. Just to launch that discussion would probably doom reform.

The Core Curriculum's answer was to advocate that students learn not specific facts or a single intellectual tradition, but "ways of knowing." Students would be exposed to a range of disciplines in order to reach an understanding of how scholars in different fields thought, evaluated, and analyzed their own material. How did historians work? What about scientists, literary critics, and economists? "Broadly stated," Rosovsky's report said, "the goal of the Core is to encourage a critical appreciation of the major approaches to knowledge, so that students may acquire an understanding of what kinds of knowledge exists in certain important areas, how such knowledge is created, how it is used, and what it might mean to them personally." To that end, the Core divided the range of study into ten "core" areas, such as historical studies, literature and the arts, moral reasoning—this was largely Derek Bok's doing—quantitative reasoning, and science. Students would have to take a set number of courses from most of the core areas.

Reaction to the Core was mixed. Liberals saw it as a political attempt to impose structure and control upon a freewheeling student body, even as "a class struggle between student masses and the faculty-administration elite," as one commentator put it. Conservatives bashed the Core on the grounds that it didn't prioritize Western thought and civilization. Scientists on the one hand thought that the Core insufficiently emphasized their fields, while on the other hand were not much interested in teaching science to undergraduates who were happily daydreaming of Jane Austen or American reactions to the Stamp Act.

In the end, the Core had to be approved by a vote of the faculty, and the faculty did approve it, for several reasons. First, thanks to Rosovsky's assiduous courtship, they felt that they had been included in the process and had a stake in its outcome. Second was their loyalty to Rosovsky himself; Rosovsky had turned down the presidency of Yale to complete the curricular reform, and they did not want him to come away from the process with nothing to show for it. Perhaps this was not the best reason to support a new curriculum, but in a university, as in a legislature, human relations influence policy decisions. Third, there was a sense that while the Core might have been an experiment, it was a serious and well-considered experiment, and worth trying.

Outside Harvard, the Core had an immediate impact; it focused new attention upon undergraduate education in an era when universities had been moving more toward research and the training of graduate students. The New York Daily News called it "a refreshing contrast to the sophomoric whims and caprices that marked the do-your-own-thing revolt on campuses in the '60s." Few schools had the resources to duplicate the Core, which, when it was introduced, contained an astonishing sixty new courses. But it did set many on the path of revitalizing their own curricula.

If the Core had a downside, it was that the new curriculum was a high-maintenance machine. It required the continuing close oversight of the dean and engagement of the faculty to work well, and particularly after Rosovsky's retirement from the deanship in 1991, it did not have either. Students lamented that the Core was confusing, arbitrary, and restrictive. Many professors didn't like to teach Core classes, as such classes tended to include concentrators who knew the subjects well and novices taking the class only because they had to. Such disparities in knowledge and enthusiasm made teaching in the Core an often unwanted challenge.

By 2001, when Larry Summers became president, a consensus that the Core needed fixing had taken hold. But whether the program just needed to be tweaked or required a full-scale "review," as it was now being called, was a matter of some debate. Just a few years before, in the mid-1990s, a faculty committee had examined the Core and concluded that, despite a few problem areas, the curriculum was basically in solid shape. So when Summers announced that a curricular review would be a priority, some wondered if he had hidden agendas. Previous reviews had followed periods of great social change: World War II and the 1960s. This one was following the inauguration of a new president who clearly was giving much thought to his legacy. (Summers would have argued that 1990s globalization had indeed brought huge social change.) Other skeptics wondered if the launch of a curricular review was not merely a precursor for yet another massive fund drive. Harvard had just finished such a campaign in 1999. If big donors were to give still more, they needed a new reason why, and the expenses of a new curriculum could be it. The contributions that the capital campaign might generate would also help fund the construction of the new campus in Allston.

The review could not begin until new dean Bill Kirby had taken office, and in October 2002 Kirby sent a letter to the faculty initiating a conversation about the review. "What will it mean to be an educated woman or man in the first quarter of the 21st century?" the dean asked. "What should a Harvard graduate know in depth about a discipline or area? What are the enduring goals of a liberal education and how can they be provided in the setting of a modern research university?"

The review's co-chair would be Dick Gross, who was then just months away from replacing Harry Lewis as dean of Harvard College. In the spring of 2003, Gross appointed four committees whose task was to examine different aspects of the Harvard education: Concentrations, Pedagogy, General Education and Overall Academic Experience. Each committee consisted of about a dozen professors, staff, and students, and perhaps the best way to understand their work is through the experience of one of those students, Joseph K. Green, class of 2005.

Joe Green came to Harvard from Los Angeles, California. His father was a math professor at UCLA, and Green was always a serious, studious kid. During his time at Santa Monica High School, he acted in plays, was captain of the Science Bowl team, captain of the swim team, and the student representative on the Santa Monica Board of Education. He took school so seriously that, as a senior, he was profiled in a CNN documentary called *Kids Under Pressure*, about the stress of applying for college.

In truth, Green doesn't look all that disciplined. With curly black hair, a Southern California drawl reminiscent of Sean Penn's Jeff Spicoli character in *Fast Times at Ridgemont High*, and a slightly spacey manner, he comes across as an absent-minded professor in the making. At the same time, he has always taken his education seriously, and in the CNN documentary, he talked about how much pressure he felt to get into the right college. "The ideal candidate, they say, is the captain of the football team, a member of MENSA, spends his weekends running a women's shelter out of his garage, and on the side, you know, has orphan children that he's taking care of and everything. And, you know, has won a Nobel Prize and he's currently in the Sydney Olympics."

Green was applying to a discriminating group of colleges: Harvard, Yale, Princeton, Columbia, the University of Chicago, Swarthmore, Georgetown, Stanford, and Washington University in St. Louis. Even with all his extracurriculars, he wasn't taking anything for granted. After he scored 1450 out of 1600 on his SATS, he crammed more and retook the college entrance tests. The second time around, he scored a 1580.

Green worried that all this work just to get into college was like mortgaging his present to buy his future—he didn't have a girlfriend, he didn't get to hang out with his friends or parents, he just didn't have the time—but he wasn't sure he had much of a choice. "When I'm having, like, a rough time, [I think], is it really worth the effort, does which college I get into really matter that much?" Green wondered. "I mean, shouldn't who I am and what I'm able to do matter more? And then I think, well, that's not really how the world works."

Green's sacrifice and hard work paid off: he got in everywhere he applied, and he seemed to think just as hard about where to go as he had thought about how to get in. "The guidebooks all said that Harvard is great except for the undergraduate education," Green remembered. "Princeton focused more on undergraduate education, and Yale students were happier. I was really stressed about it." In the end, Green chose Harvard, because he was interested in politics and thought that the Kennedy School would provide opportunities. Still, he was never quite sure that he shouldn't have picked Princeton, his number-two choice. "I have a little bit of a Princeton complex," Green admitted. "I want to prove to myself that I made the right decision."

His freshman year was Larry Summers' first year as president, and Green's confidence was bolstered when he heard the new president say that Harvard's undergraduate education needed work. He contacted Summers' office to see if the president would need an intern to help with the upcoming curricular review, but the answer was no, the review wouldn't really start for another year or so. Still, Green couldn't stop thinking about the purpose of a Harvard education. In the fall of 2002, he went to a dinner Larry Summers threw for student leaders, and he was pleased when Summers asked the students what would be the one thing they would fix regarding Harvard? Green said that people weren't asking big questions, such as "Why are we here? What are we supposed to learn?" Summers responded that that wasn't a helpful answer, because it didn't include one specific thing that could simply be fixed.

In the second half of his sophomore year, in February 2003, Green enrolled in Economics 1010A, Microeconomic Theory, a standard introductory course. But along with other students, Green found the professor's lectures disjointed, rambling, and frequently unhelpful. He grew so frustrated that he sent Bill Kirby a lengthy e-mail about the professor, who ultimately took a four-week leave from the course to "rework" his lectures. That incident inspired a *Crimson* column headlined "World's Greatest University, World's Worst Teachers." It also put Green in touch with the FAS administration, and that spring Dick Gross invited Green to lunch at the Faculty Club and asked if he wanted to be on a curricular review committee. Green did. He chose the committee on pedagogy, because he thought that area needed the most reform.

Meeting once every other week, the four committees began their work in the fall of 2003. At the start, Green was hopeful. He wanted to ask big questions about the purpose of a Harvard education, about the way teaching was done. Why were students not asked what courses should be offered? Why do concentrations even exist? Green had heard Larry Summers talk about how important and far-reaching this review was, so he thought that asking fundamental questions was the point. Green kept thinking about a question one of his professors had put to him: "If you could either go here and get no diploma, or not go here and get the diploma, what would you do?" It bothered Green that he couldn't easily answer the question.

But the two faculty members on the committee, historian Liz Cohen and biologist Richard Losick, quickly made it clear there wasn't time for that kind of open-ended conversation. "The response was, 'If we ask big questions, we won't get concrete recommendations," Green said. There was no time for big-picture debates. Summers was impatient: Bill Kirby had to release a curricular review report by May 2004, in time for commencement. His curricular review was supposed to accomplish in one year what had taken Henry Rosovsky four. Green couldn't even talk to his friends about what his committee was considering—the students had been told to say nothing to anyone outside the review process. "It was," Green came to believe, "a fantastic way to control dissent."

The four committees produced an interim report, which the faculty discussed briefly at a meeting on December 16. Lacking specific recommendations, the report reiterated the oft-mentioned goals of internationalization, scientific fluency, more contact between faculty and students, and increased undergraduate contact with the graduate schools. No one paid it much attention, partly because of the lack of substance, and partly because the faculty wasn't paying much attention to the review in general. Unlike Rosovsky, Kirby wasn't making a full-court press to reach out to faculty members. Even if he had, it was questionable whether they would have responded. The faculty didn't believe that Kirby was really the man running the review—and by and large, they doubted that Summers seriously wanted a university-wide conversation regarding a proposed new curriculum.

By now, the sense that Larry Summers created committees merely to forestall criticism of his pre-made decisions had grown widespread. Why invest time in a curricular review when their recommendations would be ignored if Summers disagreed with them? Certainly there was no sense that the university's greatest minds, the really legendary figures, were engaged with the process, invested in it so deeply that they had a personal stake in its success, as they had a quarter-century before. "Several faculty members who were present for the 1970s review told me they remember feeling excitement in the air as questions of education were debated," wrote *Crimson* columnist J. Hale Russell in late March. "This time around nobody knows what's going on, much less feels excitement."

There were signs that even Bill Kirby and Dick Gross weren't all that involved with the process. The two men were traveling frequently, both to talk about the review at other universities and to raise money; from September 2003 to March 2004, Kirby hosted eighteen alumni events designed to give alumni a sense of inclusion and solicit their financial aid. On campus, though, people said that Kirby was oddly disengaged, that despite his rhetoric, he wasn't actively involved in the review. "Bill's feeling was that this was so obviously Larry's report, what was the point of getting involved?" said one source who knew both men. One professor familiar with the review process pointed out an important distinction between Rosovsky and Kirby. It was well known that Rosovsky, he said, had turned down an offer to be president of Yale in order to complete a review. Kirby, the source thought, wanted to become a university president, and so wouldn't risk picking fights with his boss that he probably couldn't win anyway.

Kirby's appointed overseer, Dick Gross, was traveling frequently as well, for the same purposes as Kirby. But even when he wasn't, Gross delegated much of the review's work to subordinates who lacked the clout to inspire the faculty. Foremost among them was Jeffrey Wolcowitz, a lecturer in economics and associate dean for undergraduate education. Wolcowitz, who had studied curriculum management for years, was respected and well liked. He was considered a good and smart man who took questions of curricular reform seriously. At the same time, he was not a tenured professor, much less the dean of the FAS. That someone so low in the pecking order was the most involved in the curricular review struck faculty observers as bizarre, and not a good omen for the review's future. Some suspected that Wolcowitz was really Summers' ringer. "Larry pretty much handpicked Jeff to write the report," said one University Hall source.

In the early spring, Summers invited the eight undergraduates on the review committees to Elmwood for dinner. As they sat around the dining room table talking about the review, Joe Green grew frustrated with the conversation—it was so specific, all about technicalities, with no sense of the underlying point of it all. "We're not asking the big questions," he said to the president. Green thought that the Harvard curriculum needed more than tinkering to challenge and produce great thinkers. "I'm concerned Harvard could never produce another William James," Green said.

Summers looked unhappy at the suggestion that Harvard couldn't generate another important philosopher—which was really a lament that the curricular review was insufficiently ambitious. "What about Michael Sandel?" Summers asked. (Sandel was a member of the review's Committee on General Education.) Green found it hard to take the remark seriously. Michael Sandel was a gifted lecturer and a smart, provocative thinker. But no one would have put him in a class with William James, and to do so suggested either an ignorance of the history of philosophy or a denial of reality. "I think Larry does care about undergraduate education," Green said later. "He does care about Harvard College." Nonetheless, he wasn't open to challenges to his curricular review.

By early March, the work of the curricular review committees was done, and the four groups gave their secret recommendations to Wolcowitz. Once so idealistic, Green had grown disillusioned. He realized that in the time allotted, the committees' couldn't possibly have undertaken any wide-ranging intellectual inquiry, and he believed that the aggressive schedule had been "a strategy designed to make sure that the administration got its agenda through." He was so frustrated, he even met with Henry Rosovsky to ask his advice, but while Rosovsky was happy to discuss the history of the Core, he would not get involved in the current process—no one wanted the architect of the Core looking over their shoulder as they prepared to axe the old curriculum. "I don't think the committees got to the bottom of things, or even tried to," Green said. "You couldn't have, in one year. As an intellectual exercise, it was pretty unimpressive." After being asked to meet with a prominent alumni donor, Green even began to doubt the rationale for having students in the process. "The administration needed to have us there so they could say there was student involvement" in the review, he said. The alumni liked to hear that.

In mid-April, Jeffrey Wolcowitz shuttered himself in his basement office in University Hall to finish writing the curricular report in time for release on Monday, April 26. The pressure was on. According to University Hall sources, *New York Times* education reporter Sara Rimer had told Kirby's office that the paper planned a front-page story on the review, as long as she got it early enough. But there was plenty of pressure from a source closer to home: Larry Summers.

From the very beginning of his presidency, Summers had never shied away from stating what he hoped the curricular review would do. His 2003 commencement address was devoted to the topic. But during the course of the review, Summers played an even more hands-on role. At first, he acted through a surrogate. Apparently at Summers' urging, Wolcowitz had hired for his staff a woman named Inge-Lise Ameer. Ameer had a 2002 doctorate from the Harvard School of Education, but that wasn't her only qualification for the job. Also important was that she was friends with Summers' girlfriend, English professor Lisa New. When New was director of undergraduate studies in the English department, Ameer was her "undergraduate administrative coordinator"—essentially her right-hand woman. The two liked each other very much, and through New, Ameer had met and socialized with Summers. He liked her too—and in her new role working for Jeff Wolcowitz, he used her to transmit his opinions on the curricular review. "Larry would pick up the phone and call her," said one source familiar with their working relationship. Explained another, "Through Inge-Lise Ameer, Larry was delivering messages to Jeff Wolcowitz over the course of the review," circumventing Bill Kirby and Dick Gross. Ameer's presence irritated other University Hall staffers, who considered her Summers' surrogate. She was, according to a third source, "a big problem." Some of her co-workers were reluctant to talk freely around her, lest their words be reported back to the president. (Ameer declined to comment.)

Ameer's presence in University Hall also showed the growth of Lisa New's power and influence. Though she could appear absentminded and even a little ditzy, New was neither, and she had strong opinions on issues such as undergraduate advising and teaching, and the merit (or lack thereof) of some undergraduate departments. And because Summers himself was not particularly familiar with issues in the humanities—and not always interested anyway—New filled a vac-

uum. The mild-mannered divorcée and poetry lover had become a
major, if sub rosa, player in the direction of study of the humanities at
Harvard. That her former aide was helping to shape the curricular
review was evidence of that.

As Wolcowitz approached the home stretch, Summers' involvement became still more direct. According to several sources, he began
simply calling Wolcowitz directly, telling him what to put in the final
report regardless of whether the review committees had recommended
it. "At the end," said a University Hall source, "Larry was just dictating
to Jeff, 'These are the changes and they are going in.'" Wolcowitz, said
another source familiar with the process, had become the "fall guy." If
the report bombed, then, at least internally, he would take the blame.
Other sources said that Wolcowitz was "traumatized" and "depressed"
by the experience. He would not get the chance to recover. In early
September 2004, Bill Kirby summarily relieved Wolcowitz of his
decanal duties, almost certainly ending the nontenured Wolcowitz's
decades-long service at Harvard. Kirby gave no explanation; University Hall sources said that Wolcowitz had started to chafe at the untenable position he was in, and his resulting shows of independence had
irritated Kirby. In any event, the publicly identified author of the curricular review would now have nothing further to do with it.

The end of the drafting process was not pretty. On the evening of
Thursday, April 22, members of the review committees were e-mailed
a password that granted them Internet access to a draft of the report.
They had until Sunday to read it and make comments; their comments
were expected to be minor, as there was no time for major changes; the
report was to be released to the press on Monday. "We were supposed
to see the draft report several weeks before it was released," said Joe
Green. He believed that Wolcowitz didn't want feedback from the
committee members, but it seemed equally possible that Wolcowitz
had simply run out of time.

Summers was so concerned about the report's status, he insisted that
Kirby intervene. On Sunday, April 25, according to two sources familiar
with the incident, Kirby "literally took the report out of Wolcowitz's
hands." There followed a late-night editing session in order to finish it and
deliver it to Sara Rimer, the *Times'* education reporter. It was, however, too
late; Rimer's story ran on A19—still impressive for a report whose import
had yet to be determined—but not page one. The president was not

happy. Rumors began to circulate around University Hall that he was so displeased with his dean, and so anxious that the report would get ripped in the media, that he had lost confidence in Kirby.

Bill Kirby, some thought, had done everything Summers had wanted him to. Just to prepare a publishable report in a year's time was a considerable feat. But now some of his colleagues began to suspect that Kirby's future as dean was in doubt. Replacing an FAS dean so early in his tenure would once have been considered unthinkable except in the most extreme circumstances. But Summers had shown that the traditional way of doing business mattered little. All that mattered was results.

The final document, sixty-seven pages in length, was called "A Report on the Harvard College Curricular Review," and in essence, it transcribed everything that Larry Summers had been evangelizing about since the fall of 2001. The proposed new curriculum would replace the Core with a distributional requirement. Students would still be required to take courses in a few broad categories. Gone, however, was the idea that students should study "ways of thinking." The new curriculum would try to ensure that students learned specific facts, although it did not say which ones. There was no mention, for example, of a mandatory Western civilization course, often a central thrust of general education programs in American universities. Instead, "a central component" of the distributional requirement would be the creation of a new set of courses, to be called "Harvard College Courses." Though study abroad would not be required, it was strongly recommended, and student transcripts would show whether they had undergone a "significant" international experience. (What *significant* meant was undefined, but apparently the term was intended to exclude spending a night walking the Seine with a Parisian art student or discovering an Eden-like beach in Thailand.) As Kirby would say in press accounts, "If you're going to come to Harvard College, it would be very good to have a passport." In addition, there were proposals for fewer concentration requirements, mandatory freshman seminars, and a four-week January term in which students could take intensive courses, write a research paper, or perhaps study abroad. Students would have to study more science and international affairs, and possibly science courses ought to be more "interdisciplinary," although what exactly this meant also went unspecified. Perhaps the last significant recommendation was that the system of assigning students to houses at the end of their freshman years be changed to what critics would angrily call a "Yale-style" housing system, in which students received house assignments as incoming freshmen.

And that was pretty much it. (There was a lot of padding.)

In the national press, the report garnered some early good buzz. The *Times* declared that it "is likely to have an impact on universities across the nation." In an editorial called "Rethinking at Harvard," the *Boston Globe* assured readers that the review "promises to be a bold step forward."

As it turned out, though, those two newspapers were pretty much the only ones to feel that way. The highly respected *Chronicle of Higher Education* noted that "the last time Harvard reviewed its undergraduate curriculum . . . the results influenced colleges across the country." This time, according to Carol Geary Schneider, president of the Association of American Colleges and Universities, many of the report's recommendations simply mirrored what a number of other colleges already have in place. The *Crimson* added that "university administrators across the country say they are not expecting anything as radical or as influential from the current curricular review" as the Core had been. The promotion of study abroad, for example, was new to Harvard, but it was certainly not new at many other colleges around the country. The proposal for Yale-style housing, to build a stronger bond between freshmen and the houses, came, of course, from Yale. The idea for a January term seemed to come from MIT, which included a "J-term" in its calendar. This was one reason why the *Crimson*'s J. Hale Russell, a consistent critic of the review process, called the report "60 pages of stunningly bland and half-baked recommendations" and "the rather unsurprising product of a one-year process conducted behind closed doors and largely driven by the narrow-minded agenda of a university president who . . . seems intent on turning Harvard into his alma mater, MIT."

There was perhaps only one item in the report that felt unique to Harvard, and that was the so-called "Harvard College Courses." The oddly generic name was followed by an equally generic description. The Harvard College Courses were "to be foundational . . . to cut across traditional disciplinary boundaries, and to define the basis of an educated citizenry." But apparently they also were to teach something that sounded very much like the Core's ways of thinking. "Faculty in related areas would come together across disciplinary boundaries . . . to speak with one another and with students in a common language and to define the most important concepts and approaches that students should know about their fields." If the reader was not clear as to what exactly that meant, the report attempted to get more specific. "A world literature course might look at cultural representation in different places and periods, and cultural flows across traditional national boundaries and among hierarchies of culture." The description was still less than clear.

The vagueness may have been intentional; two lines in the report hinted at the real reason for Harvard College Courses. They were to be "flagship courses, listed at the front of the course catalog. They should develop distinctive course materials for use in, and potentially beyond, Harvard College." Those lines sounded innocuous enough, but as the *Crimson* would later report, they had a deeper meaning than appeared upon first reading. The key words were "for use in, *and potentially beyond*, Harvard College." At some point, Larry Summers wanted to market those courses to students around the world, to use the Harvard brand name to teach "foundational knowledge" to students whether they went to Harvard College or not. The Harvard College Courses were created both for profit and, as Michael Sandel might once have put it, for intellectual hegemony. To further stamp Harvard's imprint on the world's education; to promote an empire of the mind.

The most oft-heard criticism of the review was that it lacked any guiding philosophy or unifying vision. It was as if the chairman of Ford Motors had spent years promising the introduction of an all-new Mustang—but when the curtain came up on the car, it had only a few new bells and whistles, and even they were appropriated from the competitors' models. The faculty was underwhelmed. The report landed on their desks like a scoop of lukewarm mashed potatoes, and in faculty meetings and published comments, many turned up their noses at it. Put bluntly, said one esteemed professor, "people think the report is a joke."

Larry Summers had often spoken of wanting to create a curriculum that prepared students for the world of the twenty-first century. But behind his rhetoric had simmered a great impatience with the pace of change at Harvard and a burning desire to produce tangible achievements—to legacy-build, and to do so fast. In the 2004 Harvard College curricular review, that impatience seemed to have carried the day. And to the extent that the curricular review was a measure of Larry Summers' leadership style, it suggested that while being a bull in a china shop might be a great way to earn flattering press from critics outside Harvard, it was not the most effective way to build a better curriculum.

In theory, the Harvard faculty had to approve the new curriculum, and it would debate the review proposals in the 2004–2005 school year and beyond. (Indeed, throughout that school year the review committees would essentially re-do the work of the year before.) They would probably approve some ideas that were, while unremarkable, harmless or worthwhile; others they would surely dislike and reject. But their support or opposition mattered less than in past eras. It appeared that some parts of the report could be effected piecemeal through the fiat of Bill Kirby, who declined to detail which parts of the review the faculty would get to vote on.

Joe Green would not be there for much of that debate; he took the fall 2004 semester off to work for presidential candidate John Kerry. But Green and Undergraduate Council president Matt Mahan hadn't given up on getting students to fight for the future of a Harvard education. They were the main organizers of a group called Undergraduates Reclaiming Our Curriculum, which aspired to get students more involved in the review. "No matter how great the curriculum is," Green said, "if the students aren't invested in it, it's going to fail." The same, of course, was true of the faculty as well.

Summers had often spoken of the curricular review as a once-in-a-generation opportunity, and he was right. A successful curricular review could reinvigorate the university's intellectual life, reenergize the faculty, and excite the students, building a communal sense of academic purpose. By those measures, Larry Summers' curricular review was a failure.

The President on His Throne

As he looked out over another crowd of thirty thousand strong gathered for Harvard commencement, Larry Summers drummed his fingers on the arms of the centuries-old President's Chair in which he sat. Graduating senior Kate L. Rakoczy was giving the Undergraduate English Oration, a speech about the importance of pursuing your passions in life, but Summers did not appear to be paying attention—he already knew that there was nothing in the speech he needed concern himself with. Perched squarely in the middle of the stage at its highest point, he gazed out over the crowd and waited for his turn before the microphone. When the crowd applauded, he lifted up one hand and let it fall limply onto the other.

Thursday, June 10, 2004, had dawned wet and blustery, the third consecutive year it had rained on commencement, but the ceremonies were proceeding according to plan. After almost two years, Summers had replaced university marshal Rick Hunt with a woman named Jackie O'Neill, who had previously worked in Mass Hall, and O'Neill helped make sure that the student speeches were inoffensive. At Class Day on Wednesday, 2004, class marshal Shaka Bahadu had declared that "sitting amongst us are [future] candidates for president of the United States" and "now is the time to share our light with the rest of the world," both of which were perfectly routine sentiments for Harvard commencement. Thursday morning, the processions of cap-and-gowned graduates had filed into the Yard in their traditional order, according to the year in which their school was founded. Following more modern tradition, the divinity school students had adorned their caps with halos; the Kennedy School students carried globes; and when the business school diplomas were conferred, the HBS graduates hurled dollar bills in the air.

Later that afternoon, UN head Kofi Annan would give an impassioned speech about the dangers of unilateralism in foreign relations. Speaking first, Summers would talk about economic inequities in higher education, a repetition of speeches he'd been giving for months. In the spring, Summers had announced a policy by which Harvard would abolish tuition for students from families with an income of less than $40,000 a year. Previously such students had had to pay only $1,000 per year, so the policy change wasn't actually costing Harvard much money, but the symbolically powerful move had garnered waves of publicity. It was only natural that the president would speak about the policy change on this day.

As he sat on the presidential throne, wearing long black robes and a scarlet sash, Summers might have been reflecting on the controversy of just two years before, when senior Zayed Yasin spoke of his "American jihad." That talk had marked the end of Summers' first and most turbulent year. The president had come a long way since then. The university was firmly in his grasp. Except for the occasional and so-far ineffectual dissident, the faculty had been silenced. As Summers would explain to a British journalist who asked about his leadership style, "Sometimes fear does work of reason." The students were learning to live with a new level of separation from the Harvard administration. The Board of Overseers was an emasculated body, while the Corporation was even more firmly on Summers' side than it had been when it chose him as the new president. Treasurer D. Ron Daniel was retiring after fifteen years in that position, and Summers and the rest of the Corporation had selected a new treasurer, James Rothenberg, the head of Capital Research and Management, a Los Angeles–based money management firm that oversaw $450 billion in mutual funds. It was unclear how strong a figure Rothenberg would be. Even as he joined the Corporation, his firm was under investigation by the Securities and Exchange Commission for potential violations of conflict-of-interest regulations.

As Summers' grip on Harvard had tightened, the level of public controversy at the university had dissipated. Cornel West's portrait may still have been hanging on the wall of the African and African American Studies Department, but West himself was long gone. Poet Tom Paulin would never try to reschedule his unpopular speaking appointment. The first phase of the war in Iraq hadn't lasted long enough to prompt many anti-war demonstrations in Harvard Yard, and the protests over the Solomon Amendment had fizzled out with the onset of summer vacation. Even the uproar over Sheik Zayed's donation to the divinity school had died down. About six weeks after this commencement, the United Arab Emirates government would quietly withdraw its $2.5-million gift, saying that discussions with Harvard had dragged on too long. The university released this information the day before the Democratic National Convention began in Boston, burying the story underneath an avalanche of convention-related news.

Not only were most of the protests gone, so were most of the protesters. The last of the students who had taken over Massachusetts Hall in the spring of 2001 were now getting their diplomas and leaving town. Cornel West was at Princeton; Harry Lewis was on sabbatical at MIT; Tim McCarthy was in North Carolina writing his book on church-burnings; Rachel Fish had gone to Manhattan to run a group called the David Project, which promotes peace in the Middle East; Brian Palmer was headed to Sweden to teach at a university there.

Meanwhile, one of Summers' former critics, Skip Gates, was coming back in the fall for at least one more year. In the spring of 2004, Gates had come to Summers and asked for more money, telling the president that he'd gotten an offer from another university. (Gates denies this.) Summers turned him down. "Larry did not raise the ante," said one source familiar with the meeting. "He had come to terms with the prospect of Skip leaving, and that was his strongest hand. Larry is feeling very confident." If Gates left now, Summers had concluded, it would reflect worse on Gates than on him. Summers had done much to court the black community, and with his public praise for Summers, Gates had unintentionally given the president cover. Summers knew that he could spin Gates' departure as a law of nature; every so often, Skip Gates just had to move on.

Inevitably, there were rumors—very quiet this time—that Gates' return would not last long. "He went in to talk to Summers and Summers said he wasn't giving him a penny. Skip basically said, 'I've said good things about you and I'm covering for your ass, you've got to be kidding,'" according to one professor who knows both men. "Skip said [to himself], 'This man is not playing the game. If you're going to be a power player, play the game.'"

Gates had always worked on the presumption that there was plenty of power to go around, and that if you had it, you shared it. He was reluctant to stay in a place where the president appeared to believe that every drop of power possessed by someone else was power taken away from him. One more year at Harvard, and then it seemed very likely that Skip Gates would head elsewhere—probably either Princeton or Columbia. Months later, that outcome seemed even more likely when a husband-and-wife team of scholars in Af-Am, Lawrence Bobo and Marcyliena Morgan, announced that they would be leaving Harvard for tenured professorships at Stanford at the end of the 2004–2005 school year. Summers had declined to offer tenure to Morgan; Stanford did not hesitate.

Three years is not enough time to judge a university presidency, but in that short period Summers had clearly changed life at Harvard. He had promoted science initiatives, prodded a curricular review into life, and directed more money to the graduate schools that needed it the most. The outcomes of these projects was uncertain, but Summers could take credit for having started them. He had also helped elevate the urgent subject of economic class and access to higher education into the national conversation. And there was no question that, on issues ranging from anti-Semitism to Harvard's relationship with the military, he had once again made the Harvard president a figure who commanded national attention. Underlying all these things was the most important change—a massive centralization of power at the university and, more specifically, the power of the president, at the expense of the governing boards, the deans, the faculty, and the students.

But there was still unfinished business. It is human nature that we tend to remember leaders by their most tangible accomplishments— What did they discover? What battles did they win? What works of art did they create?—and in Summers' case, his most tangible legacy would surely be the design and construction of a new campus across the Charles River, in Allston. In the previous months, Summers had begun to release bits and pieces of information about the planned campus, and its broad outlines were taking shape. He had hired the celebrity architect Frank Gehry to oversee the planning process; Gehry had just completed the Ray and Maria Stata Center at MIT, a $300–$400 million building devoted largely to computer science and engineering. The president wanted to move much of Harvard's sciences into Allston, creating a complex that, Summers said, would lead to "a critical mass of scientific laboratories." He would also move the School of Public Health and the School of Education from their respective locations in downtown Boston and Harvard Square, where both were boxed in by development. And he would put from four to eight undergraduate houses in Allston, physically splitting the college housing in half. People involved with the Allston planning committees believed that, though he didn't come out and say so, Summers wanted to expand the undergraduate population from its current level of around 6,400 to perhaps 10,000. Many more of these students would come from overseas than Harvard currently accepted. "Summers wants people to no longer think of Harvard as being in Cambridge or Boston or Massachusetts or even the United States, but a place that's a *center*, a place that is everywhere but isn't really anywhere," said Matt Mahan, the 2004–2005 Undergraduate Council president.

If true, that plan would prompt a huge fight—such growth would not only place profound economic stresses on the university and its faculty, but it would also transform Harvard student life, making the possibility of a cohesive community even more remote than it is currently. At the very least, students worried, it would make less plausible Summers' rhetoric about increasing contact between students and faculty. If undergrads didn't see much of their professors now, what would happen if they were joined by another 3,600 students? On the flip side, if Harvard became a larger university under Summers, a place so big and so international that it truly became a global institution, Larry Summers would sit at the helm of the first world university. Anyone who knew Summers knew that this was a proposition he would find attractive.

Inevitably, the Allston proposals had both supporters and detractors. (Although, there was a general feeling that the School of Education was so chronically overlooked that *any* attention paid to it was a good thing.) But most of the people who would be affected by the changes didn't have strong opinions, simply because they lacked enough information. The president would never forget The Memo; he knew that thinking out loud only provided a rallying point for potential foes. By the time his planning became public, it would have acquired so much momentum that stopping it would be harder than going along with it.

In the meantime, the Allston project was adding to Summers' power because it was adding to the wealth of his office. In mid-January 2004, the Corporation extended for twenty-five years something called the Allston Infrastructure Fund, a tax of .5 percent on the endowment allocated toward Allston planning. If the endowment stood at $23 billion, that was over $100 million a year. Neil Rudenstine had been the fund's first advocate (proof that he was not always the milquetoast some considered him). Over the vehement objections of then-dean Jeremy Knowles—the tax would hurt FAS the most—the Corporation approved it for five years. If Bill Kirby opposed the fund's twenty-five-year renewal, his protest went unnoticed. It probably wouldn't have mattered anyway; Summers wanted this money. In theory, the hundreds of millions of dollars that would accumulate would be overseen by a committee headed by provost Steven Hyman. In reality, since Hyman worked directly under Summers (and physically just feet away from him), that money would be controlled by the president.

And there would be still more money pouring into Harvard, and the president's office, in the years to come. Even that commencement afternoon, as former Corporation fellow Roger Stone announced the year's fund-raising totals—the law school, $196 million! the business school, $450 million!—other Harvard fundraisers were working on a new capital campaign, sure to be the largest in the history of education. Neil Rudenstine aimed to raise $2.1 billion and wound up with $2.5 billion. Now people were whispering about an unprecedented number: $10 billion. During the Rudenstine campaign, 12.5 percent of the proceeds were automatically diverted to the central administration. One could be sure the Larry Summers administration would receive a similar or larger take.

Underneath—far, far underneath—the pomp and glitter of commencement, currents of unhappiness were making their way through the university. The president's critics would have said that it was his intangible changes that mattered the most. That he was corrupting the university with values and priorities better suited to the world of politics and commerce. That, instead of free speech and vigorous debate—

instead of *veritas*—the president of Harvard cared only about image, public relations, spin control. And that the thing they cherished most about Harvard—that in a world of never-ending competition and conflict, the university aspired to something higher, something more timeless—was rapidly vanishing. Like an extinct species, once gone, that precious quality would probably be gone forever. Those professors would either have to live in a world of Larry Summers' creation, or go elsewhere. But if Harvard couldn't remain an ivory tower, in the best, most optimistic sense of that phrase, what university could?

It is possible that, sooner or later, Summers' critics will rise to fight for the Harvard they believe in. Maybe if he makes a misstep, gives them an opening. But it is also possible that the moment to fight, the window of opportunity, has passed, and that their cause is already lost.

Still, from Summers' perspective, as he sat on his presidential chair, all seemed right with his world. Perhaps the only question in his mind was how long he would stay in Cambridge. During the 2004 presidential campaign, more and more members of the community wondered whether he might leave Harvard. John Kerry had attended Summers' inauguration; Summers was known to give the Massachusetts senator advice on economic policy. If Kerry won the election, would Summers return to Washington, perhaps for another stint as treasury secretary, this time for the full four years? Some Harvardians asked the question with hope; VOTE FOR KERRY, GET RID OF LARRY, went the slogan on campus. Others considered the possibility with dread, because so much of the university's planning centered around the president.

Even though George W. Bush was reelected in November 2004, Federal Reserve chairman Alan Greenspan was expected to retire in 2006. Summers, who had consistently refused to challenge Republicans on issues such as the Solomon Amendment, had made himself at least as palatable to members of that party as he was to Democrats. And certainly the job of Fed chairman would appeal to him. After all, the chairman of the Federal Reserve was probably the single most powerful, yet simultaneously least publicly accountable, economic policymaker in the world. It was entirely possible that George W. Bush might want Larry Summers in Alan Greenspan's seat.

But all that possibility was in front of Summers now, territory for future conquest. The man whom Harvard had once rejected had worked so hard to get this far. If for only this moment, Summers could take a deep breath, relax ever so slightly. Part of his legacy was already assured. There was no question that whenever Larry Summers decided to step down as president of Harvard, he would leave the university bigger, richer, more powerful, and more influential. The only question was whether he would leave it better.

Acknowledgments

Last time around, I inexplicably failed to thank my uncle, Michael Bradley, who is the kind of lawyer—and uncle—you want on your side in a tough spot. This time, let me apologize in advance to anyone I neglect to thank. So many people helped with this book, it's a challenge to give them all the appreciation they deserve.

Dan Solomon and Mindy Berman housed me during my preliminary research. Throughout snowstorms, home remodeling, and an impending birth, they never complained about the writer in the attic.

In a different locale, Evan Cornog and Lauren McCollester offered sage advice, not to mention a weekend escape from the computer screen. Andrew Auchincloss, Peter Critchell, and Townsend Davis are fine lawyers and intellectual provocateurs whose counsel is always welcome.

Sasha Smith helped check the facts in this book. Any mistakes that slipped past her eagle eye are, of course, my own. The indefatigable Tina Peak and Gregory Pearce gave immensely of their time and expertise to help with research.

The *Harvard Crimson* is a student paper that's better than many professional newspapers, and I relied on the hard work of its editors and reporters to help me understand the culture of Harvard University, as well as some of the specific events covered in this book.

Larkin Warren delivered wise editorial advice during the homestretch and helped me to say what I wanted to say with clarity, speed, and the benefit of her prodigious intelligence.

I want to thank Susan Weinberg, David Hirshey, Nick Trautwein, Miles Doyle, and everyone else at HarperCollins who helped usher this book into the world. Amid unexpected crises and down-to-the-wire deadlines, they were unflappable. From the beginning, Susan and

David believed in a book about the power, influence, and importance of a university and its president, and that's the greatest support a writer can ask.

This is the second book I've written with the help of the William Morris Agency, and I'm fortunate to have such a dedicated and smart group of people in my corner. Many thanks to Tracy Fisher, Andy McNicol, Libby O'Neill, and Sarah Pollard.

Joni Evans, my agent, is a legend in the publishing business, and anyone lucky enough to work with her understands why. Patient, understanding, tolerant, encouraging, tough when necessary, and always there when needed, Joni is truly a writer's advocate. From the start she encouraged me in my idea of writing about the university I once attended. I've asked a lot of Joni during this process, and she has never let me down.

My family, which rallied to the cause with my first book and rose to the occasion again with this one, never ceases to impress me.

Living with a writer isn't always easy. In fact, it's rarely easy. Nonetheless, Cristina Roratto was a constant source of inspiration, strength, support, advice, constructive criticism, and love. *Amo voce*, Cris.

Finally, I want to thank all the people at Harvard who gave of their time, often at professional risk, to help me understand how a great university works. Unfortunately, I can't name most of them. My research assistant was invaluable in digging up documents, answering odd questions, tracking down arcane statistics, and helping me to understand the culture of Harvard College. Whoever hires her after she graduates will have made an extremely wise move. And to all the people who put up with my repeated telephone calls, late-night e-mails, and nagging questions, I can't thank you enough. The Harvard community is filled with astoundingly smart, thoughtful, and caring citizens, and many times during the course of reporting this book I felt as though I was enrolled in a Harvard seminar, an experience everyone should be fortunate enough to enjoy. I am particularly grateful to the students, who were always willing to share their thoughts about and insights into life at Harvard. They are all they are cracked up to be, and more.

Richard Bradley
New York City
December 2004

A Note on Sources

Harvard Rules is primarily a work of journalism, and as such it is based upon hundreds of interviews with members of the Harvard community, including students, faculty, staff, administrators, and alumni. Wherever possible, the information that came from these interviews is clearly attributed, though in many cases the sources did not wish to be named. In this section I have attributed specific historical information and quotes from other sources that are not identified in the text.

President Lawrence Summers declined to be interviewed for this book. The quotes attributed to him whose source is not identified in the text are identified here.

INTRODUCTION: THE EMPEROR'S NEW CLOTHES

Page

ix   *With every breeze:* "Installation: A Summers Day," *Harvard Magazine* (November–December 2001), 57.

xi   *I would never have expected Larry:* *Harvard Crimson*, October 15, 2001.

xiii   *To the right of the stage was University Hall:* Much of my knowledge of Harvard's architecture comes from Douglas Shand-Tucci's excellent *Harvard University: An Architectural Tour* (New York: Princeton Architectural Press, 2001).

xiv   *The alumni of Harvard dominated every field:* For an impressive list of prominent Harvard alumni from 1636–1985, see *Glimpses of the Harvard Past* (Cambridge, Massachusetts, and London: Harvard University Press, 1986), by Bernard Bailyn, Donald Fleming, Oscar Handlin, and Stephan Thernstrom.

xvi   *What's outrageous? Harvard wages:* *Harvard Magazine* (November–December 2001), 57.

xx   *Only the Catholic Church had more money:* *Boston Globe,* January 27, 2000.

xx   *Harvard "was in society but it was set apart:* Nathan Marsh Pusey, "Out of War, Peace Gains Stability," *Harvard Alumni Bulletin* (June 9, 1969), 22.

CHAPTER ONE: THE REMARKABLE, CONTROVERSIAL CAREER OF LARRY SUMMERS

Page

2   *The New York Times cited Harvard:* Enrique Hank Lopez, *The Harvard Mystique: The Power Syndrome That Affects Our Lives from Sesame Street to the White House* (New York: MacMillan, 1979), 2.

3   *The potential to be the greatest president:* *Boston Globe,* January 30, 2001.

4   *I was a curious kid:* *Harvard Crimson,* May 4, 2001.

5   *Would that eliminate the traffic jam:* *New York Times,* August 24, 2003.

5   *I also liked leaving:* *Harvard Crimson,* May 4, 2001.

5   *This is not about fun:* *USA Today,* January 18, 1999.

6   *Mental gymnastics:* The line is quoted in a biographical essay on Paul Samuelson posted on the Nobel Prize website, at http://nobelprize.org /nobel/.

6   *More than any other contemporary economist:* From the Bank of Sweden Prize in Economic Sciences presentation speech, 1970, also on the Nobel Prize website.

8   *He was shunted off:* Morton Keller and Phyllis Keller, *Making Harvard Modern: The Rise of America's University* (Oxford: Oxford University Press, 2001), 81–82.

8   *The failure to appoint:* Ibid.

8   *Changed their surnames:* Couper Samuelson, "No Relation No. 8," *Slate,* July 6, 2000.

9   *There were country clubs:* Lawrence Summers, "Address at Morning Prayers," September 17, 2002.

10   *I traveled all over:* "Interview with a Public Servant: Larry Summers speaks with Gene Sperling," *Washington Life,* Summer 2001.

12   *I did some of my best research:* John S. Rosenberg, "A Worldly Professor," *Harvard Magazine,* May–June 2001, 30.

13   *A hive of activity:* New York Times, August 24, 2003.

13   *A provocative 1986 paper:* Daniel M. G. Raff and Lawrence Henry Summers, "Did Henry Ford Pay Efficiency Wages?" National Bureau of Economic Research, "NBER Working Paper Series," December 1986.

17   *Development failures are the result:* Rob Norton, "Economic Intelligence: The Third World Gets the Message," Fortune, April 6, 1992, 30.

18   *When I make a mistake:* "Toxic Memo," Harvard Magazine, May–June 2001, 36.

19   *Lant Pritchett admitted publicly:* John Cassidy, "The Triumphalist," The New Yorker, July 6, 1998, 58.

20   *The gravest sin:* Lawrence H. Summers, "International Financial Crises: Causes, Preventions, and Cures," Richard T. Ely Lecture of the American Economic Association, May 2000.

20   *Gore was really pissed off:* Summers made the remark in a freshman seminar, "Globalization: Opportunities and Challenges," he taught in the fall of 2003.

21   *A new kind of geopolitician:* "Larry Summers, Global Guru," The Economist, October 18, 1997, 32.

22   *I could just say good-bye:* Robert Rubin, In an Uncertain World: Tough Choices from Wall Street to Washington (New York: Random House, 2003), 62.

23   *Larry, what do you think?:* Ibid., 13–14. The story has also been told by Summers on numerous public occasions.

23   *The notion . . . didn't register:* Ibid., 15.

23   *By extending a large loan:* Summers made this statement in Brian Palmer's class, "Personal Choice and Global Transformation," on March 17, 2004.

24   *Human capital was peso-denominated:* Rosenberg, "A Worldly Professor," 31.

24   *Summers . . . volunteered to resign:* Rubin, In an Uncertain World, 31.

24   *The Marshall Plan . . . was never focus-grouped:* "Larry Summers, Global Guru," The Economist, 32.

24   *Larry's brain was like a tank:* Strobe Talbott, The Russia Hand: A Memoir of Presidential Diplomacy (New York: Random House, 2003), 48.

25   *The essence of issues:* "The World According to Larry," Foreign Policy, July 1, 2002, 30.

26   *It made me look good:* Robert Rubin, In an Uncertain World, 204.

27 A caricature of Summers: Cassidy, "The Triumphalist," 55.

27 Larry just got sick: Ibid., 56.

27 I play a lot better: Rosenberg, "A Worldly President," 31.

28 He waits till the end of the meeting: Mara Liasson on "Special Report with Brit Hume," Fox News Network, May 12, 1999.

28 I took a trip to Africa: Interview with Lawrence Summers, "Commanding Heights," the Public Broadcasting Service, April 24, 2001. Found at http://www.pbs.org/wgbh/commandingheights/shared/minitextlo/int_lawrencesummers.html. (Summers has told the story on other occasions.)

29 Too little globalization rather than too much: "The World According to Larry," Foreign Policy, 30.

30 More than any other single person: Robert Rubin, In an Uncertain World, 298.

31 The master chef was Larry Summers: Strobe Talbott, The Russia Hand, 84.

31 Battlefield medicine . . . is never perfect: "The World According to Larry," Foreign Policy, 30. (Summers used the line on numerous occasions.)

31 If it were up to me: Wall Street Journal, April 3, 1998.

31 Blame the doctor: Los Angeles Times, May 24, 1998.

33 A larger audience for his papers: "The World According to Larry," Foreign Policy, 30.

33 Even small degrees of information imperfections: Columbia Daily Spectator, October 11, 2001.

34 Crashes are that much more spectacular: "Clinton's Intellectual Power Broker," The International Economy, March–April 1999, 8.

34 You really should calm down: Joshua Cooper Ramo, "The Three Marketeers," Time, February 15, 1999, 34.

34 He and Summers would cut a deal: Robert Rubin, In an Uncertain World, 202–205.

35 A very good Treasury secretary: John Cassidy, "The Triumphalist," 54.

36 There are trade-offs in life: Summers speaking at "Personal Choice and Global Transformation," March 17, 2004.

CHAPTER TWO: NEIL RUDENSTINE'S LONG DECADE

Page

39 This has been a good run: Boston Globe, May 23, 2000.

50 I see in retrospect: Harvard Crimson, June 6, 1996.

50   *The frail Renaissance scholar:* Lynnell Hancock, "Exhausted," *Newsweek*, March 6, 1995, 56.

51   *University presidents . . . are eunuchs:* David Plotz, "Larry Summers: How the Great Brain Learned to Grin and Bear It," *Slate*, June 29, 2001.

51   *Incredible shrinking college president:* David Greenberg, "Small Men on Campus," *The New Republic*, June 1, 1988, 24.

56   *Harvard's goal is to die:* New York Times, June 24, 2001.

58   *Rudenstine's tenure has stripped:* Harvard Crimson, May 22, 2000.

CHAPTER THREE: SEARCHING FOR MR. SUMMERS

For those interested in Harvard history, Morton and Phyllis Keller's *Making Harvard Modern* is remarkably comprehensive, and Richard Norton Smith's *The Harvard Century* is informative and accessible. I drew from both. *Harvard A to Z*, by John T. Bethell, Richard M. Hunt, and Robert Shenton, is an excellent source for specific information about Harvard history and culture.

For further information on the Harvard presidential search, the best source is the *Harvard Crimson*, which conducted excellent reporting on a secretive process.

Page

65   *Some of it just seemed comical:* Harvard Crimson, June 5, 2003.

65   *Highly contested presidency:* Harvard Crimson, November 9, 2000.

69   *Somebody more aggressive, more pushy:* New York Times, August 24, 2003.

70   *I rather doubt [Gore] will get it:* United Press International, December 19, 2000.

71   *I look back ten years ago:* Harvard Crimson, October 16, 2000.

73   *Your best friend's father:* Michigan Daily, September 10, 1998.

74   *They are terrific students:* New York Times, March 29, 1999.

76   *We saw . . . a powerful intellect:* New York Times, August 24, 2003.

78   *A "rough edges" issue:* Ibid.

79   *Rubin made us confident:* Boston Globe, March 18, 2001.

80   *You don't need a degree:* This quote comes from the film, "Occupation," directed by Maple Raza and Pacho Velez, a Harvard student film about the Massachusetts Hall sit-in.

81   *An almost feudal relationship:* Morton Keller and Phyllis Keller, "Making Harvard Modern," 138.

81   *Such courses were the best way:* Maple Raza and Pacho Velez, "Occupation."

83   *I'll resign before I give in:* Ibid.

CHAPTER FOUR: THE PRESIDENT VERSUS THE PROFESSOR

Page

87   *A sign on my back: New York Times,* April 1, 1990.

87   *We all wanted to be spooks: New York Times,* January 20, 2004.

89   *A famous* New York Times *editorial: New York Times,* July 20, 1992.

96   *Conant wanted the University Professor to roam:* Richard Norton Smith, *The Harvard Century: The Making of a University to a Nation* (New York: Simon & Schuster, 1986), 117.

97   *Black musicians play such an important role:* Cornel West, *Keeping Faith: Philosophy and Race in American Life* (New York: Routledge, 1994), 289.

99   *There is no crisis in America:* Leon Wieseltier, "All and Nothing at All," *The New Republic,* March 6, 1995, 31.

106 *Harry Truman said:* Lawrence Summers, "Freshman Orientation Address," September 2, 2001. Located at http://www.president.harvard.edu/speeches/2001/freshman.html.

107 *This pulpit was not one of them:* Lawrence Summers, "Morning Prayers Address," September 21, 2001. Located at http://www.president.harvard.edu/speeches/2001/morningprayers.html.

108 *The C stood for compassion: Harvard Crimson,* June 2, 2003.

108 *Imbibing the spirit of affirmative action:* Harvey C. Mansfield, "Educational 'Therapy,'" *Harvard Crimson,* February 27, 2001.

109 *Gossip is a dangerous basis:* Harry R. Lewis, "The Racial Theory of Grade Inflation," *Harvard Crimson,* April 23, 2001.

109 *Universities are sometimes derided:* Lawrence Summers, "President's Installation Address," October 12, 2001. Found at http://www.president.harvard.edu/news/inauguration/summers.html.

111 *I want you to help me:* My accounts of the two meetings between Cornel West and Lawrence Summers are drawn from on-the-record interviews with West, interviews with people to whom he told details of the meetings around the time they took place, notes West made in his journal, public statements by West, and press accounts. In his 2004 book, *Democracy Matters,* West has written his own account of his encounters with Summers.

114　*In the book, Rosovsky explains:* Henry Rosovsky, *The University: An Owner's Manual* (New York: Norton, 1990.) I draw on various sections of Rosovsky's book, but particularly useful is Chapter 10, "Tenure: The Meaning of Tenure."

116　*There is no middle ground:* Smith, *The Harvard Century,* 79.

116　*Brilliant and creative people:* Derek Bok, "Reflections on Academic Freedom: An Open Letter to the Harvard Community," Supplement to the *Harvard University Gazette,* April 11, 1980, 2.

116　*Universities—as distinct from the scholars:* "A Wunderkind Goes Home," *Newsweek,* March 26, 2001, 94.

121　*A single compelling idea:* Sam Tanenhaus, "The Ivy League's Angry Star," *Vanity Fair,* June 2002, 220.

122　*One needs an enemy:* John Kenneth Galbraith, *Name-Dropping: From F.D.R. On* (Boston and New York: Houghton Mifflin, 1999), 18.

CHAPTER FIVE: WASHINGTON ON THE CHARLES

Page

127　*I would travel all over the world:* Lawrence H. Summers, "Remarks at the President's Associates Dinner," November 16, 2001. Found at http://www.president.harvard.edu/speeches/2001/presidentassoc.html.

128　*What will shape this world:* Lawrence H. Summers, "Remarks to the Harvard College Fund Assembly," October 25, 2003. Found at http://www.president.harvard.edu/speeches/2003/college_fund.html.

128　*The world is really shaped:* Lawrence H. Summers, "Some Thoughts on Undergraduate Education," Commencement Address, June 5, 2003.

128　*Nothing that would give greater support:* Harvard Crimson, March 10, 2003.

128　*Harvard exists for only one reason:* Lawrence H. Summers, "Remarks at Tobin School," January 9, 2002. Found at http://www.president.harvard.edu/speeches/2002/afterschool.html.

129　*A "passion for Athenian law":* "John Harvard's Journal," *Harvard Magazine,* January–February 2002, 65.

130　*We couldn't be choosy:* Smith, *The Harvard Century,* 205.

130　*Harvard's loss is Wisconsin's gain:* Kai Bird, *The Color of Truth: McGeorge Bundy and William Bundy: Brothers in Arms* (New York: Simon & Schuster, 1998), 119.

130　*Serene and quiet courage:* Smith, *The Harvard Century,* 208.

131 *Undergraduates who get excited:* Ibid., 210.

131 *I was tougher then:* Ibid., 244.

137 *The most important problems in the world:* Lawrence H. Summers, "Remarks at Harvard School of Public Health," October 26, 2001. Found at http://www.president.harvard.edu/speeches/2001/sph.html.

138 *An "American decade":* Interview with Lawrence Summers, "Commanding Heights," the Public Broadcasting Service, April 24, 2001.

139 *If you read Gandhi:* From Brian Palmer's class, "Personal Choice and Global Transformation," on March 17, 2004.

141 *When they think of police:* Lawrence H. Summers, "Remarks at Public Service Awards Dinner," October 26, 2001. Found at http://www. president.harvard.edu/speeches/2001/ksg.html.

141 *Their work is America's work:* The video can be seen at http://www.goarmy.com/flindex.jsp.

145 *Sex between the Bushes: Washington Post,* July 1, 2001.

149 *They literally look terrible:* Vasugi V. Ganeshananthan, "Image Is in the Eye," *The Harvard Crimson,* May 17, 2002.

149 Above average in fatness: "Larry Summers Is Fat," *The Demon,* March 2003, 2.

151 *The most arcane subjects:* J. Madeleine Nash, "The Geek Syndrome?" *Time,* May 6, 2002, 50.

151 *The person with AS:* Barbara L. Kirby, "What Is Asperger Syndrome?" from O.A.S.I.S., Online Asperger Syndrome Information and Support, at http://www.udel.edu/bkirby/asperger/aswhatisit.html.

155 *Being a good baseball scout:* Summers made the remark at a forum sponsored by the School of Education on April 23, 2004.

160 *As a Muslim:* Zayed Yasin, "Of Faith and Citizenship: My American Jihad," reprinted in *Harvard Magazine,* July–August 2002, 65.

162 *Jayed . . . Zayed: Today,* NBC News Transcripts, June 5, 2002.

166 *We venerate at this university:* Lawrence H. Summers, "ROTC Commissioning Ceremony," June 5, 2002. Found at http://www. president.harvard.edu/speeches/2002/rotc.html.

CHAPTER SIX: LARRY SUMMERS AND THE BULLY PULPIT

Page

171 *History teaches us that:* From "Harvard President Lawrence Summers Speaks at Health Care: East and West," from *HMI World—A*

Bimonthly Newsletter Published by Harvard Medical International, June 27, 2001. Found at http://www.hms.harvard.edu/hmi/wnew/summers_transcript.html.

173 *His idea of study abroad:* Kirby made the remark at a lunch for Harvard alumni in London, England, on November 15, 2003, but often delivered variations of it when meeting with alumni.

178 *The* Crimson *staff hope: Harvard Crimson*, November 18, 2002.

178 *I've been thinking about retirement:* Ibid., September 9, 2002.

178 *He just wanted to stand up:* Ibid.

179 *Rick has served Harvard: Harvard University Gazette*, August 22, 2002.

180 *The petition called for divestment:* The full petition can be found at http://harvardmitdivest.org/petition.html.

180 *A counter-petition:* The petition was online at harvardmitjustice.org, but is no longer available online.

181 *One of those tormented Jewish girls:* Andrea Shen, "Elisa New Weaves Literary Strands into One Web," *Harvard University Gazette*, September 23, 1999.

183 *An unlimited number of Jews:* Morton Keller and Phyllis Keller, *Making Harvard Modern*, 49.

184 *Snowballing New York contingent:* Ibid., 51.

185 *I speak with you today:* Lawrence H. Summers, "Address at Morning Prayers," September 17, 2002. Found at http://www.president.harvard.edu/speeches/2002/morningprayers.html.

188 *Respect and admire moral clarity:* Lawrence Summers, "ROTC Commissioning Ceremony," June 5, 2002. Found at http://www.president.harvard.edu/speeches/2002/rotc.html.

190 *To single out the Jewish state of Israel:* Alan M. Dershowitz, "A Challenge to House Master Hanson," *Harvard Crimson*, September 23, 2002.

190 *With an empty chair:* Ibid.

190 *Criticizing the actions and laws:* Rita Hamad, Shadi Hamid, and Yousef Munnayer, "Free Speech or Intimidation," *Harvard Crimson*, November 4, 2002.

192 *Unpopular opinions have become:* "Morning Edition," National Public Radio, October 22, 2002.

192 *Killed in Crossfire:* Tom Paulin, "Killed in Crossfire," *The Observer*, February 18, 2001.

193 *I think they are Nazis:* Al-Ahram, April 4–10, 2002.

193-4 *My views have been distorted: Daily Mail*, April 19, 2002.

194 *Lousy but famous poet:* Martin Peretz, "The Poet and the Murderer," *The New Republic*, April 29, 2002, 38.

195 *That sounds pretty bad:* Jeffrey Toobin, "Speechless," *The New Yorker*, January 27, 2003, 32. I am indebted to Toobin's thorough and excellent article, upon which I drew to describe the controversy surrounding Tom Paulin's invitation to speak at Harvard.

195 *The people who selected him:* Ibid., 32.

195 *You should ask Larry Summers:* Ibid., 33.

196 *The invitation does not represent:* Neil Rudenstine, "Statement about Visit of China President Jiang Zemin," *Harvard University Gazette*, October 30, 1997.

197 *Widespread consternation that has arisen:* Lawrence Buell's statement was posted on the Harvard Department of English's website, but can no longer be found there.

197 *What is truly dangerous:* Alan M. Dershowitz, Charles Fried, and Laurence H. Tribe, "Withdrawing Paulin's Invitation Unnecessary," *The Harvard Crimson*, November 15, 2002.

198 *The department in no sense:* From "Harvard English Department's Invitation of Tom Paulin to Give Poetry Reading—Supplementary Information," November 21, 2002. Found at http://www.fas.harvard.edu/~english/events/announcements.html.

198 *Invitations to Harvard departments:* Lawrence H. Summers, "Statement Regarding Invitation to Tom Paulin," November 20, 2002. Found at http://www.president.harvard.edu/speeches/2002/poet.html.

199 *The programme though:* Tom Paulin, "On Being Dealt the Anti-Semitic Card," *The Guardian*, January 8, 2003.

203 *Our rottweiler Larry:* Monica Collins, "Ask Dog Lady," *Cambridge Chronicle*, March 1, 2003.

CHAPTER SEVEN: THE UNEXPECTED EXIT OF HARRY LEWIS

Page

207 *A 2001 Boston Globe survey:* *Boston Globe*, February 4, 2001.

209 *Nearly half of the Harvard College student body felt depressed:* *The Harvard Crimson*, March 31, 2003.

210 *Harvard's mental health crisis:* *Harvard Crimson*, January 12, 2004.

211 *You're here by mistake:* William C. Kirby, "Remarks at the Opening

Exercises for Freshmen," September 7, 2003. Found at http://www.fas.
harvard.edu/home/administration/kirby/opening_exercises_2003.html.

219   *In Yale time:* Richard C. Levin, *The Work of the University* (New
      Haven: Yale University Press, 2003), 57.

219   *The greatest danger for a university:* *Washington Post,* June 24, 2004.

219   *Camp Harvard:* Anthony S. A. Freinberg, "Debunking Camp
      Harvard," *The Harvard Crimson,* March 21, 2003.

220   *I did once use the phrase 'camp counselor':* Ibid.

221   *That has staggering potential:* Lawrence H. Summers, "Remarks at
      Spring Members' Meeting of the Zell/Lurie Real Estate Center," April
      22, 2004. Found at http://www.president.harvard.edu/speeches
      /2004/wharton.html.

227   *Part of a broader university:* *Harvard Crimson,* December 3, 2002.

233   *They are gracefully unambiguous:* Jeremy Knowles quoted on "Wild
      About Harry—Recollections from Colleagues and Friends," a DVD in
      honor of Harry Lewis' service as dean of Harvard College.

234   *A review taking place post–Sept. 11:* *Harvard Crimson,* September 30,
      2002.

234   *Lewis' introduction of American values:* Ibid.

237   *Newton and Einstein did their main thinking:* Lawrence H. Summers,
      "Baccalaureate Address," June 4, 2002. Found at http://www.
      president.harvard.edu/speeches/2002/baccalaureate.html.

237   *Not to put too much pressure on you:* Lawrence H. Summers, "Remarks
      at Opening Exercises," September 8, 2002. Found at http://www.president.
      harvard.edu/speeches/2002/welcome.html.

237   *Autumn was the time for executions:* William J. Kirby, "Self-Cultivation,
      Self-Criticism, and Self-Renewal," September 27, 2002. Found at http://
      www.fas.harvard.edu/home/administration/kirby/speech_092702.html.

239   *Dean Lewis has done a great deal:* *Harvard Crimson,* March 18, 2003.

242   *Gross was overwhelmed:* *Harvard Crimson,* June 10, 2004.

CHAPTER EIGHT: WAR

As much of this chapter is about Timothy McCarthy, I should note
that I knew McCarthy before commencing the writing of this book.
While a graduate student at Harvard from 1989 to 1992, I served as a
tutor in the department of history and literature, and in that capacity I
taught McCarthy in his junior year tutorial during the 1991–1992

school year. We did not stay in touch over the next eleven years, and it was to my surprise that I discovered, upon beginning this book, that McCarthy had become a scholar and was teaching at Harvard.

Page

256 *Race Is Never Neutral:* Lawrence H. Summers and Laurence H. Tribe, "Race Is Never Neutral," *New York Times*, March 29, 2003.

258 *I do believe in affirmative action:* Lawrence Summers during a question-and-answer session at the Harvard Club of New York, March 20, 2004.

259 *Smell the roses: New York Times,* May 30, 2004.

275 *This has been a good year:* Lawrence H. Summers, "Some Thoughts on Undergraduate Education," June 5, 2003. Found at http://www president.harvard.edu/speeches/2003/commencement03.html.

277 *Different people have different views: Harvard Crimson,* May 21, 2003.

CHAPTER NINE: SILENT CAMPUS

Page

284 *Five reader letters: New York Times,* September 7, 2003.

288 *What good did I do?:* Boston Globe, August 23, 2003.

289 *Anytime Peter Gomes ascends:* Lawrence H. Summers, "Address at Morning Prayers," September 15, 2003. Found at http://www.president. harvard.edu/speeches/2003/prayer.html.

292 *This is your university:* Lawrence H. Summers, "Remarks at Black Alumni Weekend," October 4, 2003. Found at http://www.president. harvard.edu/speeches/2003/blackalum.html.

293 *My wife lives alone:* "Editor's Commentary," *Mother Jones,* July–August 1996, http://www.motherjones.com/commentary/ednote/1996/ 07/klein.html.

299 *HLS Lambda filed a friend-of-the-court brief:* In late November 2004, a federal appeals court ruled in the FAIR lawsuit that the Pentagon could not block funding to universities that restricted military recruiting. Harvard Law School dean Elena Kagan promptly reinstated the school's ban on military recruiting; Larry Summers had no immediate comment.
     The Bush administration was expected to appeal the court ruling.

301 *There is a feeling in the faculty: Harvard Crimson,* November 19, 2003.

303 *No journalist is ever satisfied:* David H. Gellis and Kate L. Rakoczy,

"The Iron Curtain Lowers Over University Hall," *Harvard Crimson*, February 5, 2004.

304 *The comment was regrettable:* The South Korean Health and Welfare Minister posted the comment on his homepage, at http://english.mohw. go.kr/html/01greetings/sub01.htm.

307 *I just left that class thinking:* *Harvard Crimson*, January 11, 2003.

309 *The university will spit me out:* Camille Dodero, "Class Notes," *The Boston Phoenix*, March 13–20, found at http://www.bostonphoenix. com/boston/news_features/this_just_in/documents/02753363.htm.

318 *Our purpose . . . is to cultivate:* James Bryant Conant, *General Education in a Free Society* (Cambridge: Harvard University Press, 1945), xiv.

319 *A very close call:* Peter Engel, "Harvard's Soft Core," *The Washington Monthly*, January 1980, 43.

319 *No very substantial intellectual experience:* Ibid., 191.

320 *The student has passed an uneventful period:* Kenneth S. Lynn, "Son of 'Gen Ed,' *Commentary*, September 1978, 61.

321 *A very good menu:* *Harvard Crimson*, June 9, 2004.

322 *The only workable solution:* Phyllis Keller, *Getting at the Core* (Cambridge: Harvard University Press, 1992), 135.

323 *A class struggle:* Ibid., 139.

325 *The ideal candidate:* "Kids Under Pressure," CNN, April 20, 2002.

325 *Is it really worth the effort:* Ibid.

326 *World's Greatest University:* Arianne R. Cohen, "World's Greatest University, World's Worst Teachers," *Harvard Crimson*, November 4, 2002.

328 *They remember feeling excitement:* J. Hale Russell, "The Curricular Misnomer," *Harvard Crimson*, March 25, 2004.

333 *An impact on universities across the nation:* *New York Times*, April 27, 2004.

333 *A bold step forward:* *Boston Globe*, April 28, 2004.

333 *The last time Harvard reviewed its undergraduate curriculum:* Thomas Bartlett, "What's Wrong with Harvard," *The Chronicle of Higher Education*, May 7, 2004, 14.

333 *University administrators across the country:* *Harvard Crimson*, April 16, 2004.

333 *Stunningly bland and half-baked recommendations:* J. Hale Russell, "Nobody Likes a Bad Review," *Harvard Crimson*, April 29, 2004.

334 *The key words were:* J. Hale Russell, "A Hard Sell," *Harvard Crimson*, May 17, 2004.

CONCLUSION: THE PRESIDENT ON HIS THRONE

Page

341   *The president wanted to move:* Lawrence H. Summers, "President's Letter to the Harvard Community on Allston Planning," October 21, 2003. Found at http://www.president.harvard.edu/speeches/2003/lhs_allston.html.

Selected Bibliography

Bailyn, Bernard, and Donald Fleming, and Oscar Handlin, and Stephan Thernstrom. *Glimpses of the Harvard Past.* Cambridge, Massachusetts, and London: Harvard University Press, 1986.

Bethell, John T., and Richard M. Hunt, and Rober Shenton. *Harvard A to Z.* Cambridge, Massachusetts, and London: Harvard University Press, 2004.

Bethell, John T. *Harvard Observed: An Illustrated History of the University in the Twentieth Century.* Cambridge, Massachusetts, and London: Harvard University Press, 1998.

Bird, Kai. *The Color of Truth: McGeorge Bundy and William Bundy: Brothers in Arms.* New York, Simon and Schuster, 1998.

Blustein, Paul. *The Chastening: Inside the Crisis That Rocked the Global Financial System and Humbled the IMF.* New York: Public Affairs, 2001.

Bok, Derek. *Universities and the Future of America.* Durham, North Carolina, and London: Duke University Press, 1990.

———. *Universities in the Marketplace: The Commercialization of Higher Education.* Princeton and Oxford: Princeton University Press, 2003.

Bowen, William G., and James L. Shulman. *The Game of Life: College Sports and Educational Values.* Princeton and Oxford: Princeton University Press, 2001.

Brown, Dan. *The Da Vinci Code.* New York: Doubleday, 2003.

Buckley, William F., Jr. *God & Man at Yale: The Superstitions of "Academic Freedom."* Washington: Regnery Publishing, 1986.

Chase, Alston. *Harvard and the Unabomber: The Education of an American Terrorist.* New York and London: W.W. Norton and Company, 2003.

Clotfelter, Charles T. *Buying the Best: Cost Escalation in Higher Education.* Princeton: Princeton University Press, 1996.

Conant, James Bryant. *General Education in a Free Society: The Report of the Harvard Committee.* Cambridge: Harvard University Press, 1945.

Galbraith, John Kenneth. *Name-Dropping: From F.D.R. On*. Boston and New York: Houghton Mifflin, 1999.

Gates, Henry Louis, Jr. *Colored People*. New York: Vintage Books, 1995.

Gates, Henry Louis, Jr., and Cornel West. *The Future of the Race*. New York: Vintage, 1997.

Giamatti, A. Bartlett. *A Free and Ordered Space: The Real World of the University*. New York and London: W.W. Norton and Company, 1990.

Greenlee, Sam. *The Spook Who Sat by the Door*. Detroit: Wayne State University Press, 1990.

Halberstam, David. *The Best and the Brightest*. New York: Ballantine Books, 1992.

Hershberg, James G. *James B. Conant: Harvard to Hiroshima and the Making of the Nuclear Age*. Stanford, California: Stanford University Press, 1993.

Hesburgh, Theodore M., and Jerry Reedy. *God, Country, Notre Dame*. New York: Doubleday, 1990.

Hope, Judith Richards. *Pinstripes and Pearls: The Women of the Harvard Law Class of '64 Who Forged an Old Girl Network and Paved the Way for Future Generations*. New York: Scribner, 2003.

Kahn, E. J., Jr. *Harvard: Through Change and Through Storm*. New York: W.W. Norton and Company, 1969.

Keller, Morton, and Phyllis Keller. *Making Harvard Modern: The Rise of America's University*. Oxford: Oxford University Press, 2001.

Keller, Phyllis. *Getting at the Core*. Cambridge: Harvard University Press, 1982.

Kennedy, Donald. *Academic Duty*. Cambridge, Massachusetts, and London: Harvard University Press, 1999.

Kerr, Clark. *The Gold and the Blue: A Personal Memoir of the University of California, 1949–1967*. Berkeley and Los Angeles, California: The University of California Press, 2003.

Kirp, David L. *Shakespeare, Einstein, and the Bottom Line: The Marketing of Higher Education*. Cambridge, Massachusetts, and London: Harvard University Press, 2003.

Knowlton, Winthrop, and Richard Zeckhauser, eds. *American Society: Public and Private Responsibilities*. Cambridge, Massachusetts: Ballinger Publishing Company, 1986.

Kors, Alan Charles, and Harvey A. Silverglate. *The Shadow University: The Betrayal of Liberty on America's Campuses*. New York: HarperPerennial, 1998.

Krugman, Paul. *Peddling Prosperity: Economic Sense and Nonsense in the Age of Diminished Expectations*. New York and London: W.W. Norton and Company, 1994.

Levin, Richard C. *The Work of the University*. New Haven and London: Yale University Press, 2003.

Lopez, Enrique Hank. *The Harvard Mystique: The Power Syndrome That Affects Our Lives from Sesame Street to the White House*. New York: MacMillan Publishing, 1979.

McCarthy, Timothy Patrick, and John McMillian. *The Radical Reader: A Documentary History of the American Radical Tradition*. New York and London: The New Press, 2003.

Morison, Samuel Eliot. *The Founding of Harvard College*. Cambridge, Massachusetts, and London: Harvard University Press, 1995.

———. *Three Centuries of Harvard, 1636–1936*. Cambridge, Massachusetts: The Belknap Press of Harvard University Press, 1964.

Nelson, Cary, ed. *Will Teach for Food: Academic Labor in Crisis*. Minneapolis and London: University of Minnesota Press, 1997.

Pearl, Matthew. *The Dante Club*. New York: Random House, 2004.

Pelikan, Jaroslav. *The Idea of the University: A Reexamination*. New Haven and London: Yale University Press, 1992.

Rosenblatt, Roger. *Coming Apart: A Memoir of the Harvard Wars of 1969*. Boston: Little, Brown and Company, 1997.

Rosovsky, Henry. *The University: An Owner's Manual*. New York and London: W.W. Norton and Company, 1990.

Rubin, Robert, and Jacob Weisberg. *In an Uncertain World: Tough Choices from Wall Street to Washington*. New York: Random House, 2003.

Rudenstine, Neil. *Pointing Our Thoughts: Reflections on Harvard and Higher Education, 1991–2001*. Cambridge, Massachusetts: Harvard University Press, 2001.

Rudolph, Frederick. *The American College and University: A History*. Athens, Georgia, and London: The University of Georgia Press, 1990.

Shand-Tucci, Douglas. *Harvard University: An Architectural Tour*. New York: Princeton Architectural Press, 2001.

Smith, Richard Norton. *The Harvard Century: The Making of a University to a Nation*. New York: Simon and Schuster, 1986.

Stiglitz, Joseph E. *Globalization and Its Discontents*. New York and London: W.W. Norton and Company, 2003.

———. *The Roaring Nineties: A New History of the World's Most Prosperous Decade*. New York and London: W.W. Norton and Company, 2003.

Sollors, Werner, and Caldwell Titcomb, and Thomas A. Underwood. *Blacks at Harvard: A Documentary History of African-American Experience at Harvard and Radcliffe*. New York and London: New York University Press, 1993.

Talbott, Strobe. *The Russia Hand: A Memoir of Presidential Diplomacy*. New York: Random House Trade Paperback, 2003.

Thernstrom, Melanie. *Halfway Heaven: Diary of a Harvard Murder*. New York: Plume, 1997.

Train, John. *The New Money Masters*. New York: HarperBusiness, 1989.

Trumpbour, John, ed. *How Harvard Rules: Reason in the Service of Empire*. Boston: South End Press, 1989.

West, Cornel. *Keeping Faith: Philosophy and Race in America*. New York: Routledge, 1994.

———. *Race Matters*. New York: Vintage, 2001.

———. *Democracy Matters: Winning the Fight Against Imperialism*. New York: The Penguin Press, 2004.

Woodward, Bob. *Maestro: Greenspan's Fed and the American Boom*. New York: Simon & Schuster, 2000.

Index